Banquo on Thursdays

Iain Crawford, the author

Banquo on Thursdays

THE INSIDE STORY OF FIFTY EDINBURGH FESTIVALS

Iain Crawford

Edinburgh

First Published 1997
© Iain Crawford 1997
Published by GOBLINSHEAD
12 Merchiston Crescent
Edinburgh EH10 5AS
Scotland

British Library Cataloguing in Publication Data
A catalogue record for this book is available from the British Library.

ISBN 1 899874 13 5

Typeset by GOBLINSHEAD using Desktop Publishing
Typeset in Garamond Narrow
Cover design – Stewart Hislop
Printed by Bell & Bain, Glasgow

Dedication

For Kathy
the youngest Festival veteran in the family
with love

Contents

By the same author

The Burning Sea
The Sinclair Exclusive
Scare the Gentle Citizen
What About Wine?
Gateway to Wine
Wine on a Budget
Make Me a Wine Connoisseur
The Profumo Affair
The Cafe Royal Story
London Man
The Havana Cigar
The Open Guide to Royal St George & Sandwich
The Open Guide to Royal Troon & Kyle
The Open Guide to the Old Course & St Andrews
The Open Guide to Royal Lytham and St Anne's
Capital Golf (with Keith Mackie)
Edinburgh, the Capital City
Held in Trust
The Open Guide to Turnberry & Carrick
The Sea Dominies
Gourmet Golf – a guide to the best golf courses and restaurants in Europe

Introduction

In August Edinburgh is now a city of many Festivals, but in 1947, just two years after the end of World War II, there was only one: the International Festival of Music and Drama – almost immediately on announcement joined by another, the Film Festival. Since then there have been many accretions – 'barnacle events' they were called first, before the coining of the definition 'Fringe' – and the Scottish capital now hosts the largest, most comprehensive and most diverse summer celebration of the arts in the world.

This is the story of its central and original ingredient: the Edinburgh International Festival of Music and Drama – the tree from which all the diverse branches grew. It tells, from a continuously present and often privileged viewpoint, the story of the development, survival, flourishing, trials, tribulations, try-ons and triumphs of that Festival, observed carefully, critically and affectionately over 50 years.

It is the story only of the original and central Festival, not its myriad offspring, although they are not ignored but come into the story as they relate to the International Festival. To tell the story of all the Edinburgh Festivals together would be well-nigh impossible – and require an encyclopaedic number of volumes. This is my view. Not everyone will agree with it but it is as accurate and comprehensive as memory, research and an abiding interest can make it, a tribute, a record and an assessment of one of the most astonishing things the Scottish capital has ever done. I wish it long life and much more joy for us all.

Acknowledgements

I am grateful to the staff of the Edinburgh Room in the Central Library, Edinburgh, for their help and unfailing patience and courtesy in checking and discovering documents and cuttings relating to the many facets of the Edinburgh Festival. Also to the Edinburgh Festival Society, particularly Penny Mills, for help in tracing photographs of recent Festivals. Also to all Festival publicity staff down the years for the generosity and lavishness with which they provided photographs of people and events; and particularly to my old friend, Alex 'Tug' Wilson, with whom I worked when I was on the Festival strength, who has taken so many splendid Festival pictures. It is not possible to name all the friends, acquaintances, colleagues and artists who have offered opinions, advice, anecdotes and comments on Festival matters over those 50 years, but I should like to thank especially those Festival Directors who have given of their time, wisdom and experience to talk with me about the Festival and their part in its amazing progress from 1947 infancy to 1997 greying maturity, *Mille grazie a tutti*.

I.C.
North Berwick
1997

SIR RUDOLF BING 1947-9
The 'Cosmopolitan Extravaganza' Has Lift-Off

I

The Edinburgh Festival began 50 years ago as a strange amalgam of cultural banditry, civic enterprise and idealism, an intriguing – even bizarre – but singularly effective combination.

The banditry was supplied by the general manager of Glyndebourne Opera, Rudolf Bing, an Austrian who had come to Britain in 1934 from the Charlottenberg Opera in Berlin. There is a romantic story about him strolling along Princes Street during the war with the soprano, Audrey Mildmay, wife of Glyndebourne's founder, John Christie, while on a tour with *The Beggar's Opera*. Looking up at the castle sailing against the torn clouds of the night sky, Bing said: 'This is an ideal city in which to have a Festival' – but this is generally discounted as a piece of amiable fiction.

Bing's greatest distinction as an opera administrator (he went straight from starting the Edinburgh Festival to the Metropolitan Opera in New York) was his hard-headed practical sense. 'About as romantic as a cobra' was the description of one famous Metropolitan soloist, who for some strange reason wishes to remain anonymous.

A typical story, current in New York during Bing's highly successful if controversial 23-year reign at the Met, concerns his long-standing feud with the Hungarian conductor, Georg Szell. After Bing had been vilifying Szell at a Park Avenue dinner table, his nervous hostess remonstrated with him gently.

'But Rudi, you exaggerate. Georg is not as bad as that. He's just one of those people who is his own worst enemy.'

'Not as long as I'm alive, 'said Bing crisply.

Such intense and unyielding single-mindedness was one of the qualities needed to launch the Edinburgh Festival and that was one of several ingredients the man from Glyndebourne supplied. He realised at the end of the war in 1945 that – with the great European festivals like Salzburg, Munich and Bayreuth still struggling to re-emerge from the smouldering ruins of the Third Reich, and with the heightened cultural awareness which many servicemen and women brought back from their battles and their occupation of the continent – there lay a great opportunity for a gifted and determined impresario like himself.

At Glyndebourne he had an existing, talented and intact artistic organisation of the highest class and, in the year before the war ended, he began to think about how this could be used to create an event of international status.

Oxford or Cambridge, acknowledged cultural centres within easy reach of London, first suggested themselves to him but neither university town showed much

Sir Rudolf Bing

interest. Then he met Harry Harvey Wood, the artist, author and editor who had been for a time on the lecturing staff of Edinburgh University and who was then the Scottish Representative of the British Council in Edinburgh. During the war, Harvey Wood had organised lunch-time concerts in the National Gallery and poetry and prose readings and discussions by and between writers from all over Britain, catering for the servicemen and others who passed through one of Britain's least bombed and most beautiful cities.

They met at a talk given to British Council officials by Bing about his ideas for post-war cultural developments in Britain. Prominent among them was the idea of an international festival in the summer of 1946. In an article in *The Scotsman* on August 7, just a little more than two weeks before the first Edinburgh Festival, Harvey Wood wrote about the meeting and Edinburgh's qualifications as a Festival centre:

> *Certain preconditions were obviously required of such a centre. It should be a town of reasonable size, capable of absorbing and entertaining between 50,000 and 150,000 visitors over a period of three weeks to a month. It should, like Salzburg, have considerable scenic and picturesque appeal and it should be set in a country likely to be attractive to tourists and foreign visitors. It should have a sufficient number of theatres, concert halls and open spaces for the adequate staging of a programme of an ambitious and varied character.*
>
> *Above all, it should be a city likely to embrace the opportunity and willing to make the Festival a major preoccupation not only in the City Chambers but in the heart and home of every citizen, however modest.*
>
> *Greatly daring but not without confidence. I recommended Edinburgh as the centre and promised to make preliminary investigations.*

Edinburgh certainly qualified on the first two counts. As to the third, it was largely hopeful rodomontade and the only thing was to obey the time-honoured Scots mother's injunction to her bairn 'Sook it and see'.

It was a curious situation. Britain was still in a period of belt-tightening austerity; food, clothes and many other things including fuel and soap were rationed and there were further cuts in 1946 when the true nature of the shortage of food and other supplies in Europe became apparent.

The watchword was austerity and the idea of a Festival of Music and Drama, scintillating with up-market international stars, many of them natives of countries with whom we had been at war only a year or so before the Festival began, was singularly un-austere.

Perhaps that is why it worked. Certainly, it was also a time when far-sighted and thinking people were anxious to restore some of the better aspects of civilised living. Elegant clothes, foreign travel – except in uniform – and gourmet meals had become unheard of luxuries.

In their place we had had shapeless garments made from poor material stamped with the awful austerity black broken-biscuit mark, a thousand regulations which said in all kinds of ways 'You can't go there' and 'Not that much', rather nasty low-gravity beer and a curious variation on the corned beef theme called Spam.

However, good music, fine acting, dance and the things of the imagination which had been an international language before the holocaust of World War Two were not subject to quality restrictions.

Harvey Wood sought the support of prominent Edinburgh citizens, among them Lady Rosebery, James Murray Watson, editor of *The Scotsman*, Dr O. H. Mavor (the playwright, James Bridie) and Lord Cameron and they invited Bing to Edinburgh to discuss his Festival ideas with them. 'I could not have found a more congenial and helpful group,' Bing said later.

He was rather more acerbic about his first meeting with the Lord Provost of Edinburgh, Sir John Falconer. 'It was a strange meeting,' Bing wrote, 'for he was not too well informed of the things I was talking about; Bruno Walter and the Vienna Philharmonic Orchestra were not familiar names to him but he did immediately recognise that here was an idea that might have cultural importance for the British Isles and economic importance for Edinburgh.'

John Falconer was a pragmatic idealist, a man who was prepared to fight for what he thought was worthwhile, and he felt deeply about bridging the gaps between peoples caused by the war.

Bruno Walter and the Vienna Philharmonic – the capture of which, as one of his programme ingredients, was Bing's first great triumph – may not have been household words in the Falconer family, but Sir John was not ashamed to accept a good idea from someone else and he set about using his considerable political skills to ensure that the Festival – planned for the summer of 1947 because Bing's original target of 1946 was obviously over-imminent – should take place.

The first announcement was made in November 1945 and was received with cautious acclaim, although it is fair to say that in many quarters it was regarded by level-headed Scots folk as an act of consummate folly and pretentiousness of a kind fairly typical of a capital city often regarded (outside Edinburgh) as too big for its brogues.

Glasgow still has a sense of puzzlement about the emergence of the Edinburgh Festival, despite breaking out with its own Mayfest in 1983 and – 43 years after Edinburgh's startling leap onto the international cultural scene – becoming Europe's City of Culture for the Year 1990. The city which is the home of Scottish Opera and the Scottish National Orchestra, the Citizens' Theatre and Scottish Ballet, has never quite understood how the weakling infant which was half an idea in 1945 should have grown to the mature age of half a century.

In that first year too there were plenty of doubts about the Festival among the douce citizens of Scotland's capital, many of whom regarded the idea of starting a major international festival in their city as not just civic folly but more akin to certifiable lunacy.

Although in 1947 there was an urge to travel and exchange ideas among different peoples brought together by war, Edinburgh had not recently considered itself as a place with the intellectual stature of Salzburg or Bayreuth, Vienna or Paris. The notion that an international festival capable of competing with the cultural beanfeasts of these supremely civilised *locales* could be mounted in Edinburgh seemed to many people to be overweeningly ambitious and dangerously impractical.

There is a cruel but true dictum that the worst things you can say about a fellow-Scot on whom fortune seems to be shining are 'Ah kent his feyther' and 'Ah knew him when he was but a laddie'. Even after the tremendous success of the first Festival there was a lot of that about. 'It couldn't have been us that did it,' Edinburgh citizens smirked at each other. 'It must have been a fluke!'

In fact there was quite a lot of truth in this disparaging civic sentiment for the impetus for the Festival came largely from outside and such support as there was for the scheme initially was limited to a few citizens.

However, Edinburgh was not exactly the cultural desert it has sometimes been made out to be before the glorious enlightenment of the Festival broke like a sunrise over Arthur's Seat – admittedly a funny direction for it to appear but it is true that the Festival sun rose largely in the south. Yet in the year before it began, Edinburgh theatres and concert halls were not moribund. When one of the theatres on which the suitability of Edinburgh as a Festival venue was based, burned down on the night of 30 March 1946, the show running at the time was Tommy Morgan in *Hail Caledonia*, a red-nosed comedian in a tartan frolic, and the Theatre Royal at the top of Broughton Street was never rebuilt.

But there were enough sizeable theatres, more than there are today. In addition to the King's and the Lyceum, there was the Empire (for long a bingo hall but recently gloriously metamorphosed into the new and splendid Festival Theatre), the Palladium, the Gaiety Theatre in Leith, several spacious halls and a number of cinemas. Still to be discovered was that the drama side of the Festival would always show itself particularly ingenious in the use of new and, on the face of it, unlikely venues for theatrical performances.

That there was an audience in Edinburgh for the kind of material that the Festival was to provide is clear from the visits paid to the city in 1946 by the Hallé Orchestra conducted by Barbirolli, singers like

3

Elisabeth Schumann, Richard Tauber and Jeanette Macdonald, instrumentalists like the viola player, William Primrose and the pianist Eileen Joyce; the London Symphony Orchestra, the *Ballets Negres*, Sadlers Wells Ballet, the Liverpool Philharmonic, Glyndebourne Opera with Britten's *The Rape of Lucretia* and plays like Shaw's *St Joan*, Ibsen's *Ghosts* and Jean Cocteau's *The Eagle has Two Heads.*

Behind the scenes programme planning went on apace while in the City Chambers Lord Provost Falconer and his successor, Andrew Murray, then the City Treasurer, lobbied for official civic support which had not yet been given by the ruling body, the Corporation of the City of Edinburgh. A meeting was held in the City Chambers on 10 August 1946 about Festival plans, at which Lady Rosebery did her best to rally the ladies of Edinburgh into, temporarily, becoming landladies. She urged them to welcome visitors into their homes for the Festival period. There had been complaints about the standard of tourist accommodation available in the city and it was felt that existing hotels and boarding houses would not be able to cope with the influx of visitors the Festival would bring.

'People in Edinburgh have not heard enough about the Festival,' Lady Rosebery said. 'Ten thousand offers of accommodation are needed. People must be told more.'

She told her somewhat bemused audience that the programme would include first-class symphony orchestras, quartets and soloists, French theatre companies and the very best of ballet and opera, a week of Shakespeare and a week of Scottish drama. Everyone was very energetic about accommodation. The brand-new Scottish Tourist Board was trying to charter a cruise liner to be berthed at Leith, a permanently parked sleeper train was also suggested and the camping ground at Silverknowes was, as it were, canvassed.

This activity was all very well, but although the Lord Provost and the City Treasurer were both strong supporters of the Festival idea and the editor of *The Scotsman* ceaselessly advocated it in the columns of his newspaper, the whole plan had to be approved by the City Fathers, Edinburgh Corporation before it could be truly launched. Meanwhile, behind the scenes, what has always been the most crucial and most controversial element of the Festival was being earnestly sought: money.

In those far-off days there was no such thing as the Scottish Arts Council, so an appeal for funding was made to the newly formed Arts Council of Great Britain. On 22 August 1946, just a month before the crucial meeting of the City Corporation which was to decide whether a Festival should in fact take place in 1947 or to be consigned for ever into limbo, an answer and an offer were received from the Arts Council. The sum offered was £20,000. £10,000 in the year beginning 1 April 1947, and £10,000 during the year beginning 1 April 1948. But the offer was conditional. The condition was that a sum of not less than £40,000 should be provided from other sources 'before the project is launched'.

At the meeting of the Corporation on 26 September, Lord Provost Falconer handled the delicate matter of finance with consummate skill. The calculations were, he told the councillors of Edinburgh Corporation, that the concert performances in the Usher Hall, the drama and ballet in the theatres and the chamber music and recitals in the Freemasons' Hall would square themselves. There was an estimated deficit of £15,000 on the opera and administration and advertising would cost £20,000. The calculated ticket sales were 80% of capacity and the net cost of the Festival would be £35,000.

While the Edinburgh councillors were blundering about among these rather alarming figures (albeit in a country which, just over a year before, had been paying several million pounds a day to fund a war), Sir John proceeded to explain how the money was already in the bag.

'Owing to the generosity of Edinburgh citizens, we have been promised £20,000 – not a guarantee but a gift to the Festival Fund.' He explained the Arts Council grant and that it was payable in two instalments. 'That is £20,000,' he said. 'In all, therefore, we have in hand £40,000.'

Then – with all the dexterity of an expert salesman producing a gold brick from his Gladstone bag – he went on to let them in on it.

'I propose,' he said, 'to ask the City of Edinburgh to take a share in this work, which would certainly benefit the city and also to contribute £20,000, which should give us enough to stabilise a Festival Fund so that the Festival may get firmly established.

'If one estimates 10,000 persons for three weeks at say £4 a week, it gives £120,000 coming into the city in all at one Festival.'

It was irresistible, a beautiful piece of 'You can't afford not to join us' salesmanship. The only difference to the usual pitch of this kind was that the brick on offer was actually made of gold.

Coincidentally with this splendid piece of fiscal legerdemain, which gave the Festival the £40,000 from other sources on which the Arts Council grant was conditional, the programme was announced.

It included 18 performances of two operas, Verdi's *Macbeth* and Mozart's *Le Nozze di Figaro*, ten orchestral concerts, four by British orchestras and six by foreign orchestras, chamber music and solo recitals in the Usher Hall and the Freemasons' Hall by world-famous artists; a two week season at the Lyceum by 'one of the best-known British drama companies' and one week by 'an outstanding French company'.

'I have little hesitation in saying that the programme compares favourably with anything that has ever been produced at any festival,' said the Lord Provost, who had evidently made quite a lot of progress from not knowing who Bruno Walter and the Vienna Philharmonic were just a year before.

'Further,' he continued, 'the Festival will only be a success if the city enters into the festival spirit wholeheartedly, laying itself out for the benefit of the visitors for these three weeks. But given that enthusiasm, given the desire to make it go, the proposal should have success.'

HM Queen Elizabeth and HRH Princess Margaret with Sir John Falconer at the Usher Hall, 1947

Perhaps there have been some dents in the enthusiasm down the years but citizens have now almost lived down the later snide fable that everybody leaves Edinburgh during the Festival and rents their houses to foreigners.

In his peroration the Lord Provost outlined the constitution of the Festival Council and spoke of the advantages of the Festival to tourism and its benefit to the rest of Scotland. Even Glasgow got a mention as a possible base for Festival visits.

'We have the programme,' he said. 'We have the money and the rest depends on our own efforts.'

He got a great reception and deserved it. Councillor Adam Millar was ecstatic, Baillie Poole (who owned a cinema) pleaded for cultural films. Councillor Jack Kane, who was to become one of Edinburgh's most distinguished Lords Provost and the first Labour one, desired that the music should not be 'too classical', that the popular theatre movement should be better represented and that ballet and music from the Soviet Union should be included.

The Corporation unanimously approved the Lord Provost's proposals which included the appointment of Mr Rudolf Bing of Glyndebourne as Co-ordinating Organiser (were people in those days shying away from any title as dictatorial as 'Director'?) and of Mr W. F. Maclennan – the only Festival official other than myself who appeared regularly in a kilt – in connection with the organisation of accommodation, travel facilities, booking arrangements etc.

The Festival was off the ground and – almost – flying.

II

My first encounter with the Edinburgh Festival (although I didn't know it at the time) began one day early in 1946 when I walked into Stricklands, the Savile Row tailor in London and ordered myself a new suit. Fed up with six years in black barathea and brass buttons, I had determined to return to civilian life in style – something I considered the hideously misshapen blue pin-stripe suit I had been allocated by the Demob Centre at Wembley football stadium did not offer.

When I got it about three weeks later, I was pleased. An elegant creation in discreet grey Prince of Wales check, it was my idea of what the non-stereotyped modern gent was wearing. It cost £35, a lot of money in these days, but it proved to be one of the best investments of my life.

I wore it to my first job, trainee reporter on the *Edinburgh Evening Dispatch* (salary £4.10s a week) and it rapidly became clear that in the era of baggy out-at-elbow austerity wear, I was easily the best-dressed man in the office – not excluding the chairman of Scotsman Publications, Sir Edmund Finlay.

So after a short period offering some indication that I could write the English language forwards, I became the *Dispatch's* smart party and socially cultural correspondent. The fact that my war service had taught me to speak French and Italian and that I knew how to spell Shostakovich meant that (very exceptionally for anyone as humble as a trainee reporter) I became part of the Festival squad.

Although I was usually given the jobs that most other people in the *Dispatch* reporters room considered boring, I revelled in them and by the time D-day, August 24 1947, the first day of the first Festival dawned, I was in it up to my neck.

I was lucky because I was given the daily 'Festival Gossip' column to do as well as a certain amount of reviewing. The mobility and out-of-the-office circumstances of the job meant that I was able to do some cultural moonlighting on the side – partly working with Glyndebourne to generate publicity for artists who were appearing in the operas; and in the final week, trying every night to translate between the stage staff from the Théàtre de l'Athenée in Paris and the back-stage crew at the Lyceum Theatre – a linguistic task of hilarious complexity. Try translating 'Tell the wee fella's gaffer he'll hiv tae put it ona bogey' into the language of Molière.

This undercover activity even included an appearance in one of the first Fringe events (albeit before the title 'Fringe' had been invented). In the YMCA theatre in St Andrew Street, the Christine Orr Players presented Shakespeare's *Macbeth* on a stage just 12 feet deep. On Thursdays I played Banquo (a role which allowed me to sneak away after the first scene in Act IV to cull a few more gossip pars from the Festival Club). I stood in for the well-known Edinburgh actor and poetry recitalist Ian Gilmour, who worked in a bank which kept him late on Thursdays. It was my first and last performance on the Festival boards. Our *Macbeth* was reviewed by no lesser luminaries than Kenneth Tynan and E. M. Forster.

Forster found it 'remarkable' and said it managed to convey 'colour and horror'. In his book *He Who Plays the King* Tynan perspicaciously pointed out that Macduff clearly thought he ought to be playing Macbeth. I have never found out if either of them came on a Thursday.

In addition to French for the Théàtre de l'Athenée company, the Italian came in useful. During that first Festival I spoke a lot of Italian.

One of the problems with rationing was that, in addition to such negligible commodities as clothes and furniture, the restrictions embraced food. Being a naval man I don't know much about Napoleon's dictum that an army marches on its stomach but as an opera fan I can assure you that those exquisite *tessiture* flowing from dewy-eyed sopranos and cavernous *fortes* booming from gigantic basses depend mightily on high-piled plates of *pasta*, mammoth steaks and the kind of calorific intake which would make Mike Tyson blanch.

Under the rationing regulations such sumptuous repasts were illegal. That is not to say they were unobtainable.

So I spent quite a few of my evenings (while not collecting gossip or playing Banquo) knocking furtively on back doors of Edinburgh restaurants, murmuring necromantic passwords in Italian to fix the best black-market meals in town, to keep the glorious sounds at the King's Theatre in full production.

It is only fair to say that the local Italian population, doubtless from their enthusiasm for Verdi, Rossini *e altri* were of great help in this particular exercise. One who ran a favourite restaurant in Fountainbridge used to point proudly each evening at the photograph of a very pretty girl on the wall. 'My daughter,' he would say, 'an actress.' Later, we recognised her as Adrienne Corri.

More loftily, I recall meeting Bruno Walter one morning in Princes Street Gardens and getting into a long conversation with him (which made me late and nearly got me fired from the *Dispatch*). Our talk was shot through with dismay on his part because I confessed I had never heard any music by Mahler (after all the Third Programme – now Radio 3 – had only begun the year before!) Most kindly he sent me tickets for his unforgettable performance of *Das Lied von der Erde* with the Vienna Philharmonic, Kathleen Ferrier and a promising young tenor called Peter Pears – thus starting a life-long addiction.

However, long before any of this happened, once the green light had been given to the Festival idea in September 1946, the Festival had to be planned and organised and, as always, there were problems about that.

Rudolf Bing, making whatever is the Austrian cabalistic sign for crossed fingers, had of course plotted a good deal of it in advance of the fateful day of 26 September, on the assumption that the Festival plan would be approved. It was easier in those days to ensure the participation of major artists, orchestras and theatre companies over a short time span because the competition for their services was not as fierce as it is today. It was, nevertheless, a formidable task.

Today, when every hamlet with a population running into three figures has a 'Festival' at some time of year, commemorating the ancient practice of lass-upping, haggis-downing or the Feast of Lambert Simnel, the rumble of sousaphones, the piping of reed-burpers and the booted clatter of Morris dancers has deafened us all to the fact that a major festival involving thousands of artists and, hopefully, tens of thousands of visitors and natives to make up the audiences, is a major administrative and planning operation.

The Edinburgh Festival has always been parsimoniously understaffed compared with other major festivals (e.g. permanent staff: Salzburg 120, Edinburgh 20). But the miracle of conjuring a vintage lake of bubbling entertainment out of a pint pot of resources has been achieved for 50 years.

Over these five decades we have become wearily familiar with the spectacle of one Festival Director after another confronting his Finance Committee, steaming with impotent rage as the real money on which he has to plan and run the greatest festival in the world is slashed and mangled, trying to keep his temper as he broods wistfully on Salzburg subsidies and the bounty of Bayreuth.

All this Bing faced first. In 1947 there may have been more goodwill and more people ready to pitch in and lend a hand out of enthusiasm, but the problems were horrendous and would have daunted all but the stoutest hearts.

One of them was starkly and obviously simple. What was the Edinburgh Festival going to be *about*? Salzburg had Mozart (even if he did hate the place) and Bayreuth had Wagner; Malvern, for some strange reason, had George Bernard Shaw.

But Edinburgh had no local composer or dramatist of world renown around whose works the Festival could be assembled. So Bing decided to 'go for broke'. This was to make a virtue out of not being a festival linked narrowly to the works of one composer or writer nor with its emphasis on just one group or one view of the arts.

7

Edinburgh was to be the great all-embracing festival. 'An overflowing fountain of grace and beneficence,' as Sir John Falconer said in one of his more fulsome moments, 'so that the human mind can confirm its weak faith and anchor it to something higher than itself.'

In the grey aftermath of war with rationing and restrictions on everything in sight seeming the only fruits of a hollow victory, the announcement of the plans for the Edinburgh Festival was pure euphoria. I can still remember the thrill at the splendour and scope of the whole idea.

However, while the Festival was being planned the world was recovering from turmoil. The Nazi leaders were being tried and hanged in Nuremberg; the first partisan guerrilla leader, Yugoslav Royalist Draza Mihajlovic was executed by his own countrymen in Belgrade; two atomic bombs were tested by the Americans at Bikini atoll in the South Pacific; Italy threw out King Umberto; Israeli terrorists blew up the King David Hotel in Jerusalem.

Many people in Europe were homeless or starving or both and in Britain there was darker bread, fewer biscuits and spaghetti and macaroni were rationed along with cake mixtures and oatmeal. Haggis was exempt although mealy puddings needed coupons. The fruits of victory seemed meagre indeed.

The wage for a good responsible job – such as Inspector of Works in Aberdeen City Engineer's Department – was advertised in *The Scotsman* at £363 per annum. MPs salaries were raised from £600 to £1,000 a year. Some things do not change however. In 1946 they were arguing yet again about what to do with Prestwick Airport.

Against this background – and plenty of it was darker than the few examples listed above – the organisation of a major arts festival could seem almost a studied frivolity.

There were protests, most of them murmurings over weak beer in dark bars, but oddly enough those which saw the light were cultural rather than sociological.

After the Corporation approved the Festival, there was a letter from John Sleigh in *The Scotsman* criticising the City Fathers for being prepared to spend £20,000 in three weeks but only 1/40th of that for an orchestra to provide music all the year round. Glasgow, the writer pointed out, gave £5,000 to the Scottish Orchestra, Manchester gave £2,500 to the Hallé and Birmingham gave £14,500 to its city orchestra. Edinburgh gave the Reid Orchestra (about to be disbanded for lack of fiscal support) only £560.

Mr Sleigh quoted the 90-year old Bernard Shaw:

> *Just as the river is useful to men who do not row, the bridges to West Enders who never cross them and the railways to the bedridden, so the provision of good music and plenty of it smoothes life as much for those who do not know the National Anthem from Rule Britannia as for those who can whistle all the themes of the Ninth Symphony.*

Hugh MacDiarmid, Scotland's leading poet (and polemicist), described the Festival as 'luxury entertainment, jamborees of the well-to-do and cosmopolitan extravagance'.

There were other carpers and denigrators and Bing wanted to reply to them in the press but he was restrained by the Lord Provost and John Imrie, Edinburgh's City Chamberlain. He had no need to get into a public fight: he had troubles enough of his own.

Some of them were minor, like the fact that every orchestral conductor appearing at the Festival wanted to play Vaughan Williams's *Fantasia on a Theme of Thomas Tallis*. This was simply enough resolved by allocating it to Bruno Walter and the Vienna Philharmonic who had asked first and for whom it was the only piece of British music in their offered Festival repertoire.

Others were not so simple. When the first Festival brochure appeared in December 1946, there was a shrill scream of rage from the Festival Council. Harry Harvey Wood, chairman of the Festival Programme Committee, summed up the outraged feelings of design-conscious members in a letter to James Bridie:

> *It is preposterous that so much money should have been spent in printing a brochure which, in general design and typography, is a disgrace to the City and the traditions of*

Scottish printing. And absurd that we have Sir Frank Mears and Stanley Cursiter on the Council and consult neither of them on a matter of this kind.

Stanley Cursiter was the King's Limner (painter) in Scotland and Sir Frank Mears was the President of the Royal Scottish Academy. Mears resigned from the Council on this issue but was later persuaded to return.

There was trouble with the Old Vic, who were scheduled to do two weeks at the Lyceum, over a new play by Bridie. Tyrone Guthrie, the distinguished Anglo-Irish theatre director was a close friend of Bridie's and had produced the Scottish playwright's first play and the first play of Bridie's to be seen in the West End of London. Bridie wanted Guthrie to produce his new play but John Burrell, the director of the Old Vic wanted to have the choice of producer left to him.

Bing, trying to mediate, wrote to Bridie on the day after the programme was announced:

For me it seems vital to hear whether you would be prepared to let someone else but Guthrie do your play, if for one reason or another we couldn't have him: if you should not be prepared to allow that then I must begin to wonder whether it is worth having the Old Vic: we are not getting Olivier, we are not getting Richardson, we are probably not getting some of the other actors who will go with Olivier, we are not getting Guthrie and we may not be getting the Bridie play – so what are we getting after all?

And after a few more complaints about negotiating difficulties with the Lunts – the American husband and wife acting team who had been pencilled in as part of the Festival programme – he ended:

What a life and what a profession!

It was all highly embarrassing. Bridie was Scotland's leading dramatist and the only contemporary playwright from north of the border who had made any impact outside Scotland. He was also one of the original members of the Festival Committee and a valued voice in its programme planning.

The Old Vic hummed and hawed about the play *John Knox* and, after some months of wrangling, decided against it on the grounds that they could not afford the number of Scots actors it demanded and they did not think it would fit into their repertoire when they returned to London.

Bing had already taken quite a lot of stick about the lack of Scottish content in the Festival and there can be no doubt that he was anxious to have Bridie's play as part of the programme.

At one point Bridie offered to forego his royalties on *Knox* and the Festival Council volunteered to fund one-third of the play's production cost (£850) but the Old Vic would not be moved and eventually the idea of a Bridie play was abandoned and, just two months before the Festival, it was announced that the Old Vic's programme would be all Shakespeare, *Richard II* with Alec Guinness as the king and *The Taming of the Shrew* with a cast which included Trevor Howard, Bernard Miles and Patricia Burke.

There was considerable disquiet about the omission of a Scottish theatre contribution to the Festival. In 1947 the Scottish segment consisted of five concerts, one by the BBC Scottish Orchestra conducted by Ian Whyte, whose Piano Concerto was given its first performance at the Festival, a second by The Scottish Orchestra conducted by Walter Susskind, another by the Glasgow Orpheus Choir under Sir Hugh Roberton, two recitals of Gaelic songs and Lowland songs in the Freemasons' Hall and Piping and Dancing on the Castle Esplanade for ten nights, organised by Scottish Command, the forerunner of the celebrated Tattoo which assumed its present form in 1950.

Bridie was tactful about the rejection of *Knox* by the Old Vic but there is no doubt that he resented it – he would hardly have been human if he had felt otherwise and his humanity is manifest in all his plays.

As a kind of challenge, it was presented at the opening of the Glasgow Citizens' Theatre season in 1947, on the eve of that first Festival. Among the first-night audience was Sir John Falconer, the Lord Provost, who had fought so hard to have the Bridie play included in the Edinburgh programme.

Unfortunately, all the indignation aroused by the Festival rejection was somewhat defused by the play itself. The critics found it too wordy, over-historical and not sufficiently dramatic. The Scots actor John Laurie who played Knox was accused of ranting – hardly a valid criticism one would have thought of a character who is historically famous as one of the greatest ranters of all time.

A letter from Bridie to John Laurie, reveals the playwright's disappointment and resentment at the play's reception but also his concern and admiration for the Festival.

You know, I think, he wrote, *how much I admired your Knox. Quite honestly it was one of the memorable performances of my life ... in the really big things.*

I put you above Forbes Robertson and far above Matheson Lang who, I suppose, are (or were) our best leaders. You are a poet, you see.

And now you and I have piped to them and they have not danced. We have mourned to them and they have not wept. Englishmen, Hungarians, Jews, Americans have told me how deeply they were impressed and moved by our Knox, but we are not, apparently, good enough for the smart Alecs and spivs of (so-called) industrial Scotland. Edinburgh, in her present mood, would have swallowed us hook, line and sinker. But Edinburgh's dormant imagination has burst its chrysalis case and she has become a living city overnight. A great miracle, John, I assure you. I hope there is a carry-through, though I doubt it.

What I should like to do now is to get together an ad hoc team of the best Scottish actors in the world for the next Edinburgh Festival. I shall talk to Cruikshank about it soon and try to book the Lyceum NOW. I don't know about a manager but perhaps Stephen Mitchell would be interested. The Festival is a really big thing and has come to stay. I'm truly grateful to you. We have done a big thing (like the Edinburgh Festival) between us whether the bloody fools realise it or not.

Despite Bridie's faith in *John Knox*, it never really took off. Tyrone Guthrie was not keen on it, although Bridie offered several times to adapt it and Robert Donat, who was the original choice to play Knox at the Festival (he had played the lead in one of Bridie's most successful plays *The Sleeping Clergyman*) in a charming letter wriggled out of the offer because he was 'not attracted by the character'.

Thus ended the first great Festival row about the place of Scotland in its capital's festival. There were many more to come. In the meantime, the curtain was about to go up on the most important event to happen in Edinburgh in this century, the first International Festival.

III

No matter what backstage rumblings might be going on behind the multifarious Edinburgh scenes and despite any internal doubts the burghers of Edin might have about an enterprise as dashingly ambitious as an International Festival of Music and Drama, the opening of the first Festival was a happy and joyous occasion.

In his introduction to the first Festival Souvenir Programme, Sir John Falconer wrote:

The idea is a new one for Edinburgh, but I feel confident we will succeed in establishing our fair city as one of the pre-eminent European Festival Centres. To succeed, we require the help and co-operation of lovers of art the world over, especially as one of our objects is to foster and maintain the international character of the event. We wish to provide the world with a Centre where, year after year, all that is best in music. drama and the visual arts can be seen and heard amidst ideal surroundings.

Heady and ambitious stuff, which cannot have been reassuring to those citizens who looked for an element of Scots canniness in civic planning. Such outright commitment was not Edinburgh's style at all. But Falconer was an enthusiast and a man of powerfully held ideals and when he decided to back the Festival idea, his support was whole-hearted and his ambition for it large and generous.

Even he, however, sounded a note of caution, suitable to the times perhaps but with hindsight ominously foreshadowing all those 50 years in which the City Fathers of Scotland's capital failed to lay one stone on top of another to create a single new building to serve what was to become its greatest international civic asset, the Edinburgh Festival.

At the present time, Falconer wrote, *all the amenities and ancillaries so essential for the visitors' full enjoyment and appreciation cannot be provided. For example, this year it is not possible for accommodation and catering facilities to be of the very highest standard, but we ask all who are interested to bear with us in these difficult times. In the course of time all these things will be rectified, but we are determined to make a start this year to establish the tradition of Edinburgh as a Festival Centre.*

The programmes for the first year are unfolded in the pages which follow and I hope you will believe that in the organisation of the many attractions, we have ever before us the highest and purest ideals of art in its many and varied forms. May I assure you that this Festival is not a commercial undertaking in any way. It is an endeavour to provide a stimulus to the establishing of a new way of life centred round the arts.

For the three weeks of the Festival, Edinburgh will be wholly given up to Festival affairs – she will surrender herself to the visitors and hopes that they will find in all of the performances a sense of peace and inspiration with which to refresh their souls and reaffirm their belief in things other than material.

If these lofty sentiments were not always reflected by the citizenry of Edinburgh – who for many years and in some quarters still, regard the Festival as an intrusion on their high summer privacy – they were given unqualified support by the weather.

The first Festival was held in brilliant sunshine and Italian opera singers, brought up on generations of gloomy, weather-torn sets for *Lucia di Lammermoor*, arriving swathed in their Dolomite skiing woollies, sweltered in Princes Street Gardens and swore blind that whatever might be the Scottish capital's Athenian pretensions, Edinburgh was *definitely* the Naples of the North. The pattern for the festival was set on Sunday, 24 August 1947, when Paul Paray raised his baton in the Usher Hall to launch L'Orchestre des Concerts Colonne into Haydn's G Major Symphony, not inappropriately known as *The Surprise*. There were several surprises, only the first of them being opening the Festival with a concert on a Sunday (it was to be many years before anything as profane as a theatre was to open its doors to Sunday audiences) but chief among them was unquestionably the range of talent and artistic quality which Rudolf Bing had assembled for Edinburgh.

L'Orchestre Colonne was followed by the Vienna Philharmonic, the Hallé, the Liverpool Philharmonic, the Scottish Orchestra and the BBC Scottish Orchestra. Glyndebourne Opera offered Verdi's *Macbeth* and Mozart's *Le Nozze di Figaro*. Famous names glittered throughout the programme – Bruno Walter, John Barbirolli, Kathleen Ferrier, Peter Pears, Josef Szigeti, Artur Schnabel, Pierre Fournier, William Primrose, Arturo Benedetti Michelangeli, Elisabeth Schumann, Malcolm Sargent. At the Lyceum Louis Jouvet from Paris was playing Molière's *L'Ecole des Femmes* and Giraudoux's *Ondine* in French with the enchanting Dominique Blanchar. The Old Vic staged *The Taming of the Shrew* with Trevor Howard, Bernard Miles and Patricia Burke and Alec Guinness's portrayal of *Richard II* in a production by Ralph Richardson. At the Empire Margot Fonteyn danced Petipa's choreography to Tchaikovsky's music in *The Sleeping Beauty* above the baton of Constant Lambert.

It was all there, the basic Festival pattern as it still shows today – opera, concerts, chamber music. English and foreign language theatre and dance. Exhibitions were added by Ian Hunter in 1950 and major choral works and the creation of the celebrated Edinburgh Festival Chorus also came later.

But there was a Scottish choir at that first Festival. The Glasgow Orpheus Choir conducted by Sir Hugh Roberton gave a concert in the Usher Hall on the middle Saturday of the Festival, singing one of its distinctive programmes mingling Highland and Lowland Scots songs with Elizabethan madrigals, Irish and Welsh songs and Bach, Elgar and Stanford.

Ian Whyte, the conductor of the BBC Scottish Orchestra had the première of his Piano Concerto at the Festival with Cyril Smith as soloist. There were also concerts of Gaelic songs and Lowland songs and the Scottish Orchestra (the forerunner of today's Royal Scottish National Orchestra) played in the Usher Hall under its conductor, Walter Susskind, with Michelangeli as the soloist in the Ravel Piano Concerto as well as playing for the opera at the King's.

Louis Jouvet in L'Ecole des Femmes *(1947)*

Despite the cautious carping of many of its citizens, the Scottish capital fizzed with excitement. In any weather Edinburgh offers visual drama from almost every street corner, vistas over hills and sea, spiky skylines along ridges, the ordered elegance of the New Town's Georgian squares and crescents. In that splendid summer of the first Festival, the city proved irresistible. Critics who had come to evaluate performances of Verdi and Mozart, Shakespeare, Giraudoux and Brahms wrote golden prose in the manner of travel brochures about the beauties of the city and the surrounding countryside, justifiably enthusing about Edinburgh as a travel destination as well as a centre for the arts.

And this was in the days before gilded travel brochurese was in vogue or indeed could be said truly to exist outside the pages of Kinglake and Freya Stark. When the Festival began in 1947, tourism as the industry we know it today had hardly begun. The first package tour from this country was still three years from take-off.

Edinburgh's holiday season ran from mid-July to mid-August and the Festival was tacked on to the end of that period as a means of extending the season.

Instead of being at the end of the tourist season, the Festival is now in the middle of it and the event itself and the publicity which it attracts annually is undoubtedly one of the principal reasons for the popularity of Edinburgh as a tourist destination.

But all that, and the discussions, debates and arguments it caused, was still to come. The atmosphere at the first Festival was a kind of bemused joy, the feeling that you were unexpectedly attending a lively, very classy party – epitomised perhaps by Margherita Grandi, the soprano singing Lady Macbeth in the opera at the King's, last seen by the audience sleepwalking mournfully in her nightie, who took her curtain call one night in a brilliant crimson evening dress and a mink stole because she was going out to dinner.

12

Plastered poets ululated behind the potted palms at the Festival Club in the elegant Assembly Rooms in George Street, where drink was being sold until the un-Scottish hour of one o'clock in the morning. Margot Fonteyn danced the fox-trot at a dinner party in the Music Hall; Constant Lambert's aphorisms were repeated and elaborated upon all over town; members of the Glyndebourne chorus sang in Rose Street pubs at lunch time (they were shut by the time they had finished singing at the King's in the evening) and people kissed each other in the street, pretending it was an old Edinburgh habit or that they were insouciant continentals who couldn't tell the difference between Edinburgh and Paris.

There was an unfettered feeling, as if the city had suddenly been released from bondage and allowed to rejoin the civilised world at large. Foreigners were at a premium – I remember someone who discovered a Bulgarian girl in the Festival Club and produced her everywhere for the next week as if she were a rare orchid. Public internationalism was *de rigeur*. There were at least 20 nations – some of them recent ex-enemies – represented among the principal artists performing at the Festival and the town was full of foreigners from all kinds of strange places. Everyone had to have one.

It was also full of critics who were having the kind of bonanza they had not been let loose on for a decade. Most of them were highly complimentary – even indiscriminately so – but not all of them.

I recall, as a brash young reporter, going to interview Alec Guinness, whose performance as Richard II with the Old Vic at the Lyceum had been generally lambasted in the press and, more daringly than I realised, asking him what he thought of the reviews. He fixed me with a mild but beady eye and said: 'Dear boy, I always try to remember that there is no such thing as an unemployed audience'.

Although the music was almost universally praised, some musical events were more vividly memorable than others. There was a great deal of Brahms, a lot of it given by the sublime quartet of Artur Schnabel, Josef Szigeti, William Primrose and Pierre Fournier (a true Festival ensemble of an Austrian, a Hungarian, a Scotsman and a Frenchman) who played two Brahms works in each of their three concerts in the Usher Hall to mark the 50th anniversary of the composer's death. The fine texture and the lyrical quality of their playing together set a standard of chamber music performance which the Festival has maintained for 50 years.

Despite having often felt that the Usher Hall is really too large for chamber music concerts, I cannot remember thinking that in 1947. Perhaps it was inexperience; perhaps they really were the greatest quartet ever assembled, as has been claimed.

Certainly they set the pattern of chamber music being an important and vital part of the Festival programmes and one of the most enduringly satisfying features, although today such recitals are usually more compatibly housed in the Queen's Hall.

To me the great revelation of the Festival was the opera at the King's. I had heard operas before – at school I had carried a spear in Erik Chisholm's Glasgow production of *La Clemenza di Tito* and at the San Carlo in Naples during the war I had become an addict. But I had never seen anything that had such dramatic unity and style as Carl Ebert's Glyndebourne Opera productions of Mozart's *Le Nozze di Figaro* and Verdi's *Macbeth*. That my amazement and delight were not naive I discovered when I became friendly with the tall and marvellously expressive Italian bass Italo Tajo, who sang the Figaro and Banquo in *Macbeth*. As two of the only three Banquos currently in town we became close companions and I remember Italo saying that he had learned more about opera in three rehearsals with Ebert than in his entire career to date.

For all the elegance and stylishness of the *Figaro* with splendid performances not only from Tajo but from the Australian baritone, John Brownlee as the Count – still the most superbly autocratic singing of this role I have ever heard – and from Giulietta Simionata as Cherubino, it was *Macbeth* which provided the first genuine Festival frisson and that visual and dramatic as well as musical magic which makes opera a separate and particularly enthralling theatrical spectacle.

From the moment the curtain went up on the gauze-misted blasted heath designed by Caspar Neher, there was the authentic feeling of greatness. I doubt if the opera – despite its local links – had ever been given in Scotland before. Indeed, it was not then often given anywhere, although it is one of Verdi's masterpieces, the greatest work of his early period and so cherished by the composer that he revised it 18 years after its première. It has been done twice at the Festival (the second time in a controversial but in my view highly effective production by David Pountney for Scottish Opera) but that first Ebert version was a unique experience.

The weirdly atmospheric witches' music, the close adhesion to Shakespeare's text, the superb chorus after the death of Duncan, the nervous tension of the banquet scene, the chorus of Scottish exiles, Macduff's splendid aria *O figli, O figli miei!* and the great sleepwalking scene for Lady Macbeth in Act Four remain in the memory from that first production as vividly as if I had seen it yesterday.

And with it the realisation that great words and great music were not necessarily inimical, as they can often seem to be when put together in opera, the insistent drama of the music taking the structure but falsifying the subtlety of the words. From the first scene where the witches chant *Un tamburo! Vien Macbetho* (A drum, drum! Macbeth doth come!) and the dagger scene where the baritone Macbeth sings *Mi si affacia un pugnal?* (Is this a dagger that I see before me?) right through to the end where he bemoans that *Pietà, rispetto, amore* (Compassion, honour, love) he must not look to have and dismisses life as:

> *Il racconto d'un povero idiota*
> *Vento e suono che nulla dinota!*
> *(... a tale*
> *Told by an idiot, full of sound and fury*
> *Signifying nothing!)*

There was music theatre which related vividly to a known piece of drama, heightening the characterisation, the tensions and the impact of the piece with brilliantly interpretative music.

I might, I suppose, have got the same kind of thrill out of Mozart's musical version of Beaumarchais's play *Le Mariage de Figaro* if I had known it as well. But I didn't. I was much closer to *Macbeth*, especially in these three weeks, and one of my dottier Highland relatives even claimed that we were directly descended from him – the real one of course, not the power-mad, hen-pecked bandit portrayed by Shakespeare.

This performance, the Schnabel, Szigeti, Primrose, Fournier quartet, Bruno Walter reunited with the Vienna Philharmonic Orchestra for the first time since he had left Vienna in 1938 as a result of Nazi persecution, the Théâtre de l'Athenée with Jouvet provided the greatest innovations in material, quality and taste for me and, I suspect, the majority of Festival audiences, and set a standard which the already promised second Edinburgh Festival would struggle to match – or so we thought at the time.

There were a few struggles going on behind the scenes too. The battle for the Scottish theatre contribution to the next Edinburgh Festival had been re-engaged by Bridie, Tyrone Guthrie, Harvey Wood and a few others. For 1948 there was a new Lord Provost, the former chairman of the Finance and General Purposes Committee, Andrew Murray. Like Falconer, he was an enthusiast for the Festival idea, now happily backed up by the fact that the 1947 Festival had sold 180,000 tickets

The prophets of doom who had foretold 'a complete fiasco' conducted by 'long-tailed squanderbugs' (the polemic has always been good and acid in Edinburgh) were confounded. The euphoria lingered on and as the Arts Council – in making their grant – had really committed Edinburgh to having at least two festivals, the programme-makers – Bing and his Scottish assistant Ian Hunter with Harvey Wood and his committee – put their halos into moth balls and got down to doing it all again.

The atmosphere at that first Festival was unique, in the truest sense of the word. It was not the shatteringly memorable single performance that stayed in the mind as much as the excitement of the whole, the feeling of total magic, that *everything* was exciting – including you.

IV

On Sunday 14 September 1947, we experienced for the first time the sinking feeling of non-Festival: that terrible vacuum which for many years was to follow the three weeks of frenzied activity, spectacle, music and matters for analysis and delight.

The people who had been our companions, our heroes and heroines, the talented familiars of the previous 21 days, went off to sing at La Scala, act in Paris, make music or dance in London or New York, films in Hollywood; those bright-eyed out-of-town people with whom we had so avidly discussed performances and values of an infinite variety of dimensions just went home to the far-away places from which they had come.

Edinburgh abruptly stopped being the capital of the world and we felt as if a rug had been pulled from under our feet. There was an ominous feeling that it had all been some kind of dream, that it might never happen again despite the promises and plans for 1948.

But amazingly, it could and it did.

In 1948, there was confrontation between the Festivals. There was, already, more than one Festival. The Fringe may hardly be said to have begun in 1947 (although my Banquo on Thursdays in the YMCA, the Gateway in Leith Walk with two plays by T. S. Eliot and Gorky, Bridie and Robert McLellan in the Pleasance and *Everyman* in Dunfermline Cathedral are evidence that there was something fluttering on the outskirts of officialdom) but the Film Festival, opened by the redoubtable John Grierson, had a definite presence from the first year.

John Grierson, apart from being the only man I have ever met who could produce a two-fingered whistle which brought every taxi in Sauchiehall Street to a grinding halt, was the father of the documentary film. 'The creative treatment of actuality' he called it and he had begun the genre with *Drifters*, made in 1928 with the fishermen of the North Sea.

The documentary film had been adopted by every cinematic country in the world and the Edinburgh Film Guild, led by Norman Wilson and Forsyth Hardy and with Grierson's co-operation, organised in 1947 the International Festival of Documentary Films, shown over four performances on Sundays and given in the 3,300-seat Playhouse cinema at the top of Leith Walk. There were films from Russia, France, Denmark, Sweden, Czechoslovakia, Belgium, Italy and the United States and there were also feature films at other cinemas, among them the British films *The Brothers* and *A Matter of Life and Death*, *Les Enfants du Paradis* from France and the Italian *Paisa*.

Jean-Louis Barrault, Hamlet *(1948)*

In 1948 the Film Festival showed Laurence Olivier's stark, black and white *Hamlet* and one of the previous year's cinema stars, Jean-Louis Barrault – everyone's favourite male waif from *Les Enfants du Paradis* – appeared on the stage of the Lyceum Theatre as the

Prince of Denmark in André Gide's French translation. History does not record whether there was a Fringe *Hamlet* that year but if there wasn't, it was one of the few years without one.

My impression was that Barrault's vivid, tense and nervy prince won hands down and that Shakespeare suffered extraordinarily little in Gide's translation but that could be because Olivier in a blonde wig made me feel I was watching Danny La Rue being serious and the cutting of 'Oh, what a rogue and peasant slave am I' offended my youthful pedantry.

The musical director of the Barrault troupe was a thick-haired young man called Pierre Boulez and another member of the company was an actor named Marcel Marceau. The Festival was to see them again, as it was Barrault, one of the actors who returned most regularly to Edinburgh.

By this time the performances which in the previous year had laboured under the ponderous grouping 'Festival Adjuncts' had acquired a name. In an article which appeared in the Edinburgh *Evening News* on 14 August 1948 as a preview of theatre offerings to come, Edinburgh dramatist Robert Kemp christened the Fringe in one phrase: 'Round the fringe of official Festival drama there seems to be more private enterprise than before'. Not everyone leapt on this particular semantic bandwagon instantly however and Kemp had a more important contribution to make to the second Festival and several others to come. He was to be the architect of a Scottish Festival triumph.

Harvey Wood, the chairman of the Festival's Programme Committee had signalled it from a distance in early August 1947 in a defensive article in *The Scotsman* about the first Festival:

> *It may also be hoped that we may find a Scots equivalent of* Jedermann *to be a recurrent and characteristic element in future programmes. It does not seem beyond the power of possibility that Bridie might do for Lyndsay's* Satyre of the Thrie Estaites *what he did for Chaucer's* Pardoner's Tale *or that* The Gentle Shepherd *which held the Scottish stage for generations, might be susceptible to the same arts of revival that were so successfully employed on Gay's* Beggar's Opera.

But it was Robert Kemp, BBC producer and a prolific and accomplished playwright who adapted Lyndsay. Ever since the Festival idea had been made public Kemp had campaigned for a part in the programme for the Scottish theatre, even if Bridie was to say later 'the Scottish theatre is not yet born'.

There had been a meeting with the leading practitioners in Scotland, David Steuart from the Perth Repertory Theatre, A. R. Whatmore from Dundee, Colin White from the Citizens' Theatre in Glasgow and Robert Mitchell who had already brought Unity Theatre, the left-wing Glasgow group, to the first Festival with an 'Adjunct' offering Maxim Gorky's *The Lower Depths* and Robert MacLellan's *The Laird of Torwatletie*.

All had submitted ideas to the Festival committee, varying, as I recall, from joint productions to single performances by each of the main Scottish companies. But the idea of a repertory season from the Scottish theatres never really took off and in 1948, the choice fell on an ancient Scottish classic which most people had barely heard of, almost no-one had read and which had not been performed for 396 years.

Despite a certain amount of literate enthusiasm, it did not seem too promising a project. Written by Sir David Lyndsay of the Mount, Lyon King of Arms to James V, the royal official responsible among other things for arranging Court entertainment, it had run for more than nine hours when it was first presented before James and his Queen, Mary of Guise at the Palace of Linlithgow.

But its patrons Kemp, Harvey Wood, Bridie and Tyrone Guthrie believed in it. Although written in the densest Lowland Scots and much too long, it said things about people and the structure of life in Scotland which Guthrie thought could be adapted to provide not merely a fascinating revival of the earliest Scottish play to make a major public impact, but to have relevance and meaning for people today.

Ane Satyre of the Thrie Estaites was a bold political and social statement for its times and must have had a few eyebrows shooting up into the hairline when it was presented to the powers-that-be at Linlithgow in 1540.

Obviously, James V, that curiously tortured, devious king who moved among his people in disguise like Harun al- Rashid to find out what they thought, liked its acid wit, its lampooning of the church, its earthy humour, and even perhaps its plea for the rights of the common man, for it had several performances. Guthrie saw it as a compelling spectacle, using the vigorous tonality of the Scots tongue as a kind of purposeful and satirical music.

So Robert Kemp pruned and remoulded the 16th-century text to a manageable three hours – a brilliant work of scholarship and craftsmanship for which it has always seemed to me he never got enough credit, swamped as the final presentation was by the direction and the acting. A musical score was commissioned from Cedric Thorpe Davie, a collaborator with Kemp in previous radio ventures. The only problem was to find a place in which to present such a sprawling, multi-cast spectacle. Guthrie later wrote:

> *We visited big halls and wee halls. Halls ancient and modern, halls secular and halls holy, halls upstairs and halls in cellars, dance halls, skating rinks, lecture halls and beer halls. Darkness was falling, I was beginning to be acutely conscious that I had led them all a wild goose chase. Then spake Kemp in the tone of one who hates to admit to something unpleasant: 'There is the Assembly Hall'.*
>
> *The minute I got inside I knew we were home. It is large and square in the Gothic style of about 1850. It has deep galleries and a raked floor sloping down to where, in the centre, the Moderator's throne is set within a railed enclosure. The seats have sage green cushions; there are endless stone corridors. Halfway up the steep black approach – it stands on one of the precipitous spurs of the Castle Rock – is a minatory statue of John Knox.*

Guthrie's fine theatrical eye took in the sweeping possibilities of the building. The others in the inspection party, Bridie, Kemp and Willie Grahame, the Assistant Administrative Director of the Festival were not as certain and were dubious about the consent of the Church of Scotland to its use for theatrical purposes.

The Assembly Hall is used by the Kirk for its annual 'Parliament', the General Assembly at which ministers and elders meet to debate and discuss not only church matters but the social and political state of the nation. Both Kemp and Guthrie had family associations with the Kirk and may have feared more from its strictures than was justified. There were no problems, no attempt at censorship of the often bawdy text, no inhibiting restrictions on use. Only one condition was made – that no nails should be hammered into the Moderator's throne.

In such a manner, the only play to survive the Calvinistic moral proscription against the theatre of the Scottish 17th and 18th centuries came to the Festival. In Kemp's vigorous and racy text the 'commendation of vertew and vituperation of vyce' became a 20th-century smash hit. But not at once.

Although the cast of Scottish actors assembled for the performances were enthusiastic and stirred by the flair and brilliance of Guthrie's direction of the piece, there was not much advance information about *Ane Satyre of the Thrie Estaites* and booking was poor.

It was one of the first instances of what was to become a Festival truism. The sense of experiment in Festival audiences is low. You can tell them how good something is going to be, produce reams of documentary and other evidence of its quality, garner quotes ranging from hyperbole to hysteria from the glitterati commending it but no-one will buy a ticket until Mrs McWhauchle next door has seen and been amazed by it and tells all her friends.

They then rush to the box office like demented lemmings and if the performance is only on for three days, you find that on the last night you could have done it five times and on the first night you needn't have bothered.

This phenomenon has the important counter-merit that the Edinburgh Festival enjoys the greatest word-of-mouth recommendation anywhere. It has happened many times down the years and is particularly needed by the Fringe at the size it is today, so large that it is only barely untrue to say that by the time you have finished reading the programme (never mind the reviews) it is too late to go to anything.

There has never been a more vivid instance of how the local tom-toms carry the message than the 1948 *Thrie Estaites*. Rudolf Bing, who must have had his doubts about it, as even his fluent and eloquent command of English hardly encompassed 16th-century Scots, brought the Lord Provost, Sir Andrew Murray and his sister the Lady Provost to a rehearsal and went away genuinely enthused. Even so the first night was heavily 'papered' with free tickets given to students and nurses. After the final, splendidly staged exit of the 60 characters, the audience rose and stamped and cheered and rushed out into the night to tell others. (What the Festival owes down the years to these anonymous legions of word-spreading nurses and students is incalculable.)

The critics raved. Guthrie's sweeping and inspired direction won the most accolades but the power and attack of Scottish actors like Douglas Campbell, Archie Duncan, James Gibson and James Sutherland were also highly praised and the sinuous ingratiation of Duncan Macrae was lauded to the skies.

John Duncan Graham Macrae was the greatest Scottish actor of his day, an ex-schoolmaster who had abandoned the classroom to become one of the pillars of the Citizens' Theatre in Glasgow, an extremely intelligent, highly expressive and marvellously gifted Glasgow Highlandman, who was to use his ability and his not inconsiderable polemical powers to fight for the Scottish theatre to the day he died in 1967. I remember long journeys back to the west end of Glasgow with him on a red tram in the year before the war, when he was still a schoolmaster at Finnieston and I was a schoolboy and we were both involved with the Rutherglen Theatre, founded by another great Scottish theatrical character, Molly Urquhart.

The trips took at least an hour and were devoted to passionate dissertations on the meaning and validity of artistic endeavour of many sorts besides the dramatic. For the most part I just listened but I used to go to Scotstoun Showground on spring Saturday afternoons to train his school classes in athletics for which John (as we called him in those days) did not have much aptitude or dedication.

The passion survived to such a degree that when I was the theatre critic of *The Scottish Field* and wrote in one annual review that the Macrae influence on the previous year had been negligible because he had appeared in nothing but revivals of former triumphs, he didn't speak to me for two years! I was forgiven in the end for what could only have been a juvenile indiscretion (I never quite lost with John the image of the youthful postulant on the red tram) and was able to join his enthusiasm for plays like *The Queen's Comedy, Gog and Magog* and

Don Giovanni *(1948)*

Johnny Jouk the Gibbet in which he appeared at the Festival and elsewhere. A great man, the flavour of whose talent, conversation and caring knowledge lingers yet.

The Thrie Estaites was a sell-out, the first great original triumph of the Edinburgh Festival. The word spread like flame on dry moorland. Queues of people were turned away. In a strange and deeply satisfying way Scotland had discovered something about itself it had not known before. Only boasted about.

The enormous, unexpected success of *The Thrie Estaites* swamps the memory of the second Festival but there were other splendid things as well. The opera at the King's was again Glyndebourne with a powerful production of Mozart's *Don Giovanni* and an elegant *Così Fan Tutte*, both directed by Carl Ebert. The Don was a splendid, vividly lecherous Italian baritone, Paolo Silveri and the Donna Anna, Ljuba Welitsch, a well-curved Bulgarian lady with a magnificent voice and a temperament like a scorpion.

Unlike the first Festival the weather was not at all Neapolitan and Ljuba was cold in the draughty, unheated King's Theatre during rehearsals. ('It's August,' the manager said, 'Ah can't justify the heating being on in August!') So I took Ljuba down to the Scottish Wool hosiery shop at Tollcross to buy some thick socks.

Various gaudy, chunky specimens were produced in thicknesses varying from exquisite cashmere to fishermen double-knit by two nervous middle-aged ladies who were unused to a customer with quite Ljuba's *panache*. The socks were waved around the shop and she also wantoned variously be-socked legs at me and the assistants and sought their opinions. With her bright red hair, archly flashing smile and her voluptuous figure, she was hardly the type of customer this shop, an essentially sober establishment generally catering for Morningside ladies and their knitting wool, was used to.

When she was certain she had caused everyone the maximum amount of embarrassment, she chose six pairs and then discovered she had no money to pay for them. While I fumbled in my pockets for coins with milled edges (the cost of the socks was about three-quarters of my weekly salary) she said in a voice that was wont to make the chandeliers rattle in the Staatsoper in Vienna:

'But you trust me, Eee-yan! You know my name.' And laughing uproariously, she turned to the pink-faced ladies. 'You know what it means?' she asked them. 'Ljuba Welitsch? Welitsch – it means "great" – Ljuba it means "loh-ov. Great loh-ov".' And shrieking with extrovert mirth, she enveloped me in a bosomy embrace. I got my money back all right but I shopped elsewhere for my socks after that. There were enough Don Giovannis in town without my being added to Morningside's mental roster.

Another younger and much prettier Morningside lady also had a bit of DG trouble. She was rightly a great admirer of Paolo Silveri and when I introduced her to him at a party, his highly attuned perceptions took delighted stock of her brilliant blue eyes, lovely face and lissom figure. When I discovered that he had invited her to dinner in his hotel, I said: 'Well go, but remember that Don Giovanni is a role he plays off-stage with as much devotion as on' and she looked at me with one of those coquettish smiles pretty girls are so good at, and went.

A panicky phone call from the lobby of The Caledonian Hotel the following evening had me galloping down there on my metaphorical white steed to the rescue. It transpired that the excellent education of this charming and intelligent lawyer's daughter had not provided her with the information that Don Giovanni is the Italian for Don Juan. Festivals are full of semantic traps.

There was another occasion when I was with John Pritchard (later, Sir John and a distinguished conductor but then a *repetiteur* with Glyndebourne) and a Glyndebourne group asked to lunch at Drumlanrig Castle on a Festival Sunday. John and I noticed, as we were being given a conducted tour by the Duchess of Buccleuch, that Paolo had vanished with one of the pretty Buccleuch daughters. Anxious not to cause needless alarm but anxious nevertheless, we hived off from the main party and began to search through the large and rambling building which neither of us knew, only to find Paolo ensconced in the music room innocently playing the piano and singing the enchanted girl Neapolitan songs.

I have always thought the most fervent rendering I ever heard of the Don's response to Leporello's plea at the beginning of Act II was from that season's Don Giovanni.

Lasciar le donne? Sei pazzo!
(Give up women? You must be mad!)

The saga of angry women was continued in the Lyceum Theatre where the Scottish actress who had leapt to fame as the Queen in Jean Cocteau's *The Eagle Has Two Heads* played the title role in John Gielgud's production of Euripides's *Medea* in a translation by Robinson Jeffers.

Eileen Herlie had acted at the Rutherglen Theatre with John Macrae and me in the very first production in 1939 and it was clear even then that she was star material. Her Medea was a striking and passionate performance.

She was to appear again in the 1954 Festival in Thornton Wilder's *The Matchmaker*, his Americanisation of one of Nestroy's Viennese farces which subsequently became the musical *Hello Dolly!*, before she went to America and stayed there. 'Beautiful, talented and terrifying' someone once described her but she was always very nice to me and I remember her with admiration and affection and have always counted her a great loss to the British theatre.

In 1948 there were again two foreign orchestras, the Augusteo from Rome conducted by Furtwangler, Carlo Zecchi and Vittorio Gui with a number of Italian soloists including the violinist, Gioconda de Vito, the cellist, Enrico Mainardi and Michelangeli.

Arturo Benedetti Michelangeli was a reclusive pianist of genius and high individuality, who later became one of the Festival's great 'cancellers', but he turned up all right at the first two Festivals and I remember him vividly because of the genuine, totally absorbed intensity with which he played and because he was annoyed with the Festival authorities for not letting him practice in the Usher Hall for nine hours before each performance he gave !

I shall never forget Michelangeli playing Chopin with a deep intellectual fervour not usually accorded to this composer and which I have heard in few other interpretations but the impression I retain of the great Chopin occasion of the 1948 Festival is less well focused.

This was when the celebrated Swiss pianist, Alfred Cortot, editor of Chopin's piano works, played the programme of the recital given by Chopin himself in the Hopetoun Rooms in Queen Street, a hundred years earlier.

Cortot had a reputation for a romantic but musicianly delicacy of touch and was considered one of the great Chopin interpreters but by the time he gave the concert in Edinburgh he was over 70 and the magical clarity of expression had become rather muddied and uncertain. The air of hushed expectancy with which the aged pianist was greeted itself created a memorable atmosphere but it grew less hushed and somewhat impatient as the concert wore on.

This was a lesson that the Festival, like all ambitious projects, had to learn. You can't win 'em all.

However, with the triumph of *The Thrie Estaites*, the splendid nervous dynamism of Barrault's *Hamlet*, excellent opera productions at the King's, which as well as *Don Giovanni* presented a charming production by Ebert of *Così Fan Tutte* in elegant sets by Rolf Gerard and with a cast which included the incomparable Erich Kunz as Guglielmo, the second Festival did something very important. It gave the whole institution continuity and an air of permanence. It sold even more tickets than its predecessor – 237,000. It made the Festival an *established* success.

V

Early in 1949 things were beginning to change. In March of that year the Festival Director went to New York to try to raise some finance to re-open Glyndebourne properly with a full season. Glyndebourne was then only appearing at Edinburgh and Bing was still its General Manager. The English opera company still commanded his first loyalty – indeed he later admitted in his highly entertaining autobiography *5,000 Nights at the Opera* that his primary purpose in creating the Edinburgh Festival had been to keep the Glyndebourne Opera in being.

But the American finance for the Sussex opera house turned out to be an illusion at that time. Bing even had his shoes stolen from the corridor of the seedy hotel in which the potential sponsors put him, when he left them out to be cleaned. He did not, however, return empty-handed. Before he left the United States he had been offered one of the most important musical jobs in the world.

In May he signed a contract to be General Manager of The Metropolitan Opera at a salary not far short of the first Edinburgh Festival's budget. Edinburgh was both proud of the honour done to its newly created Festival by Rudolf Bing's appointment and somewhat worried about his successor.

Bing's assistant Ian Hunter remembers having lunch with him just after he returned from New York and, on hearing the news, saying to Bing: 'What a pity you weren't offered it five years later because I'm not going to have any chance of following you.'

Bing said in his crisp way: 'Oh yes you are. I'll make sure that you do.'

He put it to the Lord Provost Sir Andrew Murray, who in turn put it to the Committee, which, after deliberation, and with devastating Edinburgh logic, took the line that as Bing was Viennese perhaps they had better look to Vienna to provide a new director. Hunter was just 30 and could justifiably have been considered rather young for such an important post but support for him came from a very influential quarter, Stewart Cruikshank, the chairman of Howard and Wyndham Theatres who probably had more experience of assessing managerial capability in the world of the arts than anyone else on the Festival Committee. He told them: 'Oh no, I think you are quite wrong. You should give the young lad a chance.'

It was a very wise choice. Ian Hunter, now Sir Ian, is a Scot who had been educated at Fettes, a stocky, dark-haired man with a rapid blink-rate which sometimes gives the impression of diffidence. Nothing could be farther from the truth. Hunter is a highly gifted, intelligent and sensitive man who combines the multifarious selective talents of an impresario with real administrative ability and a great deal of honest straightforward charm.

Even when he came to be the director of the most important and wide-ranging festival in the world at the early age of 30, he had a considerable amount of experience behind him. As a 15-year-old schoolboy at Fettes in Edinburgh he knew he wanted a life in music, inspired by Henry Havergal who had started him off playing the French horn in the school orchestra a year earlier. Through another music master and that staunch pillar of Edinburgh musical life Tertia Liebenstahl he met Sir Donald Tovey, the English composer and musicologist who was Professor of Music at Edinburgh University and studied with him for two years.

Hunter wanted to be a conductor so Tovey sent him to Fritz Busch at Glyndebourne in the summer of 1938. A year later Britain was at war. During the war he served with the RASC in North Africa and Italy and became a

Sir Ian Hunter

staff officer as a Lieutenant-Colonel with the Sixth Armoured Division. When the war in Italy was drawing to a close his corps commander, who knew he had been at Glyndebourne, asked him to form an orchestra to entertain the troops and, after the Allies entered Austria, he was asked to open the Klagenfurt Opera. Typically, Hunter knew what he wanted. He said: 'Yes – on three conditions'. One: that he was allowed to fraternise (occupying troops were not at that stage of the war allowed to associate with the enemy); two: that he should have the support of the Royal Engineers to make the scenery; three: that he had the co-operation of the Intelligence Corps to comb through prisoner-of-war camps to find musicians.

'So I had the experience of being a sort of intendant early on,' Hunter told me, 'and when I went back to Glyndebourne after the war and saw Rudolf Bing and said to him I was out of the army and looking for a job, he said "Well, I've got one young man working for me who is running the opera – that was Moran Caplat, who had come out of the Navy six months before me – but there is a job going being my assistant. And," Bing added, "There's this idea of starting a festival – we're thinking of Oxford and we're thinking of Edinburgh." The minute he mentioned Edinburgh he remembered that I knew it well and I got the job at £10 a week.'

Thus it was that after working with Bing for three years between May 1946 and May 1949, Ian Hunter inherited the Festival. At first the canny Edinburgh Corporation only allowed him to be called Artistic Administrator. A year later that he was granted the title Artistic Director for doing the same job.

Hunter felt he had learned a lot from Bing, who was good at delegation and allowing his assistants responsibility and his problem really was to do something different. All Festival directors have felt this compulsion and although all of them have made changes and additions perhaps the most fascinating aspect of Festival structure is how sound the initial pattern was. Although things have been added from time to time and different directors have stressed their own preferred aspects of programming, nothing has been taken away from the 1947 plan. Fifty years later concerts, opera, chamber music and recitals, English-speaking and foreign theatre and dance are still at the core of Festival programming.

The first thing which Hunter added in the first festival for which he was directly and wholly responsible in 1950 was a major art exhibition. There had been exhibitions at Festival time in the previous years notably a Bonnard and Vuillard show mounted by the Royal Scottish Academy at the first Festival but painting and sculpture and what are generally called the visual arts – as if there were nothing visual about theatre, opera or ballet – had never been officially featured.

Before the Hunter regime, the brief reign of Bing culminated in the third Festival in 1949 in a programme which, while it remained within the pattern, was a development of previous years.

The triumphant *Thrie Estaites* was repeated and there was another adaptation of a Scottish classic by Robert Kemp, Allan Ramsay's *The Gentle Shepherd*. This 18th-century Scottish pastoral written by the wigmaker, bookseller and poet who opened Scotland's first regular theatre in the Royal Mile in 1736 (typically, it was closed by the magistrates in 1737) also caused problems in choosing a venue for it. Tyrone Guthrie its director thought its modest proportions and delicate ballad opera texture too fragile for the Assembly Hall.

Bing wanted it presented as a kind of late-night cabaret but was disappointed when he found it was precious rather than naughty, because he clearly felt that Edinburgh needed some light relief after the concerts and the plays were over.

Finally, it was given in the Georgian Hall of the Royal High School on the Calton Hill and although it did not quite have the bite of some subsequent late-night entertainments, it provided a charming and nostalgic end to the evening. At the 40th Festival, as part of the 1987 theme of the Enlightenment – Edinburgh's golden age of the 18th century – it was revived.

A gesture of international forgiveness saw the bicentenary of Goethe's birth marked by the appearance at the Lyceum Theatre of the Dusseldorf Theatre led by the celebrated German actor and director Gustaf

Grundgens in Faust. On the ever-growing Fringe, Joan Littlewood's Theatre Workshop was presenting a programme which included the première of *The Other Animals* by Ewan MacColl, a play about a political prisoner in a concentration camp.

Grundgens had leaflets and abuse hurled at him accusing him of having been a Nazi. Ironically, he had not long emerged from a Russian prison camp, released after passing a de-Nazification tribunal. He was a memorable Mephistopheles, sardonic, handsome and sinister in the Dusseldorf production but clearly not a happy man for he killed himself while on tour in Manila in 1963.

The other Germans at that year's festival were the members of the Berlin Philharmonic Orchestra, who played in the Usher Hall wearing lounge suits instead of the traditional orchestral uniform of white tie and tails because such luxuries were not available in Germany in 1949. The suits were rather shabby but there was nothing down-at-heel about their playing under Sir John Barbirolli and Eugene Goossens.

The musical diet was enriched by two other foreign orchestras, the Orchestre de la Suisse Romande under Ernest Ansermet and the Orchestre du Conservatoire with the Belgian conductor André Clutyens and Bruno Walter. One of the soloists with the Paris orchestra was the contralto from Blackburn in the north of England, Kathleen Ferrier who had won rapturous praises for her singing of Mahler's *Das Lied von der Erde* with the Vienna Philharmonic and Bruno Walter in the first festival. Bing had suggested her to Walter when he was dubious about finding the right voice for Mahler's song-symphony of which Walter had conducted the première six months after the composer's death in 1911. Walter became an instant admirer.

'I recognised with delight,' he wrote of their first *Sir John Barbirolli* meeting, 'that here was potentially one of the greatest singers of our time; a voice of rare beauty, a natural production of tone, a genuine warmth of expression, an innate understanding of musical phrase – a personality.'

He described his association with Kathleen Ferrier as 'one of the happiest experiences of my life as a musician'. She appeared in six Festivals, several times with Walter, until her tragic death from cancer at the early age of 41 in 1953.

The 1949 Festival also produced a convert. A small, spiky, witty and opinionated convert in the unique shape of Sir Thomas Beecham who just the year before, while in Glasgow to conduct the Scottish Orchestra, had said with characteristic forthrightness: 'The people of Scotland are damned fools to throw away £60,000 on a musical festival.'

Sir Thomas considered that the money would be better spent on supporting Scotland's own orchestra but when he was invited to bring *his* own orchestra the Royal Philharmonic to the third Festival, he was gracious enough to accept. He even recanted his Glasgow views in a BBC broadcast.

I have very largely modified that first view because I can see that one of the results of this Festival after three years has been to stimulate curiosity in the whole of the country and will rouse a much greater interest in music of all kinds.

He also expatiated on the Festival's social virtues:

It is quite obvious that at this period in the history of Europe, there are few things more desirable and more necessary than bringing people together in amity and allowing them to meet on perhaps the only common ground of meeting, where there can be no likely chance of them disagreeing for more than two minutes or coming to blows, and that is music.

However Sir Thomas's own concerts did not escape the charge of banality also levelled at the BBC Scottish Orchestra for playing D'Albert's Cello Concerto with the great Portuguese cellist, Guilhermina Suggia (most famous perhaps for her magnificent portrait by Augustus John) as soloist. The critics were getting tougher and the honeymoon period for the Festival as an institution was over, although the carping at the D'Albert was an excellent example of the 'you can't win' syndrome because D'Albert was born in Glasgow and Ian Whyte and his orchestra were presumably trying to cast some kind of native hue over the programming.

Certainly the concert programmes for 1949 made a serious attempt to break new ground as well as offering the classical war-horses. In addition to the D'Albert Concerto which was perhaps a rarity for the best of all reasons, there was a new Concerto Symphonique by the Swiss composer, Ernest Bloch, an intriguingly spiky piece for orchestra and piano based on Jewish liturgical themes, conducted by the composer, a serene, bald little man with great style. There was a new symphony by Ian Whyte also conducted by the composer. Two world premières with the composers on the podium was bold stuff and there were other items by living British – even Scottish – composers such as Hans Gal, Arnold Bax and Cedric Thorpe Davie.

Nor was the heady air of experiment confined to the concert hall. At the Lyceum Theatre a new play had been commissioned from the leading poet of the day, Thomas Stearns Eliot.

In 1948 T. S. Eliot had been awarded the Order of Merit, the most exclusive honour given by the Queen, limited to 24 members, and had won the Nobel Prize for Literature. *The Cocktail Party* was awaited with real excitement. It was his first play since the war and many people had never seen an Eliot play, although those who had, remembered *Murder in the Cathedral* and *The Family Reunion* as highly original pieces of verse drama.

The Cocktail Party puzzled everyone, with its loose conversational verse structure, its plot tangled with cross-references to Euripides's *Alcestis* and Eliot's own tenets of Anglo-Catholic morality and psycho-analysis – one of America's other religions – all couched in London drawing room mannerism *chez* Grosvenor Square.

It was brilliantly acted by Alec Guinness and Irene Worth heading a distinguished cast and, as it felt like the kind of thing you ought to be able to understand if you had any pretension to intellectualism (and there was plenty of that around at the early Edinburgh Festivals), it was a hit.

This was the first of three plays which Eliot wrote for the Festival and it went on to score successes in London and New York but apart from a performance by the Gateway Company in Edinburgh a few years later, it has curiously resisted revival, although *The Family Reunion* and *Murder in the Cathedral* reappear from time to time.

It was an important play because it was central to the brief flourish of poetic drama on the English-speaking stage just after the war, which gave us the banner-waving verse plays of Christopher Fry like *The Lady's Not for Burning*, *Venus Observed* and *The Dark is Light Enough* as well as Eliot's more pedestrian strophes.

Both styles now seem to have been driven from the theatre by the later surge of 'kitchen sink' and other determinedly didactic and socially conscious plays which began with John Osborne's *Look Back in Anger*. I wonder if I am the only person who mourns their passing.

I have always envied (who hasn't?) Peter Ustinov's unique ability to be intelligent, intellectually analytical and devastatingly accomplished at the same time as being uproariously funny but even he is rather terse about the other play at the Lyceum that year, his *The Man in the Raincoat*. In his deliciously entertaining autobiography *Dear Me* he says: 'It was played by Mary Ellis and George Colouris, who disliked each other so heartily during rehearsals that there was nothing left over for the performance.'

When he returned to the Festival in 1982, I asked Ustinov about *The Man in the Raincoat*. 'It was very popular in Norway,' he said with mock defensiveness, 'where it was known,' he added with relish in a fluting Scandinavian accent, 'as *Mannen i Regnfrakken*.'

It was in these first years too, that the principle and the practice of taking the Festival to the people to whom it was inaccessible began. It was iniated by a curious combination of a great Scottish baritone, my bank manager and me – and despite the intrusion of the bank manager it had absolutely nothing to do with money.

During the second year that I worked with Glyndebourne, getting their singers some extra local publicity and acting as a kind of liaison officer between Moran Caplat, the Glyndebourne manager and the city, I met a man who became and has remained one my closest friends and who, for nearly 50 years, has effortlessly maintained my first assessment of him as one of the nicest men in the world.

This is Ian Wallace who in 1948 provided a Scots voice on the opera scene when he came to Edinburgh to sing Masetto, the much-put-upon husband of Zerlina in Mozart's *Don Giovanni*. Ian and I got on famously from the first meeting and together we cooked up the first Festival venture at 'taking the Festival to the people'.

My other friend, the bank manager – well, I'd been in the Navy with him – Bill Young really started it off by telling me one day of his wife's disappointment at missing the Festival. She was in hospital with tuberculosis. I told this to Ian and together we formed a Glyndebourne 'concert party' which visited hospital wards and sang and played to patients who could not leave their beds to attend performances.

The first hospital we visited was the one in which Bill's wife was a patient. When you recall that in 1948 tuberculosis was regarded as very much the same sort of plague as AIDS is today, I thought it was singularly brave, public-spirited and generous of the singers to join in – and what a marvellously entertaining and distinguished bunch they were.

John Pritchard played the piano and in addition to Ian there was Sena Jurinac, the lovely and superbly gifted Yugoslav soprano, Paolo Silveri, Petre Munteanu the Romanian tenor and the beautiful Hilde Gueden and Erich Kunz from Vienna and, in later years, the fine American tenor, David Poleri, the English bass Hervey Allen, the incomparable Geraint Evans, Italian soprano Alda Noni and the Spanish tenor, Juan Oncina.

In every way it was a star-studded cast and over the early years we visited several hospitals each festival. None however, was quite as touching as that first one.

When we left after numerous encores, and were getting into our cars in the hospital yard, all the patients to whom we had been singing who could walk and some of the nurses, came out onto the hospital balcony and sang to us:

'Will ye no come back again?' There weren't many dry eyes in that audience.

SIR IAN HUNTER 1950-5
The Young Lad's Chance – the Festivals Multiply

VI

Ian Hunter's first Festival, Edinburgh's fourth, saw the whole concept truly come of age. The honeymoon period with the critics was over; there was a new young director in the driving seat. Other festivals were beginning, some new and fired by Edinburgh's example, some old and recovering from the devastation of war. Salzburg and Bayreuth were once more in full swing – Salzburg to the innovatory extent of having already premièred three operas in addition to its usual Mozart programme. Bayreuth stuck to Wagner.

It had not, at that point, reached the current stage when festivals are as common as flag-days but the festival business was definitely getting competitive in money, artists of international calibre and audiences. Something special was required from the fourth Edinburgh Festival if it was to stay in the top league. And that was just what Ian Hunter provided.

I wrote an account of it at the time for the American magazine *Theatre Arts*.

The Scots are renowned for their love of argument. It is almost the only part of their international reputation which they cultivate assiduously and, for that reason alone, they must be content with the fourth Edinburgh Festival. There have been talking points in all Edinburgh Festivals of course, but never has there been offered such a variety of subjects on which to differ from one's neighbour as this year.

Musically, the merit and faults of Richard Strauss's Ariadne auf Naxos *will be fuel for the fire of debate well into the New Year. Dramatically, Eric Linklater's* The Atom Doctor *and, to a lesser extent, Bridie's* The Queen's Comedy *promise to provoke controversy at the drop of a hat until the 1951 Festival at least. The American Ballet Theatre, Spanish dancers Antonio and Rosario, the standard of acting in a small Festival side-show,* Never Get Out *which was a critic's rave, the Tattoo, the flowers, the fireworks – all will have their devotees to keep their memories burning in the heat of discussion.*

Two things only gained universal and unstinted admiration – the playing of the Orchestra of La Scala, Milan and the exhibition of 36 paintings by Rembrandt in the National Gallery of Scotland. I put them in order of impact rather than of merit.

To say that La Scala made an impression is a gross understatement. They left a dent – even in the hide-bound souls of the Edinburgh bourgeoisie who have spent years cultivating an impenetrable resistance to indelicate emotion in public. But La Scala got them.

I met them outside Edinburgh's beautiful Usher Hall, reeling speechless into the night, brushing terribly unfurtive tears from their cheeks, and I laughed from the sheer exhilaration of it – it was all I could do. I was no more capable of words than they were.

Even now, in the calmness of reflection, it is difficult to find words to describe the effect of this magnificent orchestra. One was not merely listening to music, one was taking part in it – in its ecstasies, its exhilarations its tragedies and terrors so that at the end of the concert one was emotionally, mentally and almost physically épuisé.

As one of my friends remarked after the final concert 'Thank God in a way they're going. I don't think I could live through another week of this!'

La Scala appeared during the last of the three weeks of the Festival. With the orchestra, there came from Milan the chorus from the opera house and four soloists, Renata Tebaldi, soprano, Fedora Barbieri, mezzo-soprano, Giacinto Prandelli, tenor and Cesare Siepi, bass. In Edinburgh the concerts were conducted by Victor de Sabata and the 30-year old Guido Cantelli. During their triumphant opera season in London which followed the Festival, Franco Capuana was added to the conductors and almost every other modern Italian singer of note to the list of singers.

Naturally, choral works predominated at Edinburgh. The week opened and closed with the Verdi Requiem. *The theatricality and operatic nature of the work was much in evidence but nobody cared. Such crashing blows of sound were achieved in the* Dies Irae *and the serene glory of the final* Libera Me *with the incomparable voice of Tebaldi floating superbly above the chorus not merely disarmed but destroyed criticism.*

By itself, the orchestra provided some of the most exciting music I have ever heard. It did this without much help from the programmes. Even such an over-played and exaggerated work as Tchaikovsky's Fifth Symphony *took on a new grandeur in their hands. The only excuse for including such a work in the programme at a Festival is to make of it something new and splendid. This, under young Cantelli's baton, incredibly,* La Scala *did.*

The entrance of the brass with the motif in the final section had a dramatic splendour which I have never heard equalled and, although I remain adamant in my dislike of this symphony, I would travel many miles to hear it played like that again.

It would be easy to go on talking of La Scala *but for the limitation of English superlatives. How I long to be able to use the Italian -issimo ending to describe their playing of Rossini or Respighi's* Pini di Roma *– or but why go on? If I have not made my point by now I never will.*

In a quite different way, the Rembrandt exhibition was of the same stature. In these 36 examples of every stage of Rembrandt's career as a painter, there is no assault on the emotions, no almost intolerable but ecstatic drama but only a great and deep humanity. In every canvas there glowed that sympathy and comprehension of human frailty which pardons all because it completely understands. The passions which La Scala's music aroused could be sweetly assuaged by the serenity which Rembrandt's paintings radiated.

The way in which the painter achieved his intensely realistic effects by being deliberately dramatic contains a lesson for every playwright. Although the first impression of Rembrandt's work is of the naturalness and vitality of his subjects, this reality is produced by the most theatrical means.

The lighting in most of his pictures savours more of the theatre electrician's spotlight than of any natural means and the balance of light in such pictures as Lady at a Window *might well cause even a stage lighting expert a headache.*

The treasures of the show were the almost unknown Family Group *and the famous* The Shipbuilder and His Wife, *both newly cleaned, the first lent by the Herzog Anton Ulrich Museum in Brunswick and the second by His Majesty King George VI. Both are family pictures, both radiate that tranquil tenderness which is the ideal of family life and which no-one has ever portrayed like Rembrandt.*

Where – after a moment for recuperation – La Scala made one feel like rushing out and taking Edinburgh Castle single- handed, the Rembrandt exhibition pointed out clearly that there was more enjoyment to be had from standing in Princes Street watching the grey battlements sail against the clouds over the city.

But during the Festival such tranquillity could not last long. Outside the peace of the National Gallery a conflict raged and sooner or later, all who had seen the plays at the Lyceum Theatre were drawn into its vortex.

The storm raged around the bald head of Scots novelist and playwright, Eric Linklater, who had written for the Festival a 1950 adaptation of Ben Jonson's The Alchemist *which he called* The Atom Doctor.

This witty farce made a lot of people laugh and I am inclined to prophesy that it will make even more people laugh before its time is out, but with the distinguished exception of the two most eminent British theatre critics Ivor Brown and Harold Hobson, the press tore it to shreds.

Leading the assault were the Scottish critics trumpeting with indignation. How dare Linklater write a farce for the Festival? The deep belly-laugh accords ill with the cultural aspirations of the Scots theatre. Something more fitting was expected – and so on.

The simple fact that when one writes a farcical comedy it is intended to make people laugh and that if it does so, it has every right to be considered a success, escaped them. There were I think, two reasons for this. First the new Scots creed that theirs is an intelligent almost an intellectual theatre, and second, Duncan Macrae.

James Bridie's The Queen's Comedy *was fairly well received, partly because it is very nearly a good play – and is certainly a better one than Daphne Laureola – in spite of sententiousness at the end, and also, one could not help feeling, because you could not appreciate all the jokes unless you were acquainted with* The Iliad.

In The Atom Doctor *a knowledge of Ben Jonson undoubtedly sharpened your enjoyment but you could take it from scratch and still laugh with great heartiness throughout.*

Then Macrae. Duncan Macrae is the greatest actor in Scotland. In The Thrie Estaites *last year and in 1948 he was an international success. He played the lead in* The Atom Doctor *and was acted off the stage and into the aisles by Patricia Burke, an actress imported from London who is better known for her musical comedy roles than as a straight player, although she has been successful in what the British snobbishly call 'the legitimate theatre' before.*

The Atom Doctor *(1950)*

Miss Burke played the Doctor's slatternly mistress, whom he uses to entice clients into parting with their money, with all the stops out – to such an extent, in fact, that it caused a little uncomfortable shuffling among the more puritanical Scots critics – but no-one denied that it left Macrae looking rather pale and vapid. Too many of the Scottish hopes are pinned on Macrae and this reversal, taken in the right spirit, should do nothing but good.

The Queen's Comedy *had its moments – and here Macrae in a ten-minute sequence as a Clydeside Vulcan was a riot. Taking as its theme the relationship between Gods and men and with the siege of Troy for its setting, it promised much and for the first act fulfilled that promise most entertainingly.*

Unfortunately in the second act the tempo slowed noticeably, particularly in the long scene between Juno, superbly played by Sonia Dresdel and Jupiter, acted by Walter Fitzgerald in a much less satisfying manner. At the end came anti-climax. The mortals, snatched from life, confront the Gods and an impassioned soldier berates them for their indifference to mankind.

The play then closed almost inaudibly with a long and unexciting speech by Jupiter of the kind in which unsuccessful politicians specialise 'Hang on, things will get better some time – maybe'.

There may well be more in this speech than Mr Fitzgerald got out of it but, as it was played in Edinburgh, it was a disappointing ending to a play which had moments of brilliance and which, for at least half its length, raised high hopes.

By contrast, the disinterred Scots classic Douglas *by John Hume, given its first performance for 150 years, for which no hope was held out before the first night, was at least a moderate success. The lines which when read had seemed tedious, came to life in a great performance of the Mrs Siddons' part, Lady Randolph by Sybil Thorndike. Dame Sybil's family indeed came out of Douglas with all the credit for not only did she herself give a noble and moving performance but her son-in-law, Douglas Campbell played the title role with a most effective strength and vigour while her son, John Casson was the producer who had the courage in face of criticism which would have deterred more famous theatre figures, to put on the play and stage it in the grand manner.*

Perhaps Douglas *will not have many more performances but if not, it will have gone out in a blaze of glory as it began and it gave us the chance of seeing a play which is a landmark in the history of the Scottish theatre.*

Whether or not there will be another revival of Douglas *is a debatable point but I think we can say with confidence that the Edinburgh Festival saw the dernière of Ben Jonson's* Bartholomew Fair *which the Old Vic gave at the Assembly Hall for three weeks.*

There were some fine performances in it but the play is so dull and uneventful that only a genius like Tyrone Guthrie, who used the same apron stage so brilliantly in The Thrie Estaites *and who directed the Bridie and Linklater plays this year, could have made anything of it.*

George Devine did his best but the enormity of the task defeated him from the start and one could not but feel sorry for him and the talented cast who were wasted on this Elizabethan fiasco.

From Greek classic à la Bridie to Greek classic à la Strauss/Hofmannsthal. Not that classical mythology was by any means all that was offered in Ariadne auf Naxos *at the King's Theatre. It came under the Festival classification of opera but that is a term of ready reference rather than a description because in form and content, I should think* Ariadne *is unique.*

The version presented at Edinburgh by Glyndebourne Opera was that of the original conception by librettist, Hugo von Hofmannsthal and composer Richard Strauss. The first act was made up of an English translation of Molière's Le Bourgeois Gentilhomme, *acted not sung by Miles Malleson as Monsieur Jourdain and a fine cast of English* *actors with balletic interludes danced to music from Stra*uss's Bourgeois Gentilhomme *suite.*

In the second act, after a prelude of quarrelling singers – still not singing – the opera was presented as the after- dinner entertainment offered by Monsieur Jourdain to his guests.

On the excuse that Jourdain wanted the whole thing over as quickly as possible, the two parts of the evening's diversion are mixed up – heroic Greek tragedy interrupted by the commedia dell'arte *of Zerbinetta, Harlequin, Brighella, Scaramuccio and Truffaldin.*

Musically, the whole thing is amazingly ingenious. The contrasting themes are cleverly interwoven and the orchestration is a delight. But what does it all add up to? For me, I am afraid the answer was – nothing.

In spite of first-rate performances all round – a wonderful Zerbinetta with a tremendous vocal range which encompassed an aria containing a top F with ease, from Ilse Hollweg, a beautifully sung Ariadne by Hilde Zadek and a pathetically funny Jourdain from Miles Malleson – the final impression was one of immense cleverness which could not but be admired but which aroused no other emotion. In spite of the success of the component parts Ariadne *failed to achieve that unity which is essential to a successful art form. It remains in the mind as a brilliantly executed highbrow cabaret show – but not as an opera, a play or a ballet or anything else which is complete in itself.*

Over the other opera Le Nozze di Figaro *it is kindest to draw a veil. Conductor Ferenc Fricsay's idea of Mozart* tempi *would have baffled the most gifted of singers and apart from a charming performance by Sena Jurinac as Cherubino and Ian Wallace's nicely rounded Bartolo, none of the singers overcame the handicap which* maestro *Fricsay imposed on them.*

Ending something as compact and exhilarating as the Edinburgh Festival has always presented its organisers with a problem. This year they solved it with complete success.

After the last concert had finished and the final curtains had come down on the plays, opera and ballet, all the world and his wife made their way towards the great Castle which crouches watchfully on its rock in the centre of the Scottish capital.

*There, in a pool of light in the centre of the Castle esplanade, Britain's diminutive, thrustfully bearded, dynamic first conductor, Sir Thomas Beecham directed massed military bands in a performance of Hand*el's Music for the Royal Fireworks, *scored for brass, woodwind, strings – and cannon!*

Sir Thomas had the time of his life. As he lunged towards the Castle battlements, cannon boomed in response to his baton thrusts and when the music was over, from the turrets and buttresses of the Castle there rose a succession of rockets and fireworks which sprayed the clear skies with stars of gold and red and green. drifting across the city in a gay and splendid shower of light as a Festival farewell.

As the last of the artificial stars faded and the crowds walked down the hill towards their homes and hotels, the heat of discussion barely raised a flicker after the simple pleasures of noise and light which even the most sophisticated had enjoyed. The arguments would be taken up again in the morning but, as they walked home arm in arm that night, everyone was convinced that it had been a fine Festival.

I have included all of this rather arrogant youthful assessment of one of the early Festivals because I think it reflects some of the wonder and excitement we all felt in these days – and also the stressful necessity, if you were appearing in print, to be seen to stand up intellectually and culturally to the many fascinating and occasionally wonderful performances with which we were being bombarded!

Ian Hunter told me that when Sir Thomas Beecham conducted the massed bands at that final concert on the Castle esplanade, Lady Beecham insisted that he should wear a tin hat on the podium to protect him from being struck by a falling rocket. As a recent Army officer, Ian signed the right form and obtained it.

After the concert, in which the new Festival Director had been playing his part by crouching below the podium and pressing the button which signalled to the gunners on the battlements when to fire the cannon at appropriate points in the score, Ian found himself virtually alone on the esplanade when a soldier stamped up, came to attention and said: 'Surr, Ah have a requisition order fur Sir Thomas Beecham's helmet – and Ah must hiv it back!' Retrieving tin hats is just one of the lesser-known facets of a Festival Director's job.

I have rather revised my opinion about Bridie's *The Queen's Comedy* since I first saw it in 1950 and now think of it as probably his best play and one which the Festival should think of reviving. It seems a great pity they did not take the opportunity to do so on the centenary of his birth in 1988.

Also about Tchaikovsky. Although, in defence of my pretty snobbish comments on the Fifth, I would beg to point out that it was the current view at the time, epitomised by Scott Goddard, music critic of the *News Chronicle,* who was sitting next to me in the Usher Hall when Guido Cantelli led the Orchestra of La Scala, Milan into the stupendous climax which they made that night of the Fifth Symphony.

As the echoes of the last shattering brass and drum rolls faded, there was a moment's stunned silence from the audience before it broke into wild and clamorous applause.

Into that pulsating moment of hush, Scott, with tears streaming down his face into his grey beard, said very loudly in his strong Northern accent. 'Christ! It's not nearly as good as that!'

The finest piece of music criticism I have ever heard.

VII

1951 was the year of the Festival of Britain and the plethora of festival-type events all over the country gave Edinburgh very serious competition; but by now the Festival was acquiring a unique atmosphere, an ethos of its own. And festival-goers were developing an ethereal stamina of their own which enabled them to attend more diverse items in those three weeks than they normally did in the rest of the year.

But there were still times, of course, when we earnest seekers after culture found ourselves gasping for breath. The glittering sea of the assembled arts seemed at times to be closing over our heads. In each direction you turned a new wave was bearing down threatening to engulf you completely. It was at this stage of avid festival exhaustion in 1951 that I slept through an entire performance of *Le Rendezvous de Senlis* by Jean Anouilh given by the Théâtre de l'Atelier from Paris at the Royal Lyceum but, undaunted, I returned to see it awake at the matinee next day!

What is it about the Edinburgh Festival that gives festival-goers this dogged stamina? Is it just the natural cussedness of the individual who, having bought his Festival tickets, is determined to enjoy himself even if it kills him – or is there something else? I think there is.

Nowadays, of course, we are all so blasé about the Festival phenomenon that we just take satiation for granted. But I think there is a Festival ethos special to this city. It is the most heady mixture you can imbibe and even the most sober visitor to Edinburgh at Festival-time must swallow a drop or two which builds up his resistance to concert-fatigue, opera-neurosis and dramatic apathy. Festival addicts, of course, inhale it in gallons and become virtually impervious to normal human frailties for three weeks. One American critic Gerry Berkowitz even got into the Guinness Book of Records by attending 132 Festival and Fringe performances in one visit.

The mixture is composed chiefly of three things. The first and least of these is Edinburgh itself.

There is always an appeal about Scotland's capital, with its grey castle crouching with massive watchfulness over the city, the lands and vennels along the windy ridge of the Old Town which descends towards Holyroodhouse and the grace and Georgian splendour of the 18th-century New Town. These physical attributes are enhanced at Festival-time by the vivid life which flows around them and, curiously enough, by floodlighting.

This device, often so garishly employed, is strangely effective in Edinburgh. The Castle, seemingly perched on cloud, leaps at you out of the night sky, the crown of St Giles steeple floats like a portent above the High Street and even the terrible Bank of Scotland building on the Mound takes on a kind of necromantic splendour. The natural grandeur of the city is also exploited by the Tattoo, held on the Castle esplanade, against the magnificent backdrop of the Gatehouse, the Half-Moon Battery and the ancient palace where the first king of Scotland and England was born to Mary, Queen of Scots in 1566. What was once a simple display of piping and dancing by the soldiers of Scottish Command, had by 1950 grown into a military extravaganza masterminded by Brigadier Alasdair Maclean, an international spectacle and the biggest single show on the Festival scene.

The Tattoo is not part of the 'official' Festival programme but Ian Hunter has always felt that it should be more involved with the central Festival.

'If the Festival Director were to sit down with the Director of the Tattoo, they must be able to dream up some way in which they can work together. There are some enormous musical works after all – there's Beethoven's *Wellington's Victory* for example with cannons and bands and fireworks – and that's only scratching the surface.

'There must be other enormous works which could be presented in the Tattoo setting and with their help. They could even be specially written, I suppose.'

But the spectacular nature and the beauty of Edinburgh is only one of the ingredients of the Festival ethos and, I would be rash enough to suggest, the least of them. I say this not out of any disregard for the city's charm, to which I am certainly as susceptible as anyone, but because Edinburgh is there all the year round but the Festival atmosphere is not. It vanishes with the last visitor and with the exception of occasional events like the Commonwealth Games and rugby internationals is absent for most of the other 49 weeks of the year.

The second component of the Festival ethos is the people who come to Edinburgh for the Festival and the effect they have on the douce burghers of Scotland's capital.

From all over Europe and America and even farther afield come men with high-domed foreheads and women with the determined spark of intellectual fire in their bright eyes. They generate heat, they are full of ideas, opinions, theories about almost everything you can think of – and even a few things which might not easily have occurred to you.

They dress extravagantly, sometimes in the extravagance of Roman or Parisian elegance, sometimes with the scruffy international individuality of the Left Bank, Greenwich Village or San Francisco, sometimes like perambulating protests. They talk extravagantly, once of Mozart, Picasso and Eliot now of women's rights, black power, drug trips, green issues and the latest manifestations of the 'underground' or alternative theatre which the Fringe helped to create.

And those impassioned, uninhibited people strike sparks off the Scots who go to the Festival. They arouse the ingrained Scots passion for argument and we launch forth on the kind of intense intellectual discussion which our neighbours and over-influential friends – the English – still secretly consider to be rather embarrassing bad form.

Sometimes to our surprise, we find that we are rather good at it and the discussions linger on for weeks after the Festival. Occasionally some of the visitors have stayed on and got involved in founding things like the Traverse Theatre, the Scottish Chamber Orchestra, Stills Gallery, 7.84 or a new vegetarian restaurant.

Over the last couple of decades the Festival has often managed, like a turbulent stream, to leave something behind when it has passed, throwing up a few boulders here and there for the timorous to stub their toes on, irrigating an often briefly flourishing patch of growth.

For what the Festival does, of course, is to turn Edinburgh for three weeks into a major European capital. Only this can explain the frenzied desire on the part of every manifestation of the arts of communication and persuasion to add within the same three weeks yet another mini-festival to the giant carbuncle that the Edinburgh Festival has become!

In addition to the central Festival and the myriad activities of the Fringe, the Film Festival and the Tattoo, we now have a Television Festival, a Jazz Festival, a Radio Festival, a Book Festival and from time to time a Photographic Festival or a Textile Festival, a Youth Orchestras' Festival, a Crafts Festival and what appears to be a scaffolding festival starting on the heights of the Castle Rock and spreading its steel web down into the entrails of the city.

All these, with the possible exceptions of books, are about as indigenous to Edinburgh as *chili con carne*. So far we have managed to avoid having a Tory Party Conference in the middle of the Festival but that could be just a Saatchi-type inspiration away.

The concerts, the opera, the plays, the paintings, the ballet, the pulsating indignant life of the Fringe, the pond which became an ocean; the gossip, the penchant for outrage and Richard Demarco all give us common ground for discussion and dissension and for three exotic weeks we live in an extraordinarily concentrated and potent atmosphere.

Rikki Demarco has always said that he wants to make Edinburgh a Festival city all the year round but I don't know if we could stand it. The daily dose of cultural press-ups might prove fatal rather than rejuvenating.

However, what is undoubtedly true is that in Festival time Edinburgh becomes not merely a European capital city but temporarily the artistic capital of the world.

To anyone who cares about the arts this is a giddily enlivening experience – and the people who go to the Festival, all half-million or so of them, *do* care and even the most Morningsidely moribund of councillors is forced to have *some* opinion about it.

But I said there was a third constituent and although it is the least pragmatic and the most romantic and idealistic, it is also the most important of the three, the *raison d'etre* of the Edinburgh Festival.

The constant hope of glory is not an ingredient of everyone's everyday lives but it is an integral and paramount part of the Edinburgh Festival. At the first Festival it was only hope. Today, to those of us who are regular Festival addicts, it is hope backed by 50 years of experience.

The Edinburgh Festival has brought an incomparable richness to Scotland and it would be impossible to recall all the moments of glory it has offered since it began in 1947. But there are some of unusual splendour.

I remember the day on which the fifth Edinburgh Festival began. At lunch-time on that Sabbath morn, before even the first fanfares of the opening service at the High Kirk of St Giles , the highlight of that Festival was named and chosen.

Our group of Festival veterans – four years or more service with the capital's cultural colours – had gathered together for a glass of something warming to the heart and welcoming to the Festival and we were searching for a phrase expressive of the rigours, the unexpected joys and sorrows, the ecstasies and calamities which befall us at Festival-time. Unerringly and unanimously we chose our catch-phrase, the words with which we could greet the nerve-chilling spectacle of Peter Westwater refusing his second whisky, Sydney Goodsir Smith unpolemical in a pub and which would be equally appropriate to crown an unattended pleasure or a chance encounter. We picked the phrase from the Festival programme. It was *La Forza del Destino* – 'The Force of Destiny'.

It was a happy choice for not only did it serve our frivolous purpose nobly but it endowed us all with the mantle of the prophet. Glyndebourne's production of Verdi's monumental melodrama *La Forza del Destino* was one of Edinburgh's most spectacular triumphs.

On the first night when the curtain had come down for the last time after everyone who could possibly be imagined to have any connection with the performance had taken at least five curtain calls and the singers' reappearances were well into double figures, my old friend Lionel Daiches (whom I had virtually dragged to the performance) and I staggered out into the chill Edinburgh night in a babbling crowd aglow with glory.

On reflection, perhaps the opera has its demerits; it may be that the plot is both involved and improbable, but no-one cared. It was magnificent, superb and wonderful. Unashamed tears stained our cheeks and *Bravos!* had burst unchecked from our lips. We were drunk with a divine intoxication which owed nothing to liquor and we reeled away in the direction of the Festival Club (which in these days was still worth reeling towards) ablaze with Latin exaltation.

That was glory – and it is very far from being an isolated example. Who could forget the performance of the *Verdi Requiem* by La Scala, Milan? Or Tchaikovsky's *Fifth Symphony* conducted by a then unknown young man called Guido Cantelli? Or the first night of Eliot's *The Cocktail Party*? Or Ferrier's *Alto Rhapsody*? Or *The Thrie Estaites*? Or Strehler's stunning production of *Arlecchino* with the brilliant Marcello Moretti? Or Edwige Feuillière as *La Dame aux Camelias*? Or *Orlando Furioso* as created by Ronconi at the Haymarket Ice Rink? Or Rembrandt? Or Bernstein's *Mahler Second*? Or Dickie Buckle's two great exhibitions *Homage to Diaghilev* and *Epstein*? Or the Japanese Ninagawa Theatre's spectacular *Macbeth* and *Medea*? Or Abbado's *Alexander Nevsky* and the great *Carmen* production at the King's which he conducted with such passionate fire and grace?

And for every one of these searingly memorable performances there are at least a couple of alternatives and often more. The list, like Macbeth's apparitions, can seem to stretch out to the crack of doom.

The constant hope of glory: that is the most powerful ingredient in the Edinburgh Festival atmosphere. The knowledge that in the next concert hall or theatre, the next cellar or adapted church hall, you may hear or see something which you will remember all your life. The 'unforgettable moment' has become an advertiser's cliché but much of the magic of the Edinburgh Festival is due to the fact that there is always at least one genuinely unforgettable moment, one instant of pure fused emotion and delight which in memory will recapture the thrill with which you first experienced it. Of course, it is often a different moment for different people. Everyone brings their own acceptance and astonishment to such occasions but the Festival survives because such moments are always there. That is also what makes each Festival such a hard act to follow.

Unlike Bayreuth which always presents only Wagner operas and Salzburg which, as Mozart's birthplace, centres its programming on the works of its native son, Edinburgh has no such anchor and this makes choosing the programmes especially difficult as the Edinburgh Festival has, from its inception, competed in quality with the greatest festivals in the world.

It means that in Edinburgh, items can rarely be repeated year after year, as is done in these other two great festivals. It has been done occasionally with *The Thrie Estaites* and, when Peter Diamand was running what was in fact Edinburgh's own festival opera company in the 70s, all the opera productions created over these six years were repeated but this is the exception rather than the rule. In all the approximately 8,000 performances given at the Festival there have been very few successive repetitions.

In 1952 Ian Hunter, who had already changed and enlarged the Festival pattern by including art exhibitions within its framework, changed the mould again. He did not use Glyndebourne, which had been the lynch-pin of the Festival and the original organising body, but invited a foreign opera company from Hamburg.

It was a hard decision for him to take because he had always been closely associated with Glyndebourne and John Christie had really given him his first chance in the music business but in the course of he travels Hunter had seen, and been impressed by, the work of the remarkable German director, Gunther Rennert with the Hamburg State Opera.

Hamburg, despite the drawbacks of the King's as a venue for major opera, brought six of their most important productions, which provided an historical cross-section of German opera from Mozart to Hindemith and Edinburgh with the most comprehensive opera programme it had ever seen.

Although the Hamburg visit created or highlighted problems, it was a triumphant success. The limitations of the King's Theatre were sufficiently apparent when productions were specially designed to be shown there, as Glyndebourne had done in the first four years. But when productions designed for much larger continental opera houses had to be truncated for the King's, the primitive back-stage facilities became more of an irritant.

The lack of an orchestra pit meant that rows of expensive stalls had to be taken out to accommodate a sizeable orchestra and be filled by rows of even more expensive musicians – who appeared on the opposite side of the balance sheet!

Nevertheless, under the direction of Josef Keilberth, Leopold Ludwig and Georg Solti, they gave us 150 years of German opera from Mozart's last work *Die Zauberflöte* (1791) through Beethoven's only opera *Fidelio* (1805), Weber's *Der Freischutz* (1821) and Wagner's *Die Meistersinger* (1868) to Richard Strauss's *Der Rosenkavalier* (1911) and Hindemith's *Mathis der Mahler* (1938).

All of them except the Hindemith were reasonably familiar and they were performed by a company full of great names such as Lisa della Casa, Inge Borkh, Elisabeth Grummer, Anneliese Rothenberger, Martha Modl, Rudolf Schock and Gottlob Frick. *Mathis der Mahler* (Matthias the Painter) was the only 'new' opera the Festival had offered up to that time. It was not exactly contemporary in setting as it was the story of Matthias Grunewald, the great German painter famous for his grim and magnificent altar-piece at Isenheim in Alsace and his part in the Peasants' Revolt of 1524 and, if the music proved to be dramatic and declamatory rather than lyrical and tuneful in the manner of Verdi, it seemed adequate enough proof that modern composers could write music that was different but within the great operatic tradition. I think its romantic setting and the fine staging by Rennert had something to do with its impact but I have always remembered *Mathis* kindly and have long wanted to see it again without ever having had the chance to do so.

I remember Paul Hindemith too whom I met at some Festival social gathering either that year or another when his works were being played, a large cheerful bald man in a grey suit who told me the only German joke about Scotland he knew. It must have been popular on the continent because Marcel Marceau told me the same story in French in 1953. *Accident de deux taxis à Glasgow. Douze morts, quarante-six blessés.*

In 1951 we had the Festival's most consistent playwright, William Shakespeare, represented by a cool, elegant, almost elegiac production of *The Winter's Tale* directed by the 26-year old Peter Brook. The play, which includes the most dramatic stage direction which the Bard ever penned – 'Antigonus's Exit, pursued by a bear' – moved very slowly but was beautifully spoken by John Gielgud, Diana Wynyard and Flora Robson – and the bear duly made his singular appearance.

Lack of vigour, however, was not something of which you could accuse Hugh Hunt and the Old Vic when they presented *Romeo and Juliet* at the Assembly Hall in 1952. This was the first of many Shakespearean productions in the setting which had been pioneered by Guthrie for *The Thrie Estaites* and it raged about the open stage area with such pace and violence that, sitting anywhere near the front, you felt almost in need of a sword to defend yourself from the brawls of the Montagues and the Capulets in the passionately humid atmosphere of Verona.

Alan Badel made Romeo more lustful than languishing, his lines ringing with the petulance of frustration rather than the gentle *arpeggios* of romantic love, Peter Finch was a splendid, wearily cynical Mercutio and the 20-year old Claire Bloom – always and still one of the most beautiful women on the English stage – was a meltingly desirable Juliet with a sensuous innocence which I can remember hauntingly to this day.

She returned to the same venue the next year to play Ophelia to Richard Burton's emphatically masculine and deeply torn Hamlet in another Old Vic production by Michael Benthall. For once Ophelia became something more than an instrument of Hamlet's single-minded paranoia and between them the 'Get thee to a nunnery scene' fuelled, I suspect, by not a little genuine mutual attraction, became composed of the tugging madness and despair which breaks the heart.

It too was a fine production, using the sweep and space of the Assembly Hall to give new visual dimensions to Shakespeare's text and although as Ophelia, her part was largely a foil to Burton's vibrant, eloquent, tortured Hamlet instead of the ardent star she was as Juliet, it was enough to confirm that here was an actress of true quality and enormous potential.

There was more Shakespeare at the 1953 Festival in French. Jean Vilar's powerful company from Le Théâtre National Populaire mounted an austere but effective *Richard II* with Vilar himself in the title role. Although it was impressively staged, I missed the colour of the language in this French adaptation (as I had not in the Gide-Barrault *Hamlet* of 1948) and it was Molière's *L'Avare* and the other contribution from the French theatre which gave the greatest pleasure.

This was Marcel Marceau, the great French mime, who had appeared with the Barrault company at the 1948 Festival. Here, in silence, was total theatrical magic – the death-defying teetering along the tightrope with the audiences gasping at the precipitous sway, the amiable drunk leaning wordlessly against the gradually-harder-to-find bar, the pursuit of the butterfly, the terrible tragic struggle of the despairing face fighting to get out of the ever-smiling mask. All done on the flat boards of an empty stage with illusion complete.

Here were the basics of theatre, the stark, comic, grotesque contrasts between reality and illusion, very trusting and very cynical; almost always leading to the proof that trust (and therefore love) is a phantom and that just round the corner lies the banana-skin of humiliation. What seemed just a brilliant refinement of technical skills became a philosophical, analytical interpretation of the way we lived – or failed at it.

And yet Marcel made us laugh at our inadequacies, at our failures through a medium older than words. I remember one evening when he came back for something to eat and drink to our flat in Coates Crescent – a star abandoned, as so many of them are, in the moment of triumph at the dressing-room door by the appalling inhospitality of the Festival authorities – I remember him drawing a tree with his hands in our sitting-room, spectral and bare in winter, then gently budding, then in full leaf with birds singing in it.

Not a sound, pure visual magic, needing no theatre tricks, no lighting, just a genius for depicting things, emotions and situations which went back to the beginning of time and still speaks in a silent, totally comprehensible language now.

In the years between 1950 and 1955, Ian Hunter had the task of consolidating the Festival, making what had been a bold, even rash enterprise secure and established. To do this without making it dull and unimaginative was a major achievement and the way in which he broadened the Festival and made it more splendid and international and more world-renowned will always compel my admiration.

There is a tendency to think that the early directors had a wider choice of programmes and that it was only as time went on that innovation became more difficult. But in 1951, Festival of Britain year, Hunter faced the problem that not only was every other town in Britain competing for performers but that virtually all the great orchestras, ballet companies, theatre companies and soloists of Europe had *already* been to the Edinburgh Festival.

So he crossed the Atlantic for his orchestra and, with the aid of an additional grant, negotiated for the New York Philharmonic to come to Edinburgh and give no less than fourteen concerts in one of the best orchestra series Edinburgh has ever mounted – and these concerts were exclusively Edinburgh's. There was no question of the New York orchestra using Edinburgh as a stop-off on the way to the Proms in London or a tour of Europe, as has been too often the case with transatlantic performers who have come here in recent years.

Nor was this massive concert programme simply a parade of the popular classical war-horses, known to be sure crowd-pullers. It contained two superb choral performances in which the chorus was the Edinburgh Royal Choral Union, trained by its chorus-master, Herrick Bunney. The choral concerts were each given twice, with an all-Brahms programme in the first, including the *Song of Destiny*. The second was Beethoven's *Ninth Symphony* with four American soloists and Bruno Walter as conductor.

Other concerts were conducted by Dimitri Mitropoulos, the Greek principal conductor of the Philharmonic-Symphony Orchestra of New York (as it was then somewhat ponderously known) and included some American music – a *Short Symphony* by Swanson, *Philharmonic Waltzes* by Morton Gould and an extraordinary piece *Symphonic Elegy* by Ernst Krenek, written in memory of Anton Webern, the Austrian 12-tone composer who was accidentally shot dead by an American soldier during the occupation of Salzburg in 1945.

Mitropoulos also appeared as a soloist in the Fourth Piano Concerto by Gian-Francesco Malipiero, the rediscoverer and transcriber of Monteverdi, and there were works by Mahler, Prokoviev and Bruckner, by no means as common names on concert programmes then as they are today.

To hear two very different conductors direct the same orchestra in several performances was a memorable and educating experience. Mitropoulos, a wildly waving, batonless figure, drew music of a vibrant, almost steely precision from the wonderfully gifted forces of the American players while the gentle, august gestures of Bruno Walter produced a quite different sound, more lyrical and reminiscent of the Vienna Philharmonic..

It was a perfect refutation of the foolish theory that 'conductors don't matter, it's the orchestra that counts'. Both played Beethoven, both played Brahms but the interpretations were from different ends of the musical spectrum – one was not better than another, just different, perfect examples of what makes concert-going such a fascinating business.

VIII

It is a characteristic of Festival Directors that when they go, they like to go out in a blaze of glory and when Ian Hunter relinquished the post in 1955 to become the managing director of the musical impresario firm of Harold Holt, he took his leave at the end of one of the finest Festivals Edinburgh had ever seen.

There had been plenty of splendours before. Among those not already mentioned was the emergence of the Amadeus Quartet at several festivals (and many since) as one of the best chamber music groups in the world, recitals by Pierre Bernac and Francis Poulenc and a colourful performance by the Yugoslav Ballet in *The Legend of Ohrid*.

In 1952 the Concertgebouw Orchestra from Amsterdam (managed by Peter Diamand) appeared for the second time, the Curzon-Szigeti-Primrose-Fournier quartet repeated the chamber music triumph of 1947 with Clifford Curzon taking the place of Artur Schnabel who had died the previous year. There was also the première of a play, *The River Line*, by Charles Morgan, one of the literary gurus of the day, now almost forgotten. I remember it chiefly for a fine performance by John Westbrook and the fact that there

was a line in the second act when someone said 'How quiet it is,' which was immediately followed by a boom of cannon from the Castle battlements above the Lyceum Theatre announcing the start of the Tattoo.

Another verse play by T. S. Eliot, *The Confidential Clerk*, was commissioned for the 1953 Festival and its wry complexities ingeniously elucidated by Denholm Elliott, Margaret Leighton, Isabel Jeans and Paul Rogers. Glyndebourne returned with two operas by Stravinsky, *The Rake's Progress* and *The Soldier's Tale*, a work which is a kind of cuckoo's egg in the opera nest as there

The Player King *(1952) by Christopher Hassall – one of the Festival's drama commissions*

are no singers but it was elegantly mime-danced by Moira Shearer and Robert Helpmann and narrated by Terence Longdon. More conventionally Glyndebourne offered in 1953 and 1954 two delicious and then little-known Rossini operas *La Cenerentola* and *Le Comte Ory*. Herbert von Karajan made his first appearance at the Festival in three concerts with the Philharmonia which included a majestic performance of Beethoven's Seventh Symphony and the Violin Concerto with Yehudi Menuhin and works by Britten, Debussy, Mozart, Ravel, Bartok and Tchaikovsky.

The Vienna Philharmonic returned with Furtwangler and Walter, there was some marvellous ballet from American, French and Spanish companies and in 1954 a great exhibition marking the 25th anniversary of the death of the great Russian impresario, Serge Diaghilev. *Homage to Diaghilev*, masterfully created by Dickie Buckle, was one of the greatest-ever Edinburgh exhibitions, full of striking imaginative touches worthy of the *maestro* himself.

It was a true theatrical experience of tremendous virtuosity, with music, sets and costume designs by Picasso, Utrillo, Cocteau, Benois, Bakst, Derain, Matisse and Braque, fantastically lit and brilliantly evocative of the special magic of the theatre of dance.

Almost breathtakingly at the same time, in the Royal Scottish Academy there was the most complete and comprehensive exhibition of the works of Cézanne ever shown in Britain – another unlikely-ever-to-be-repeated experience of the revolutionary impact of a great painter, a sweeping view of the manner in which Paul Cézanne took the ideas of the Impressionists into another dimension within his philosophical concept that 'Art is a harmony parallel to nature'.

An extraordinary visual year was complemented by a new production of Stravinsky's *Firebird* danced by Margot Fonteyn and the Sadlers Wells Theatre Ballet and by the Comédie Française with Louis Seigner as the greatest Monsieur Jourdain I have ever seen in a superbly stylish and divinely funny performance of Molière's *Le Bourgeois Gentilhomme*. His rendering of the phrase *Ah, quelle belle chose de savoir des choses*! sticks in my mind to this day, not only as a beautifully delivered comic line but as a perfect delineation of the bumptiously ambitious Monsieur Jourdain. Molière, of course, must also take some of the credit.

Anyway, with all that and the dazzling range of exhibitions which had marked his regime – Rembrandt, Spanish Painting from El Greco to Goya, Degas, Renoir plus Medieval Yugoslav Frescoes, Diaghilev and Cézanne – Ian Hunter was likely to find it difficult to make his last Festival programme the equal or the peer of the others.

His task was further complicated by the fact that at the end of the 1954 Festival, the Festival Society had to draw on its reserve fund to meet steadily rising costs and, not for the last time, money was tight.

However, the measure of all great festival directors is that they are able to accomplish miracles of financial legerdemain without sacrificing the quality of the programmes. Indeed some of Edinburgh's artistic directors must often have thought ruefully that they had been appointed for no other talent. In 1955 Ian Hunter became the first Festival Director to exercise this particularly frustrating fiscal skill.

A new play was commissioned from the American dramatist Thornton Wilder, whose *The Matchmaker* (later in its career to become the musical and to reappear in another guise at the 1981 Festival as Tom Stoppard's *On the Razzle*) had been one of the hits of the 1954 Festival.

Richard Burton Hamlet *(1953)*

Glyndebourne brought three operas, Rossini's *Barbiere di Siviglia, La Forza del Destino* and Verdi's last and perhaps greatest opera, *Falstaff*. One of the conductors in charge of Forza was my old friend, John Pritchard, who had in fact conducted opera with Glyndebourne at two previous Festivals in 1953 and 1954. Vittorio Gui, who was to have conducted *Falstaff*, became ill during rehearsals and in his place came the music director of Radio Italiana, an Italian conductor little known outside his own country, 41-year-old Carlo Maria Giulini.

Giulini made his international reputation at Edinburgh, as many artists have done down the years, by his brilliant handling of Verdi's sensitive and complex score.

The Berlin and New York Philharmonic orchestras returned, conducted by Eugene Ormandy, Wolfgang Sawallisch, Hindemith and Josef Keilberth with the German players and Mitropoulos, Cantelli and Bing's *bête noire*, Georg Szell with the Americans. The Royal Danish Ballet appeared at the Empire Theatre where they offered a very classical repertoire, much of it based on 19th-century choreography, an appropriate contribution from the second oldest ballet company in the world, but also a new *Romeo and Juliet* by Frederick Ashton.

At the Royal Scottish Academy the exhibition illustrated and illumined the life, work and philosophy of Paul Gauguin, the painter whose life story has always appealed most to arty romanticists, abandoning the career he had made as a successful stockbroker as well as his wife and family because the urge in him to paint and to change the painting of his day was so strong.

In the bountiful collection on view in Edinburgh the whole gigantic canvas of his struggle to learn to paint, to master the technique and change it so that it might express what he wanted to say, was on display.

You might leave the gallery still not altogether sympathising with the man who deserted his five children and his Danish wife (even if she was 'bourgeois and philistine' as the catalogue insisted) to paint every day instead of just at weekends, but you were nearer understanding him and closer to realising that such an anti-social and inhuman attitude might have its rewards and even justifications.

At the Lyceum Theatre there was another link with the Creole strain, which added such strange and exotic touches to 19th-century French artistic life. Like Gauguin, Alexandre Dumas *fils* had Creole blood through his grandfather, although it never captured his imagination as it did the painter's.

It is odd that he should be remembered by his least typical play *La Dame aux Camélias*, because the younger Dumas was a bit of a prig, over-sensitive about his illegitimacy and envious of his flamboyant and more successful father.

Most of his theatrical output was of a socially conscious and improving nature but the original lady of the camellias, Marie Duplessis, a courtesan of the days of Louis-Phillipe, particularly touched his heart and, just a few months after her death in February 1847 at the age of 23, he wrote a novel about her which he subsequently made into a play.

She seems to have been an exceptionally appealing girl who numbered Franz Liszt among her admirers and the play in which she is depicted as Marguerite has outlasted everything else the younger Dumas ever wrote and still provides an impressive vehicle for a star actress.

At the 1955 Festival it got one, Edwige Feuillère, the greatest French actress of her time, for some critics the greatest actress in the world. Sir Harold Hobson, eminent theatre critic of *The Sunday Times* said of her:

> *Of these, the impression that most vividly remains is that of Madame Feuillère: tall, languorous, incomparably magical. Madame Feuillère is the only actress I have seen who unites extreme physical allure with the highest mastery of her art. Her movements have a slow incantatory grace, her voice is grave and enchanting. She can give the feeling that she has bewitched the entire universe so that it is caught in a net from which there is no escape. She breathes an atmosphere of the warm, spell-binding, perhaps demoralizing South, bringing into her theatre that lotus-eating world of sensuous delight from which one would not depart even if one could.*

Edwige Feuillère (1955)

In cold print the adulation seems almost too much to take but I have kept that quotation from one of Sir Harold's reviews of her Ysé in Claudel's *Partage de Midi* all these years because it reflects accurately my own memories of Feuillère's enchantment.

In Edinburgh she played *La Dame aux Camélias* flat out for dramatic effect, dying in the final scene by falling backwards, centre stage, on to a circular white rug. It was pure ham but it was magnificent and if there was a dry eye in the house when the curtain came down, it certainly wasn't mine.

The other play at the Lyceum was an Old Vic production of Shakespeare's *Julius Caesar* by Michael Benthall which contained fine performances by Paul Rogers as Brutus, Richard Wordsworth as an exceptionally cynical Cassius and John Neville, ahead of his time, playing Mark Antony as a film star politician. But my most persistent memory associated with this production was of Rosemary Harris's determined encounter with Edinburgh non-salesmanship.

Rosemary, who played Calpurnia in the play, was a spirited and highly attractive redhead who wanted to buy a red hair-net after we had lunch. We went into shop after shop and to Rosemary's growing exasperation (red-haired girls are not noted for their patient disposition) in every one we got the same bland reply 'I'm sorry, we don't stock them' which eventually provoked her in the last shop into saying angrily:

'But there must be a demand for them. There are lots of red-haired girls in Edinburgh. Why don't you stock them?'

To which the middle-aged saleswoman replied in a tone of subdued triumph: 'Oh yes, we're often asked for them. But we don't stock them.'

More imposing theatrical moments in Edinburgh can also end on a note of bathos. In his last year as Festival Director, Ian Hunter was asked by the Azuma Kabuki Dancers and Musicians – who were appearing at the Empire Theatre in the final week – to attend the ceremony when the stage of the theatre was blessed before performances, Hunter devoutly removed his shoes to walk on the stage. The ceremony was recorded for posterity by the *Daily Express* photographer, revealing in the paper next day that he had a hole in his sock!

Ian Hunter is one of the most experienced Festival Directors in the world – Bath, Brighton, Canterbury, Hong Kong and the City of London are among others he directed after Edinburgh – and when I talked with him in London, I asked him what would he do with the Festival now:

'I think the day Edinburgh gave up Glyndebourne was a very sad day. I suppose if I hadn't talked them into taking Hamburg in 1952, it might have gone on longer but I did it, as I told you, for very specific reasons. And I did bring Glyndebourne back afterwards and in my time we did several really outstanding productions in the King's Theatre, which were done specifically for the Festival. Afterwards they went on to Glyndebourne as a second opera – I'm thinking specifically of *Le Bourgeois Gentilhomme* with *Ariadne auf Naxos* with Carl Ebert and Sir Thomas Beecham. You had to go to Edinburgh to see that.

'Now I think the festival is in such competition with Salzburg and everywhere else and Salzburg puts on one or two new opera productions every year and you can only see them by going to Salzburg. Opera is the jewel in the crown and although those productions of Peter Diamand with Barenboim and Claudio Abbado became very expensive they were worth it.

'I think the Festival has to keep – has kept despite all the blah-blah – an elitist centre. It is far more difficult to run the Festival now than it was in my days in some ways. Even in 1955 there was no National Theatre – the Old Vic, the Stratford Royal Shakespeare Theatre were operating pretty low key. There was the Glasgow Citizens, the Birmingham Rep and the Royal Court, where I was on the board. But there was, of course, also the commercial theatre and I had very good relationships with Binkie Beaumont and Henry Sherek and through those we got some, I think, extremely good plays – the Eliot plays, Charles Morgan's *The River Line*, Thornton Wilder's *The Matchmaker* and his specially commissioned play for the Assembly Hall, *A Life in the Sun*, which Montgomery Clift was meant to have done but didn't. And I developed the Assembly Hall, getting the Old Vic to do *Romeo and Juliet, Hamlet* and *Bartholomew Fair* there.

'What would I do if I go back? Well, I would use the Scottish opera chorus, workshop, orchestra and everything else and bring them together with great conductors and great casts and do something that would be totally new and would be memorable for the Festival. Not performances to go into Scottish Opera's repertoire as a routine production, although I suppose it might be pulled out in two year's time so that the costs were amortised. That is something I feel is awfully important.

'The Festival should commission more. New performances pull in the critics and the critics are important in enthusing public opinion. For example, Maxwell Davies talked Isaac Stern into giving the first performance of his new violin concerto in Orkney. That's something Edinburgh should have had. As far as the music is concerned, it could be more creative. It could offer commissions to composers, I mean top composers, world composers to write new things for Edinburgh. If I were to go back I would commission in the theatre as well as in the concert hall.'

I asked him what he thought Edinburgh, apart from its setting, had contributed to the Festival. Did Edinburgh deserve it? Sir Ian Hunter thought for a moment.

'I would have said that I don't think it's contributed a great deal," he said.

'I think the Festival has acted as an enormous stimulus. I don't think Scottish Opera would have existed if it had not been for the Festival. The

Romeo and Juliet *Royal Danish Ballet (1955)*

Scottish National Orchestra would certainly not be as good as it is if the public in Edinburgh and from all over Scotland had not heard all these great orchestras and become more aware of international standards. And it has helped to keep the Lyceum Theatre alive – there is a permanent company there now.

'I think the Festival has done quite a lot for Edinburgh but I don't really think Edinburgh has done an enormous amount for the Festival. I mean, Glasgow would have done far more if it had been held there!'

ROBERT PONSONBY 1956-60
On with the Elitist Plot – Tottering to the Edge of Satire

IX

Looking back, I suppose that we should have been more surprised when, on 29 April 1955 three months before Ian Hunter's last Festival, it was announced that Robert Ponsonby would succeed Hunter as Festival Director – or rather Artistic Administrator as the director was then called for a probationary period before he was upped to being Director. Not because we did not know Ponsonby. He had been Hunter's assistant for more than three years, a graduate through the Glyndebourne appointment system – and you can hardly miss someone who is 6'6".

Even nowadays when it would seem that youth is all and you are washed up on the flotsam-strewn shores of time at 40, being appointed to run the world's largest and most comprehensive festival at the age of 29 would raise a few eyebrows. But I cannot recall much criticism of the appointment.

Robert Ponsonby

The Corporation had sailed past their initial belief that Festival directors ought to come from Vienna or somewhere foreign and exotic and had not arrived anywhere else. Edinburgh Tory councillors were always very impressed by the kind of Eton and Scots Guards background which Ponsonby offered and the tradition of a dynastic succession was the next safe port so they dropped anchor there. The general public were not supposed to know about such lofty matters and in 1955 were not too aware of who the Festival Director was. If he delivered the goods as far as the programme was concerned that was all right. A great many of them were still highly suspicious of the Festival anyway as an elitist plot to foist alien culture on a baffled bourgeoisie. They could not quite understand how it had happened or why it was rated a success and would really have preferred if the City's contribution had been spent on new public lavatories in Leith.

The City Fathers were not much more knowledgeable but they didn't want to look foolish by making a mistake for which they might be held accountable. Robert Ponsonby clearly knew how the job was done so, sighing with relief, they accepted Ian Hunter's recommendation and appointed him. For what I suspect were mostly the wrong reasons, they made a very good decision.

The man they had chosen had very definite ideas of his own about how the Festival should be structured and where it should be going. Behind Ponsonby's patrician manner was a lively mind, a shrewd show-biz intelligence, a lot of innovative ideas and a sharp sense of humour.

These qualities began to show in the first programmes he organised for the Festival. The year he took over was the tenth festival, the first significant calendar landmark in its history. By 1956 it was clear it was not just a transient phenomenon – as Lord Provost Sir John Banks put it with unwonted candour: 'an interesting but rather troublesome interlude in Edinburgh during the summer season'. It showed irritating signs of becoming a fixture and therefore thought had to be given as to how it was to be developed, more thought than just planning for next year when the current year's programme was complete.

Uncomfortable evidence was being produced that the Festival was truly important to Edinburgh. William Nicholson, manager and secretary of the Scottish Tourist Board, published a report:

> *There is convincing proof that no other event in living memory has done more than the Festival to bring people to Edinburgh from all parts of the world. From 1950-6 the number of visitors rose from 57,032 to 89,570 with overseas visitors rising from 11,226 to 37,357.*
>
> *It is estimated that the first ten Festivals produced at least 500,000 extra passengers on city transport – worth £5245 each year. Thus in transport revenue alone one-third of the £15,000 (paid to the Festival) from the rates was recovered. There were also revenues from the letting of halls and theatres, the growing volume of trade for hotels, shops and restaurants. An average of less than £8,000 a year was spent on publicity, including brochures, leaflets, posters and all programmes.*
>
> *One European centre which seeks to emulate Edinburgh in Festival promotion incurred publicity costs of £60,000 in 1956. The value of the publicity obtained for Edinburgh and Scotland by the Edinburgh International Festival is not less than £100,000 per annum.*

However such happy optimism had to be placed alongside such items as the letter in *The Scotsman* following an article by painter and art critic, Peter Westwater suggesting that Princes Street Gardens might have a continental style cafe.

'What meets with approval on the Continent,' an indignant reader warned sternly, 'could hardly be expected to receive encouragement over here!'

But the *Scottish Daily Express* published an estimate that the Festival attracted to Scotland no less than £3 million per year.

All this was part of the problem confronting Robert Ponsonby. I remember writing about it at the time.

> *Ten years is a long time in the life of anything as large and all-embracing as an International Festival of Music and Drama. It is not altogether possible to evade the fact that with years running into double figures something more than mere longevity falls to be accounted. Since 1947 the Edinburgh Festival has certainly grown but has it grown up?*
>
> *I remember vividly the excitement of the first Festival. At the press conference at which the launchers revealed their plans even the press reacted. Around the windswept grey buildings of the Scottish capital the awesome lunacy of the City Fathers who had backed this fantastic project was the subject of much derisive comment. But as the event itself grew near, excitement mounted. Douce Edinburgh burghers secretly read books about opera and when the sun shone for almost the whole three weeks and Edinburgh magically found itself a capital city again, many converts were made.*
>
> *For those whose tastes did not run to concerts, opera and ballet, there was always the Festival Club. There in the palatial George Street Assembly Rooms where Sir Walter Scott coyly confessed to the authorship of the Waverley novels in 1827 – in Scotland (!) the bars were open till 1 am and there was dancing and music and poets lying plastered among the potted palms. All that has now been put a stop to – and the Festival Club is almost as dull and respectable as Edinburgh itself and the poets have found elsewhere to carouse. But the Festival has survived all that.*
>
> *It even survived the discovery that the first year made a loss of £20,777. It survived the obstinate denials by the tradesmen and hoteliers of Edinburgh that the Festival had made any difference to their takings. It survived the sneers of the cynics and the*

wallowing enthusiasm of the culturally feeble-minded. At the end of the first decade it is sleek, prosperous, well-oiled and seemingly indestructible – on the surface. But down below there are troubled waters which must give Edinburgh's young Artistic Administrator, Robert Ponsonby plenty to think about.

It seems to me to be rapidly approaching a point when some serious thinking will have to be done about its future. Every year it has gone on growing bigger and more comprehensive in its scope until now it is unquestionably the biggest annual cultural circus in the world.

From the point of view of the Festival-goer with catholic tastes, Edinburgh is a splendid place in which to have a yearly cultural splurge. In the short space of three weeks he can hear a great deal of good music well played, view some excellent art exhibitions, see theatre 'in the round' and behind the proscenium arch, ballet, a film festival and a host of side-shows which come under some or none of these categories. In most performances he can expect a high level of execution – there have been some wonderful performances at the Festival but Edinburgh's annual cultural jamboree has been memorable rather for the brilliance of its executants in the concert hall, opera house and theatre than for exciting new discoveries in the creative field.

In his first year of office no Festival Director ever has a completely free hand. There are always commitments made before he was appointed. In Robert Ponsonby's case he was, of course, involved in their making.

So for the tenth year Hunter and Ponsonby between them had organised the return of the Hamburg State Opera, the only foreign opera company ever to have appeared at the Festival. But in 1956 the programme was very different.

Günther Rennert's highly-praised production of *Zauberflöte* was repeated but most of the rest of the programme came from the 20th century. The exception was *Der Barbier von Bagdad*, a charming and light-hearted tale from the *One Thousand and One Nights* made into an opera by the minor composer Peter Cornelius, which was surprisingly the occasion for Liszt's departure from Weimar in 1858. The row was about Cornelius's support for the 'New Music' advocated by Liszt and Wagner but there is nothing Wagnerian about *Der Barbier* but I suppose the revolutionary history of both operas made some programmatic sense as well as providing some light relief.

Stravinsky's *Oedipus Rex* and *Mavra* also provided contrast, the one an ironic comedy based on a Pushkin poem with a plot even more idiotic than most comic operas but some agreeable music in Stravinsky's less spiky mode and *Oedipus* a static but costumed oratorio-like performance of one of the great classic tragedies. Sung in metal masks in Latin with a Narrator recounting the lack of action in English, this, the first staged performance of the work in Britain, was a strange almost eerie experience. Stravinsky was very opposed to opera being sung in languages for which it had not been composed. 'Translation changes the character of a work and destroys its cultural unity' he maintained. Just how this objection is answered by having Jean Cocteau translate Sophocles's play into French, have

Richard Buckle (1954)

45

the singing libretto made into Latin by Professor Daniëlle while the Narrator is instructed to speak his lines in the language of the audience, I am not sure.

But for all those intellectual and textual obfuscations, one thing was clear. This Oedipus, set to its strangely pagan music reminiscent of Monteverdi in some stylised structural aspects but much less sinuous and elegant than the 16th-century Italian master, told the terrible blighted history of the king doomed unknowingly to kill his father and marry his mother in pitiless musical language which underscored the pettiness of control men and women exercised over their destiny and the elements beyond which can predestine disaster, now as then.

At the same time in the great black hall of Assembly for the Church of Scotland looming over the centre of Princes Street, which Tyrone Guthrie had appropriated as the ideal venue for *The Thrie Estaites*, there was another *Oedipus Rex* played by a Scottish actor, Douglas Campbell, and brought from Guthrie's latest bold theatrical venture, the Stratford Ontario Festival. This striking open stage production, in a translation by W. B. Yeats, played in tandem with Shakespeare's *Henry V*, a performance of charismatic flair by a 27-year-old Canadian actor Christopher Plummer.

Back at the King's, pagan sensuality was taken to its operatic apotheosis in *Salome*, Richard Strauss's one-acter based on Oscar Wilde's play. When it was first performed at the Court Opera in Dresden in December 1905, it attracted nearly as much outraged protest as the play itself. It had just one showing at the Metropolitan Opera in New York in 1907 and was withdrawn in the face of public outcry. The Dance of the Seven Veils was considered particularly salacious and one American critic described the work as 'a moral stench'. Even Strauss's most eminent fan Kaiser Wilhelm II expressed dismay at Strauss having set *Salome* to such voluptuous and dissolute music. 'It will do him a lot of damage' he prophesied gloomily. 'The damage' Strauss quipped some years later, 'built me a villa at Garmisch.'

The ambiguous attitude to the power of the text and the music was still evident 50 years later. *The Times* music critic wrote:

The whole fascination of Wilde's libretto, the attraction made stronger by the leverage of repulsion, closed its grip, while the music, still astonishing after 50 years, wove itself strand by strand, motif by motif into a texture that felt as though it would soon have smothered us if Salome herself had not first been smothered by the soldiers' shields.

The excitement of the evening at the King's Theatre was heightened by back-stage drama when the soprano who was to sing the Princess of Judea fell ill and her place was taken by the young Helga Pilarczyk, who fulfilled this fairy-tale back-stage plot by singing the role with great brilliance and passion and going on to make a most distinguished career, particularly in modern roles such as Marie in Berg's *Wozzeck* and the Woman in Schoenberg's *Erwartung*.

The most fascinating part of the tenth festival for me, however, lay not in the opera house nor even in the concerts provided by Beecham and the Royal Philharmonic, the Boston Symphony Orchestra under Pierre Monteux and Charles Munch, the two Scottish orchestras, the National Youth Orchestra of Great Britain and the Vienna Hofmusikapelle in the Usher Hall, but beyond the proscenium arch in the Lyceum theatre.

I had got myself even more than usually involved in the whole thing by writing a feature for what was then known as the Third Programme (now Radio 3) called *Teatro*, an account of the Italian theatre which was to be the foreign language contribution to the 1956 festival in the form of the Piccolo Teatro from Milan. Additionally, I had wished on me by an actor friend Alan Judd, with whom I had served in the Navy, the After Dinner Opera Company, a mini-company from America which was appearing on the Fringe with a repertoire of contemporary American one-act operas. Alan had promised to manage the company while they were making their foray to Edinburgh but was called away at virtually the last moment to play Horatio in a production of *Hamlet* at the Baalbek Festival in Lebanon. This involved a great deal of organisation including finding lodgings, arranging publicity, making sure bookings had indeed been made and so on in addition to placating the natural but jittery anxieties of the company's intendant who rejoiced in the not very reassuring name of Richard Stuart Flusser. To assist in these multifarious tasks I had taken on the strength a friend, then an out-of-work actor (but not much since) Iain Cuthbertson. Which is how Iain Beag and Iain Mhor got involved in the Italian theatre.

The beginning was not auspicious. When my *Teatro* programme was broadcast a substantial chunk of it was missing. When I telephoned the producer, James Mactaggart, somewhat flown with authorial rage, I found that while I had been arranging After Dinner Opera U. S. Style, and therefore rather difficult to locate in festival-ridden Edinburgh, *Teatro*, Jimmy Mactaggart and I had been involved in an international copyright drama.

The two plays being given by the Piccolo Teatro were Goldoni's *Arlecchino* and Pirandello's *Questa Sera si Recita a Soggetto* (Tonight We Improvise). To illustrate my programme I had translated short scenes from both plays into English, excerpts to be acted on radio. There was no problem with the Venetian dramatist Goldoni, who had been dead since 1793 but with Sicilian Nobel prize-winner, Luigi Pirandello it was quite different. When he died in 1936, it transpired that he had left the copyright in several of his plays including *Questa Sera* to his leading lady, Marta Abba. The BBC – super-meticulous about copyright (even for just two pages of dialogue) – found that la Abba was still alive, in an old folks' home and still articulate enough categorically to refuse permission for anyone but her to translate a line of the play. So Pirandello, the playwright of the

Arlecchino *(1956)*

'relativity of truth' struck from the grave. I had thought of devoting some time after the Festival to translating *all* of the play but faced with the formidable Diva Abba, I put such vaulting ambition aside.

However my contact with the Italian theatre was by no means over. In the course of preparing *Teatro* I had corresponded with Paolo Grassi, administrator of the Piccolo Teatro in Milan and with Giorgio Strehler, the director. They sought me out when they came to Edinburgh and so Iain Cuthbertson and I became involved in helping to ease the Italian theatre on to the Edinburgh stage.

As usual with such moves nothing seemed to go right. Everyone declared the theatre a physical disaster area, nothing fitted, the rehearsals and the lighting were inadequate and the company out of sorts and despondent. With such laments ringing in our ears and hope at zero, we went to the ill-attended first night, Goldoni's *Arlecchino*, bravely prepared to make excuses for our new friends to Edinburgh theatregoers.

There was never a more fruitless qualm. Well perhaps fruitless was not quite the right word. As Ponsonby described it in the Souvenir Programme for the 25th Festival in 1971:

> *Strehler's* Arlecchino *for the Piccolo Teatro of Milan, with Marcello Moretti in the title role was unforgettable. At one point after a scene of quicksilver chaos and dialogue fugato con fuoco, total silence suddenly descended and the stage was discovered to be occupied only by a small blancmange quivering gently by the footlights.*

This was theatre we had missed – if we ever knew it existed. A brilliant stylisation based on the *commedia dell'arte* from which Goldoni had taken most of his characters, staged with dazzling flair, speed and a seemingly endless facility of invention by Giorgio Strehler and his company, trained like an immaculately functioning sports team in skills like acrobatics, mime and ensemble playing which we had forgotten were supposed to be part of the dramatic repertoire.

In addition to the quivering jelly there were the endless athletic subterfuges resorted to by Arlecchino to justify his status as the servant of two masters, somersaulting into the boothed restaurant with tureens of steaming soup, juggling, making love and mischief, pathos and magic in one of the greatest displays of the craft of theatrical arts either Iain or I had ever seen.

Afterwards I asked Marcello Moretti how he had learned all these astonishing tricks. He looked up at me with a quirky smile fringed with incomprehension. 'I train for five hours every day,' he said.

The *commedia dell'arte* also made its influence felt on *Questa Sera si Recita a Soggetto* for one of its alternative names in the 16th century was *commedia a soggetto*, a play to a given scenario around which the actors made up their speeches as they went along. In his usual tortuous way Pirandello added another dimension – a play said to be improvised but with written dialogue and arias borrowed from Verdi's *Trovatore*.

Here, the central impulse of Pirandello's theatre – the limitless uncertainty of the present, the obvious, the immediate – made convoluted drama when infused with the traditional jealousy and vehemence of his native Sicily, grown from the past his literary predecessors had rejected. Futurists like Pappini and Marinetti, rebelling at the snail-like progress Italy was making into the 20th century, had proclaimed that the heavy Italian past of art and history with its weighty traditions should be discarded and eliminated. (Marinetti carried it even further by writing a futurist cook-book which demanded the abolition of *pasta*!)

Pirandello believed that the past was at least one clue to the present, the structure of which could dissolve before your next breath. Combined with Sicilian passion and *Il Trovatore* it was a heady mixture but it made marvellous theatre especially when contrasted with the scintillating professional and artistic structuralism of *Arlecchino*.

It was a marvellous year – to which the American mini-operas played in a hall in George Street, made their contribution although the tuneful folksiness of the dramas of Lizzie Borden's axe and *Sweet Betsy from Pike* and even Menotti's witty *The Telephone* struck very different notes from Stravinsky and Richard Strauss and Pirandello's soul-probing analysis to music.

Plans for 1957 were just as ambitious and once again Italy provided a focal point. The opera company at the King's Theatre was La Piccola Scala from Milan. In August 1943 when the Allies were consolidating their invasion of Sicily and Italy was negotiating its surrender, the most famous opera theatre in the world, Il Teatro alla Scala, was almost totally destroyed by bombs.

By 1946 it had been rebuilt in all its former glory and nine years later it opened another theatre next door, a part of the building which had also been severely damaged, to provide a venue for works which needed a smaller auditorium than the 3,000-seat La Scala and which would serve both as a performance place for 18th-century opera and for new works which did not require the scenic scale of a full-size opera house.

So La Piccola Scala had been open for just 18 months when it brought its repertoire of operas to Edinburgh. Although it was the second house of La Scala there was nothing downgraded about either its casting, musical direction or production. It was only the operas which were smaller in scale. The talents touched the heights.

To Edinburgh the Italians brought four operas by Cimarosa, Bellini, Donizetti and Rossini, their star composers of the turn of the 19th century. The singers included Maria Callas, Rosanna Carteri, Fiorenza Cossotto, Renata Scotto, Graziella Sciutti, Luigi Alva, Carlo Badioli, Fernando Corena, Nicola Monti, Giuseppe di Stefano and Nicola Zaccaria: the conductors were Gianandrea Gavazzeni, Nino Sanzogno and Antonino Votto: the producers Franco Enriquez, Giorgio Strehler, Luchino Visconti and Franco Zeffirelli. A dazzling line-up.

As it always was anywhere she went, the focus was on Callas. She was in one of her great stamping-out periods and was known recently to have had a much-publicised falling out with di Stefano, so there was great speculation as to whether she would ever actually appear on the stage of the King's Theatre or would make Edinburgh yet another venue for a display of diva temperament.

Inevitably, there was a walk-out story when it was announced in the second week that La Callas would not sing in the final performance of *La Sonnambula* at the beginning of the third week. Temperament, back-stage strife and contractual confusion were all cited by the media as the reason for this withdrawal. There was also a miasma of an excuse about 'indisposition'. Naturally, the diva got the worst of it but a subtle campaign of sympathy was worked up for the 23-year-old Renata Scotto who replaced her and Scotto's interpretation of the mild, long-suffering sleepwalking Amina in Bellini's pastoral tragi-comedy was hailed as a triumph. Frustrated Festival opera-goers who had tickets for the 3 September performance swore with insistent self-delusion that she was better than Callas (most without having seen the diva in the role) and it certainly helped to make Scotto's subsequent successful career.

The circumstances of that final performance of *Sonnambula* remain somewhat obscure but the most inside-track account of it winkled from both the Festival authorities and senior management of La Scala is that Callas had never agreed to sing on 3 September because she had already accepted an invitation for that night to a party in Venice, given in her honour by American celebrity hostess, Elsa Maxwell.

Later, the press found out about the party and there was some more Callas vilification for deserting Edinburgh in its hour of need. To which Maxwell's overblown ego added fuel. 'I have had many presents in my life ... but I have never had any star give up a performance in an opera house because she felt she was breaking her word to a friend,' she exulted.

What seems to have been a cunning if somewhat dishonest ploy on behalf of the Festival and La Scala not to kill the box-office on the last night, simply added to the diva legend. Those who proclaimed that Scotto was better anyway were hoist with their own verdicts.

What is certainly true is that they should have been disappointed. This is no reflection on Scotto who is a remarkable singer with a fine and intelligently used lyric soprano voice – but Callas remains unique.

Although the gentle Amina, given to sleepwalking round the village at night in circumstances which cast doubts on her chastity, was not exactly in the classic mould of the great Callas roles like Floria Tosca, Norma or Medea, she brought to it all her extraordinary magnetic qualities of passion and commitment. She was also in fine voice, moulding her phrasing to the rather saccharine character of the heroine with amazing finesse and dazzling unforced technique.

Her final cabaletta *Ah! non giunge*, when she emerges from her sleepwalk over the dangerous mill-wheel bridge and wakes to find her previously suspicious lover Elvino grovelling amorously at her feet, was unforgettable. As she awoke and saw Elvino and the gawking villagers, the stage *and* the house lights went up and she strode triumphantly down stage trilling Amina's triumph as if she was brandishing a spear. Totally out of character but wonderful!

Meeting Maria Menighini Callas showed another side to her personality. Through connections with La Scala and Radio Italiana and after a great deal of negotiation, I had managed to arrange to interview her on behalf of BBC Radio. A list of questions had to be submitted and the diva's approval sought. It was rather like arranging a private audience with a cross between royalty and deity and I will not conceal that when permission was granted I felt a curious mixture of triumph and apprehension.

There was no lack of people to tell me that la Callas ate interviewers for breakfast and that, together with my own admiration for her, ensured that I was not lacking in awe.

On the appointed afternoon I picked up the tape-recorder, an unwieldy heavy green box in those days, from the BBC studio in Queen Street. To my consternation I was also allocated Anna Instone, the formidable presenter of London's *Music Magazine*, whom I was instructed was to accompany me as a kind of duenna.

Already nervous and having gone to a great deal of trouble to arrange this privileged encounter and tremulously aware of the strict parameters within which all had been set, I felt obliged to impress on Madame Instone that I must be allowed to conduct the interview and that she should not try to interrupt or take over the proceedings or all might end in disaster. This attempt to clarify diplomatically what I saw as a delicate situation was hardly a success, received in tight-lipped silence as vain posturing barely masking calculated insult. So, mutely dragging tape-recorders like lead balloons, we set off for the Caledonian Hotel.

There we were shown up to Callas's room. Surprisingly slight for a diva, she was smiling and agreeable, rather taller than I had imagined, rather more coarse-featured than she looked on the stage but very striking with her large eyes and imperious Florentine nose and expressive sensual mouth. She was surprisingly relaxed, friendly and unpretentious, and slightly disdainful of the unscheduled Instone presence, but making no direct comment. Her husband Giovanni Battista Meneghini, a small square white-haired man with a passing resemblance to Mussolini, lay on the bed and made disparaging remarks in Italian as we chatted through the preliminaries to the interview. Madame Instone said not a word.

Meneghini's banter aroused the imperious diva. She rounded on him with an impatient 'Ma che!' and told him to get out, saying his chatter was disturbing everyone. He shrugged and left the room. When the door closed behind him she offered a conciliatory smile.

We began to record the interview and she was in sparkling form, speaking forcibly about artistic standards in music, acting and production, defining her own beliefs as an artist and having a snide go at various singers who might be considered in any way her rivals. We came to the end of the allotted questions and I asked if she would like to hear the tape played back.

I reeled back the tape and turned it to 'Play'. There was a distant rumble of traffic, a wheezing noise and nothing else. I had just failed to record the interview of a life-time.

Callas arched her dark eyebrows and looked at me, smiling mischievously.

'So,' she asked, 'what do we do now?'

'Be the tempestuous diva,' I said, hopelessly trying to make light of it, 'and throw me and my box of tricks out the window.'

She laughed very genuinely with a reassuring note of conspiracy. 'Send that woman,' she said dismissively, nodding at Anna Instone, 'for another machine and we will do it again.'

Anna Instone had left her recorder in the hotel lobby at the hall porter's desk. She went to fetch it and returned grim-faced while La Callas and I had a glass of wine. We did the recording again and the diva was better than ever. Twice as vehement about standards of operatic integrity and singing and the few places you can find them. Three times as scathing about 'singers with little voices and those who can only sing Puccini' and altogether quite sweepingly splendid.

I was very grateful. I thanked her profusely and next day sent her flowers. Anna Instone never spoke to me again.

However a diva's favours are not given lightly. The following week Giuseppe di Stefano decided to give a party in his suite at the George Hotel. He decided that for this special occasion he would buy himself a kilt, the full evening dress outfit and because I always wore a kilt during the Festival, he appointed me to arrange all. We spent several hours at Anderson's the tailors and outfitters opposite the hotel, sorting out the intricacies of Highland garb and an appropriate tartan – Royal Stewart was the final choice – and he was kitted out in full Caledonian splendour.

He was kind enough to invite me to his party but I was given strict instructions that I was *not* to wear a kilt, just a dinner jacket like everyone else!

Apart from Pippo di Stefano's natural warm-hearted Sicilian ebullience, one of the purposes of this gathering was to mark or effect a reconciliation between Maria Callas and the host. In Edinburgh they were in different operas. Di Stefano was singing Nemorino in *L'Elisir d'Amore* and it was said that they had not spoken since the spat over curtain calls in Milan.

I went to the party with Graziella Sciutti, the enchanting Carolina from *Il Matrimonio Segreto* who professed not to know me unkilted. However Pippo and his kilt were a big hit. He looked very handsome and posed in the centre of the room greeting his guests and was showered with compliments and admiration.

But after an hour or so the atmosphere became a bit taut. People were eating, people were drinking, the air was full of the mellifluous chatter of Italian voices but Pippo was still hovering centre-stage, somewhat distractedly, his anxious brown eyes on the door through which all the guests seemed already to have arrived.

Finally the bell trilled, a waiter opened the door and there she was. In a dress of black lace with a touch of colour in a flower and iridescent with jewels and a kind of mantilla, she looked magnificent, imperial, stunning. As she stopped and looked around the room di Stefano came forward, all swishing Highland charm, to greet her.

She looked at him, with a smile like a regal tiger,

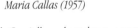

Maria Callas (1957)

patted him on the cheek and said 'Ciao, Pippo'. Then she came over to where I was sitting on a small settee with Graziella and sat down, accepted a glass of champagne, talked to me desultorily but uniquely for half an hour and left.

I didn't stay much longer myself. My status as Highland dress adviser to tenors and escort to doe-eyed mezzo-sopranos appeared to be irreparably damaged. The price of a diva's amiable tolerance had been exacted. Fortunately I was able to cajole forgiveness for being down-staged from Graziella who has a notable sense of humour to add to her other charms but when I talked to Pippo di Stefano many years later when he came to sing in an Italian flood relief concert at Scottish Opera, it was clear that his enthusiasm for the kilt was in a condition of permanent wane. With divas you can't win any of them.

X

All the focus was on Callas and *La Sonnambula* and everyone but the critics raved: 'Her repertory of vocal colour is restricted' wrote Martin Cooper in *The Daily Telegraph*; 'the reservations about tone and pitch are forgotten,' said Andrew Porter backhandedly in *The Financial Times*. 'Her tone above mezzo-forte is often painfully hard,' wrote another carper and only Christopher Grier in *The Scotsman* ranged himself alongside the ecstatic public with 'Callas inflamed the audience to a fever of enthusiasm, without parallel in the history of Festival operatic annals'.

I have never been very clear what it is about music critics which makes them recoil from total approval like horses shying from a hissing cobra but it is dispiriting after a great performance to listen to and read their emphasis on the superior qualities of their own judgement, pricking holes in something which has been a wonderful experience for everyone else. There are even those who never applaud at any concert or opera so as not to commit themselves to a public verdict before they can get it down on paper.

But *per contra*, I recall Gerald Larner telling me of a lady who wrote indignantly to the editor of *The Guardian* complaining that: 'Mr Larner obviously never pays any attention to the performance because every time I see him in a concert-hall he is always reading a book!'

So critics studying scores are also excoriated as was Rosanna Carteri for being 'too pretty' to play Adina in *L'Elisir d'Amore*, which with Rossini's *Il Turco in Italia* was dismissed as 'frivolous' and 'slight' as if the beauty of the heroine (praised in the very first tenor aria) was unimportant in a love story or Zeffirelli's vivacious and colourful production of *Il Turco* was not an object lesson in the presentation of comic opera.

'Slight' even cropped up in several reviews of Cimarosa's *Il Matrimonio Segreto* which for me was the most completely satisfying operatic offering of the Piccola Scala season. This was the opera with which La Piccola Scala had opened on 26 December 1955, written by Domenico Cimarosa, a contemporary of Mozart, who succeeded Antonio Salieri in Vienna as Court Kapellmeister. When it was first performed in 1792 it was so successful that the Emperor Leopold II invited the cast to dinner after the performance and then asked them to do it all again!

It was an imperial privilege much envied in Edinburgh. Giorgio Strehler's brilliant production of *Matrimonio* merged ensemble playing of the highest quality with staging exquisite in style and comedy, full of verve and invention and impeccably sung by Luigi Alva, Carlo Badioli, Franco Calabrese, Gabriella Carturan, Eugenia Ratti and Graziella Sciutti. Although this post-Restoration comedy based on an English play by David Garrick and George Colman is not perhaps the greatest lyric comedy in the repertoire, the music has great charm and spirit and in this presentation it remains in my memory vividly as one of the most perfect opera productions I have ever seen.

So in two years we had seen three brilliant productions from the 36-year-old Giorgio Strehler, still one of the greatest theatre directors in the world. It seems very strange that he has never been invited back to Edinburgh.

Certainly the theatrical offerings in 1957 could have done with the redeeming touch of a great director like Strehler because they were almost all uninspired. Looking at the programme there seemed no very good reason for this as on paper the drama seemed full of interest. At the Lyceum was *Nekrassov* by Jean-Paul Sartre in an English translation produced by George Devine and starring Robert Helpmann and Harry H. Corbett (not at that time eternally branded as TV's Steptoe junior).

It was followed by *Man of Distinction* by the German dramatist Walter Hasenclever directed by Denis Carey with Moira Shearer, Anton Walbrook, Eric Porter, Peter Bull and the young Prunella Scales and then by Madeleine Renaud and Jean-Louis Barrault in Anouilh's *La Répétition ou l'Amour Puni*.

A playwright turned critic, Alexander Reid, wrote in the *SMT Magazine*:

> *Two plays of so slight a character as Sartre's* Nekrassov *and the Henry Sherek production of Hasenklever's* The Man of Distinction *in the Lyceum would have been acceptable as light relief to two more substantial items; that either should be considered the 'best' of the 1957 Festival drama makes one wonder what sort of advisers on drama the Festival Society have.*

He didn't even like the Anouilh – which I enjoyed for Barrault's riveting performance as the sinister count with evil designs on Simone Valere's wide-eyed innocent Lucille – and he dismissed the Compagnie Renaud-Barrault's brilliant prose anthology, *Connaissance de Claudel* as 'more interesting for the interpretation than the matter interpreted' which put this poet-dramatist, disciple of Rimbaud and definer of poetry as 'to plunge into the finite to find the inexhaustible', firmly on his continental shelf.

Personally, I have always thought of Claudel as a kind of holy Roman Catholic Oscar Wilde in his epigrammatic way but no less of a sensuous prober into divine relations and skilled turner of a good phrase for that. Illustrated succinctly by the spat between Claudel and André Gide in which Gide said: 'Claudel thinks he will be carried to Heaven in a Pullman car'; and Claudel replied: 'And Gide believes he can get to Hell in the Metro.'

But Reid like everyone else turned the full fury of his theatrical rage on the play specially commissioned for the Festival, described by Ponsonby in a pre-Festival article in *The Queen* as 'Jonathan Griffin's astounding play *The Hidden King*'.

Quite why anyone had ever conceived the idea of commissioning Griffin, a minor poet with little or no dramatic experience, to write a large-scale play for production in the Assembly Hall, is difficult to imagine. It had an incredibly muddled plot, static in everything except constantly changing venues, written in colourful but convoluted verse centring on the mysterious Don Sebastian, a King of Portugal reputedly killed in battle in North Africa but who kept re-appearing all over Europe after Phillip II of Spain had annexed his country. It had been a drama by Eugène Scribe and an opera by Donizetti and a failure as both and had best been left that way. But where Scribe and Donizetti had been quite workmanlike about their plotting of this Iberian Perkin Warbeck, Griffin jumped about in place and time in totally bewildering and singularly undramatic fashion:

> It is no thesis: rather a myth. A play may, by bringing together many diverse experiences find a truth which any simple statement would distort. A play about our own times in terms of another may enable us to see over manners and catch sight of Man. Be for a moment Man knowing himself, wrote Griffin in his programme note and this extract catches fairly exactly the wordy overload and jumbled philosophical thinking which pervaded *The Hidden King*.

Far from finding a truth it couldn't even find an exit and although cut and pulled about over its dispiriting run of three weeks at the Assembly Hall it failed miserably to pull in the audiences. Put on entirely under Festival auspices, it lost £16,418.

Strangely enough in a book of verse, *The Rebirth of Pride*, published later that year, Griffin re-stated more powerfully his fascination with the divinity of Man in a bitter statement of agnostic faith. It would have made a better if intellectually more controversial plot than *The Hidden King*.

So in 1957 the Festival had its first complete self-inflicted flop. It was a pity because it gave ammunition to the philistines, encouraged the Festival Council's all too entrenched attitude against innovation and underlined commissioning as a dangerous departure from the norm.

When we talked about this many years later Robert Ponsonby said that in his view the Eliot plays had not really been commissioned but just made available to Edinburgh by Henry Sherek.

'Eliot was certainly encouraged to write them because they were going to open at Edinburgh. Eliot is now a very unfashionable writer,' he added, 'and of course the play which caused the greatest stir in my time was also by a very unfashionable writer, Jonathan Griffin. *The Hidden King* caused such a stir that we had a public forum on the stage of the Assembly Hall and Jonathan Griffin, Michael Macliammoir, Lady Rosebery and I and all the actors appeared before 300-400 people to argue the toss about whether it was a great play or simply an aberration.'

He felt very strongly that you had to take a chance on the occasional 'aberration' but that what he achieved in his five years as director was a sustained high quality of events in the Usher Hall, in the theatre and in art exhibitions. 'But I was aware every year of greater and greater constraints on the budget and the impossibility of a more creative approach to planning for the Festival.'

I asked him about relations with the Corporation.

'It's never been very good,' he said. 'Not I think because the directors have not been Scottish but fundamentally because the local authority aspect of Edinburgh has always been unimaginative, concerned with immediate and obvious topics and traditions whereas the Edinburgh Festival was an imaginative stroke of genius really. The committees expressed a generally philistine indifference towards artistic aspirations and policies.'

'The reason I resigned was that I could see no way out of the trap of local authority money to support the things which I knew the Festival had to do. Which were to aspire to book the greatest artists, give the greatest commissions, have the greatest visits by the greatest companies and orchestras.'

'The most successful festivals,' he went on, 'are the most independent of local authority influence, pressure and financial wherewithal. The Festival Council should be a wholly independent body to which a small number of those who contribute to it should be appointed. It's hamstrung by its incestuous relationship with local government. The really enlightened authority – and Edinburgh has never really been enlightened in that particular matter – lays down the quality it wishes its money to contribute towards and then lets the thing alone.

'Resignations have always been about the same things – money, pride, impossibility to run.'

But although there were intriguing uproars about the departure of Callas and the retention of *The Hidden King*, the 1957 Festival had other highlights. In the Usher Hall, Barbirolli and the Hallé Orchestra made a celebration of the centenary of Elgar's birth; Klemperer, difficult as ever to get on to the concert platform, but when he got there 'manically marvellous' in Beethoven, Brahms and Stravinsky, Mozart and Mahler; Ormandy in one-composer concerts with the Concertgebouw devoted to Tchaikovsky and Richard Strauss.

That year Rudolf Firkusny (who made his final appearance at the Festival some 33 years later at the age of 78) played three piano concertos and Victoria de los Angeles in sublime voice sang Berlioz's great song cycle *Les Nuits d'Eté*. At the Empire there was the Grand Ballet du Marquis de Cuevas and the Royal Swedish Ballet with a sensational production of *Miss Julie* starring Else Marianne von Rosen and Les Ballet Africains de Keita Fodéba, stylised tribal dancers, bare-breasted on a Scottish stage (but they were black and French to boot, so the Edinburgh bourgeoisie unpursed their lips and flocked to see them). At the Gateway there was a fine production of Robert MacLellan's *The Flouers o' Edinburgh* with Lennox Milne, Tom Fleming and Duncan Macrae.

And to end the '57 Festival, on the final night at the almost witching hour of 11pm at the Freemasons' Hall there was a taste of the Festival innovation for which Robert Ponsonby was doomed to be most vividly remembered – satire.

At an official Festival event, Anna Russell presented *Satire and Song* a musical entertainment which had the audacity to poke fun at serious music, the staple of the Festival diet. *The Ring of the Nibelungs: an Analysis* explored the complexity of the relationships between the characters in Wagner's epic. She was very funny and we loved it.

Anna Russell maintains that she began as a dedicated opera singer but when sections of decor kept falling on her and other *en scene* incidents added to the perils of her career, she had to see the funny side of music or get out. So she did both. The result are her brilliant impressionistic distortions of the operatic and straight music world which have brought as much joy to audiences around the world as quite a number of performances of *opera seria* which it has been my misfortune to attend.

On the last night of the 11th Festival she had us rolling in the aisles with her guide to the Ring cycle and other gems from her repertoire and with her joyous performance the genre of Festival satire was launched on to the main programme. Levity had received the official OK.

It had of course not been unknown on the Fringe. Since 1952 the most popular performances in the Fringe's wildly varied programmes had been the late-night revues. I think The New Drama Group in 1952 were the first with *After the Show* starring Eunice Gayson and Betty Marsden. Not designed specifically for Edinburgh it was imported from London where Hermione Gingold in Alan Melville's *Sweet and Low* and Joyce Grenfell in *Tuppence Coloured* and Coward's *Sigh No More* had put this kind of barbed entertainment firmly back on the post-war theatrical map.

'Revue has always been seen as a cardinal feature of the Fringe,' Alastair Moffat wrote in *The Edinburgh Fringe*, his 1978 book about the other Festival. 'In a festival set-up late-night entertainment is in demand, especially from those seeking light relief after an enervating evening at the Usher Hall.'

In fact the first revue went on immediately following an enervating evening in St Mary's Hall – if enervating means going weak at the knees – at Donald Pleasance's dramatic adaptation of Robert Louis Stevenson's *Ebb Tide* which contained a powerfully sinister performance by the playwright. The idea that a compelling or inspiring performance on stage or concert hall disqualified you somehow from enjoying some derisive banter about social or performance pretension later was one that was not to survive long in Edinburgh at Festival time.

However it took a further two years for the point to make the headlines.

In 1958 there was the British première of a great play by a great if tortured American playwright, Eugene O'Neill. *Long Day's Journey into Night* was written in 1941 but not produced until 1956 in Sweden, three years after O'Neill's death. It had been performed in New York only the year before with Fredric March and his wife Florence Eldridge in the leads, and when the play was first announced for Edinburgh they were in the cast. Eventually an English company took over the project with an American O'Neill specialist, José Quintero, director. In spite of its stuttering progress to Edinburgh this turned out to be a theatrical event of the first rank. In his dedication to his wife, O'Neill wrote:

For Carlotta, on our 12th Wedding Anniversary.

DEAREST: I give you the original script of this play of old sorrow, written in tears and blood. A sadly inappropriate gift, it would seem, for a day celebrating happiness. But you will understand. I mean it as a tribute to your love and tenderness which gave me the faith in love that enabled me to face my dead at last and write this play – write it with deep pity and understanding and forgiveness for all the four haunted Tyrones.

O'Neill's father James, an Irish emigrant who became a celebrated actor considered to be the successor and rival to Edwin Booth, took to drink after his popularity in the role condemned him to playing the Count of Montecristo almost continuously for 30 years. The play is heavily autobiographical and the younger son in the play, Edmund, is O'Neill himself – although quite why he borrowed the name of their mutual grandfather from Tyrone Power and Tyrone Guthrie is not clear.

The four Tyrones were played by Gwen Ffrangcon Davies, Anthony Quayle, Ian Bannen and Alan Bates with an agonised brawling fervour and passion which remains in the mind clearly 40 years later. No-one put it better than film director John Grierson in the BBC programme *Arts Review:*

It is for me very beautiful – very moving and one of the theatrical experiences of my life, for which I expect to be always grateful. These Tyrones, they bicker, they backbite, take the skin off each other. They lie, they are totally disreputable. But all I can remember is that they talked to each other and really loved each other, and if they doped and drank as a result it was in the profoundest cause of all – which is to live and live abundantly, even if you are supposed be doing it all wrong. O'Neill is above all a man of the theatre. There is a sort of dramatic breathing in every space he leaves, every absence he registers. But above all, with all his concentration on the hurts of life, the disappointments, the illusion of age and disintegration – it is the inner kindness of life that he finally asserts and why his tragedy comes to you as though it were a blessing which is the way all tragedy must.

It was a superb production, wonderfully sustained throughout by the four principals. Gwen Ffrangcon Davies as Mary Tyrone gave one of the great Festival performances. I can see and hear her to this day at the end of the Fourth Act coming downstage in her dishevelled white dress and delivering that terrible last line 'And then I married James Tyrone ... and was so happy for a little while.'

The 1958 drama programme opened with T. S. Eliot's last Festival play *The Elder Statesman*, like the previous two a modern verse drama remaking a classical Greek tragedy. This time it was Sophocles's *Oedipus at Colonus* which was in the Eliot melting pot. Somehow the device of making it into drawing-room comedy in free verse seemed less convincing this time round although it gave Paul Rogers a chance to impersonate Harold Macmillan. There was also a splendidly vivacious production by the Old Vic of *Twelfth Night* in the Assembly Hall.

Again Michael Benthall was the director: Barbara Jefford was a passionate Viola, Joss Ackland a rumbustious Toby Belch and Richard Wordsworth a marvellously melancholic Malvolio.

At the Empire Theatre there was an admirable example of Ponsonby's commissioning zeal. A dance company under the auspices of the Festival Society presented twelve brand-new ballets specially commissioned for the Festival under the title *Ballets Premières*. The dance director was Peggy van Praagh and the musical director Charles Mackerras. The ballets combined a host of talents.

John Cranko created *Secrets* to the music of Francis Poulenc who had appeared at the previous Festival as pianist in a recital with the baritone Pierre Bernac; Wendy Toye choreographed and danced *Concerto for Dancers* to music by Joseph Horowitz: *Dreams* merged the dance patterns of Dimitri Parlic with the music of Alban Berg. Dancing as guests were some of the star ballet names in the world – Beryl Kaye, Gillian Lynne, Elsa Marianne von Rosen, Marjorie Tallchief, Walter Gore, Bjorn Holmgren and George Skibine – in six sparkling programmes of genuine Festival inventiveness and originality.

Opera that year was provided from Stuttgart and Madrid. The Stuttgart State Opera brought Mozart's *Die Entführung aus dem Serail*, Weber's *Euryanthe*, Lortzing's *Der Wildschütz* and Wagner's *Tristan und Isolde*. Madrid supplied de Falla for three performances at the end of the Festival in a double bill of *La Vida Breve* with Victoria de los Angeles as Salud and the ballet *El Sombrero de Tres Picos* with Antonio as The Miller.

Inevitably Stuttgart was compared with Hamburg who, having been to the Festival twice, had become Edinburgh's favourite German opera company.

But although most of the comparisons were unfavourable, there was plenty to enjoy. One was the introduction to Fritz Wunderlich who was Belmonte in *Die Entführung*, the young sailor in *Tristan* and Baron Kronthal in *Der Wildschütz*, a lyric tenor with a voice of exceptional beauty and style who was to appear at the Festival only once more a few weeks before his tragic death in 1966. Another was a brilliantly lit and splendidly mythic production of *Tristan* by Wagner's grandson Wieland, marvellously sung by the greatest post-war *heldentenor* Wolfgang Windgassen and the passionate Swedish-American soprano, Astrid Varnay.

One of the most delightful musical events of that Festival came when the Menuhin-Cassado-Kentner Trio decided to take their music to the people of Edinburgh. Although tickets for the Festival have never been expensive by international – or even national – standards, there are inevitably those who find them beyond their financial reach. Menuhin has always had an evangelical approach to music and with his two colleagues and friends, he set out to bring their music out of the concert hall to a new audience.

He wanted to make admission to the concert free but there was some kind of legal hitch to that so they hired the Embassy Cinema in Pilton, a housing estate in the north of the city and announced their concert for a Saturday morning, entry one shilling (5p). The altruism of the players was largely commended but the behind-the-hands chatter was that they would be lucky if they got more than a few dozen there – and they would all be refugees from the capital's cultural centre around Princes Street. Nobody in Pilton would come to listen to a trio playing classical music.

The faint of heart were proved gloriously wrong. The 1,000 seater cinema was packed. When I got there even in my 'important' capacity as a journalist, there was not a seat to be had. I had to sit – very happily – on the stairs.

The audience, many of them schoolchildren, listened enraptured and, to Menuhin's delight, they clapped in all the wrong places – between the movements of the Brahms B major and Beethoven's Archduke Trio. This, as he told me afterwards, proved conclusively that they were not genteel refugees from Princes Street, used to attending concerts. Outside as the three musicians left the cinema through the still applauding crowds, an old woman in a shawl shouted 'Haste ye back! Ye'll aye be welcome here.' It was a heart-warming occasion.

Back up the hill in the Usher Hall as well as the Trio (who also appeared as soloists with the Scottish National Orchestra under Hans Swarowsky, the Philharmonia with Klemperer and Ernest Ansermet and the Royal Danish Orchestra with Georg Solti), there was a series of one-composer concerts – an all-Britten programme from the Royal Opera House Orchestra, conducted by the composer and Ansermet; a Beethoven programme with Klemperer; an evening of Stravinsky under the baton of Ansermet, two recitals by Claudio Arrau devoted to the piano music of Beethoven and Chopin and Arrau playing Brahms and Mozart concertos with the Vienna Symphony Orchestra which rounded off the Festival with an exuberant Viennese evening of Johann Strauss conducted by Josef Krips.

Although the Festival has been haunted by real or manufactured financial crises throughout its history, this was the first year in which the cry of fiscal concern was really made public. Sir Ian Johnson-Gilbert, the Lord Provost launched an appeal for public support. He claimed that the Festival attracted 34,000 overseas visitors, 19,000 from North America (Americans counted virtually double in calculating imagination because of their free-spending reputation) and 57,000 from other parts of the United Kingdom in addition to thousands of day visitors who came largely for the Tattoo.

The Tattoo dates back to the very first Festival in 1947 when on nine evenings at 10 p.m. lit by searchlights from the battlements, troops of Scottish Command gave displays of Piping and Dancing on the Esplanade of Edinburgh Castle. On alternative evenings pipe bands played *Retreat* in different places in the city.

The Edinburgh Tattoo as a mixture of pageant and military spectacle was created by Brigadier Alistair Maclean in 1950, adding to the core Scottish contribution as the years went on by including units from overseas. The most cosmopolitan up to this date had been the 1957 Tattoo which contained the Danish Life Guards, the Royal Canadian Mounted Police and (coinciding, happily or fortuitously I've never discovered) with the performances of Rossini's *Il Turco in Italia* at the King's Theatre, the Turkish Army with the Corps of Janissaries, inventors of the military band, with their standard-bearers and cavalry whose drill patterns date back to the 13th century

The Tattoo is the single most popular item in the Festival – of it but not in it as it were. From the beginning it was organised by the Army's Scottish Command and it has played to an audience of getting on for ten million people down the years with another 80 million watching it on television, making Edinburgh Castle, the background against which it is set, one of the most recognisable landmarks in the world. Under an administration separate from the Festival, it is a great spectacle in its own right, a giant adjunct to the many summer spectacles going on at the foot of its mighty rock which dominates the city and a very important contributor to festival funding.

'The Festival has extended substantially the tourist season,' the Lord Provost's Appeal continued, 'and there is no doubt whatever that it is of immense commercial benefit to the city.' (A far cry from Sir John Falconer's 'May I assure you that the Festival is not a commercial undertaking in any way' of 1947!)

It was ended on a pragmatic note:

The Inland Revenue authorities will raise no objection to the allowance as expenses for Income Tax purposes of contributions by business houses to the Festival Society if the business has a direct trading interest in the continuation of the Festival and the amount of the contribution is reasonable in relation to the benefit likely to accrue to business. Any trader who wishes further information on this matter should consult his Inspector of Taxes.

In 1978 when I was involved in seeking sponsorship for the Festival, one major Scottish Princes Street store which must have been taking several thousand pounds a day during the Festival offered £400.

The newspapers ran the story of the Lord Provost's appeal as 'Festival Deficit of £22,000', and 'Is There an Edinburgh Festival Crisis?' One loudly raised voice among the City Fathers proposed that there should be a major festival only every three years with a series of lesser events in between. Ronald Mavor, James Bridie's son and *The Scotsman's* drama critic pointed out trenchantly that the city's share of Festival funding was under three-farthings on the rates. But the 'Festival Crisis' story had taken root and we have had one every year as regularly as the Tattoo but with fewer fireworks and a great deal less pleasure to the eye or ear.

1959 was the 200th anniversary of the birth of Scotland's national poet, Robert Burns, one of the great phenomena of literature because the lively veneration and affection which Scots the world over have felt for his verses lyrical, satirical and narrative has survived all kinds of invasions and generalisations of the national psyche, language and style in a way that has happened to no other poet. However much the Burns supper type of celebration may be derided or sneered at, the pleasure in the work of this 18th-century maker of verses persists. Lines from Burns have passed into the language – even the English language – and his songs remain favourites to this day.

Auld Lang Syne (in various translations) has even become a kind of international national anthem and his staunch advocacy of the brotherhood of man is more fashionable today than when he proclaimed it in *Is there for Honest Poverty?* in 1794.

> *Then let us pray that come it may*
> *As come it will for a' that*
> *That sense and worth, o'er a' the earth*
> *May bear the gree and a' that*
> *For a' that and a' that*
> *It's comin yet for a' that*
> *That man to man, the warld o'er*
> *Shall brothers be for a' that.*

Naturally the Burns Federation were keen on there being some celebration of the National Bard in the 1959 Festival. There had been a few Burns songs and a well-crafted play by Robert Kemp, *The Other Dear Charmer* about the poet's Edinburgh affair with the sugar-cane widow, Nancie Maclehose, at the Gateway in 1955 but not much else. Robert Ponsonby persuaded the Federation to join with the Festival Society in commissioning a new major orchestral work by the Scottish composer, Iain Hamilton to mark the occasion.

Hamilton was at that time deeply interested in serial techniques and his *Sinfonia for Two Orchestras* exploring a starkly structured series of notes around which the main themes were built, aroused no echoes of the Burns verses and melodies with which the poet had rescued Scottish song in the ears of the outraged Burns Federation listeners – or indeed anyone else – when it was played at the first concert given by the Scottish National Orchestra under Alexander Gibson.

For once the policy of 'sandwiching' – inserting a new work in the programme between established sure-fire winners – did not work.

Hamiltonian dissonances side by side with Wilhelm Kempff's serenely romantic playing of Beethoven's *Emperor Concerto* simply added impiety to insolence.

There was some consolation for the Fans of Rabbie in the splendid late-night entertainments at the Lyceum where Joan Alexander, Meta Forrest, Ian Gilmour, Roddy Macmillan, Roberta McEwan, James Kelman and Iain Cuthbertson offered the Bard in more acceptably presented song and verse and the matinee readings by the Gilmours, Sir Compton Mackenzie and James Gibson.

The most original celebration of the Burns anniversary (if you discount the controversial Hamilton *Sinfonia*) was Cedric Thorpe Davie's setting of Burns's wild and rebellious tavern cantata *The Jolly Beggars* given in the Lyceum with The Saltire Singers, Patricia Clark, Constance Mullay, Duncan Robertsom, Frederic Westcott and the Amici Quartet, directed by Hans Oppenheim.

'*The Jolly Beggars* is the most immoral poem in all literature. It does not merely defy morality. It treats morality as a fantastic fable,' wrote James Douglas in his introduction to the 1906 *Everyman* edition of Burns's poems. In Thorpe Davie's setting it did not seem quite as cataclysmic as all that but the anarchic defiance of authority and convention rang as true as when the French Revolution gave it stimulus and the rage of truth.

> *A fig for those by law protected!*
> *Liberty's a glorious feast!*
> *Courts for cowards were erected,*
> *Churches built to please the priest*

There were, of course, other things in the Festival. The first visit of the Royal Opera from Stockholm brought back Wagner with the second opera of the Ring cycle *Die Walkure* with Svet Svanholm as Siegmund and Birgit Nilsson as Brunnhilde in an impressive performance crushed into the inadequate space of the King's Theatre. And there was *Rigoletto* and *Un Ballo in Maschera* in Swedish with all the names changed.

This was of course justifiable on historical grounds as *Ballo* had encountered a lot of trouble with the Neapolitan and Papal censors when Verdi first wrote it for the San Carlo Opera in Naples in 1857. The story, based on the assassination of the Swedish King Gustav III at a masked ball in 1792, was taken from a play by Eugéne Scribe which had been made into an opera by Daniel Auber in 1833. Verdi and his librettist, Antonio Somma, had changed the locale and period to 17th-century Pomerania and altered the title to placate the Neapolitan censor. But on 14 January 1858 a bomb was thrown at Napoleon III's carriage while he was on his way to the Opera in Paris and when Verdi arrived in Naples to prepare *Ballo*, it was to find the censors in a major twitter about the whole subject.

The opera house produced a new libretto which completely nullified the original plot and changed the title of the opera and the names of all the characters (including that of the page Oscar to Orsini, the name of the Italian who had attempted to kill Napoleon III!) Verdi rejected the amended version and there was a lawsuit which was settled out of court.

In the meantime *Ballo* had been offered to the Teatro Apollo in Rome subject of course to the approval of the Papal censor, who insisted that the setting should be moved out of Europe. After tinkering with exotic locations all round the world from Russia to the Pacific, Verdi and Somma settled on Boston as a British colony before the American War of Independence. That a splendid opera survived all this censorious knock-about is a real tribute to Verdi's genius, as we had already seen in Edinburgh in Carl Ebert's fine Glyndebourne production of 1949.

In view of all the disorientation the opera had already suffered, it seemed piling confusion on disharmony for the Swedes to insist on transferring everything back to Sweden, a practice I regret to say has since been practised elsewhere, including the Royal Opera, Covent Garden.

Thus, historically correctly, Riccardo became King Gustav, Renato, his chief courtier and husband of the desired Amelia, Count Anckarström, Ulrica the fortune-teller Madame Arvedson, Tom and Sam the conspirators Counts Horn and Warting.

None of this would truly have mattered but for the fact that being historically correct about the names dehistoricised the story. The production's attempt to account for the historical fact that Gustav III was homosexual and much more likely to make a pass at the page Oscar than sing one of the greatest love duets Verdi ever wrote in the second act with his friend's wife, destabilised the plot. But it was great to hear Nilsson sing Amelia.

In August Strindberg's play *Gustav III,* the Gothenburg City Theatre gave the 1974 festival a different social and sexual interpretation of the ill-fated king in prose.

The most interesting opera which Stockholm brought was *Aniara* by Karl Birger Blomdhal, based on the epic poem written in 1956 by Harry Martinson and set in a space-ship, fleeing radio-active Earth for Mars. The emigrants remember war horrors and peer into the unknown future in a meld of traditional harmonies, serial orchestral writing, taped voices of Pasternak, Hitler and Mussolini and messages on a super-computer with a name and personality. The mixture of styles was disconcerting but the concept fascinating and it contrasted strangely with the grim purposeful personal tragedy of the other modern idiom piece, Alban Berg's *Wozzeck* powerfully sung by Erik Saeden and Elisabeth Söderström.

In the Usher Hall the Czech Philharmonic Orchestra conducted by Hans-Schmidt-Isserstedt and Karel Ancerl gave us Dvorak in every programme. Tribute was also paid to British musicians by the Royal Philharmonic in a Walton programme conducted by the composer and Sir Adrian Boult conducting a memorial concert of music by Ralph Vaughan Williams who had died during the previous Festival, which included the Sea Symphony and the Concerto for Two Pianos and Orchestra.

There was a strong and interesting dance programme with Finland providing mainly classical ballet and Les Ballets Babilée with *Le Jeune Homme et la Mort* a haunting image of loneliness and despair. Jerome Robbins's Ballets USA offered vigour, vitality and optimism with vibrant dancing, upbeat sets and heady rhythm in *NY Export-Op Jazz.*

It was not a great year in the theatre. Michael Flanders and Donald Swann brought their own late-night humour to the Lyceum and Anna Russell returned in six nights of such gems as *Wozzeck (An Analysis), Schreechenhauf* and *Guarda la Bella Tomato.* The Assembly Hall staged another Guthrie production of *The Thrie Estaites,* as popular as ever, with Macrae being even more deviously Doric and Tom Fleming giving new dimensions to Divine Correction. At the Gateway a season by Scottish repertory companies from Perth, Dundee and Glasgow had a new play from Linklater, *Breakspear in Gascony* which never really got off the ground, Bernard Shaw and a spirited revival of one of Bridie's best dramas *The Baikie Charivari* well done by Ann Gudrun, Iain Cuthbertson and Leonard Maguire.

There was more Bridie in the Fringe's first published programme along with *The Firstborn* by Christopher Fry; Gordonstoun School in an operetta *Beastie Beware* written by two young masters, John Gillespie and Tony White; Oxford Theatre Group in the première of *Why the Chicken* by John McGrath and St Andrews University with Douglas Young's Scots translation of Aristophanes *The Burdies.*

There was also a zany sounding pair of musical programmes at Gartshore Hall, *New Pills to Purge Old Melancholy* and *The Tear and the Smile,* featuring an unknown baritone Frederick Fuller and an obscure pianist called Dudley Moore. There was no whiff of protest and no sign of anyone taking off their clothes and the word 'sex' was never mentioned. I wonder what happened to Frederick Fuller.

In October Robert Ponsonby resigned and the prospective Lord Provost, Jack Dunbar and City Treasurer Duncan Weatherstone sped south to talk to Lord Harewood, the Queen's cousin who was Controller of Opera Planning at the Royal Opera House, Covent Garden to see if he would be interested in running the Edinburgh Festival. A new Festival era was on the immediate horizon.

GEORGE, EARL OF HAREWOOD 1961-5
Theme and Variations – Czechs and Cash

XI

George, Earl of Harewood was 36, a tall, ruggedly handsome, outspoken and determined man, the eldest son of the Sixth Earl and Princess Mary the Princess Royal, sister of King George VI. Although educated at Eton his interests had always been primarily in the arts, principally music. After an unlucky war – as a captain in the Grenadier Guards he was badly wounded near Perugia in June 1944, taken prisoner and held in Colditz – he sought a musical career. He became the editor of the magazine *Opera* in 1951 and joined the staff of the Royal Opera, Covent Garden in 1953.

When approached about the Festival job he had just been appointed Controller of Opera Planning at Covent Garden and had established a serious reputation in the music world, having overcome earlier suspicions of being merely a royal dabbler by his knowledgeable application, energy and enthusiasm. He had been President of the Aldeburgh Festival ever since it began when he was an undergraduate at Cambridge in 1948, andwas also President of the English Football Association. A man of diverse interests with a strong and positive personality, he could of course also be presumed to have influential friends everywhere.

Edinburgh was delighted when he accepted not only because the Earl of Harewood as Festival Director appealed to the vein of ingrained snobbery in the city but also because the few people in the inner circle of the Festival who knew anything about the arts were aware of the esteem in which he was held in London and Aldeburgh. It was certainly a good appointment in a publicity sense and Harewood was known personally at the Festival because he had been a regular attender during its first decade. But it was undeniably a risk.

Lord Harewood

Harewood was to take over in 1961: in the meantime, Ponsonby had the 1960 Festival to plan. It was in no way a negligible contribution, underlining the sterling qualities both innovative and traditional which Ponsonby had brought to the task.

The Scotsman did not think, however, it was innovative:

> *This year's operatic programme contrasts strongly with that of 1959,* it said sternly at the beginning of the Festival, *and the accent this year is on entertainment and more commonplace predicaments.*

Just what was being complained about is rather hard to fathom. The opera supplied by Glyndebourne consisted of Verdi's *Falstaff*, Bellini's *I Puritani* both conducted by Vittorio Gui and a bill of three one-act operas, Wolf-Ferrari's *Il Segreto di Susanna*, Poulenc's *La Voix Humaine* and Busoni's *Arlecchino*. *Falstaff* is an undisputed masterpiece and the other four operas had almost certainly never been seen before by 90 per cent of the audiences who attended the Festival. Verdi's only comic opera, apart from the early and disastrous *Un Giorno di Regno*, was in the Carl Ebert production we had seen in 1955 directed by Ebert's son, Peter. In it Geraint Evans played Falstaff:

His dexterity of voice was as prodigious as his figure, recorded a less judgmental critic,
*but there was a glint in his eyes which suggested a younger shrewder and less lugubrious
Falstaff. A remarkable performance rich in humanity and voice.*

Despite allegedly being based on Sir Walter Scott's novel *Old Mortality*, *I Puritani* (originally *I Puritani
di Scozia* for no reason made clear in the libretto as it all happens in Devon!) was not received with any
great acclaim apart from the singing of Joan Sutherland as Elvira, the Roundhead's daughter who wishes
to marry a Cavalier and spends most of her time from the end of Act I in lyrical fits of madness.

The three one-act pieces, however, were a hit. *Il Segreto di Susanna* is a trifle but musically pleasing,
'a soufflé flavoured with nicotine' as someone described it – for Susanna's secret, roguish in Wolf-Ferrari's
day and not socially subversive as in ours, is that she smokes! Busoni's satirical *Arlecchino* is a comparatively
jolly piece from a very serious composer, set with *commedia del arte* characters in 19th-century Bergamo
and was splendidly sung by Ian Wallace, Helga Pilarczyk and Carlos Feller. A capriccio with bite.

The third piece was Francis Poulenc's brilliant *La Voix Humaine* from a play by Jean Cocteau who also
designed the sets and directed. A tense and moving solo sung by Denise Duval in a one-sided telephone
conversation from a woman whose lover is leaving her, it gave you the almost shameful sense of unwillingly
intruding on private desperation and grief. A *tour de force* in every sense and a stark contrast to Gian-
Carlo Menotti's witty and frivolous *The Telephone*, written ten years earlier, which we had seen with the
After-Dinner Opera Company in 1956.

'A very successful evening's entertainment and not to be missed,' as Christopher Grier, *The Scotsman's*
music critic noted.

Cocteau was also in the news for presenting the Festival with a new logo free of charge – a pallid
Orpheus peering pensively through the strings of his lyre looking as if he had done a harrowing stint in
the underworld. It was featured for a year or two until it was discovered that the French man-of-all-arts
had presented the same logo to several other festivals!

It was another big year for Scottish drama with the Citizens' Theatre from Glasgow giving the British
première of Swiss Friedrich Dürrenmatt's *Romulus the Great* and the Gateway Company a new translation
of Norwegian Bjørnstjerne Bjørnson's 1862 *Mary Stuart in Scotland*.

There was some competition about which contained the most bogus history but the Norwegian plod
through the Scotch mists of the 16th century won on dullness.

Outstanding theatre performances (all of them 'premières') were achieved by Scots being Scots, French
being French and English being English. Sydney Goodsir Smith's epic drama *The Wallace*, designated 'a
triumph in five acts' was on the open stage of the Assembly Hall – not always an advantage in intimate
scenes – but his swinging vital Scots blank verse made its own vivid impression and Peter Potter's handling
of the big scenes was spectacular. In the title role Iain Cuthbertson gave one of the finest performances
of his life, passionate, 'a rantin' roarin' boy' of real power and magnetism although one critic from south
of the Border observed:

> *Mr Sydney Goodsir Smith is almost entirely preoccupied with the treachery, cruelty
> and barbarism of his countrymen. If the author were an Englishman, I should gravely
> fear for his safety in Princes Street.*

Another, impressed by Wallace as 'a dominant figure, the powerful common man whose nobility is
innate', complained petulantly: 'It's half in a foreign language.'

The Duke of Edinburgh, however, on one of royalty's rare visits to the Festival, praised it highly –
perhaps it's the Gordonstoun education. A noisy group calling themselves The Scottish Patriots hissed
the *National Anthem* and tried to get the audiences to sing *Scots Wha Hae* at the end. This started the
usual crop of indignant newspaper letters from England's last North British colony in Morningside.

It was a good year in the concert hall too with a virtuoso performance of the Verdi *Requiem* from the Philharmonia Chorus and Orchestra, soloists Joan Sutherland, Fiorenza Cossoto, Luigi Ottolini and Ivo Vinco under the inspired and inspiring direction of Carlo Maria Giulini.

Musica Viva, a kind of concert/lecture followed by a public discussion which had been evolved by Karl Amadeus Hartmann in Munich, imported by John Pritchard to Liverpool and successfully tried out by Alex Gibson in Glasgow earlier that year came to the Festival with Berg's *Lulu Suite* and Humphrey Searle's Third Symphony. Lulu – never at that time been performed in its entirety – made:

> *... a shatteringly impressive and expressive effect, made the more intense by two magnificent vocal contributions (plus one terrifying scream) from Helga Pilarcyzk and the Searle Symphony was judged to have a very strong emotive content and in the last resort the fact that it is cast in the 12-tone discipline is irrelevant.*

Walton's Second Symphony also received a world première, played by the Royal Liverpool Philharmonic and conducted by John Pritchard. Despite a great ovation, it was noted:

> *Not music that explores new paths of tonal or rhymthic experience but rather enriches a territory with whose salient features most concert-goers are tolerably familiar.*

Four concerts with the Leningrad Symphony Orchestra under Eugen Mravinsky and Gennadi Rozdestvensky explored the popular canvas of Russian music including the British première of Shostakovich's *Concerto for Cello and Orchestra* with Mstislav Rostropovich. At the Lyceum was Chekhov's *The Seagull*, with the Old Vic, celebrating the centenary of the Russian playwright's birth.

Almost the most Russian performance however was given by Rostropovich playing Brahms, Bach and Prokoviev in the Freemasons' Hall. The aggressive intelligence and dazzling technical skill with which he tackled the Brahms F major Sonata and the Bach Suite in C major underlined the particular qualities of contrasting tone and dynamics, articulation and phrasing and the integral rhythmic sense which were inherently Russian no matter what was being played and which had been the hallmarks of Mravinsky's direction of the Leningrad Orchestra.

The effect of Robert Ponsonby's most remembered contribution to Festival programming, however, was seeping into criticism. The shade – as it were – of Anna Russell hung over one Usher Hall review of a concert by the Philharmonia under Wolfgang Sawallisch which included Mahler's Songs from *Des Knaben Wunderhorn*. The performance of the powerfully voiced soloist, Ursula Boese, a lady cast in heroic mould, 'would have been enhanced by greater variety of emotional play,' one critic said, adding:

> *Without being irreverent it was difficult to forget Anna Russell's description of German lieder as 'mushy poetry set to magnificent music'.*

At the Lyceum Theatre there was incipient crisis and scandal. La Compagnie Roger Planchon found themselves in hot water because they had not paid their three guineas trade union fee to Equity's Scottish secretary Alex McCrindle, and Mr McCrindle was threatening to call out all Equity members in the Festival unless they came up with the cash.

One group who might not have minded being on strike were the cast of Frank Dunlop's production of the world première of Bernard Kop's play *The Dream of Peter Mann*, the reception of which qualified actor Michael Warre for the Grand Order of Optimistic Lunacy (always seriously contested at the Festival) when he said: 'People walking out of the theatre is a healthy sign.'

Appeasing the menacing wrath of Alex McCrindle did not solve all of La Compagnie Roger Planchon's problems. In those days we still had censorship and the Lord Chamberlain, responsible for keeping public morals in exposed places like theatres on a leash, demanded to see a script of the French company's play *Les Trois Mousquetaires*. This would not have posed any problems for the company's free adaptation of Alexandre Dumas's famous tale but they didn't have a script because the essence of their comedy was that they made it up as they went along.

So the stage director Jean Malaterre drew the short straw and sat down in the wings with a typewriter and wrote one for his lordship's perusal. Thus in the end, approved by plebs and patricians alike, the show went on. And just as well for it was a joyous occasion.

I would regret that anyone who has ever taken pleasure in a theatrical performance should miss Les Trois Mousquetaires, whether from plague, poverty, parsimony or ignorance of the French language, wrote Ronald Mavor. *So much entertainment can seldom have filled a stage. Cocteau said* Waiting for Godot *was like* 'une pensée de Pascal interpreté par les Fratellini'.

Les Trois Mousquetaires *is like a wilder Guthrie production of Shakespeare interpreted by the Marx Brothers. It would be an understatement to say that there is never a dull moment. And yet the production eminently merits a Festival performance because there is an originality of approach to the telling of a story on the stage and a vigour in the acting which one would like to hope will influence productions in this country for a long time.*

And then there were the English being English in *Beyond the Fringe*. It was of course fringe English – the wit came from the traditions of Swift, Pope, Hogarth, Chesterton and Coward – even perhaps, in deference to their top university origins, from Horace and Juvenal; but the purpose was mockery or take-the-mickery not reform.

No hint here of Pope's *Epilogue to the Satires:*
Yes I am proud, I must be proud to see
Men not afraid of God, afraid of me
Safe from the Bar, the Pulpit and the Throne
Yet touched and shamed by Ridicule alone.
O sacred weapon! left for Truth's defence
Sole Dread of Folly, Vice and Insolence.

'I knew Dudley Moore, I knew Jonathan Miller,' Ponsonby said '*Beyond the Fringe* stole the show. We thought at first we'd call it the *Oxford Revue* but it grew beyond that. The dress rehearsals were a disaster. It broke down, they giggled at each other, jumped their lines, camped it up. I thought: "Oh my God! What have I done?", but it opened the floodgates to all the satire that followed.'

Whether you remember Miller pricking the pomposities of academe in his A. J. Ayer popular philosopher mode, Peter Cook as the miner who wanted to be a judge but didn't have the Latin for it, Alan Bennett in the pulpit or Dudley Moore at the piano, it was hilariously wonderful.

In *The Weekly Scotsman* before the Festival, under the heading *Around the Fringe,* Sydney Goodsir Smith, playwright, poet, prophet and polemicist wrote:

From a' the airts they come, home and abroad and put on their shows – classics, experiments and world premieres, solos, recitals, exhibitions, late night revues, anything and everything – often in appallingly

Beyond the Fringe *(1960)*

undramatic conditions in cold draughty halls where they do miracles with primitive lighting and half the audience expect to see nothing anyway but miraculously do; all in the wild crazy hope (which every now and again actually does come off) that some visiting talent scout will spot them and carry them off in his gilded chariot to London where the bright lights will go up and names are made for evermore.

For *Beyond the Fringe* 'the wild crazy hope' really came true. After the first night the show received two offers to go straight into London's West End and Jonathan Miller started agonising about his career as a pathologist in Cambridge where he had recently begun work. But as we all know he solved that problem.

In an endearingly eccentric gesture, Robert Ponsonby advertised his Rolls Royce on the Festival Press notice board and prepared to go off to run another festival on Hog Island in the Bahamas, linked to Nassau by a high-arched bridge and now known as Paradise Island. A man beset by many illusions not his, and one or two disillusions entirely personal. He had taken the Festival resolutely in the direction in which he believed it should go, in the process offering more first performances of new or never-before-seen-or-heard works in all the artistic disciplines than anyone else (the 1960 Blue Rider show of German Expressionists at the Royal Scottish Academy, full of light, hope and rebellion was the most *outré* of the Festival's visual art shows to date).

For all this his reward was to be remembered as the man who helped to launch *Beyond the Fringe* – which most people think was on the Fringe anyway. His successor Lord Harewood had the Director's salary raised by £500 to the lordly sum of £2,500 a year and was given another £20,000 of programme money to play with, a contribution of £50,000 in total from Edinburgh Corporation. This for an enterprise from which the city earned substantial rents and which was reckoned to earn Scotland's capital more than £3,000,000 per year – to say nothing of the knock-on tourist effect.

There was, of course, opposition to this lavish benevolence. The grant was made despite strong opposition from Councillor Pat Rogan who wanted an investigation into the affairs of the Festival Society and from Councillor Murdo Mackenzie who claimed the organisation was 'tottering'.

Even Councillor Magnus Williamson, who seconded the Lord Provost's approval proposal, could not forbear to carp:

We want a bigger control of Festival affairs, he said, by the business people of Edinburgh and the Corporation. There comes a time in every organisation when there must be a wind of change. That time has almost been reached in the Festival Society. The Society should be run by the Corporation, helped by a number of 'artistically clever' people. The present rather arty-crafty collection of people on the Society who have given us a great deal of assistance in the past should be replaced by new people.

In City Chambers debates about the Festival there had always been plenty of wind tempered by the excuse that they were running out of change, but this was tampering not tempering. 'We have had a Festival now for 13 years so now we know all about festivals. Let us then get down to doing what local authorities do best – meddling.' What Bernard Levin was later to christen 'the annual Ritual of the Grudging of the Money' was hardening into a Festival Rite.

At the final 1960 press conference Lord Harewood promised 'new talent' for the next Festival. The new era was tottering on its way.

XII

Harewood opened his Edinburgh Festival career with what in cultural terms could certainly be counted as a 'bang' but there were not too many new faces around. The bang was making Schoenberg the theme composer of the Festival by giving 25 performances of his works ranging from the massive scale of *Gurrelieder* to the minimalism of the string quartets.

Gurrelieder was the opening concert with the augmented London Symphony Orchestra. It needs ten horns, eight flutes, four Wagner tubas, six timpani and iron chains in addition to three male choirs, a large mixed chorus, five soloists and a speaker. The work is based on a collection of Danish poems by J. P. Jacobsen about Castle Gurra, home of the 14th-century heroine Tove. Composed at the turn of the century it is very much Schoenberg in his high romantic, Wagnerian style rather than the dreaded later atonalist.

One of the faces new to the Festival – although hardly to the general public – was the conductor Leopold Stowkowski. He had become famous in the cinema in the 1930s and 40s playing himself in a Deanna Durbin film *A Hundred Men and A Girl* and as the conductor in the Walt Disney classical music full-length cartoon *Fantasia*, as well as the *maestro* of the Philadelphia and other American orchestras. His relentless showmanship and his phoney accent (he was born in London of a Polish father and an Irish mother and studied at Oxford and the Royal College of Music but had a well-developed mittel-European intonation) irritated purists. ('He is a very fine man I am sure and interested in many things,' Sibelius said, 'but not, I think, in music.')

However all his flamboyant qualities masked a very real musicianship. He was about 80 in 1961 (like many legends his exact age was something of a mystery), and was as dynamic and demanding of excellence as ever.

Stokowski on the podium conducted *Gurrelieder* with Dutch soprano Gré Brouwenstijn, Americans Nell Rankin and James McCracken as soloists and the BBC news-reader Alvar Liddell as narrator in the finale, was a triumph.

Its success encouraged audiences to hear other Schoenberg items such as the Five Orchestral Pieces, the Op 31 Variations, Six Songs sung by Elisabeth Söderström and the Film Music suite. Unfortunately there was no Schoenberg opera, but there was a good deal of 20th-century music in the concert programmes. This included items by Schoenberg's disciples such as Webern, Berg and Blacher, as well as works by Britten, Tippett, Stravinsky, Bartok and Hindemith. There was a stunning Ravel Piano Concerto from Arturo Benedetti Michelangeli under Colin Davis, and Shostakovich's Fifth Symphony from Stokowski, both with the London Symphony; plus a stirring *Heldenleben* from von Karajan and the Berlin Philharmonic.

Opera was provided by the Royal Opera House, Covent Garden – Gluck's *Iphigénie en Tauride* with Rita Gorr as the guilt-stricken heroine and Robert Massard as Oreste, conducted by Georg Solti who was also on the podium for Britten's *Midsummer Night's Dream*. Giulini conducted a sparkling performance of *Il Barbiere di Siviglia* with Rolando Panerai as Figaro, Luigi Alva as the Count. Boris

Carlo Maria Giulini

Christoff as Basilio and Fernando Corena as Dr Bartolo but there was a problem with the Zeffirelli production of Donizetti's *Lucia di Lammermoor*. In one of her most celebrated roles Joan Sutherland was not in good voice:

> *There was dryness and a slight sense of strain*, one critic commented. *Perhaps a sign of the danger that Miss Sutherland might be tempted to seek out rarely performed 19th-century operas in this style, works which are sheer piffle. We want to see her tackle the great roles in the standard repertory such as Puccini's* Manon *and Minnie in* The Girl of the Golden West. *No-one, not even Miss Sutherland, the world's greatest singer, can go on forever playing Mad Bess of Pencaitland.*

This was one of the odder pieces of Festival criticism: not only by casting Donizetti beyond the bounds of standard repertoire as 'sheer piffle' and elevating Puccini's two least acclaimed operas to masterworks, but also by suggesting that *Lucia*, an opera set in East Lothian by Sir Walter Scott (whoever Mad Bess of Pencaitland may be) was unworthy of Edinburgh's attention. *Lucia* contains the finest mad scene in lyric drama and *bel canto* writing for ensemble in the sextet, which has been much admired.

It was also unjust for Miss Sutherland was ill and suffered from an ear abscess – on the eve the next performance of *Lucia* was cancelled. This resulted in one of those frantic behind-the-scenes orgies of panic organising which are a fairly regular feature of Festival life.

A last-minute presentation of another work in the Covent Garden repertoire was hastily conjured up so that audiences should not be deprived of lyricism. Desperate phone calls combing the Highlands summoned back Boris Christoff and Fernando Corena from motor tours of the north. Edward Downes was called in from London to replace Giulini who was conducting the Philharmonia in the Usher Hall that night and a performance of *Il Barbiere di Siviglia* was scrambled on to the stage of the King's Theatre. Nearly 300 people asked for their money to be refunded and the young French diva Mady Mesplé was rushed from Paris to sing Lucia on the last night of the Festival.

One indignant letter in *The Scotsman* the following week *complained* that Madame Mesplé gave a magnificent performance (which she did) and demanded to know why the Festival authorities did not arrange for her to do it at the previously scheduled *Lucia*. To audiences great Lucias grow on trees but no-one pointed out just what rare fruit such singers were. Everyone just smiled rather tightly from beneath their recently mopped brows.

So with its usual ingredients of drama and incipient crisis Lord Harewood's first festival got under way. With funding from Jack Lyons and brilliant imaginative design and conceptual staging from Richard Buckle, the Waverley Market was turned into a spectacular homage to *Epstein* in what is still remembered as one of the most stimulating and impressive exhibitions staged at the Festival – along with Dickie Buckle's other presentations of Diaghilev and Shakespeare making an astonishing trio of visualisations of genius.

When he began planning his first Festival Harewood was keenly aware that drama had come to be seen, for one reason or another, as the poor relation of Festival programming. So in 1961 he boldly offered a bit of everything.

On the open stage of the Assembly Hall darkness reigned. Two of the blackest plays in the English classical repertoire were presented by the Old Vic: Shakespeare's *King John*., his most prolix denunciation of tyranny; and Marlowe's *Dr Faustus*, the ultimate template for ambition's descent to hell. John Osborne's *Luther* in the vituperous personification of Albert Finney raged against ecclesiastical bigotry in the Lyceum, Molière's *Le Misanthrope* made a more sardonic comment on the human condition and only Lawrence Durrell's *Sappho* which gave Margaret Rawlings a chance to wallow in exotic prose and a specially commissioned play from Nigel Dennis, *August for the People* with Rex Harrison being semi-politically semi-satirical offered any light relief.

In 1962 the featured composer was Shostakovich. The composer himself, nervous and suspicious of his position and standing in the pernicious West, attended. He mellowed somewhat when Lord Harewood introduced him to haggis with whisky gravy – for which throughout his spell as Festival Director Harewood was an unflagging and enthusiastic propagandist – and seemed to enjoy some of the 25 items of his music, performed mainly by Russian artists.

Among the 25 – clearly a magic number – items by the featured composer were half of Shostakovich's extant symphonies (by 1962 he had published 12 later to grow to 15) and all the string quarters then written. Shostakovich straddled the political-cultural-musical problem of artists in the Soviet Union rather uncertainly and he was not very sure about how or why his music was appreciated in the West. He had had various brushes with the Soviet authorities who regarded his more adventurous forays into modernism as too experimentalist or formalist, and were forever demanding music which enshrined the sincere expressiveness and democratic nature of musical idiom natural to the Russian soul. So it was puzzling to this embittered man of searing genius to find works condemned at home acclaimed abroad and sincere expressions of the Russian soul considered rather dull and plodding outside his native borders.

There were however works which crossed all frontiers. The Fifth Symphony, given at the 1961 Festival, was certainly one, in many ways a traditionally romantic Russian work reminiscent of Tchaikovsky, Borodin and Mahler but with its own 'high voltage nervous electricity' as someone said at the première in 1937, and great

Dimitri Shostakovich (1962)

power. Then the Seventh – written while the composer was a fire-fighter as his native city of Leningrad was being besieged in 1941 and broadcast all over America in 1942 – was the other major work which drew attention to Shostakovich in the West although it was damned as 'over-publicised and over-praised' by a 1962 programme note.

The 1962 Festival introduced many people to the other symphonies the five-movement Eighth written at the time of the Battle for Stalingrad with its evocation of mock empty triumphalism and the bleak brutality of war – a resounding contrast with the Beethoven Eighth with which it shared a programme – and the savage denunciation of Stalin in the second movement of the Tenth as well as excerpts from *Lady Macbeth of Mtsensk* and the superb quartets.

At a press conference shortly before leaving the great composer seemed to have relaxed a little and discussed the performances of his work with some vigour and even asperity – he admitted to having enjoyed the Festival:

> I *have never before heard such a concentration of my works in so short a period he said. And I might, like Mendelssohn, write something about Scotland and Edinburgh in time. But I am not in the habit,* he added with a smile, *of issuing promissory notes unless I know I can pay them.*

This semi-promissory note was, alas, never redeemed but there was a bit of musical exchange in the other direction when Ronald Stevenson, music teacher at Broughton school and a distinguished Scottish composer, presented his *Solo for Piano in honour of Shostakovich* to his Russian confrère in the George Hotel.

History was the theme and the Devil the most popular character in the year's rag-bag of dramatic offerings with Dylan Thomas's *The Doctor and the Devils* at the Assembly Hall and *The Devils* by John Whiting at the Lyceum. The first was a another look at the celebrated Edinburgh grand guignol tale of the anatomist, Dr Knox and the suppliers of corpses (some of them over-fresh), Burke and Hare; the subject of a famous play by James Bridie which might have made a better choice than Thomas's reworked film script. John Whiting's play was based on another gruesome historical event which has not lost its fascination down the years. The most recent manifestation was the Ken Russell film but Whiting's play was based on Aldous Huxley's account of the scandalous events of 17th-century Loudon when the 27-year-old priest, Urbain Grandier, was charged with the bewitching of the nuns in the local convent and burned at the stake.

Shakespeare's *Troilus and Cressida* and Christopher Fry's *Curtmantle*, another look at the Henry II/Thomas à Becket story, were the other plays at the Lyceum. The Gateway Theatre had a Scottish offering in Robert MacLellan's *Young Auchinleck* with John Cairney as Boswell seeking a well-dowered bride prior to his romps in London and the acquaintance of Dr Samuel Johnson. The *Troilus* directed by Peter Hall was notable for a luminous and touching performance from Dorothy Tutin as the heroine and *The Doctor and the Devils* was locally cast with Leonard Macguire as a powerful Dr Knox, Tom Conti as Daft Jamie and the one-time scourge of the Roger Planchon Company, Alex McCrindle as Davie Forsythe.

There was a Writers' Conference in the McEwan Hall, organised by publisher and author John Calder. It discussed 'The Basic Approach to the Novel' – whatever that might be – under the chairmanship of Sir Compton Mackenzie; 'Scottish Writing Today' with David Daiches, Hugh McDiarmid, Alexander Reid, Robin Jenkins, Neil Gunn and Douglas Young; 'Is Commitment Necessary?', 'Censorship' and 'The Future of the Novel', all subjects of hardy perennial interest in those days but which have become rather overgrown in the groves of contemporary academe.

There was no discussion of the impact of the Russian novel on contemporary writing although that might well have been expected in view of the heavy emphasis on East of Iron Curtain items in the rest of the programme. There were Yugoslav Modern Primitives at the National Gallery. The opera came from Belgrade with Borodin's *Prince Igor* in the Rimsky-Korsakov version, Mussorgsky's *Khovanshchina* arranged by Shostakovich, with the great bass, Miro Cangalovic outstanding in each; Prokoviev's *Love of Three Oranges* and *The Gambler* and non-Eastern oddities in Massenet's *Don Quixote* (not seen in Britain since 1912) and Britten's marvellously sinister *The Turn of the Screw* conducted by Meredith Davies and presented by the English Opera Group.

The Belgrade Ballet was a hit with a splendid performance of the unknown *Kostana* by the Serbian composer Petar Konjovic, choreographed by Dimitrije Parlic and featuring what now seems the inevitable Eastern European *Miraculous Mandarin*, then derided as decadent and sending delicious frissons of the forbidden through Edinburgh audiences. There were large audiences at Murrayfield Ice Rink for *The Four Sons of Aymon*, a kind of heroic dance pageant created (not on ice but in the space the building provided) by Maurice Bejart from a medieval French romance, made in Belgium and narrated in English by Paul Anriew and Iain Cuthbertson.

The Scotsman caricaturist Coia drew Harewood as a fur-hatted, prancing, knee-kicking Cossack dancer. Allowing for the odd Slavic bit of temperament from Rostropovich and others it all seemed pretty *culturny*. The leader-writer of *Edinburgh Evening News* certainly thought so:

> *There can be no doubt that Edinburgh has benefited spiritually as well as materially from the Festival. There used to be the feeling, not quite eradicated perhaps, that we were provincial, rather narrow, and that the city was no place for high culture.*

Emilio Coia

Certainly it is not as well equipped as it might be – we don't even have a proper opera house – but we manage and can put on a show for everyone. Granting that other forces are at work, it cannot be denied, nevertheless, that the Festival has had an enormous effect on the city's amenities. Good restaurants with a wide bill of fare have increasingly opened up in recent years and the city's list of hotels is extending. Edinburgh as a conference centre is recognised more and more and its popularity as a tourist centre is daily more evident. Long may the bustle continue.

Despite this and other notes of approval and chalking up the highest-ever ticket sales, there was still more than a hint of civic disapproval. On the insistence of the councillors who had claimed that the festival organisation was 'tottering', Festival office methodology and practice was put under the beady eyes of a Time and Motion study investigator.

In his entertaining autobiography,*The Tongs and the Bones* (Weidenfeld & Nicolson, 1981), Lord Harewood relates how the dapper and dark-suited investigator spent three days in London going through the books, discussing expenses and the fees paid to festival artists and others at Edinburgh and comparing them with other festivals. The investigator then went on to Edinburgh and grilled the administrative director, Willie Grahame for 13 hours to check the truth of what he had been told in London!

When the report from the interlocutor arrived a few weeks later it was neither highly critical nor hostile but it contained what Lord Harewood, with commendable restraint, noted as 'some rather odd comments'.

One was that the artistic direction appeared not to follow accepted business practice in its dealings with artists: it should not, for instance, let a musician know that he was the first or only choice for a particular engagement, but should leave him with the impression that others were being sounded out, so that a more competitive price might be obtained.

Harewood's comment was: 'Try that on Klemperer or Karajan!', followed by 'something rather less parliamentary'.

The practice of planning festivals around the works of particular composers remained as a Harewood theme. 'After all,' he said cheerfully, 'in a festival the size of Edinburgh it is perfectly possible to have 25 works by a single composer and for a visitor to fill a week without hearing any of them.'

In 1963 however the pattern was changed and augmented. There were once again two 'featured' composers, Berlioz and Bartok but there was also a strong emphasis on music from India, something for which Harewood had a particular passion.

There had been Indian performances before. The Ram Gopal Ballet had been at the tenth Festival with a repertoire of classical and folk dances from the sub-continent and the Little Ballet Troupe from Bombay had danced at Ponsonby's last festival but was not received with any great enthusiasm, 1960s audiences preferring eastern promise westernised by the Ballet Nervi dancing in Bakst's peacock-coloured sets and costumes to Rimsky-Korsakov's exotic music in *Sheherazade*.

But the 1963 programmes from India were more than a genuflection in the direction of multi-cultural internationalism in a single event. With the co-operation of Dr Narayana Menon, Director-General of All India Radio and a graduate of Edinburgh University who had studied Western music under Sir Donald Tovey, a series of performances were spread over the three weeks in Leith Town Hall, Freemasons' Hall, the Royal Scottish Museum and St Cuthbert's Church covering a wide range of Indian music and dance as well as certain events of cultural commingling.

Balasaraswati, introduced in the Souvenir Programme by Lord Harewood as 'one of the three greatest living dancers', danced in the Royal Scottish Museum to the *tambura*, the long-necked Indian lute, drums, flute and cymbal: Ravi Shankar's virtuoso sitar with Alla Rakha's tabla and Subbulakshmi, the Carnatic Callas, accompanied by violin, mridangam, ghatan and tambura gave concerts in the Freemasons' Hall.

In two concerts east met west in sometimes bewitching sometimes bizarre harmonies with Larry Adler on harmonica, Julian Bream on guitar, George Malcolm on harpsichord, Ravi Shankar on sitar, Louis Luff on clarinet and Dr Menon on veena, a seven-stringed plucked instrument, playing Bach, eastern music transcribed western style, Bartok, raga improvisations, and a specially written new work by Vanraj Bhatia.

Critics struggled to encompass these new musical structures. One of the more successful was John Currie, later to be the chorus master of the Edinburgh Festival Chorus:

Anyone who has felt the emotive power of the long weaving line of plainsong, for example could hardly fail to be moved by this singer's control and shaping of similar melodic outlines. Specially moving were the long ecstatic, vibrate-less notes which would suddenly end in a deliciously-shaded flourish before handing over to an echo effect on the violin (played and tuned in the Indian manner).

Madame Subbulakshmi presents her small voice (by Western operatic standards) in an endless variety of timbres, nasal, gently throaty, pianissimo, dolcissimo which blend alarmingly with her accompanying instruments. Sometimes on a hummed note she will imitate precisely the sound of the violin who takes his cue and enters musically invisible.

There was also an Indian art exhibition from which Harewood was asked to censor two of the miniatures as being over-erotic! In fact it was very much a year in which the hide-bound social *mores* of the Scottish capital clashed with artistic aspirations – or pretensions.

The Drama Conference in the McEwan Hall during the last week of the 1963 Festival is now remembered chiefly for the 'happening' of a naked girl being wheeled on a trolley across the organ loft – possibly the first instance of a 'streaker' at a literary conference but far from being the most important statement made in the week's debates about the future and significance of the theatre.

As far as theatrical significance was concerned not a lot was offered in the programme. At the Lyceum there was a new play by Ray Lawler, who had put Australia on the drama map with *The Summer of the Seventeenth Doll* before the national focus shifted to TV soap operas, but *The Unshaven Cheek* failed to make the impact of its predecessor. The Assembly Hall epic of the year was the British première of *The Rabbit Race* by the Swiss Martin Walser, adapted by Ronald Duncan. In the last week John Dexter's production of Bernard Shaw's *St Joan* from the Chichester Festival took its place to considerably more acclaim particularly for Joan Plowright's shining performance in the name part.

In the same week at the Lyceum, Alec Guinness returned to the Festival with a wonderfully vulnerable study of disintegrating royal impotence as King Elie Berenger in the British première of Ionescu's *Exit the*

King with a distinguished cast including Googie Withers, Natasha Parry and Eileen Atkins directed by George Devine.

The Berlioz/Bartok featured-composer programmes were played by the Royal Opera House orchestra under Solti and John Pritchard and the London Symphony with Colin Davis and the young Hungarian conductor, Istvan Kertesz, the BBC Symphony with Lorin Maazel and Norman del Mar and the Concertgebouw with Bernard Haitink and Georg Szell, together with recitals featuring Yehudi Menuhin, John Ogdon and Brenda Lucas and the Amadeus and the Tatrai String Quartet from Hungary in concerts at the Usher Hall, the Freemasons' and Leith Town Hall.

Bartok came out of it rather better than Berlioz – always an expensive composer to programme – who featured only in bits and pieces like the Shakespearean and Byronic overtures apart from the inevitable *Symphonie Fantastique* and a fine concert performance under Solti of *La Damnation de Faust* with Josephine Veasey, Nicolai Gedda and George London.

There was an all-Bartok programme at the Empire – which Harewood temporarily rescued from its lately acquired role as a Bingo hall – by the Budapest Opera and Ballet with a somewhat untidy *Bluebeard's Castle* followed by the ballets *The Wooden Prince* and *The Miraculous Mandarin* – made forgivable however by a loutish anti-Communist attack on the theatre which opened top floor taps and flooded the stage.

For me, as for many, the central opera programme that year was something of a sentimental reunion for the company was the San Carlo from Naples. After the hard-fought Salerno landings in the autumn of 1943, Naples fell to become the major forward port in Italy. After massive harbour clearance and salvage it filled up with Allied naval vessels and troops. The British took over the splendidly baroque Teatro San Carlo which, although bombed, succeeded in resuscitating its opera programme. Part of the building became the most glamorous officers' club any of us had encountered to date and the rest proceeded to educate the Allied forces in the delights of the *teatro lirico*.

We were stuck there for quite a long time because the port had to be cleared of more than 200 ships sunk and mined by the retreating Germans.

The Allied plan to cut the roads to Rome by landing at Anzio farther up the Tyrrhenian coast was frustrated by Kesselring's ferocious counter-attack for four months. So, in intervals between being shelled and bombed doing escort and other duties off the landing beaches at Nettuno and Anzio, uncivilisedly within range of the German long-range guns on the Alban Hills, we returned to Naples and went to the opera.

There was understandably no Wagner but I remember Bizet's *I Pescatori di Perle* Italianated, and the great duet sung by, to the best of my memory, the two *taglias* Ferrucio Tagliavini and Carlo Tagliabue as well as Carosio as Violetta and Gilda and the young Silveri as a bass. From the reopening of the theatre in 1944 to the end of the war it is reckoned that more than one and three-quarter million members of the Allied forces attended performances at the San Carlo – almost certainly a major factor in the post-war popularity of opera.

In Edinburgh the operas were Verdi's *Luisa Miller*, Cilea's *Adriana Lecouvreur* and Donizetti's *Don Pasquale*. Although strongly cast with Margherita Roberti as Luisa, Renato Cioni as Rodolfo and one of Italy's finest baritones, Piero Cappucilli as Miller, *Luisa Miller*, the last opera Verdi wrote for the San Carlo, was not well known and what one critic called 'the baffleboard complexities of the plot' (the original Schiller play was called *Kabale und Liebe* 'Intrigue and Love') and the texture of the music moving from Verdi's first rum-ti-tum period to something more orchestrally and harmonically demanding and from a large canvas to a domestic one foreshadowing *La Traviata*, puzzled audiences. Cioni's famous Act II aria *Quando le sere al placido* was enthusiastically applauded and everyone recognised in Cappucilli a great new baritone voice but there were complaints that the scenery (built of course for San Carlo and not the King's) seemed 'overpowering'.

Adriana Lecouvreur was much more the fustian of acceptable opera. Magda Olivero, who had been coached in the role by the composer a few years before his death in 1950, made the doomed actress appropriately diva-like and was as such acclaimed but the production was tricked out with an excess of pastoral interludes and ballet which tended to obscure what was disdainfully sidelined as 'Cilea's near-miss score' doing the melodious lyricism of the music considerably less than justice. Someone even said of it 'rather as if Puccini had written the last act of *Traviata*' elevating injustice into blasphemy.

The real hit of the San Carlo season was Gaetano Donizetti's *Don Pasquale*, the lively *opera buffa* directed by the veteran Neapolitan actor/dramatist, Eduardo de Fillipo with great élan and style and wonderfully sung and characterised by Fernando Corena as Pasquale and Renato Capecchi as Dr Malatesta and the Italian-American soprano Gianna d'Angelo and Spanish tenor Alfredo Kraus as the lovers. As the most recognisable of the three operas it had been a sell-out for weeks:

'Verged on ham – but very stylish ham,' was the kindly critical verdict.

In addition to the furore when 19-year old Portobello model Anna Kesselaar was wheeled naked across the organ gallery of the McEwan Hall, there were other troubles with the Drama Conference. The Berliner Ensemble were refused visas to attend by the British government; Bernard Levin was rude and savage; Kenneth Tynan was cutting about the Home Office and playwright Ronald Duncan offered to give the royalties for the two shows he had on at the Festival (the libretto for Britten's *The Rape of Lucretia* and the adaptation of *The Rabbit Race*) towards the building of an opera house. As these were calculated to amount to £100-£200 no-one took him up on his offer and no-one did anything about the opera house either. Next year's projected Poetry Conference was hastily cancelled to ensure that no more such libertarian excesses should again besmirch the fair name of the Scottish capital.

XIII

Berlioz reappeared at the 1964 Festival in more massive form. Charles Munch conducted the *Requiem* with the Orchestre National de Radio Television Francais in the opening concert. Later the same orchestra under Maazel gave us that curious blend of symphony, cantata and opera which Berlioz wrote with the princely gift of 20,000 francs given him by Nicolò Paganini shortly before the great violin virtuoso died in 1840, the mighty *Roméo et Juliette* with Joseph Rouleau and Anna Reynolds among the soloists. The Scottish National Orchestra under its inspiring new young conductor, Alexander Gibson, who had just founded Scottish Opera, completed the Berlioz monumental cycle with the *Te Deum*. For this one performance Arthur Oldham, composer, pupil of Benjamin Britten, choir master of St Mary's Roman Catholic Cathedral and augurer of the Festival future, got together a large choir from his own choristers, Scottish Opera and the Scottish Junior Singers for the occasion.

And just as everyone was thundering on about the overblown orchestral demands of the French composer, Colin Davis jogged memories about another aspect of Berlioz in the gentle, meditative and exquisite *Childhood of Christ* as did Marilyn Hortne in a ravishing performance of the song cycle written to Theophile Gautier's poems, *Les Nuits d'Eté*.

While enthusing about Czech music, a large feature of the 1964 programme, Lord Harewood – interviewed by *Scotsman* music critic, Conrad Wilson – released a few barbs in the direction of the citizens of Edinburgh:

> *One of the main problems*, he said, *is that an image of the Festival is difficult to create. Salzburg created its image before the war with Toscanini and Bruno Walter conducting Mozart. But it's not so easy to find the OK image for Edinburgh and I do think the*

citizens of Edinburgh make it more difficult because they say on all occasions – to visitors and to the press – that the Festival is of no interest to them.

They keep grumbling about it and say the Festival doesn't offer anything for the ordinary masses (though I'd like to know who packs out the hall for the Beethoven cello sonatas if not the ordinary masses). They say the whole thing is a hindrance to them and they can't get on the buses and the city is swamped by dreary tourists and so on. This feeling of resentment that boils up in so many people gives the city a not wholly festive image, you know.

Ronald Mavor also in *The Scotsman* agreed with him:

The Edinburgh citizen – I speak as a Glaswegian – has his virtues but why does the Festival bring out only his vices, his philistinism, his xenophobia?

The music and the artists from Czechoslovakia, however, pulled in the masses in quite sufficient numbers to create new record attendances at the Usher Hall and the biggest last-minute run on opera tickets in the 17-year history of the Festival. When planning for the 1964 Festival there was yet another financial crisis which the Council asked Harewood to resolve by sticking to a very tight budget. He warned that this could only be done for one year otherwise the parsimony would become painfully visible but he scored a great success by packing the programme with big-name recitalists who were cheaper than orchestral concerts. The veteran Rudolf Serkin played no fewer than seven Mozart piano concertos with the English Chamber Orchestra in three inexpensive concerts memorable for the Bohemian pianist's wonderful silvery touch and poised grasp of rhythm, style and shape.

It was also a great year for *aficionados* of vocal music with choral pieces and works for soloists and orchestra by Berlioz and Janacek; Henze's Festival commission *Ariosi* conducted by the composer and recitals of rarities such as Donizetti's *Summer Nights at Posillipo*, Schumann's *Gedichte der Maria Stuart* based on poems by Mary, Queen of Scots, Berlioz's *Chansons d'Irelande* and Mussorgsky's *Nursery Songs*.

The operas were outstanding. Prague National Theatre brought two Janacek operas *Katya Kabanova* and *From the House of the Dead,* Dvorak's *Rusalka,* Smetana's *Dalibor,* and at Lord Harewood's special request, a work by a contemporary Czech composer, Jan Cikker's *Resurrection,* based on a Tolstoy story. Not everyone was enthusiastic about the Cikker: 'opera moments in the last act: a snatch of the chorus, a few fragments of melody – which suggested an old-fashioned composer aching to escape from his Bergish trappings and to return to the songs of his youth', identifying a native talent too heavily influenced by Berg's *Wozzeck.* But Smetana's *Dalibor,* Dvorak's opera once dismissed by a member of the Covent Garden board as 'a bloody bore', was hailed with delight. 'Mainly pure gold,' said Conrad Wilson, 'richly and glowingly melodic, grandeur and fervour, a honey of a work.' Following roughly the same plot line as Beethoven's *Fidelio* to a different ending, it seemed strange that so fine and passionate an opera had been ignored for so long. Desmond Shawe-Taylor wrote:

After the big prison scene at the end of Act II, with the hero's rapt invocation to the spirit of his murdered friend and the exalted love scene with his disguised Fidelio-model rescuer, followed by the lovely orchestral peroration and 'after glow' (a model of operatic writing) hardened opera-goers were seen to dab their eyes.

There has been such a fervent recent interest in composers like Janacek, Dvorak and Smetana that it is difficult to recall that in 1964 Czech music was virtually unknown in Britain. *The New World Symphony* (then the Fifth but now the Ninth for some foggy musicological reason), *Songs My Mother Taught Me* and Joan Hammond's recording of *O Silver Moon* from *Rusalka* were about the extent of the British Dvorak repertoire, the overture to Smetana's *Bartered Bride* occasionally appeared as a filler in concert programmes and a few privileged audiences had recently heard Janacek's celebrated orchestral brass blare *Sinfonietta*.

So the 16 works by Janacek and the other Czech contributions came as something of a surprise. *Sinfonietta* and the *Glagolitic Mass* were given in the concert hall but it was in opera (and the constantly-complained-about Edinburgh non-opera house, the King's Theatre) that Janacek really made his impact.

The House of the Dead, set in a Siberian prison camp, bleak, stark and lacking in any warmth other than the prisoners' human compassion for one another, Dostoyevsky anticipating Solzhenitzyn, is virtually plotless but written in music of such spare dramatic and emotional texture, running the gamut of misery and oppression and somehow adding humanity and pity in a way that makes it a masterpiece. It was given in a flawless production that was stunningly truthful and sincere.

Of *Katya Kabanova* Edmund Tracey wrote in *The Observer*:

> *The Prague Opera production of Janacek's Katya Kabanova was one of the most perfectly integrated pieces of teamwork in my experience.*

Opinions were divided about *Rusalka* which was generally agreed to be sweetly melodic but a bit vapid in plot and staging, but everyone went for *Katya* in a big way. This tempestuous tale of temptation, love and guilt with assonances of Madame Bovary on the banks of the Volga, was played and sung with such pathos and passion that phrases like 'an intense and moving experience' and 'bowled us all over' were tossed around like scraps of paper in a high wind.

The music passed everyone's test and but the drama had no such acclaim. Joan Littlewood's production of Shakespeare's *Henry IV* at the Assembly Hall as a hacked-about adaptation to render it 'people's theatre' was on the whole enjoyed by the public but ruthlessly savaged by all the critics.

> *I have rarely seen*, wrote Bamber Gascoigne in *The Observer*, *Shakespeare slapped on to stage with so little love, rarely heard speeches raced through with so little sense. The greatest pity is the lack of humour. Falstaff's are the best scenes of comedy ever written.*
>
> *I have never heard them greeted with anything so near to silence.*

Another Shakespearean production *Love's Labour Lost* was damned as dull. Richard Buckle's spectacular exhibition on the Bard in the Waverley Market, despite a publicity stunt which draped 'Bacon' stickers all over the entrance posters, was considered muddled and bitty and the rest of the official theatre programme was branded uninspiring. Even the Delacroix exhibition at the Royal Scottish Academy, mounted as a kind of visual counterpoint to Berlioz, failed to arouse much enthusiasm

A student called Michael Palin got good notices for his part in *The Oxford Revue* at the Cranston Hall and the one undisputed drama hit was also on the Fringe.

The Observer's Edmund Tracey went to the Brecht-Weill *Happy End* at the Traverse – the Richter/Rostropovich recital was cancelled because Richter had flu – and noted:

> *... a beautifully committed account of the heroine, Hallelujah Lillian by Bettina Jonic who brings the house down with the ravaged innocence of her singing in Surabaya Johnny.*
>
> *No-one in Edinburgh should miss it.*

Happy End *is the greatest fun imaginable*, said *The Sunday Times's* Jack Lambert, *and put over with a dash and skill and spirit which easily vanquish the worst excesses of the Edinburgh climate.*

It was from the success of the music that the following year, 1965 the combination of Arthur Oldham and Alexander Gibson and Harewood's bold programming led to the formation of one of the Festival's most precious and prestigious assets, the Edinburgh Festival Chorus. Looking, as every Festival Director does for a dramatic and memorable way to launch his final festival, Harewood asked Alex Gibson and the

Scottish National Orchestra to present Mahler's Eighth Symphony *The Symphony of a Thousand* on the opening Sunday.

This, the most ambitious concert ever devised for the Edinburgh Festival, demanded a choir of around 400, eight soloists and an orchestra of 105 players. Arthur Oldham was given the formidable task of recruiting a chorus of at least 240 adult voices plus 120 boys and he scoured Scotland's amateur choral societies and held auditions all over the country. The result – the Edinburgh Festival Chorus which has appeared in every Festival since.

During the winter the members of the Festival Chorus rehearse weekly but separately in groups in Edinburgh, Glasgow and Aberdeen, visited by the chorus master from time to time and given togetherness at joint weekends when all assemble in Edinburgh to sing together. Travel from Aberdeen and Glasgow to Edinburgh is organised as is any other travel to sing in Paris, Salzburg, Berlin, Munich, Israel, Cologne or Rouen, but apart from these nominal expenses they are paid nothing. They use up their holidays from their daily jobs for rehearsals and tours; they provide their own strictly uniform concert clothes; they put up with long and tiring practice sessions and the fact that they only rehearse a couple of times for each concert with the conductor who is going to be responsible for them 'on the night'.

Yet somehow they retain their musical skills, their sense of humour and their sanity and are cajoled, bullied, bewitched and exhorted into giving some of the greatest performances of peaks from the most challenging musical mountain ranges in the international repertoire.

They sing with the world's leading orchestras and soloists in Russian, French, German, Italian, various kinds of Latin, Spanish and even sometimes English. The world's most eminent conductors are among their fervent admirers. They can sound like the wrath of God demolishing the roof of the Usher Hall, lyrical as linties, sombre as monks, vengeful as warriors, anguished as the cruelly bereaved and they have an amazing corporate whisper which flickers *pianissimo* through the hall like the brush of an angel's feather.

In the 32 years of its existence the Festival Chorus has given more than 120 concerts and worked with almost every great conductor in the world from Abbado, Barenboim and Bernstein through Giulini and Karajan to Rozhdestvensky, Solti and Temirkanov. Most often they have been conducted by the late Sir Alexander Gibson with Claudio Abbado and Carlo Maria Giulini as close contenders for second place. The chorus members have sung in every Festival since their formation, usually several times – only in the 1965 Festival did they give just one performance – three or four is more common and in 1986 they gave eight!

Almost every choral masterpiece is in their repertoire including such unlikely or bold choices as Kodaly's *Psalmus Hungaricus,* Stravinsky's *Oedipus Rex*, Verdi's *Oberto, Conte di Bonifacio* and Schoenberg's *Moses und Aaron.*

From the then virtually unexplored territory of the operas of Janacek in 1964 there was a return to a more mainstream programme the next year. The Holland Festival, whose director Peter Diamand was to succeed Harewood in Edinburgh, sent co-productions of Mozart's *Don Giovanni* and Haydn's *Le Pescatrici* and the Bavarian State Opera from Munich gave the first stage performance in Britain of Richard Strauss's *Intermezzo* and managed also to squeeze Mozart's *Così Fan Tutte* onto the stage of the King's Theatre. The new chorus was received with acclaim and even wonder.

Ten years ago, wrote Conrad Wilson in *The Scotsman, it would have been inconceivable, an Edinburgh Festival opening with the Mahler Eighth performed by a Scottish orchestra and chorus. The Scottish National Orchestra and Alexander Gibson's achievement were joined by the 380 voices of the new and splendid Festival Chorus in a performance that will surely be remembered as a milestone in the history of the Edinburgh Festival and of music in Scotland.*

It was the centenary of Jean Sibelius and Scandinavian music was well to the fore. In the Usher Hall Sir John Barbirolli with the New Philharmonia gave a crisp and exciting rendering of Carl Nielson's Fifth Symphony complete with thunderously aleatory drumming. The Scottish National Orchestra with Gibson, who developed a particular rapport with the Finnish composer, gave a stunning all-Sibelius programme combining the terse epigrammatic Fourth Symphony, perhaps the most individualistic of all major Sibelius works, with a lithe and lyrical account of the violin concerto by Henryk Szeryng and the heroic, romantic Fifth Symphony.

The Hamburg Radio Symphony Orchestra brought its warm and excitingly uninhibited string tone and the silky skills of its conductor Hans Schmidt-Isserstedt playing Haydn, Brahms, Tippett and Beethoven. It also brought Pierre Boulez back to Edinburgh. Since he had first been at the Festival with Jean-Louis Barrault's company from the Théâtre Marigny in 1948 he had developed as a conductor of orchestras of international stature and made a considerable reputation as an *avant-garde* composer. Interviewed on television about his compositions, he said memorably of his years at the Paris Conservatoire at the end of the Second World War: 'At that time there was nothing. That was our great chance'.

With the Hamburg Orchestra he showed his mettle as a conductor in classic pieces like Beethoven's Second Symphony and Debussy's *La Mer* and baffled nearly everyone with the British première of his own *Pli selon Pli* (Fold upon Fold), a complex work for soprano and orchestra. designed as a five part portrait of the symbolist poet, Stephane Mallarmé, one of whose poems had inspired Debussy's prelude *L'Après-midi d'un faune*.

One critic said: 'I find I want to hear more and more of his music but not necessarily the same work twice' and described 'batonless Boulez gesturing like a Boy Scout with an efficiency badge for semaphore' with the work later dismissed for its rhythmic stagnancy.

On his first point Boulez almost certainly agrees with him because he is constantly altering, developing and recomposing his major works, so you rarely have the chance to hear the same piece twice.

Peter Heyworth made a cooler assessment:

> *I think the critics who in their anxiety to explain their reactions talk about Boulez in terms of his predecessors, who invoke a succession of Debussy, Webern, Messiaen and thus Boulez, rather as one might say Beethoven, Wagner, Brahms and thus Schoenberg are missing the most important (and obvious) thing about him: that where Schoenberg came before the deluge, Boulez comes after it. Whereas Schoenberg was trying to withstand that deluge, Boulez accepts it as his starting point.*

Unfortunately the Holland Festival contribution was beset by problems. Haydn's gentle lyrical romance based on a libretto by Goldoni about the fisher-girl who is really a princess and the prince who comes in search of her was dismissed as 'charming' and 'provincial like Haydn' despite a fine performance from Yugoslav mezzo Roza Pospis as the heroine.

The praise given to the tenderly swaying melodies by some local critics alarmed the *Observer's* music man, Edmund Tracey. After comparing Haydn unfavourably to Mozart and Rossini and admitting that:

> *... he writes melodies of great beauty and the orchestral accompaniments although over-inclined to a sort of stately chugging, have many points of interest.*
>
> *But I cannot for the life of me see that this piece has the stamina to take a regular and profitable place in the repertoire of either of our metropolitan opera houses and I read with alarm that there are about two dozen of his operas waiting for our attention.*

Oddly enough no-one challenged this outburst of metropolitan arrogance.

The fuss about *Don Giovanni* had a quite different origin. When Giulini saw the opera at the Holland Festival, he disliked the production and staging intensely and flatly refused to conduct the opera in Edinburgh unless both were changed. The director Virginio Puecher and the designer Luciano Damiani would not agree to alterations and eventually left in high dudgeon. Giulini himself took over the production and with the help of a lighting expert and new costumes from Covent Garden the opera was staged at the Festival.

Opera is for both ears and eyes, said Giulini, *but today's generation of opera producers do too much for the eyes. Though they are brought up on cinema and television, they must not forget what is due to the music.*

But the critics did not subscribe to such a purist view. *Don Giovanni* on a virtually bare stage made little appeal. 'Visual boredom' was one verdict and although the handling of the orchestra was generally praised, the singers, particularly Renato Capecchi as 'a scampering graceless Don' were heavily criticised.

The only person everyone liked was Paolo Montarsolo as Leporello. Even Giulini, one of the icons of European music, was not spared.

'He made it clear,' said *The Observer,* 'by the passion with which he conducted the overture, Mi tradi and the final confrontation between Don Giovanni and the statue and the superficiality with which he conducted everything else that he wished the opera had been written by Verdi.'

So for the Director of the Holland Festival, Peter Diamand, shortly to appear on the Edinburgh scene, it was not the happiest of auguries.

The Traverse, the entrepreneurial Edinburgh theatre group founded in 1963 by American Jim Haynes, darling of the Fringe, became part of the official Festival in 1965 by being transferred from their tight little space in the Grassmarket to the wide-open pastures of the Assembly Hall. Haynes had come to Edinburgh in 1956 with the American Air Force, had fallen in love with the city and stayed. At first he started a bookshop and later moved into club theatre, attracting 3,000 members and surrounding himself with the most innovative of Edinburgh's culture vultures who shared his conviction that the city should do something local and positive to reinforce its role as a place worthy of an international festival. By 1964 the Traverse had become the centre of the city's artistic life and was widely regarded as the best *avant-garde* theatre outside London. Harewood and Haynes thought highly of each other and the accolade (if such it was) of being part of the 'official' programme was inevitable.

Almost as inevitably it was a disaster. If there is anything that Edinburgh can do to dull the edge of enterprise it will do it by committee.

The Traverse made several suggestions, one of them *The Assembly* a 300-year old satirical play about the General Assembly of the Church of Scotland (in whose meeting-place on the Mound the company were to play) by an 18th-century founder of the Edinburgh medical school, Archibald Pitcairne, sometime Professor of Physic at Leyden – 'notorious as a Jacobite, an Episcopalian, a satirist of Presbyterian men and things and, according to his opponents, an atheist and scoffer at religion'. The idea of presenting such a work in the home of the Kirk sent the committee into a maidenly flutter. So they insisted the Traverse play a drama about regicide, bloodshed, tyranny and ruthless ambition. In defiance both of their fiercely established anti-classical tradition and their technical small-space expertise the Traverse conformed for one of the few times in its corporate life and presented the committee's choice, *Macbeth.* There were protests about the naked witches and the fact that Lady Macbeth had a Welsh accent and no-one was very happy about the result.

Duncan Macrae, gaunt muse of the Scottish theatre, who played the Porter was scathing:

The Edinburgh Festival is just a flash in the pan, he said. *What does Edinburgh do the other 49 weeks of the year to encourage theatre? Nothing. If it did the Empire wouldn't have become a bingo hall. The trouble with the Festival is that it's almost entirely second-hand goods and none of our own. Unless you've got something yours, it's no use having imported goods The bringing-in of Scottish actors to do a show is nonsensical. The Festival should be a Scottish event – a Scottish Festival which reaches its peak at tourist time. The artists should be regarded as the hosts and not Edinburgh Corporation who know nothing about the arts anyway.*

Macbeth was a tribute to the impact the Traverse had made on matters theatrical in Scotland but although it had its moments, the experiment was not a success. Better theatrical fare came at the Lyceum where an American company made gospel song into a new dramatic dimension with James Baldwin's *The Amen Corner*, set in the moral complexities of the Holy Rollers in Harlem.

As Sister Margaret floating on an emotional tide of gospel songs, Claudia McNeil gave one of the great festival performances, carrying with tears and anger the message of gospel loving and family ties in the claustrophobic black religious community.

In a spiky Festival preview in the *Evening News*, Alexander Reid had his doubts:

But what oddly enough, remains to be proved is that this new work is a play at all: for brilliant writer though Baldwin is, there is little evidence in his published writings that he has the dramatist's ability to lose himself in his creations.

Harold Hobson, the distinguished critic of the *Sunday Times* had no such reservations. After recording the objections of an American visitor who demanded his money back from the Festival authorities with the words 'You never told me there were niggers in this play', he wrote:

For the rest of us it brought about an unconditional surrender to its pathos, its charm, to the thrilling excitement of its spirituals and to the overwhelming performance of its principal actress, Claudia McNeil. Miss McNeil is the lightning and the tempest, the avalanche and the voice of God thrown in for good measure. Justly her reception by the audience was thunderous. I thought the cheering would never stop. I thought that I myself would never stop cheering.

At *Macbeth* Mr Hobson found himself next to a child, very audibly horrified by the copious bloodshed. Seeking another seat he found himself in the street outside the Assembly Hall. He did not bother to return.

He did, however, slaver over Marlene Dietrich appearing for the second year running in late-night cabaret at the Lyceum and had no problem being enthusiastic about the final week's occupants of the Lyceum, the Teatro Stabile di Genova and their version of Goldoni's *I Due Gemelli Veneziani*.

It was a memorable evening, he wrote, *and the whole house rose at the company in uncontrollable enthusiasm and delight. I Due Gemelli Veneziani and The Amen Corner have brought Festival drama back to a level it has not attained since Henry Sherek produced* The Cocktail Party *and* The Confidential Clerk *and Edwige Feuillère played Marguerite Gautier.*

In the meantime, the art critic of *The Observer* Nigel Gosling was having a more tranquil Festival:

Quietness, he wrote, *is the thread which unites the main shows at Edinburgh this year. The artist appears as a gentle creature,*

I Due Gemelli Veneziani *(1965)*

79

withdrawn from mundane hurly-burly, soothing and patient, a putter of slippers before the fire of life.

He found Corot at the Royal Scottish Academy 'plumb in the middle of the bourgeois belt' with 'too many undistinguished sketches and a number of large and very dubious studio-manufactured canvases' and the Swiss-French painter's recessive attitude reflected in shows of Giorgio Moramdi and Julius Bissier at the Scottish National Gallery of Modern Art 'perfect illustrations of small but real talent coming to a fragile flowering'.

The marriage of private contemplation to public celebration is superbly consummated in the Rumanian Art Treasures in the Royal Scottish Museum – moving icons, sumptuous silver, noble carving. The ritual of Byzantine art has turned quietness into emotion and splendour.

In consummation outside the galleries, however, things were getting much more authentically Byzantine.

Although Lord Harewood was on record in stating that he did not believe that a Festival Director's term of office should be longer than six to eight years, it was not a premature invocation of this principle which had led to the announcement of his resignation after just four and a half years in December 1964. He left because of a domestic crisis in his private life. In the year he first joined the Edinburgh Festival his first marriage was disintegrating and in 1964 the lady who was to become his second wife had given birth to a son and a divorce was on the horizon. Someone on the Festival Council found out about this and felt it his duty to tell Sir Duncan Weatherstone who as Lord Provost of Edinburgh was *ex officio* chairman of the Festival Council.

There had been no elaborate efforts made at concealment on Harewood's part but obviously, in the circumstances, there had been no public announcement. When Harewood went to see the Lord Provost he was told that Weatherstone felt that this could have a very serious effect on the Festival so he offered to resign. Just what Lord Harewood's private life had to do with his considerable abilities as Artistic Director of the Edinburgh Festival is not clear. What is certain is that the December announcement was totally botched.

On December 15 Lord Provost Sir Duncan Weatherstone said that 'nothing was being done at the moment about appointing a successor'.

'A major factor to be considered before contemplating another appointment,' he added, 'was to consider the report of Urwick, Orr & Partners who were investigating the Festival administration and who would be presenting a preliminary report to the Council in January.'

Having thus managed to imply that there was something suspect lurking in the woodshed of Festival administration, he then had to spend the next few months saying what a wonderful Artistic Director Harewood had been, how it was pure coincidence that he had resigned when he did, that there was no dispute between the Festival Society and Lord Harewood, that Harewood had not held out for either a higher salary or more programme money and then added to the fog of unreason by announcing on 26 January 1965 that the ponderous labours of Urwick, Orr & Partners had come up with a momentous decision. The overlord of the Edinburgh Festival was no longer to be called Artistic Director but Festival Director.

After that it only took a few months to announce that Lord Harewood would be succeeded as Festival Director by Peter Diamand at the end of the 1965 Festival. However there were other aspects of Edinburgh's annual cultural jamboree which were coming under fire. In 1963 Jack Lambert had written in *The Sunday Times*:

Whether or not Lord Harewood continues to find a place for the theatre in future festivals, for the good name of this one he would have been better advised not to rally as he has done to the defence of the indefensible which can only undermine faith in his judgement. Far better if he were to suspend further performances of a wretched travesty (Henry IV) *whose principal faults are not susceptible to the rapid improvement he claims for the production; it is a blot on the programme and a slap-happy disgrace to the British theatre.*

Then there was television. A lady from Craigmillar Park complained about television lights being left on at two successive concerts in the Usher Hall – the Allegri Quartet and a recital by Svyatoslav Richter and Mstislav Rostropovich which had been postponed because of the pianist's illness and was slotted in after the Allegri concert:

> *Throughout this entire marathon of music-making which began at 8 pm and did not finish till after 1 am, batteries of dazzling television lights were left switched on. What should have been a memorable evening was ruined by the intense discomfort which resulted from the blaze of the lights – some of the audience were even reduced to wearing sunglasses!*

> *The Festival Society should get its priorities right. Festival concerts are presented primarily for the audiences who attend and pay Festival prices for their seats. To subject an audience to intolerable discomfort throughout the whole of two successive concerts for the sake of earning a television fee smacks of commercial sharp practice.*

A nostalgic moment from the distant time before TV was king of the schedules with everything arranged for its imperious slot-time. Little did she know how lucky she was to avoid a penalty shoot-out or a four-hole play-off.

Bavarian Opera's *Intermezzo* which had that year its first performance in Great Britain, is an autobiographical comedy of bourgeois life depicting a few tempestuous hours in the life of himself and his notoriously shrewish wife by Richard Strauss. The ravishing Hanny Steffeck played Madame Storch and Hermann Prey was the henpecked husband in this light, mannered and from time to time enchantingly lyrical piece which was most delicately imagined and presented by director Rudolf Hartmann.

Indeed, the only cavil was that it was perhaps too delicate and charming and that Pauline Strauss who attended the first rehearsals in Dresden in 1924 and used constantly to leap to her feet and shout at the first Madame Storch, Lotte Lehmann: 'No, no! I'm much more disagreeable than that!' had been needed in at the Munich rehearsals to inject a little acid into the performances. Steffek also sang Despina in a fine Bavarian production of *Così fan Tutte* which restored Mozart opera to a more traditional presentation style and contained a glorious Ferrando from the German tenor, Fritz Wunderlich.

Many years later when I talked with Lord Harewood about his years at the Festival at Harewood House, he was very interesting about the motivation and cultural direction of Edinburgh:

> *At the start in 1947 I asked Rudi Bing how he saw it and he said it was a framework for performance and performers and I said that wasn't enough. And he said that was how it was. When they asked me I decided it was too large to make much sense without some element of theme. It needed some kind of string to which to attach the various events – although they would not all be thematic, obviously. I thought Edinburgh had to regain its clout – its standing with critics.*

We discussed the thematic idea and in particular his boldness in making Schoenberg the featured composer in his first Festival in 1961. How did the committee receive it?

> *I don't remember anyone objecting at all,* he said, with a smile. *And when you look at it now! I am going to run the Adelaide Festival and if when asked what we should do and I say 'well, I think we should have rather a lot of Schoenberg', I think they might think that rather peculiar.*

> *So it almost makes me think that I never mentioned it to anyone – but I must, mustn't I? I think I must have explained that it wouldn't dominate the Festival. It would only be dominant for someone who wanted to be dominated. And of course that was true – and people do recognise the truth.*

All the time I was there I only remember two positive suggestions – one was notable and one was un-notable – being rejected by programme committees and therefore the Council. One was that in my last year in 1965 I should have an associated theme with Boulez and Tippett. And improvisation was to be a part of it and I had the idea of having Indian musicians who by definition do improvise on a classical framework as part of their performance technique ands some jazz musicians who also improvise – although on a very strict framework very often. In Mozart piano concertos I would have someone like John Ogdon to improvise the cadenzas. They just didn't like it and what scuppered it was the argument that when people did that in Mozart's day they all thought in the same way as Mozart – even the audiences – but people don't think like that musically any more and they wouldn't like it.

And then, he added rather sadly, *I realised that the performers would probably not really improvise – they would write the whole thing before. That was the large one and I was sorry to lose that.*

As almost the only festival director from anywhere I have met who had a good word to say for the committee system, I pressed him about its devious workings. He was very positive about it – in a way:

They did have some value because it meant that the Programme committee or the Council didn't have to waste a lot of time chewing over digested ground. I had a wonderful standard of programme committee.

Lord Cameron, he was wonderful, very supportive and helpful and understanding – and a tremendous advocate with the Council, for what he said was very persuasive. We had a very strong Arts committee in these days and it was very difficult to put anything over on that. The Drama committee depended on one or two people. So did Music and as long as you were convincing and had a proper line of thinking that was it.

I suggested that perhaps he just made the programmes and got the committees to agree to them.

I did. And I think that must be so. I think the art of working with committees is to sort of tee up the chance for a suggestion and hope that somebody makes it. Then they feel they're doing some positive work. And if you feel that things are going too much your way, you may even put up a preposterous idea for someone to contradict so that they can feel they have contradicted you.

He laughed and added: *As a totally privileged and rather amateur person, I take a very serious view of things like festivals. But keeping the amateur always in it somewhere, I try to ensure that a lot of it's fun. And I thought that the fun should be made more serious. That was why I was not in favour of Rudi Bing's platform for performers kind of thing. In that sense he ran an emporium, a big store in Edinburgh and I wanted it to have something more to say.*

I always thought that a Festival Director shouldn't stay longer than six to eight years because it's a kind of fireworks display. You could go on inventing fireworks without becoming predictable but if you run a symphony orchestra, a theatre, an opera company catering to a similar public each year, you have another kind of job.

Continuity is everything. For the Edinburgh Festival, Edinburgh is the continuity. Disparity, diversion, difference is the important thing each time.

So I think I may have been there in a lucky period. Certainly before inflation. We never seemed to have any serious shortage of money. You never have enough money of course. But if I had stayed on a few years perhaps I would have found the promises about the opera house less likely of fulfilment and there might have been a shortage of money, I don't know.

PETER DIAMAND 1966-78
Diamand Years I: Against the Odds – Fiscal and Philistine

XIV

Outwardly Peter Diamand was a very different kind of Festival Director from Lord Harewood. Born in Berlin in 1913 he was much the oldest of any of Edinburgh's artistic *maestri* and although small, bespectacled, quiet-voiced and physically unimposing, he managed nevertheless to be somewhat intimidating on first acquaintance. As Goldsmith said of the schoolmaster in his *Deserted Village*:
> *And still they gaz'd, and still the wonder grew*
> *That one small head could carry all he knew*

Before World War II he had been secretary to the great pianist, Artur Schnabel who appeared in some of the earliest Festivals. He had fled to Holland in 1933 to escape Nazi persecution but it caught up with him when the Germans invaded the Netherlands in 1940 and he was sent to a concentration camp but later released because Nazi bureaucracy slipped up and he was not on the invaders 'wanted' list. On release he went underground and spent years in hiding. When peace was restored he changed his original Austrian nationality to become a Dutch citizen. In 1946 he was assistant to the director of Netherlands Opera later managing the Concertgebouw Orchestra and being secretary and artistic director to the Holland Festival. So at the age of 53 he had unrivalled experience as a festival administrator and programme planner – at one of his first press conference he said, 'I am very used to unsatisfactory conditions for presenting opera and ballet from my days with the Holland Festival'. However beneath the token modesty and the quiet exterior manner was a will of steel, a powerful intellect allied to a positive compassion and a brilliant wit all of which were to serve him well throughout his 13 years in Edinburgh.

Peter Diamand

In 1966 he opened his Edinburgh festival career with one of the most stimulating programmes the Scottish capital had seen.

With his pedigree we might have expected this of the musical content – and indeed there was much at which to wonder and applaud in this – but it was in drama that the biggest impact was made.

It was the year of the Greeks – in Scots, English and the more-or-less original tongue. At the Lyceum was Aristophanes's comedy *The Burdies*, transmogrified into Scots by Douglas Young, a noted Scots poet and Professor of Classical Studies at St Andrews University. This play had already appeared on the Fringe, much applauded in its amateur university versions but for some reason it aroused the self-conscious nationalistic ire of Scots critics.

> *A sense of pride,* wrote *The Scotsman's* Allen Wright, *that Edinburgh could reach such heights of stage design* [the designer was Abd' Elkder Farrah] *tempered by the shame of watching the Scots again present themselves to the world as quaint uncouth clowns with a pawky sense of humour. The production had the regal appearance of roast capercailzie but it tasted like mince and tatties.*

Although in a lively newspaper correspondence Douglas Young pointed out that pawkiness was not unknown in the Athens of the South and that Aristophanes's text was full of satirical humour and racial caricature, the Scots scribes, their patriotic feathers ruffled, would not be appeased and the English critics adopted their usual attitude to the Scots tongue of patronising incomprehension. To Shakespeare's quasi-Greek drama with its Delphic intervention, *The Winter's Tale*, they were more generous, finding Frank Dunlop's Pop Theatre production: 'a noble unity of a disjointed play presented in compartments of black and gold – the dark malevolence of Leontes giving way to the gaiety and warmth of the pastoral scenes'; and praising Laurence Harvey's Leontes, Jane Asher's enchanting Perdita (off-stage coyly denying her engagement to Beatles star Paul McCartney) and Jim Dale's nimble clowning.

Euripides's great anti-war play, *The Trojan Women* in an English translation by Ronald Duncan from the Sartre adaptation was Frank Dunlop's second production in the Assembly Hall. Given a heavy resonance of the Vietnam war, with the Trojans as Vietnamese and the invading Greeks as Americans, it was not to everyone's taste but the adjectives were trotted out for Flora Robson's Hecuba and singer Cleo Laine's fierce Andromache.

The trumpets sounded unmuted however for the Athenians from Piraeus. Scots may have been incomprehensible but demotic Greek from the 5th-century BC proved rivetingly dramatic. The Piraikon Theatre's productions of Sophocles's *Electra* and Euripides's *Medea* brilliantly directed by the theatre's founder, Dimitrios Rondiris, (a pupil of Max Reinhardt who had made his first stage appearance as Florizel in *The Winter's Tale*) were sound and fury made theatre.

Though the company was said to be bereft of its leading actress, Aspassia Papathanassio, rated in the first rank of tragediennes in the world, her replacement Elsa Vergi who played both principal roles (on the final Piraikon Saturday within a few hours of each other!) was a one-woman dramatic tornado 'monumental, declaiming with a passion that would fill a vast amphitheatre'.

> *Other productions here*, wrote one critic, *have flicked the skin. This will change the shape of your bones.*

So it was all the more strange that John Russell, *The Sunday Times's* art critic who had arranged the exhibition of the Fauve-rebel, religious expressionist Georges Rouault at the Royal Scottish Academy should write:

> *Edinburgh is and has always been a hierarchical festival. Music sits at the captain's table, drama camps out in the tourist lounge, art bobs behind in the bum-boat.*

But as Peter Diamand once told me: 'There is no way you can persuade people to enjoy events they have decided they do not wish to see.'

De gustibus as the cynical old Romans used to say.

However there were few disputes about the new musical talent which Diamand introduced to the Festival in his first year. He established in perpetuity what one newspaper had called 'a chorus too large to live' by giving the Festival Chorus a greater role with three concerts. There was a repeat of the Mahler Eighth and a second concert with Gibson and the Scottish National Orchestra in Britten's *Cantata Academica* and Tippett's *A Child of Our Time*. Moving out of the British standard repertoire they also sang with Gennadi Rozhdestvensky in the British première of Prokoviev's demonic *Seven, They are Seven* – a fierce cantata on the demons who grind rather than guide the destiny of mankind – with the Moscow Radio Orchestra. The Chorus had learned the words phonetically and Arthur Oldham had sent a tape to Moscow for Rozhdestvensky's approval, thus introducing him to a work which he had never heard before! Launched by Koussevitsky in Paris on 1924 it had never been performed in Russia.

The Mahler was acclaimed as 'even better than last year' and the Festival Chorus as having 'a tone quality as vivid as their colourful dresses'. Alas no more, as they now sing in stygian black. The Prokoviev première was also a hit, 'armour-plated ostinati and swooshing vocal glissandi put over with terrific attack' and the high voltage tenor solo marvellously projected by the hero of the Prague Opera, Vilem Pribyl. Rozhdestvensky told the Lord Provost and the audience at a civic lunch that the outstanding moment in his orchestra's visit was the 'most fruitful association with the Festival Chorus'. Fortunately the first of many such collaborations.

The Stuttgart Opera at the King's brought yet another *Magic Flute* in a rather staid production enlivened by the radiant-voiced Pamina of Gundula Janowitz. Another Festival debutante was the conductor of Berg's *Wozzeck* Carlos Kleiber, talented son of a famous father who drew sounds of wondrous intensity from the Stuttgart Orchestra and established himself as one to watch. Tragically in the second *Magic Flute* we were unknowingly saying farewell to the superb lyric tenor Fritz Wunderlich who was to die in an accident just a few weeks later.

The Castle Esplanade saw another farewell when retiring Brigadier Alistair Maclean took the salute at Edinburgh's greatest spectacle, the Military Tattoo he had created in 1950 and master-minded for the past 17 years.

In compensation for the losses several new talents on view were to enliven future festivals. Not only Kleiber, the Russian orchestra and the delightful Gundula Janowitz but two artists who were to have an important influence on the Festival for many years to come.

In 1965 Israeli pianist Daniel Barenboim had substituted for the indisposed Claudio Arrau in an Usher Hall recital and in 1966 appeared in his own right. In two concerts with the New Philharmonia we had our first taste of the dynamic brilliance of a new young Italian conductor, Claudio Abbado, in a marvellously strong and vital account of Berg's Three Pieces for Orchestra and a thrilling performance of Schubert's Third Symphony. In the second New Philharmonia concert Barenboim and Abbado came together in the Beethoven C major piano concerto.

Even the hyper-critical London Sundays acknowledged that the Festival had unearthed an important new talent. After two columns of complaining about what a dull composer Schumann was and how different it might have been had he been born either French or Polish, Desmond Shawe-Taylor in *The Sunday Times* went on:

Claudio Abbado

A sudden and brilliant ray of sunshine has fallen across the gory Edinburgh scene with the arrival of the young Italian conductor, Claudio Abbado to conduct the New Philharmonia. On Friday evening his direction of a Beethoven and Schumann programme was marked by purity and vitality of melodic line, unusual clarity of texture and a logical sense of proportion and structure. The orchestra responded to his lead with a glowing account of Schumann's Genoveva and accompanied Daniel Barenboim in a youthfully exuberant reading of Beethoven's C major piano concerto.

The Stuttgart Opera's second performance of *Wozzeck* had to be cancelled because of Carlos Kleiber's illness but the second Berg opera *Lulu*, in Wieland Wagner's production of the incomplete version, matched flesh and grim fantasy to create a sensation and project another young star, 26- year-old German soprano Anja Silja in the name part displaying the most beautiful legs in opera as well as handling the complex coloratura of her role with wonderful panache.

Peter Diamand devised a new and agreeable way to end his first Edinburgh Festival. The closing concert was given by the Hallé Orchestra with Sir John Barbirolli, its centrepiece the symphony dedicated to Sir John of which he had given the first performance in 1956 with the same orchestra, Vaughan Williams Eighth with its wonderful wind-only scherzo and enterprising instrumentation. It was a splendid proof of why Vaughan Williams had called him 'Glorious John' full of lyricism and humanity through the open weave of the music. There was also Elgar's *Sea Pictures* in which Janet Baker managed to inject some magic into the setting of five rather indifferent poems by five different poets. But when the applause had died away there was more work for the Hallé and Sir John and Janet Baker in the new Festival Director's finale.

The culmination was Haydn's Symphony no 45 in F sharp minor *The Farewell* played by candlelight, in which the players, one by one as their parts end, extinguish their candles and leave the platform.

It was a highly effective and smilingly elegiac end to the 1966 Festival, preceded by a delightful cultural cabaret in which Barenboim played Les Adieux, Janet Baker sang a Mozart aria from *La Clemenza di Tito*, Bettina Jonic Brecht songs and a svelte, black-gowned Anja Silja Elizabeth's Greeting *Dich, teure Halle* from *Tannhauser*.

The biggest Fringe to date provided 33 companies and 70 productions featuring more than 1,000 players among which was a major American invasion from the University of Southern California Performing Arts Department under the formidable Professor John Edward Blankenchip with 13 productions ranging from mime, jazz and rhythm-speaking to full-blooded productions of plays by Edward Albee, Thorton Wilder and Tennessee Williams. There was also a breakaway Oxford Group, *Four Degrees Over* bankrolled by the not inconsiderable wallets of Richard Burton and Elizabeth Taylor (currently filming *The Taming of the Shrew* in Mantua with Zeffirelli). It predated evangelical modernism in such immortally daring lines as 'God is fab, God is here: God's as good as fags and beer'.

Rosencrantz and Guildenstern are Dead provided the Fringe with one of its early commercially successful transfers to London when it was taken up by the National Theatre shortly after the Festival and subsequently moved to Broadway. David Frost, star of the satirical TV series *That Was The Week That Was* had his own late night show at the Palladium, *Frost Report*. In a talk to the Fringe Club John Calder made an impassioned plea for the creation of two Fringes, professional and amateur, claiming that the Fringe had taken over drama from the official Festival.

At the final press conference of his first Festival Peter Diamand said the development of the Lyceum/ Synod hall site into a new theatre large enough and sufficiently well-equipped to handle major opera productions was 'an indispensable must'.

A special committee of the Lord Provost's Committee asked the Lyceum project's architect, W. H. Kinnimonth to scale down his estimate of £3 million. Diamand deplored the lack of festive flags and decorations in Princes Street over the Festival period. Lord Provost Brechin said 'Princes Street doesn't need decorations'. Plans for the 21st Festival in 1967 were announced.

The seeds of dissent between Diamand's endeavour to broaden the variety of Festival programmes while increasing the quality of performances and what seemed to many people Lord Provost Brechin's cultivated philistinism came to a head before the 21st Festival.

Edinburgh's coming-of-age as a festival city should clearly have been a matter for celebration but being *ex officio* the chairman of one of the greatest festivals in the world clearly meant little to Brechin. It was announced that the Corporation's grant to the Festival was to be cut by 33% for the next three years.

In an interview given in August 1967 Peter Diamand said in his quiet voice:

You know, there is nothing to stop Edinburgh scrapping the Festival if that is what people really want. The decision to hold it was freely taken by Edinburgh and the same decision to end it could be made tomorrow. My view is this. Either the people support the Festival and provide for it in the proper way – or do away with it altogether. But it must never be done by halves.

Perhaps it is a particular streak of Puritanism in the character which is prone to consider that festivals of this type are wasteful, frivolous and somehow sinful.

He pointed out that other comparable festivals – Salzburg, Berlin and Vienna along with Edinburgh making up the big four – get financial assistance vastly in excess of Edinburgh.

Salzburg which currently received £400,000 from state and local authority sources had said it could not go on next year unless another £70,000 could be found to back it.

The Edinburgh Festival gets £50,000 from the Arts Council £27,000 from donations and £75,000 from the Corporation. Companies from overseas put up more money to visit the Festival than Edinburgh Corporation provides. People do not realise the extent to which the Festival is subsidised from abroad. And in addition to cutting the grant they propose to raise the rent for the King's Theatre to £16,000 – almost one third of the total Corporation grant!

Despite all this barely veiled acrimony the 21st Festival offered seven orchestras, eight theatre companies, three opera companies and the New York Theatre Ballet, the usual number of chamber concerts and recitals and the largest-ever Fringe – in what was to be an annual spread for many years to come – of more than 50 companies.

The ballet was a particularly welcome addition because there had been none in the final Harewood Festival, partly owing to complications with the Empire Bingo venue, partly difficulty in finding a dance company of sufficient quality. In 1966 there had been a small troupe of nine dancers led by Paul Taylor, an associate of Martha Graham and Merce Cunningham, performing in what critic Dicky Buckle called a 'newly perverted' theatre (formerly Morningside Free Church) converted in 1965 to the 379-seat Church Hill Theatre. The Empire was temporarily reclaimed for dance for the New York Theatre Ballet performances.

Lord Provost Brechin was concerned about the Festival Club and the 'necking' and 'excessive drinking' which he had been shocked to observe there, so new and stricter regulations for entry were introduced to curb such excesses as the Festival came of age.

The Festival's supporters' club, the Festival Guild abandoned plans for a Festival History to mark the occasion. Lord Provost Brechin banned the showing of the James Joyce films *Ulysses* and *Finnegan's Wake* at the Film Festival. Diverse views of Edinburgh's role as a festival city simmered away like a fermenting Scotch broth.

John L. Paterson, Edinburgh architect and designer of *Two Hundred Summers in a City* the 200th anniversary New Town exhibition in the Waverley Market in 1967, called for piazzas beside the Royal Scottish Academy and in front of the Usher Hall where Festival artists and visitors could commingle and drink a festive glass or two, the creation of a Festival flag, decorations on Princes Street and for Edinburgh to mount on the Calton Hill the first-ever *son et lumière* telling the story of a city rather than an individual building.

He also suggested that the Festival should seek to provide an amenity which the Scottish capital singularly lacks to this day – a restaurant where customers can enjoy the views over one of the world's most spectacular cities. It should, he said, be a temporary structure on the Calton Hill for the three weeks of the Festival. Like the rest of his suggestions this vision of pie in the sky was never fulfilled although after

I joined the Festival staff in 1973 we did manage to have a flag designed which flew in Princes Street and at Festival venues.

Lord Provost Brechin, ever the harbinger of doom, warned that Edinburgh might have no theatres in which to present the Festival in future years if Howard & Wyndham's application for planning permission to redevelop the King's Theatre was granted and such alterations were to coincide with the plan to demolish the Lyceum and proceed with the creation of a new theatre on the Castle Terrace site. We did not then know of course that this was one Edinburgh Festival show that was to run and run.

Ironically but perhaps not unexpectedly, it was the Festival which was first to suffer from the never-to-be-realised plans to build an opera house on or adjacent to the Lyceum site. In 1968 the Corporation forced the Festival to move from its office in Cambridge Street at a greatly increased rent (from £800 to £4,000) to Market Street, former offices of *Edinburgh Evening News* recently taken over by *The Scotsman* which had moved to the daily paper's building along the road. The Cambridge Street offices were not demolished till 1990.

All this sniping at the Festival did not pass unnoticed. Critics rallied to Peter Diamand's support. At the opening of the 1967 Festival Desmond Shawe-Taylor wrote in *The Sunday Times*:

> *This is the 21st Festival. A glance through the main features of its predecessors makes a stunning impression of riches and variety and concentrated talent. The City Fathers have also noticed the occasion and celebrated with a neat sense of timing not by giving their distinguished offspring the key to the front door but by cutting down his allowance by one third from £75,000 to £50,000. It has been estimated that the United States alone will have spent about twice that amount in sending across the Atlantic half a dozen large scale groups headed by the Cleveland Orchestra and the New York City Ballet. Nor can the cost to West Germany (the Berlin Philharmonic and Karajan) or to Holland (the Netherlands Chamber Orchestra) be small. These sums are spent, not out of pure idealism but because the countries, municipalities and individuals concerned take a civilised view of the impression made on the world by the state of culture in their great cities. Edinburgh is their shop-window. Can it really be true, even on the most sordid reckoning, that the actual owners of this great international shop-window net less than £50,000 from the visitors who pack their streets and hotels and shops and restaurants for three solid weeks?*

Ever responsive to public opinion the Corporation's Civic Amenities Committee cancelled the firework display. Earlier, the Lord Provost's Committee had added to the general gaiety by withdrawing the grant of £5,000 towards Festival publicity giving as its reason that 'the Festival already benefits from the general publicity for the city' – exactly the opposite of what most expert projectors of the Edinburgh image believed.

All was not doom and gloom. Breaking on to the scene that year was a man – artist, propagandist extraordinary and impresario, Richard Demarco – who was at the beginning of his colourful career as a one-man-Fringe-and-Festival with *Edinburgh Open 100*, the first major competition open to artists throughout Britain ever to be mounted in Scotland. Even John Russell the lugubrious *Sunday Times* assessor of the arts was pleased to see him:

> *When Richard Demarco announced just a year ago his plans for the revitalisation of Edinburgh's art life, everyone was delighted to give him the benefit of any doubts that rose to mind. Eyeing his swart demonic figure, we reasoned that if it came to nothing, only his neck would be broken. It was not as if Edinburgh had much to spoil: nothing could be more cautious than the official art policy, if there is one, of the Edinburgh Festival.*

But Edinburgh Open 100, *opened by Jennie Lee, housed by the University, juried by three reverend seniors of our Establishment, (David Baxendall, Roland Penrose and Norman Reid) backed by the Scottish Arts Council had 1,500 entries. Prizes each of £1,000 to Robyn Denny, John Hoyland and Victor Newsome, £500 to Colin Lancely and £1150 shared between six others. All over Edinburgh new art is being given a run in places unused to it.*

Nigel Gosling, *The Observer's* art man, although opening with the ritual sneer, also rejoiced: *Painting stopped around 1940: this is the message normally conveyed by the Edinburgh Festival. Now largely due to one man, the Sixties have broken into the city in force and things will never be quite the same again. The Demarco Gallery itself is virtually the only show-case of modern art in Edinburgh.*

As he was so often to do in the future Rikki Demarco managed to attract what quite a lot of people considered a disproportionate amount of the limelight. However beyond the effulgent Portobello Italian Demarco glare there was plenty else going on.

Alexander Schouvaloff, leaving to be Director of the North West Arts Association, in his last year as the Festival Director's assistant had scoured the smaller theatres off Broadway, Montparnasse, Sweden, Poland and the theatre clubs of Britain looking for dramatic innovations. Pop Theatre and Frank Dunlop returned to the Assembly Hall with modern dress productions of *A Midsummer Night's Dream,* Molière's *Tricks of Scapin* and Ionescu's *The Lesson* which were received with the public rapture to which Dunlop and his company had become accustomed over the past few years. The Mods and Rockers *Dream* seemed to carry the Pop Shakespeare idea about as far as it could go but it was certainly animated. Most critics liked *Scapin.* Harold Hobson said: 'Frank Dunlop's inventive direction makes Molière's farce explosively funny and the effect of *The Lesson* is quite shattering.' An interview in the *Weekly Scotsman* by William Foster probed the new theatre wonder boy's secrets of success and the reach-the-people authenticity of his productions.

My most extraordinary production, Dunlop told him, *was in the Great Hall of the ruined Palace of Linlithgow ten years ago when we put on the death of James IV of Scotland in the play* Mary Stuart *on the exact spot where the real James IV was murdered. You couldn't get anything eerier than that.*

It certainly showed unusual dramatic sensitivity – not to say imagination – as Mary Stuart's grandfather James IV was not murdered at Linlithgow but killed at the Battle of Flodden near Wooler in Northumberland 30 years before she was born.

Prospect Theatre made a distinguished Festival debut at the Lyceum with Chekhov's *The Cherry Orchard* directed and translated by Richard Cottrell with Lilia Kedrova as Madame Ranevsky and Patrick Wymark as Lopakhin. But Toby Robertson's production of an adaptation of E. M. Forster's Florentine novel *A Room with a View* was not so well received. The mannered direction with mimed train journeys, bicycle rides and croquet games brought laughs but also anger at the loss of the irony and tenderness of Forster's tale.

The power of black theatre was demonstrated once more in Eugene O'Neill's *The Emperor Jones.* As the ex-convict who makes himself ruler of a West Indian island, James Earl Jones, tall and commanding, deep voiced and with a resonant personality, made his haunted drum-beat journey of escape through the dark forest a thing of majestic terror imbued for all its fear with the magnetism of the tyrant fleeing to his spectacular end. Off-stage the cast made militant noises about black power and its achievement but in their second production *Black New World* told the story of the emergence of black Americans from slavery to freedom with restraint, dignity and a touching sadness.

The Hampstead Theatre Club brought two plays by Barry Bermange, *Nathan and Tabileth* and *Oldenberg* clever and funny but chillingly acute observations of urban life. This was at Church Hill where they were followed by The Traverse in a new play by Paul Foster, *Tom Paine*, a sensual recreation of this intemperate republican, author of *The Age of Reason* and other inflammatory works, which somehow lost its way in the telling, being described crisply by one reviewer as 'The Rights of Man by Batman and Robin'.

There was also a trio of short plays by Olwen Wymark from the Close Theatre in Glasgow at the Gateway, a kind of twelve-tone theatre followed the next week by Marcel Marceau wordlessly much easier to understand. In the Lauriston Hall *The Complete Works*, the Cambridge Footlights Revue featured Richard Harris and Clive James, Scottish novelist James Kennaway's first play *Country Dance* peopled by decadent Scots aristos into grouse moors and what would today be called organic farming, failed to make as large an impression as *Tunes of Glory*, the film made from his first novel. *Country Dance* was also made into a film after Kennaway's early death in a road accident but it never achieved any considerable success.

The music invoked considerable critical applause – and audience cheers as well. Stravinsky and Bach were the featured composers and the two great foreign orchestras at the Festival, the Cleveland and the Berlin Philharmonic were widely admired. Their conductors, Georg Szell with the Cleveland and Herbert von Karajan with the Berlin were renowned as conservative middle-of-the-road exponents of the classical repertoire from Mozart to Strauss. Thus there was no Henze or Hindemith from Berlin and not a single note of American music from Cleveland. But Desmond Shawe-Taylor wrote:

> *Despite this disappointment, I cheerfully allow that the American orchestra has provided some of the finest music I have heard in the Usher Hall or anywhere else for that matter. Strauss's* Don Juan *made us feel all the fresh power and genius of the young firebrand who wrote it. After the interval the Sibelius Symphony sent us away exultant.*

Two premières were in the programmes of the BBC orchestras. James Loughran conducted the BBC Scottish Symphony Orchestra in the first performance of Thomas Wilson's *Concerto for Orchestra* an interesting piece of great textural variety showing affinities with Alban Berg and the late 19th-century romantics.

With the BBC Symphony Orchestra from London, Pierre Boulez made brilliant contributions to the Stravinsky theme particularly in the then rarely heard *Song of the Nightingale*, a *Rite of Spring* mind-blowing in its pagan incisiveness, as pulsatingly rhythmic as I have ever heard; and the European première of *Requiem Canticles*, nine short intense pieces for chorus, solo voices and orchestra from which Boulez drew vivid tones of startling purity and effectiveness.

Large audiences packed the High Kirk of St Giles to hear the church organist, Herrick Bunney give a monumental series of 16 afternoon recitals of the complete organ works of Bach.

Scottish Opera made its first appearance at the Festival in two Stravinsky pieces, *The Rake's Progress* directed by Peter Ebert with a series of striking stylised sets by Ralph Koltai, and *The Soldier's Tale*. Its choice recognised the place which the company had made for itself in British musical life in the six years of its existence and the production and main performances of *The Rake's Progress* were well-received with particular praise for Alexander Young's flabby, complacent Tom Rakewell and the stylish Dutch baritone Peter van der Bilt's sardonic firm-voiced Nick Shadow.

Although some disliked the elaborate moving platforms of the sets, most critics found the staging imaginative and positive in its task of setting the plot's move from the pastoral to final hopelessness and despair in Bedlam. The playing of the Scottish National Orchestra and Alexander Gibson's conducting drew general praise. *The Soldier's Tale* – that curious, non-singing opera in which Gibson conducted a chamber group of the SNO – was elegantly and dramatically staged in a Brechtian style production by

Wendy Toye. It was performed in a series of morning performances, during the last week, on the open-sided stage of the Assembly Hall with Gordon Jackson as the Narrator, Nicky Henson as the Soldier, Patrick Wymark as a sinister throaty Devil and the lithe mini-skirted Una Stubbs an enchanting Princess. The Scottish Opera contributions certainly held their own against the other 1967 opera offerings. Bellini's *I Montecchi ed I Capuleti* (The Montagues and the Capulets) had its moments. The opera – hastily cobbled together by Felice Romani and Bellini in 1830 for a commission from La Fenice in Venice (and taken rather from Matteo Bandello's version of the tale of the star-crossed lovers than from Shakespeare) – was given a rather dull production in Edinburgh. It was enlivened, however, by a sparkling London Symphony Orchestra in the pit, conducted with verve and passion by Claudio Abbado. Giacomo Aragall sang Romeo (originally written for a mezzo-soprano), Anna Moffo was a touching but rather off-key Juliet and the second tenor, Tybalt made a considerable hit with his two stirring arias sung by an unknown young man called Luciano Pavarotti.

Peter Heyworth thought Haydn's last opera *Orfeo ed Euridice* was 'a score that dribbles over rather limp action, often agreeably enough but rarely to much dramatic effect' but nobody felt that the role of the lost Euridice really suited Joan Sutherland and such praise as there was went to Nicolai Gedda as Orfeo and the bass Spiro Malas for Creon's two nobly contemplative arias.

The two heroes of the 1967 Edinburgh Festival, wrote Desmond Shawe-Taylor, *are Bach and Stravinsky and the centre of the Bach celebrations has been a pair of performances of the* B Minor Mass *under Carlo Maria Giulini, the first, it is said, he has ever conducted. The chorus was the New Philharmonia divorced for once from its own orchestra and accompanied by the Netherlands Chamber Orchestra with the addition of the famous Bach trumpeter, Adolf Scherbaum, who scaled the dizzier heights in dashing style. This was a great occasion, worthy of a great Festival. The performance I heard – the second one – was by and large of glorious quality, its elevated character in no way compromised by the sensuous beauty of the sound.*

Most of the supreme things came from the choir. Though the sopranos snatched at their notes now and again the general effect of the great series of choruses was immense: tremendous that is to say, but not overpowering.

The Observer's music critic, Peter Heyworth said:

The musico-dramatic high point of this festival has been provided not by opera but by the New York City Ballet in the wide range of their Stravinsky repertoire, all with a single exception in Balanchine's choreography – one of the historic creative partnerships of our time. No other company could equal this Agon, *the serene classical lyricism of* Apollo Musagetes *... a real musical illumination of Igor Stravinsky's vast contribution to 20th-century theatre.*

But perhaps the ambience of the Festival struggling to be preserved was best captured by Conrad Wilson:

No better evidence of the sheer range of the Edinburgh Festival was provided this year than on Saturday when one could hear Monteverdi madrigals in the morning, visit a matinee or some exhibitions in the afternoon, drop into St Giles Cathedral for a Bach recital at tea-time, hear Claudio Abbado conduct Verdi and Stravinsky in the evening and finish off at a late night concert party devoted to operatic arias, a luminous four-handed piano account of Ravel's Mother Goose Suite *from Abbado and Marta Argerich, Shirley Verrett singing negro spirituals and the strains of Cleo Laine and John Dankworth. If there is another European festival which daily offers such a cornucopia of events I have yet to find it.*

XV

The advent of the 1968 Festival was ponderous with ill omens. In January it was announced that because Edinburgh had no proper opera house the Festival had lost the chance of the premières of two new operas by British composers, Alexander Goehr's *Arden Must Die* and Humphrey Searle's *Hamlet* which the Hamburg Opera had planned to present at the Festival. The intendant of the Hamburg Opera was now Rolf Liebermann, a composer as well as a director. He had fostered the cause of contemporary opera and this had undoubtedly influenced Diamand's choice of company for the 22nd Festival which was to feature Schubert and Britten as composers, with a distinctive strand of 20th-century music.

Arrangements to bring these productions have collapsed, said Diamand, *simply and only because of the limitations of the King's Theatre. I am frustrated and disillusioned about the lack of progress on the opera house site. It cannot be said often enough and adequately enough that a city like Edinburgh with a festival of the importance of the Edinburgh Festival urgently needs an opera house.*

In February the Corporation refused to allow the Festival Society to erect a sign on the new building in Market Street to which it had been forcibly removed, on the grounds that it would spoil the view from flagless Princes Street. Martin Huggins, the Festival's recently appointed sales manager, protested. The new location, he said, is not going to help ticket sales. People will find it less accessible. After a few months council chamber bickering a sign was finally permitted 'for the period of the Festival only', ignoring the fact that a great many of the tickets are sold before the three-week period of the Festival begins.

The Pop Theatre which had packed the Assembly Hall in previous festivals had offers to go to America and Israel and decided not to appear in Edinburgh that year. It was to be replaced in the Assembly Hall by the newly formed 69th Company which would present *Hamlet* with Tom Courtenay as the Prince and Ibsen's last play *When We Dead Awaken* with Wendy Hiller as Irene and Alexander Knox as Rubek. Prospect Theatre would be at the Lyceum in *The Beggar's Opera* along with the Abbey Theatre's production of *The Playboy of the Western World* and Glasgow Citizens' version of Brecht's *The Resistible Rise of Arturo Ui*.

Other drama came from Wroclaw in Poland with the experimental Laboratory Theatre in *Acropolis* directed by Jerzy Grotowski playing in the Festival's former office in Cambridge Street to a nightly audience of 80 and The Traverse at Church Hill in O'Neill's *Mourning Becomes Electra*. It was a distinctly un-jolly programme made no better in March when the *Edinburgh Evening News* announced that a loss of £52,000 was anticipated on the 1968 Festival due to devaluation and other factors.

However there was more cheerful news in June when, in the teeth of fierce Labour opposition in the council chamber, the civic grant to the Festival was restored to £75,000. By the time the opening concert was under way a slightly more optimistic ambience prevailed. The London Symphony Orchestra, in an all-Britten concert conducted by the Hungarian István Kertész with the Festival Chorus, provided an exultant beginning with *Voices for Today*, Yehudi Menuhin's impeccable, radiant account of the violin concerto and the Spring Symphony. *Voices for Today* had been composed by Britten at the invitation of U Thant, then the Secretary General of United Nations, to celebrate the 20th anniversary of the UN in 1965. Included in its text were all kinds of references to the brotherhood of man and the need to secure and maintain world peace with quotations from Sophocles, Blake, Shelley, Yevtushenko and Albert Camus.

Camus's quotation 'The fruits of the spirit are slower to ripen than intercontinental missiles' was to prove an ironic and bitter comment on the world events which paralleled the 22nd Festival.

With Scottish Opera's *Peter Grimes* and Harrison Birtwistle's first opera *Punch and Judy* at the King's, the three Britten church parable operas, *Curlew River*, *The Burning Fiery Furnace* and *The Prodigal Son* at St Mary's Episcopalian Cathedral, two new concert works by Thea Musgrave and other 'local' items, despite the loss of the Searle and Goehr operas from Hamburg, it was the biggest representation of British music ever offered at the Festival.

The jinx element remained: American tenor Richard Cassily was due to have a nautical Festival singing the lead in the Britten opera and Erik in Wagner's *The Flying Dutchman* but he had to call off at the last minute with a viral infection from *Peter Grimes* and was replaced for the first two performances by Nigel Douglas, an English tenor recruited from Zurich, with a voice of quality rather than girth, who nonetheless gave a curiously vulnerable and unbrutal air to the character which perhaps better explained his appeal to the protective instincts of Ellen Orford.

Scottish Opera's bold and dramatic *Grimes* was well-received by critics and audiences alike. Colin Graham, the most experienced of Britten producers, directed although he had never before worked on Britten's first major opera. It was a straightforward production which brought out the virtues of the splendid Scottish Opera chorus and it was full of strongly etched vignettes of the close-knit characters of the East Anglian fishing village in which early 19th-century Suffolk poet George Crabbe set the poem on which the work is based. Alexander Gibson led the Scottish National Orchestra and the singers through the vivid score, now harsh, now lyrical, with a fervour and sureness of pace which made the action come alive tellingly in the music.

The only critic to withhold his praise was Lord Provost Brechin. On Scottish Opera's first night the year before he had irritated everyone by closing the Circle Bar in the King's Theatre to hold a civic reception. In 1968, he booked a block of seats for the European burgomasters and other municipal chain-wearers he had invited to the Festival, then cancelled the booking at the last moment and took his international group for a sail down the River Clyde instead. The rain which poured down on the burgomasters' nautical bash was greatly enjoyed vicariously by opera enthusiasts everywhere.

The outstanding Britten performance came in the *War Requiem* from the New Philharmonia under Carlo Maria Giulini with the Festival Chorus and boys from St Mary's Cathedral, the Melos Ensemble and the three soloists from the warring nations for whom conscientious objector Britten had composed his bitter reflections on war and eloquent pleadings for peace, Galina Vishnevskaya, Peter Pears and Dietrich Fischer-Dieskau. Britten conducted the chamber orchestra but for Giulini, no enthusiast for modern music, it was his first performance of the work. The result was a triumph: vivid, powerful and deeply moving in conception, highly responsive to the terrible violence and the grieving intimacy of the music, an unforgettable festival performance of supreme quality, worthy to set beside the Italian conductor's great interpretation of the Verdi Requiem.

The rest of the opera programme had a limited success. Birtwistle's unconventional and macabre *Punch and Judy*, given two performances by The English Opera Group at the King's was, although interesting, not to everyone's taste. Houses were not full and, as had happened at the work's première at Aldeburgh a few weeks before, there was some noisy walking out and a good deal of restlessness. What had been described as 'two hours of non-stop ritual accompanied by piercingly squally music' did not sound so off-putting in what was probably the gentler acoustic of the much-maligned King's Theatre.

Anthony Besch's ingenious production housed in a brightly striped box devised by Peter Rice was sinisterly effective and the young conductor David Atherton made a fine impression with the incisive playing he won from the orchestra.

After the first Hamburg rehearsals at the King's, 12 of the orchestra's string section had to be sent home because there was simply no room for them in the pit. Unable to fit their new British operas into what Rolf Liebermann described as 'the worst theatre the company has ever played in' the Germans brought two contrasting operas by Richard Strauss and Wieland Wagner's last production (he died in 1966) of his grandfather's *The Flying Dutchman*. Liebermann made early excuses:

The programme is not the choice of Mr Diamand, he said. *It is not the choice of the Hamburg Opera. It is the choice of the stage of the Edinburgh theatre.*

However no-one who had seen the superb Glyndebourne-Edinburgh Festival productions on that very stage: of *Ariadne auf Naxos* in the original version in 1950, enveloped by *Le Bourgeois Gentilhomme*, wonderfully directed by Ebert and fizzingly conducted by Beecham, and the second version in 1954 with Sena Jurinac as a hauntingly memorable composer, could enjoy the ancient and creaky staging (rumoured to date back to the Hitler era) which Hamburg presented. The *Elektra*, although somewhat cramped on the King's stage, had an impressive heroine in Gladys Kuchta with Regine Resnik and Leonie Rysanek making up what William Mann pithily described in a programme note as 'a household of mentally unhinged women'. But *The Dutchman* – with its vivid, surging sea music – had a strikingly mythic setting by Wieland Wagner and Scotland's David Ward, stepping in at the last moment for Theo Adam as Vanderdecken gave a fine doom-laden performance; Anja Silja was a wild Nordic Senta with the storm in her voice.

The one genuine musical novelty of 1968 was the first live performance in Britain of Schubert's opera *Alfonso und Estrella* premiered in Weimar in 1854 when it was conducted by Franz Liszt. Given in a lengthy concert version by the Scottish National Orchestra under Gibson (Liszt had cut it for Weimar) it nevertheless revealed some beautiful lyrical music in the Act II love scene and plenty of melodic interludes elsewhere in the muddled plot, serenely conducted by Gibson in a fluent performance although a little bloodless in the title roles sung by Richard Lewis and Phyllis Curtin.

The new company at the Assembly Hall was not exactly offered a clamorous welcome. Most critics were severe on Tom Courtenay's low-key *Hamlet*, an unhappy staring boy, sober and solemn in demeanour, tetchy with old fools and cold-eyed to the depravity of his elders. This tightly controlled production made new use of the apron stage with a moat around it so that actors did not have to make their entrances and exits through the audience. 'Middling rough Shakespeare,' said Ronald Bryden in *The Observer*.

But in *The Sunday Times* Harold Hobson took exception to the unenthusiastic critical reception of *Hamlet* in an unusual view of the Prince:

> *I was absolutely absorbed by the action of the play. Mr Courtenay's Hamlet is a man who believes in his religion and is ruined by it. A superlative* Hamlet: *a beautiful and sensitive performance.*

In genial mood he praised Norman Holland's *The Year of the Locust* given by Trinity Square Repertory Company from Providence, Rhode Island as 'a finely calculated study of Wilde in prison' and went into raptures about a new young actress who had made a considerable impression on the Fringe the year before:

> Brecht's Mahagonny *is spectacular, inventive, acrobatic and stunningly aggressive. Julie Covington as Jenny the prostitute is shattering – quiet and gentle even wistful in a short lyric scene: for the rest she is devastating in the girl's irresistible attacking sexuality and formidable powers of defence, an erotic machine-gun that shoots dead straight.*

And the Citizens' Theatre's comic-strip presentation of *The Resistible Rise of Arturo Ui* also brought out the superlatives:

> *A brilliant burlesque of the rise to power of Hitler, probably Brecht's most powerful achievement. The play, the playing and the production are full of delights, at once poisonous and sweet. Michael Blakemore's production is remarkable and Leonard Rossiter's savage portrayal of the repulsive and frightening character of Ui is a tour de force of melodrama, farce and political insight. The last caption slide however was*

not about Hitler but the Russians entering Czechoslovakia. Brecht would not have approved. He would have been with the invaders.

The Russian invasion of Czechoslovakia in the first week of the 1968 Festival had several repercussions in Edinburgh. Before he played the Violin Concerto in D in his concert with the Scottish National Orchestra under Gibson on 22 August, Yehudi Menuhin ended his emotional speech to the audience saying, 'I dedicate this performance, as Beethoven did his life, to the indomitable and defiant spirit of man.'

John Currie in *The Scotsman* wrote of the exceptional quality the occasion drew from the soloist:

There are passages in this concerto when Menuhin catches a dimension seldom glimpsed even by his technical superiors – the final calm statement of the D major tune just before the end of the first movement, the effortlessly high cantabile of almost the entire slow movement and the naive radiance of the main theme of the finale. These passages seemed to have added significance at this performance and were deepened by well-nigh impeccable accompaniment from Mr Gibson and his colleagues.

Two days later there were angry demonstrations, pickets and protests outside the Usher Hall and letters to the papers urging people to boycott the State Orchestra of the USSR under their conductor Evgeny Svetlanov who were giving their first concert that night. Conrad Wilson wrote:

Nevertheless on Saturday while demonstrators thronged outside the hall, one had only to listen to the sombre intensity Rostropovich brought to Britten's Cello Symphony and to the Bach sarabande he played as an encore, to know that the performers and the large tense but enthusiastic audience were on the same wavelength.

Despite the demonstrations – Glasgow threatening to cancel a Polish Trade Fair and the vandalism of the Russian Exhibition at Earl's Court – the recently-knighted Sir Herbert Brechin, the Lord Provost with aristocratic disdain, said he was happy to go ahead with the planned civic supper party at the City Chambers on Sunday evening for the 125 members of the USSR State Orchestra. Only three Councillors attended.

Oddly enough no calumny seemed to attach to the Poles whose armies had marched with the Russians into Prague. The first performance of the Laboratory Theatre's *Acropolis* was cancelled because three specially balanced wheelbarrows – a vital part of the production – had vanished en route to Edinburgh. As far as I know there were no dark murmurings about sabotage and replicas were flown in from Warsaw and *Acropolis* duly appeared on the second night. The play was received with almost hysterically reverent astonishment.

The applause at the end, wrote Allen Wright, *was not only incongruous but outrageous. It reduced a shattering experience to the level of a theatrical occasion. It showed us civilisation so debased and distorted that it might have been a vision of purgatory culminating in mass cremation – a grotesque ritual dedicated to despair. Instead of being set in a glorious cathedral* (as was the original Polish classic by Wyspianki) *it was transferred to an extermination camp. The Old Testament and Greek myths of the original and the triumph of the Resurrection were deformed – like sitting on the brink of the madhouse and the charnel house.*

The Observer hailed it as 'the Festival's dramatic scoop' but *The Sunday Times* demurred that Grotowski was 'in desperate bondage to the past, to ancient myth and above all to Catholic ritual' although it was difficult to accept Auschwitz 'as ancient myth'. Perhaps, one thought, all was explained by the last line of the rather too unconfined Ibsen play on the windy heights of the Assembly Hall stage:

When we dead awaken – we see that we have never lived!

XVI

Immediately after what had often seemed a Festival which lurched from one calamity to another – and which had ended with peculiar incongruity in an over-extended late-night concert of Hoffnung characters and cartoon music – there was some good news.

More people had visited Edinburgh in the three weeks: 96,548 overnight stays had been recorded, 5,000 more than the previous year. Box office receipts had been the best since 1957 at 83% of capacity and the gloomy forecast of a devaluation-assisted £52,000 loss had been reduced to a less catastrophic sounding deficit of a mere £9,500.

The 23rd Festival in 1969 was a brilliant piece of cheese-pared planning which enjoyed a bit of luck to sweeten the dish. The visit of the Florence Opera from the Teatro Communale, performing outside Italy for the first time, was a major *coup de programmation* and they came with a subsidy of £180,000 negotiated with the Italian government.

The King's Theatre which, after considerable municipal in-fighting had been bought by the City earlier in the year for £200,000 but was still charging the Festival the same outrageous rents as Howard and Wyndham, was given over entirely to the six productions from the Tuscan capital. Most importantly and almost uniquely for a visiting European company, the Italians made a real attempt to conquer the problems posed by the theatre instead of letting themselves be conquered by them.

Nor was the Edinburgh repertoire any kind of down-market popular compromise. Donizetti's *Maria Stuarda,* apart from being geographically and historically apposite, had been staged only once before in this country at the St Pancras Festival in 1966. So the Florence company offered its first major staging in Britain.

The libretto by Giuseppe Bardari dated from the early 1830s and is based on Schiller's play, a version of which had already been seen at the Festival. It contains the famous meeting between Mary and Elizabeth which historically never took place but is dramatically highly effective.

Verdi's *Rigoletto* was a more conventional choice but the two double-bill programmes, Rossini's *Il Signor Bruschino* with Puccini's *Gianni Schicchi* and Malipiero's *Sette Canzoni* with Dallapiccola's *Il Prigioniero* offered more adventurous fare. Although it looked like a pairing of romantic composers and modern composers in fact Malipiero and Puccini were quasi-contemporaries and the works of Rossini and Dallapiccola were separated by almost a century and a half.

Rossini's romp of mixed identities and twisted emotions was principally a vehicle for Renato Capecchi's *buffo* Monsieur Hulot, a tortured comedy performance as the duped parent, and for highlighting the ingenious touches of character orchestration which the 20-year-old composer had inserted in the score. Puccini's *Gianni Schicchi*, for once separated from its usual macabre and sentimental one-act partners which make up *Il Trittico*, is a masterpiece. In this performance it was presented by a master craftsman.

Tito Gobbi who produced as well as singing the title role of the arch-schemer Schicchi, was simply wonderful, one of the great singing actors of our time, cunning, endearing and compelling yet so managing the piece as to make it an ensemble, balanced by the unforced lyricism of Ugo Bennelli's Rinuccio and the sweet innocence amid a parcel of rogues of Maddelena Bonifacio's Lauretta.

Scipio Columba made Luigi Dallapiccola's searing drama of the Spanish Inquisition and the torture of hope into a personal triumph as he had at the première of the opera at the Teatro Communale in 1950.

From Gian Francesco Malipiero, the 87-year-old editor of the 16th-17th century composers, Monteverdi, Vivaldi and Frescobaldi, in his *Le Sette Canzoni* there was an extraordinarily vivid set of operatic sketches, vignettes of life in song and mime and an almost cinematic presentation which in its different way rivalled the Puccini and made of the two double bill operatic evenings memorable and particularly enlivening festival events.

Maddelena Bonifacio and Tito Gobbi in
Gianni Schicci *(1969)*

Maria Stuarda stole most of the headlines in a sumptuously costumed production by Giorgio di Lullo and the *vil bastarda* confrontation between the Queens and the execution scene were tellingly staged. Shirley Verrett was in great voice as the imperious Elizabeth, with a finely moulded outpouring of marvellously eloquent full tone and great presence, while as the sad and angry vituperative Mary, Leyla Gancer sang with style, passion and melodic tragic appeal which justified the lyrical ardour Franco Tagliavini brought to the role of Leicester. The Teatro Communale orchestra gave spirited and full-hearted accompaniment under Maria Callas's favourite *maestro*, Nino Sanzogno.

Rigoletto had a superb Gilda in Renata Scotto, in prime voice, delicate in phrasing, hopelessly vulnerable and achingly sweet in tone. The hunchback as played by Mario Zanesi showed every sign of being vocally impressive with floods of warm and generous sound but very little indication of any concept of characterisation. Unfortunately Renato Cioni as the Duke showed neither style nor class in a vulgar and inaccurate performance which made it difficult for Alberto Erede's shapely and intelligent reading of the great Verdi score to make its full impact.

But despite any reservations it was exhilarating to hear from the home of opera once more and from a wide spectrum of its delights warmed and enthused by Italian genius, vivid musicality, visual invention and that heart-lifting *brio* which you get from nowhere else.

But the essential performance quality which tingles in the blood and gives festival its special frisson of genuine excitement and thrill was not to be confined to the lyric theatre.

There was a bold opening concert with an ingenious mix of contemporary and 19th-century classical music, Britten's *The Building of the House* and Richard Rodney Bennett's racy new piano concerto crisply played by Stephen Bishop and the Festival Chorus and the Scottish National Orchestra under Gibson producing thrilling open-throated sounds and some magical *pianissimi* in Berlioz's *Te Deum*.

Earlier on the same day the Festival was given a sensational send-off from, of all places, the pulpit of St Giles. Television pundit Malcolm Muggeridge had been asked to take part in the traditional official opening service in the High Kirk and he used the occasion to attack sex and violence in the arts:

> *Have what pass for being art forms*, he asked, *ever before been so drenched and impregnated with erotic obsessions, so insanely preoccupied with our animal nature and its appetites, so remote from any other consideration, intellectual, moral or spiritual as are ours today?*
>
> *In a way the whole thing is hilariously funny; all this vast expensive edifice of public culture – the Arts Council, Miss Jennie Lee, the National Theatre, Lord Goodman, the BBC, Kenneth Tynan and Kenneth Clark; the ever-multiplying and ever-growing universities where the half-baked receive contemptuously the ministrations and instructions of the half-hearted.*

Abbado and the London Symphony Orchestra gave the world première of Luigi Nono's suite from his controversial opera *Intolleranza* with Cathy Gayer in virulently atmospheric form as the soprano soloist in this strange mixture of taped and performed song with pungent orchestral accompaniment.

Itzhak Perlman, the Israeli violinist who plays seated because of polio, with the London Symphony under Hans Schmidt-Isserstedt played Prokoviev's Second Violin Concerto with wonderful flair and virtuosity. Giulini and the New Philharmonia with the Festival Chorus and the Philharmonia Chorus made the Usher Hall ring with the two greatest Italian liturgical masterpieces, Rossini's *Stabat Mater* and Verdi's *Requiem*. Alexander Goehr had his revenge for being excluded from the previous festival with a series of late-night programmes in the Freemasons' Hall by his Music Theatre Ensemble which featured not only some stunning examples of his own music but that of Luciano Berio with Cathy Berberian and gave Edinburgh the world première of *Pharsalia*, a timely and brilliantly set-out cautionary tale filched from Lucan by Scots composer Iain Hamilton about the terrible effects of civil strife (albeit in ancient Rome).

Dame Sybil Thorndike movingly and entertainingly gave three poetry recitals in the newly refurbished St Cecilia's Hall in the Cowgate, scene of Edinburgh's first music festival in the 18th century; there was *Pomp* at the Royal Scottish Museum, an exhibition of priceless gold and silver plate, nominally valued at £1 million, organised by the Worshipful Company of Goldsmiths, 200 items dating from 1,500 and including such impressive artefacts as the crown worn by Queen Caroline of Anspach, consort of George II and the coronation crown of the 19-year-old Victoria from her enthronement in 1838. Sketches by Michelangelo, Raphael, Veronese and Caracci were on view in a superb exhibition of *Italian 16th-century Drawings* from British private collections in the Merchants' Hall.

Theatre has annually been the part of the Festival ritually lambasted by critics both professional and amateur. Over the years it has constantly been a matter of complaint from sensitive thespian enthusiasts that the drama on offer on Edinburgh stages during the three weeks does not match the quality of the music.

Offered in defence has been the argument that theatre in mid-summer is notoriously more difficult to arrange than concerts and opera. Orchestras, instrumentalists and singers plan their professional lives a very long way ahead, partly because music – being its own language – is much more international than theatre. For the most part, theatre attracts an audience which is fluent in the language presented in the play; and is a much less set-piece concern than an ensemble group, like an opera company or an orchestra. Many plays are presented by adhoc companies, formed for a particular occasion or brought together for a particular play. There are far fewer repertory companies than formerly, and leading actors come and go according to the roles they are offered and many other considerations.

So generally while the bookings of orchestras and opera companies are fixed several years in advance (a fearsome cliff-teetering problem for Festival planners who often do not know from one year to another what the budget will be on which to make their programmes) the finalising of theatre tends to take place months rather than years before the protagonists arrive to rehearse on Edinburgh stages.

There are many counter temptations. Many actors hope that in the summer they will be working in a highly paid film or television series rather than in a lowly paid play for a limited run at the Edinburgh Festival. There is not a lot of long-term investment in theatre projects as a rule and if you are dependent on a star actor or actress to fill a role, it is by no means unknown for that luminary to be coyly delaying a decision in the hope of a better offer from the large or small screen.

Despite all this, it has always seemed to me that the often savage criticism and perennial girning the drama programmes have to face are nearly always singularly unjust. One of the troubles is that very few Festival goers – or Festival staff for that matter – have any real or extensive knowledge of Festival history. Their minds go back to last year or the year before, seldom further.

There are fewer plays in the Festival programme than concerts or recitals but generally not fewer performances. Plays run for several days, often a week or longer, whereas concerts are very rarely repeated. But I have never understood why it should be that the annual carpers have such difficulty in remembering outstanding theatre occasions as fondly as they do operas or concerts. Perhaps it is because theatre and music audiences are not necessarily the same people and that drama enthusiasts take musical acclamation at second hand in order to feel they have something to complain about. Certainly, there is little to justify the 'drama is treated as second-class art' attitude in the first two decades of Festival history.

From Louis Jouvet and Alec Guinness in the first Festival through Barrault's sensitive *Hamlet* and the vigorous rumbustiousness of *The Thrie Estaites*, half a dozen fine Shakespearean productions in the Assembly Hall by the Old Vic and Frank Dunlop's Pop Theatre, two scintillating appearances by the Italian theatre troupes from Milan and Genoa, the highly original staging of *The Four Sons of Aymon* at the Murrayfield Ice Rink, Feuillère's *La Dame aux Camelias,* the Comedie Francaise's brilliant *Bourgeois Gentilhomme*, the commissioned plays from T. S Eliot, Bridie, Linklater, Thornton Wilder and Sydney Goodsir Smith, *Long Day's Journey Into Night*, the Piraikon Theatre's astounding Greek tragedies, the power and commitment of American black drama in *The Amen Corner* and *Emperor Jones*, the biting hilarious satire of *Beyond the Fringe*, Marcel Marceau, Grotowski, Gielgud, Ashcroft, Edith Evans, Guthrie, Gründgens, Strehler, Ustinov, Vilar – here are some of the greatest names in world theatre and the most riveting performances of a generation. And there was more, much more to come.

In 1969 drama was in the hands of the newly formed Scottish Actors Company, who gave a much discussed version of Ibsen's *The Wild Duck*. The performance played rather heavily on the supposed affinity between Scotland and Norway, but produced fine performances from Leonard Maguire as Ekdal and a wonderfully well-meaning self-righteous Brian Cox as Gregers.

Opinions on *Zoo Zoo Widdershins Zoo* wavered between those who found Peter Laffan's portrayal of Birmingham drop-outs mercilessly funny or lots of groping, grappling and swearing unworthy of the talents of Frank Dunlop. Prague's Theatre on the Balustrade at Church Hill was praised as sensitive mime drama or damned by those who felt, in the words of one critic, that mime 'always gives me the feeling of watching the theatrical equivalent of those amputees who paint Christmas cards with their toes'.

At the Assembly Hall however, for Prospect Theatre's productions of Shakespeare's *Richard II* directed by Richard Cottrell and Marlowe's *Edward II* directed by Toby Robertson, with Ian McKellen playing the title roles in both plays, the keynote was unstinted acclaim and tumultuous applause.

Let no-one say, wrote *The Scotsman's* Allen Wright of the Shakespeare play, *that drama occupies a minor part in the Festival after last night's demonstration of its nobility. On the shoulders of a great young actor, it rose up to be full stature. This is one of the finest Shakespearean productions to reach Scotland for years – ablaze with royalty and splendour. Ian McKellen brings out all his sublime vanity, a beautiful young man,*

Ian McKellen in Richard II *(1969)*

poised but not equipped to rule.

Two days later he wrote:

Hard on the heels of a superlative production of Richard II, *another mighty play of Royal ruination burst upon the Assembly Hall last night in Marlowe's* Edward II. *In the Marlowe pace and passion compensate for lack of poetic grace. Edward's abdication is even more heart-rending than Richard's. The humiliation is agonising – worse than the torments and unspeakable death which he subsequently suffers. This hall has not housed such momentous drama for at least a decade.*

Ian McKellen's Edward is only a shade less brilliant than his Richard. A fresh and vital portrayal with Timothy West as powerful as Mortimer as he was as Bolingbroke.

Ronald Bryden of *The Observer* – in a curious staccato review taken seemingly un-edited from the notes he made in his sleeper on the way back to London, (which he would certainly have condemned in a playwright as unbearably sloppy) – analysed both productions at length:

Both ecstasy and performances, slightly premature, forced-ripe. In both parts feel him straining against limitations of age, technique – he'll want to play them again in ten years, find himself embarrassed by precocious legend. Too many moments when thought-out development sacrificed to thrilling vocal effect. But a taste of real meat, young but bloody, amid all the greenery. George Cukor, who should know, says on the great ones you can smell danger. It's here. More reassuring (remember Brando, Finney) splendid flow of inventive detail, never repeating itself and objective approach to character. Two clinical (but not cold) studies in royal upbringing. Richard, the artificial neurotic, created by total obedience deference and flattery from infancy up, wrapped in a dream of golden gloved kingship. When reality shatters it, spins himself a new cocoon of equally dreamy sorrow, abnegation of world. Edward, by contrast, the unchecked palace cub, never told not to pick his nose, writhing in tantrums of unbridled passion, Marlovian, unteachable, can only become more superbly wilfully his wild self, the lion rending captors and his own flesh until put out of its misery. Production ragged at edges but beefed up well beyond previous Prospect standards by strong supporting casts. Timothy West powerful as Bolingbroke, Mortimer Robert Eddison finely indecisive as York, poisonously gentle as murderer Lightborn.

Best Assembly Hall stage devised so far. A tilted metal ring around which strong boyars of our feudal semi-legend circle two sacrificial bulls. A target design demanding a bulls-eye star performance. With a bit of nervous quiver and strain it gets two.

After this percipient telegraphese it is relief to turn to the more mellifluous Harold Hobson. First saying of *Richard II* that the whole production deserves the rapture with which it has been received he was not quite so sure about the Marlowe:

McKellen was given as great an ovation as I have ever heard in a theatre – not really deserved, the audience were alerted for a masterpiece and saw what they expected to see. There is more to the passionate enslavement of King Edward to the fascinating Galveston than can be revealed by the continuous spectacle of a couple of hippies necking in Green Park. In this production the action is suited to the word with a monotonously exhibitionistic reiteration that only rarely in an occasional gash of the wanton loveliness of Marlowe's verse, gives any sense of the destructive tide of homosexual infatuation. Mr McKellen is an actor of great spiritual grace but he is not graceful to look at and all those smacking kisses before his angry nobles suggest little more than that Edward was tiresomely addicted to showing off.

It seemed a curious piece of dramatic criticism to suggest that if McKellen had been prettier the frenzied cuddling would have been more acceptable but few people in the audiences for these two plays had many doubts that they had just seen two of the greatest dramatic performances of their lives.

However Councillor John D. Kidd was one of them. This tempestuous City Father wrote to the Chief Constable demanding that *Edward II* should be prosecuted for obscenity:

> A disgrace to the city with male members of the cast kissing on stage. Shocking and degrading with the scene where the king is killed with a red-hot poker, just brutality,

he fulminated.

Meanwhile in the Town Planning Department of the Corporation, on public view for the first time, was the embryo of Edinburgh's never-to-be born dream palace of culture in the form of President of the Royal Scottish Academy, Sir William Kininmonth's model of the proposed opera house in Castle Terrace. 'No decision has been taken yet about proceeding with building which would take four to five years and is estimated to cost about £3.5 million,' read the cautious caption.

The 1970 Festival opened with mourning. Less than a month before he was due to conduct the opening concert in a festival musically devoted to the celebration of the 200th anniversary of the birth of Ludwig van Beethoven, Sir John Barbirolli died. Earlier that summer the death was also announced of Georg Szell, the Hungarian conductor who had appeared twice at the Festival with American orchestras and who had also been due to appear at the 24th Festival. Both were commemorated in the speech made by the new Lord Provost, James McKay, remembering:

> Two outstanding musicians who were, as few others were, admired and respected throughout the whole world of music for their knowledge and authority and perhaps still more, for their love and respect for music. Many will recall their memorable contributions made to the Edinburgh Festival since its inception in 1947. We had felt privileged at the thought that both would be with us again this year. Barbirolli and Szell have set standards and established values for which they will be remembered for years to come.

In fact this represented another misreading of Festival history because Georg Szell had not conducted at the first Festival as the Lord Provost implied.

His name appears in the first Souvenir Programme as conductor of the Scottish Orchestra for the Glyndebourne performances of *Macbeth* and *Le Nozze di Figaro* but in fact he cancelled just before the Festival and was replaced by the German composer and conductor, Berthold Goldschmidt, then Glyndebourne's chorus master and Walter Susskind, the orchestra's resident conductor for the Verdi opera and Renato Cellini for the Mozart. Szell first appeared at the 1955 Festival with the second visit of the New York Philharmonic Orchestra and again in 1967 with the orchestra he had made particularly his own, the Cleveland. But he had strong previous connections with Scotland. From 1936-39 he was conductor of the Scottish Orchestra, succeeding John Barbirolli who had gone to New York to take over the New York Philharmonic from Arturo Toscanini.

In 1970 Szell would have conducted at the Festival for the third time but it would have been Sir John Barbirolli's 12th appearance. I remember him from his Scottish Orchestra days, a stocky, vital and dynamic young man with a head like a Roman emperor and a mane of bouncing black hair, directing the orchestra with a wonderful ferocity which made a strong appeal to the children who attended the afternoon concerts for schools he organised in St Andrew's Hall, Glasgow, as did the way he came into the audience afterwards and talked to us about what we liked and – if we knew – why. He admirably fulfilled Ernest Newman's definition of the public's conception of a conductor as 'a cross between a hypnotist and a lion-tamer'.

It took longer of course to appreciate that not only could he provide blaze, power and excitement in the concert hall but that he was a great musician capable of tenderness and subtlety of interpretation far

101

beyond the noisy understanding of a schoolboy. At the first festival in two concerts with his beloved Hallé Orchestra he most memorably played Elgar – the Second Symphony and the Introduction and Allegro for Strings.

His highly personal interpretations had a warmth and affection which made many new friends for the composer of whom Bernard Shaw – a shrewd and knowing music critic as well as an ironically probing playwright – said had a rank 'either so high that only time and posterity can confer it, or else he is one of the Seven Humbugs of Christendom', and reinforced Shaw's subsequent judgement:

> *To the north countryman who, on hearing of Wordsworth's death said 'I suppose the son will carry on the business,' it would be plain today that Elgar is carrying on Beethoven's business. The names are up on the shop front for everyone to read: ELGAR, late BEETHOVEN & CO. Classics and Italian & German Warehousemen. Symphonies, Overtures. Chamber Music, Oratorios, Bagatelles.*

Newman in *The Sunday Times* wrote of Barbirolli and the Hallé at the second Festival:

> *Of Sibelius (Fifth Symphony) I do not hope ever to hear a more convincing performance. It was an inexpressible pleasure to see a great work gradually taking shape in performance as it must have done in the mind of its creator, developing steadily logically from acorn to mighty oak, and treated respectfully as something existing in its own right.*

At the opening concert of the 1957 Festival the birth of Elgar was celebrated by Sir John and the Hallé with a marvellous interpretation of the Concerto for Cello and Orchestra played with a slow but dynamic sense of reverence. The soloist was Janos Starker but the man on the podium had also been a cellist and that experience made its contribution to the quality. There was the great and moving occasion at the end of a Verdi Requiem dedicated to the memory of Kathleen Ferrier in 1954 when Barbirolli motioned to the audience to rise as the last *pianissimo* of the *Libera Me* died in the Usher Hall.

There were great performances with other orchestras too. Neilson's Fifth Symphony in 1965 with the New Philharmonia, the concerts with Kathleen Ferrier for the last time in 1952 in Handel's *Messiah* and in 1951 when she sang Chausson's *Poeme de l'Amour et de la Mer* in a programme which also contained a thrilling performance of Berlioz's *Harold in Italy*, the Byronic Second Symphony which he wrote for Paganini. His own last appearance at the Festival was in 1969 conducting the Scottish National Orchestra in another performance of the Sibelius Fifth, a work which has a strong appeal to Scots as it had to Barbirolli. Reviewing this concert Conrad Wilson wrote: 'They do not make conductors in Sir John's mould any more.' A fitting epitaph.

After the lamentations, the celebrating of Beethoven's birth anniversary proceeded apace. On the anniversary of his death in 1927, Shaw had written in the new-fledged *Radio Times:*

> *A 100 years ago a crusty old bachelor of 57, so deaf that he could not hear his music played by a full orchestra, yet still able to hear thunder, shook his fist at the roaring heavens for the last time and died as he had lived, challenging God and defying the universe. He was Defiance Incarnate: he could not even meet a Grand Duke and his court in the street without jamming his hat tight down on his head and striding through the very middle of them. He had the manners of a disobliging steam-roller (most steamrollers are abjectly obliging and conciliatory) and he was rather less particular about his dress than a scarecrow: in fact he was once arrested as a tramp because the police refused to believe that such a tatterdemalion could be a famous composer, much less a temple of the most turbulent spirit that ever found expression in pure sound. The impetuous fury of his strength, which he could quite easily contain and*

control but often would not, and the uproariousness of his fun, go beyond anything of the kind to be found in the work of other composers.

Greenhorns write of syncopation now as if it were a new way of giving the utmost impetus to a musical measure, but the rowdiest jazz sounds like The Maiden's Prayer *after Beethoven's third Leonora overture: and certainly no negro corobbery that I ever heard could inspire the blackest dancer with such diable au corps as the last movement of the Seventh Symphony. And no other composer has ever melted his hearers into complete sentimentality by the tender beauty of his music, and then suddenly turned on them and mocked them with derisive trumpet blasts for being such fools. Nobody but Beethoven could govern Beethoven: and when, as happened when the fit was on him, he deliberately refused to govern himself, he was ungovernable.*

A timely reminder of the sheer rebelliousness of Beethoven's music both in its spirit and the challenging complexity of its interpretation – which perhaps ought to have but did not appear in the 24th Festival's Souvenir Programme. Sometimes he is a composer approached with too much reverence, unappreciative of the element of danger which lurks in every major work. Serenity is not a prime Beethovian characteristic. Fortunately few of the performances of this bi-centennial year failed to recognise this.

Beethoven was everywhere: the Festival was opened by Colin Davis – also a conductor with Scottish connections for from 1957-59 he had been assistant conductor to the BBC Scottish Symphony Orchestra – in an all-Beethoven programme with the New Philharmonia and the Festival Chorus culminating in the Ninth Symphony. Five of the symphonies were played and all the piano concertos, Clifford Curzon the soloist in the two most mature and Radu Lupu (latest winner of the Leeds piano competition) in the C minor, Stephen Bishop in the B flat major and Alfred Brendel in the C major. In Leith Town Hall the Amadeus played all seventeen quartets, not in chronological order but in several well-structured programmes, with authority and passion

Daniel Barenboim accompanied his young wife Jacqueline Du Pré playing the five cello sonatas. Brendel combined the subtle and the imperious in a majestic *Hammerklavier* at a morning concert in the Freemasons' Hall. Fischer-Dieskau at his vocal peak with Barenboim at the piano sang *An die ferne Geliebte* in the Usher Hall with consummate artistry and style, and Giulini, taking over the concerts originally designated for Szell, fashioned a tremendous performance of the *Missa Solemnis* with the New Philharmonia Orchestra, the Festival Chorus and a fine group of soloists, which included that rarest of all discoveries, a new young tenor with superb technique and a genuine thrill in his voice, 'who from the first note brought an ardour and ease to the tenor part such as one rarely experiences'. His name was Placido Domingo.

Even the Fringe got in on the Beethoven act. To St Cuthbert's Church at the west end of Princes Street, a young Irish pianist Julian Dawson brought his own Busendorfer and played all 32 piano sonatas.

The Festival closed with the rarely performed *Choral Fantasia for Piano, Chorus and Orchestra* done with such *brio* by Clifford Curzon, the Festival Chorus, Alexander Gibson and the Scottish National Orchestra that at the end there was so much applause and delight that the whole work apart from the long piano introduction was repeated as an encore!

Of course in a Festival as diverse and diffuse as Edinburgh, it could not be all Beethoven. And of course there were the usual alarums and excursions. The most criticised excursion was made by Lord Provost James MacKay and a censorious posse from the Festival Council who sent themselves on a moral inspection tour to the Deutsche Oper am Rhein at Frankfurt to attend a Sunday performance of Prokoviev's *The Fiery Angel* to see if it was fit for genteel Edinburgh consumption. They had been forewarned by Peter Diamand that in the final act there was a scene of holy hysteria in which three nuns stripped to the waist.

On the Tuesday after their return it was decided this did not constitute a moral affront. Councillor Kidd said he would lodge a protest.

Those of us who had seen Les Ballets Africains de Keita Fodeba dancing bare-breasted on the stage of the Empire Theatre in 1957 found it difficult to comprehend what could be so corrupt about the exposure of white breasts at the Festival when black breasts had already been seen without any notable sign of moral degeneration. But Presbyterian doom lurked in the wings.

At the first performance of *The Fiery Angel* at the King's Theatre the switchboard went berserk and there were seven unscheduled black-outs on stage and the opera had to be abandoned before it was truly under way. After this first attempt it had to be re-started at 8.45. As none of the plunges into darkness had occurred during the final breast-baring scene Councillor Kidd was not suspected.

Despite the cuts in the score made by the Frankfurt Opera it was an impressive performance of a complex and difficult work, Anja Silja with the looks and stamina for the mysterious vision-haunted heroine giving a tremendous account of the distraught and tormented Renata.

Scottish Opera brought a work by a composer for whom Alex Gibson had long been one of the prime advocates in Britain, Hans Werner Henze. *Elegy for Young Lovers* unlike many of Gibson's Henze performances, was not a British première for it had been done at Glyndebourne in 1961 to no great *eclat* at a time when Henze's status as a composer of major influence had not been fully established. Despite his list of premières Gibson had never conducted a Henze opera and to give him that opportunity, Peter Diamand made Henze one of the featured composers of the Festival, with performances of his Sixth Symphony, *El Cimarron* and *Essay on Pigs*, all conducted by Henze, also in the programme.

The Festival *Elegy* was designed to restore the reputation of the 44-year-old German composer in Britain by presenting the opera with the music complete and not heavily cut as it had been at Glyndebourne and in several recent continental productions.

As Henze had already been responsible for the staging of two of his operas he was invited to produce *Elegy* at the Festival. The designer was Ralph Koltai and his collaboration with Gibson and the composer/ producer resulted in a highly distinctive and distinguished opera debut for Henze in Edinburgh. The ironically romantic plot revolves around an evilly arrogant old and famous poet, Gregor Mittenhoffer who ruthlessly exploits everyone around him for his own self-centred ends. The visions of the distracted widow Hilda Mack, whose husband disappeared on the Hammerhorn mountain on their honeymoon 40 years before, provide inspiration for his verses and when her twisted longing is fulfilled and the glacier returns her husband's body, he sends his stepson Toni and his young mistress Elizabeth out on to the treacherous slopes of the mountain to gather edelweiss to fuel his muse for an elegy on their deaths.

From a text by W. H. Auden and Chester Kallman, Henze's spiky and dramatic music against the skeletal scaffolding of Koltai's weirdly compelling mountain design made an unforgettable impact. Performances matched the originality of the music and production, above all Alexander Gibson's incisive and masterly handling of the score but also Catherine Gayer's brilliantly sung widow, John Shirley Quirk's crabbed but dangerous poet, Jill Gomez and David Hillman as the lovers and Sona Cervena as Mittenhofer's strangely submissive patron and secretary. Some of the critics were undecided about the merits of the opera but all of them rated *Elegy* one of Scottish Opera's finest achievements and one of the musical highlights of the Festival.

The National Theatre of Prague provided the rest of the opera programme with three Janacek operas. *The Excursions of Mr Broucek,* two comic and sardonic one-act pieces involving the *petit bourgeois* Broucek in space and time travel – to the Moon which he finds inhabited by fantastically posturing aesthetes and to the 15th century where he decides that life is much less terrifying in the 20th. Not quite as funny as it may have seemed in 1920.

The Makropoulos Affair from a play by Karel Capek proved a much more powerful piece. The famous singer Emma Marty whose involvement in a 300-year old lawsuit proves that she cannot die, is a strange and tortured character and this production called universal attention to this work which has since been extensively performed. As did the third Janacek offering in 1970 *The Cunning Little Vixen*, developed from a comic strip but made into something more profound and touching about the relationship between man and animals than Walt Disney. But for all the charm of *The Vixen* it is *The Makropoulos Case* which made the most lasting impression. Emma Marty is the last portrait in Janacek's strange gallery of heroines, at the same time the most abstract and the most truly realised of all, the one whose cruel dilemma of extended living touches everyone most nearly. Opera at one and the same time at its most theatrical and most poignantly human.

Other theatre in the 24th Festival brought the Nederlands Dans Theater with a strong and lively programme of recently created ballets from their celebrated repertoire – but prudently leaving back in licentious Holland their new nude work *Mutation*, deemed too strong meat for delicate Edinburgh palates. There was a fine *Much Ado About Nothing* from Prospect, switched for some eccentric Toby Robertson reason from Sicily to a Spanish colony in Central America, but with a lovely saucy Beatrice from Sylvia Sims and a sparkling witty Benedict in John Neville. Aristophanes *Peace* from the Deutches Theater in Berlin pioneered the odd continuing Festival concept of presenting plays written in one foreign language in the aspects and traditions of another unfamiliar tongue and then offering the audience irritatingly buzzing simultaneous translation machines to baffle out what is going on. However the Berliners from Max Reinhardt's old house managed to be sufficiently operatic in gesture to flog the peace message but rather missed the comedy in ponderous frolic.

In the Lyceum there was also an outstanding production of a much-neglected 17th-century English play *The Changeling* by Thomas Middleton and William Rowley directed with intelligence and sensitivity by Richard Eyre with a superb central performance from David Burke as the betrayed servant, De Flores: a rather understrength Pirandello *Henry IV* from the Leeds Playhouse at the Church Hill, enigmatic but lacking the menace in the puzzle of relative identity which makes this play so remarkable. At Haymarket Ice Rink there was real theatrical innovation in a wonderfully spectacular production of *Orlando Furioso* by Luca Ronconi and the Teatro Libero from Rome.

Based on the greatest poem of the Cinquecento by Lodovico Ariosto – the prime mover in establishing Italian as a literary language in the 16th century – it involved the audiences to a degree never seen before. *Lingua Toscana in bocca Romana* (a Tuscan tongue in a Roman mouth) the Italians say for an ideal speaking of their language but this reworking of the Charlemanic Roland legend which made Tuscan standard Italian speech was not about language but action. The knights charged through the audience on gorgeously caparisoned wooden horses on wheels. The narrative came from platforms around the arena by sighing heroines and screaming witches, proselytising priests and sonorous heroes in a dazzling display of inventive theatre which had everyone reeling with delight, emotive drama and surprise.

On this high note in a fine robust Italian hand of *panache* and theatrical splendour the Festival completed the first half of its history.

XII

As the 25th Edinburgh Festival, 1971 was always going to be a special year, magic numbers providing a good excuse for asking for more money to make an even more special occasion out of an already remarkable event. Inevitably it caused municipal ill-feeling. There had been resentment in previous years that the City could unhesitatingly spend several million pounds on the construction of a new sports stadium at Meadowbank and the Commonwealth Swimming Pool in the shadow of Arthur's Seat for the

Commonwealth Games of 1970, an event which so far has appeared in Edinburgh twice in 25 years, but would not provide for the much needed opera house for an event which brought prestige, tourists and revenue to the city every year.

There had been talk of tying the Festival grant from the Corporation to one penny on the rates so that Festival income could keep pace with the cost of living. This would have helped in the six years since Festival accounts were submitted to a civic system of budgetary control in 1964. But that calculation did not show the City Fathers in a very generous light.

In 1964 the City collected £11 million in rates; in 1969 the sum was £21 million. In that period the contribution to the Festival had risen from £75,000 to £80,000 – an increase of just £5,000. In 1969 the Italian government had spent more on the Edinburgh Festival than Edinburgh and the British government combined and of course the City was recouping from the Festival substantial rents on the Usher Hall, the King's, Royal Lyceum and Church Hill theatres, the Assembly Rooms in George Street and the Festival offices in Market Street.

When the City contribution to the Silver Jubilee Festival was debated in the Council Chamber in October 1970 Lord Provost Sir James McKay proposed that the grant for 1971 should be increased by 20 per cent to £100,000.

Councillor Peter Wilson, leader of the Labour group, proposed that it should be reduced and said of the Lord Provost's claim that the Festival had put Edinburgh on the world map: 'Perhaps this is true. But as far as being on the map is concerned, I think Edinburgh is well to the fore in the world as a sewage preservation society.' Councillor Kidd proposed that the new sports centre at Meadowbank should be used as an opera house.

This set the tone of municipal debate for several years to come in the run-up to 1974 when the local authority structure was to be changed creating regional as well as civic authorities. However McKay managed to push through his proposed new grant despite virulent protests from the opposition.

Announcing plans for the Silver Jubilee Festival, Peter Diamand praised the box-office support received from people in Edinburgh and around. 'In Salzburg and Bayreuth,' he said, 'people take great pride in their festivals but they do not participate to the same extent as the citizens of Edinburgh.'

Despite all the snide stories backed up by smirking Edinburgh householders who were prone to boast that they never went to the Festival but rented their houses to visitors at exorbitant profits, it has always been statistically true that the biggest market for Festival tickets is Edinburgh and the rest of Scotland. The city's warped sense of humour was neatly summed up in private by Peter Diamand who said 'Festival-going in Edinburgh is a secret vice. People do it but they don't talk about it.'

All five Festival Directors contributed memories and observations to the 1971 Souvenir Programme. At the end of his contribution Diamand wrote:

> *After 25 years I believe that the Festival, while having sustained and perhaps enhanced its international reputation, is even more deeply rooted in Edinburgh and Scotland than it was – also perhaps because more Scottish artists than ever are involved in it. I believe too that younger audiences take a more active interest in the Festival than they used to do. To keep their interest alive will be an important task, a great challenge for the coming years.*
>
> *The city and the citizens of Edinburgh will continue to be a splendid host to the artists and to the visitors – not the boastful flashy sometimes oppressive kind – more in that cautious yet reliable spirit in which one Edinburgh citizen summed up his feelings last year: 'I quite liked the Festival, I even enjoyed it. All in all we are none the worse for it.'*

The Silver Jubilee programme was a strange mixture. The trusted formula of a featured composer or composers was abandoned and the only anniversary which could be found to be celebrated was the bicentenary of the birth of Sir Walter Scott – an obligatory civic cheer for a city which has a Gothic rocket housing a marble statue of him dominating its main street. However the remembrances were rather low key.

Parliament House, the 17th-century building in the Old Town where the last Scots parliament met, now the centre of one of the few systems which has survived its final deliberations, the Scottish legal establishment, housed an exhibition of paintings of the author and his contemporaries borrowed from the National Portrait Gallery, Scott's house at Abbotsford and other sources, manuscripts, first editions and the sort of romantic historical knick-knacks which the writer of the *Waverley Novels* liked to collect, along with letters from Byron, Goethe, Wordsworth and other literary worthies.

In 'Writer to the Nation' appropriately set in Waverley Market, John L. Paterson attempted to re-create 'in visual and aural terms something of the quality of the writer and his work to breathe life into what is only a name to the wider public', a well-meaning but uphill task.

'Singular Grace' in St Cecilia's Hall offered, in four afternoon recitals, readings from Scott's poetry and prose by Lennox Milne, Tom Fleming and Richard Todd; while the Freemasons' Hall had 'Walter Scott in Music and Song', a morning concert in which Jill Gomez from Guiana, Peter Gellhorn from Germany and Peter Katin from England performed Scott-related works by Schubert, Liszt and Francis George Scott. Although this trio gave substance to the internationality of Scott's appeal, surprisingly there were no major musical tributes to a writer who had created the market for the romantic historical novel all over Europe and who had inspired no fewer than 40 operas, some by composers as famous as himself such as Rossini, Donizetti, Bellini, Flotow, Pacini, Nicolai, Auber, Adam and Bizet. Nor were any of the numerous plays stemming from his works part of the programme although mercifully we were spared *The Doom of Devorgoil*, Scott's only venture into the field – for him a morass – of drama.

Instead there was an opera programme which did not seem to follow any pattern but that of diversity – perhaps no bad theme for a Festival as diffuse as Edinburgh.

Under the banner of Edinburgh Festival Opera – a name that was to become more significant in the next few years but in this instance represented a co-operation with the Maggio Musicale Fiorentino – came Rossini. As an exact contemporary of Sir Walter Scott his *La Donna del Lago* or *Ivanhoe* might well have been considered as suitable anniversary material. However no-one could quarrel with the choice of *La Cenerentola*, Rossini's version of the Cinderella story, one of his most delightful and musically imaginative operas.

Produced and designed by Jean-Pierre Ponnelle, it was given a sparkling performance by the London Symphony Orchestra under Abbado, with Teresa Berganza as the much put-upon but eventually forgiving Angelina, Luigi Alva as the Prince and Paolo Montarsolo as a wonderfully bumbling Don Magnifico and the ensemble work in the scintillating vocal crescendos sung with stunning virtuosity and attack.

Cenerentola was followed by Wagner (of whom Rossini memorably said 'he has some beautiful moments but some terrible quarters of an hour') in Scottish Opera's *Die Walkure*. It emerged sufficiently from the original gloom in which it had been presented in the company's 1966 season not to remind us too often of Rossini's jibe, in an enlivened setting from designer Michael Knight and a sharpened production by Peter Ebert. The demanding leading roles were finely sung by Helga Dernesch as Brunnhilde, David Ward as Wotan and Charles Craig as Siegmund with a powerful Fricka from Anna Reynolds.

There were problems with the programme of the Deutsche Oper Berlin which had originally included an opera based on Shakespeare's only Viennese play and one of his most complexly motivated works, *Measure for Measure* by Nicolas Nabokov, which were, for once, nothing to do with the inadequacies of the King's Theatre. In its place the Berlin company brought a strange update of the water-sprite theme by

Aribert Reimann, *Melusine* which brought the luckless lake fairy up against all kinds of contemporary problems like pollution and industrial unrest in a production chiefly remarkable for providing yet another sensational role for the splendid talents of Catherine Gayer. *Die Entführung aus dem Serail* Mozart's endearing fairy tale of the abduction from the harem is the happiest of his operas. Unfortunately it did not find Erika Koth as Constanze in top form although Werner Hollweg as Belmonte and Bent Rundgren as a worthily sinister Osmin did their best to liven things up.

There did not seem to be much pattern to the theatre contributions either.

Jack Ronder's *Confessions of a Justified Sinner* was a brave attempt to make theatrical sense of the extraordinary novel by 'The Ettrick Shepherd' James Hogg, who sent ballads to Walter Scott for his collection of Border minstrelsy and who gave up farming for literature without much success. Patronised as a bumpkin by Edinburgh *literati*, Scott said of him 'The poor fellow has just talent sufficient to spoil him for his own trade, without having enough to support him by literature.'

This does Hogg considerably less than justice. *The Private Memoirs and Confessions of a Justified Sinner* was written in 1824, a powerful narrative essay on the duality of self written 30 years before Freud was born. This rigorous moral analysis was difficult to dramatise but Jack Ronder made a bold stab at it and Richard Eyre's direction certainly gave the piece considerable atmosphere and tension with Russell Hunter playing Hogg himself with sympathetic bravura. *Confessions* has reappeared on stage since as a play by Liz Lochead and an impressive opera by Thomas Wilson

There were no puzzles to be solved nor souls to be scoured at the Haymarket Ice Rink where Frank Dunlop and the Young Vic in a circus tent setting made pantomime Scotch nonsense of Shakespeare's *The Comedy of Errors*, following the all too pervasive fashion of moving the location of the play and embellishing it with local and contemporary references. 'The text becomes much clearer when spoken with a Scots accent,' said Dunlop. 'English voices make Shakespeare sound like lukewarm bathwater.'

Moving the location from Ephesus to Edinburgh proved a stroke of genius. The whole thing was a glorious romp with Denise Coffey wonderfully funny as a harassed Edinburgh housewife and Edward Fox ineffably superior as Antipholus of Edinburgh and hilariously outrageous performances from Alex McEvoy and Ian Trigger to the merry accompaniment of two pipers and an accordionist. Audiences packed it out and it proved so popular that it was repeated in 1972.

Just to recall us to the validity of the Presbyterian ethic, Prospect Theatre's *King Lear* directed by Toby Robertson in the Assembly Hall was stark and bleak, symbolically costumed in sack-cloth with a strong, agonised forsaken performance central to old tribal values from Timothy West as the deposed King.

Predicated too heavily on Gloucester's 'As flies to wanton boys, are we to the gods, They kill us for their sport', it induced a longing that Verdi's life-long desire to make an opera out of *Lear* had been fulfilled because only music could truly illuminate and transform this nobly-worded but thawless litany of misery and rejection into greatness. 'Ripeness is all,' as Edgar says in supreme irony for there is no ripeness just a terrible final withering – perhaps, in the ultimate analysis, the true message of the play.

The Romanians from the Bulandra Theatre offered slapstick in *Carnival Scenes* and a surprising romantic fantasy from the author of *Woyzeck* and *Danton's Death*, 19th-century German playwright Georg Buchner's *Leonce and Lena* done with great flair and style. The two American companies who brought plays to the Festival, Long Wharf Theatre and The Manhattan Project, failed to arouse any enthusiasm.

There was no lack of it however for Flemming Flindt and the Royal Danish Ballet whose programmes brilliantly combined the traditional ballets by Bournonville and Balanchine for which they were famous with new works by Flindt himself, John Cranko and Roland Petit, danced with formidable accomplishment and grace by a highly talented company.

The opening concert of the Silver Jubilee Festival was something of a marathon for the Festival Chorus.

With Gibson and the Scottish National Orchestra they sang his *Ave Maria* and *Pater Noster* as a tribute to Igor Stravinsky who had died in April of that year; Thomas Wilson's newly commissioned *Te Deum for Orchestra and Chorus* and Walton's *Belshazzar's Feast* with John Shirley Quirk as soloist with a respite only while Yehudi Menuhin played the Elgar Violin Concerto. The London Philharmonic Orchestra under Bernard Haitink gave an all-Russian programme and a concert with Victoria de los Angeles singing the two arias from the last act of Verdi's *Otello* before Bruckner's *Third Symphony*; Josef Krips with the same orchestra brought two largely Viennese evenings plus Pierre Fournier with the Schumann Cello Concerto and Boulez inspired the National Youth Orchestra in a lively concert of Bartok, Berg and Webern culminating in an exciting performance of Debussy's *La Mer*.

The Israel Philharmonic came to the Festival for the first time with Zubin Mehta in three very classical concerts with Barenboim and Pinchas Zukerman as soloists and the Chorus featured again in a spacious and dynamic performance of Mahler's *Resurrection Symphony* with Margaret Price and Janet Baker and Abbado conducting the London Symphony Orchestra. Scots composer Thea Musgrave's *Clarinet Concerto* with Gervase de Peyer as soloist wandering minstrel-like among the players of the London Symphony Orchestra, conducted by André Previn made an interesting evening sandwiched between the Berlioz *Rob Roy* overture and Rachmaninoff's *Second Symphony*.

The Chicago Symphony Orchestra made its Festival debut on its 80th birthday with resident *maestro* Georg Solti and principal guest conductor Giulini in four concerts which featured only one piece of American music, Elliott Carter's *Variations for Orchestra* but emphasised yet again the superb quality of the leading American orchestras and the individual character of each, marked by the sensitive and lyrical strings of the Chicago and the wonderful clarity and incisiveness of the woodwind.

Brahms, Mozart, Mahler, Berlioz, Stravinsky, Prokoviev and Ravel were all presented with that shining newness of interpretation which shows the virtuosity of a great musical instrument.

In the galleries in addition to the Scott exhibitions, the Royal Scottish Academy was home to the first large-scale post-war exhibition of its kind in Britain, *The Belgian Contribution to Surrealism* a dream show of the work produced in Belgium in response to the *First Surrealist Manifesto* by poet André Breton in 1924 'the artist revealing in broad daylight what he has seen in the night of his mind'.

The mysterious quality of the paintings, often executed with singularly stark clarity was disturbing and compelling, particularly when delineated with a lack of obvious emotion. René Magritte, Paul Delvaux, Jacques Cheamy and E. L. T. Mesens, who had died just two months before the exhibition, and a host of others represented this tortured half-world of the imagination. Rikki Demarco brought *Contemporary Romanian Art* to his gallery, claiming that this modern art was clearly derived from simple peasant motifs but the images of the eleven artists on show were most certainly vigorously contemporary.

A delightful and entertaining addition to the art shows was an exhibition of *Coia Caricatures*, drawings and sketches of Festival personalities and places which Emilio Coia, the talented Scottish/Italian artist had contributed to the pages of *The Scotsman* for the previous 17 years, a tradition most happily and most wittily continued up to his death in 1997.

For all its seeming shapelessness the 1971 Festival was a great success. When the figures were published in April 1972 there was a surplus of £21,940 and the revenue had risen to £272,530, an increase of £76,000 and the highest in Festival history.

The Festival of 1972 dodged nimbly between the centuries. In the Usher Hall the musical stress was on the 20th century, particularly on recent Polish music but the opening concert struck a more domestic note. It was the centenary of the birth of Ralph Vaughan Williams and the first concert, given by the Royal Philharmonic conducted by his old friend Sir Adrian Boult, was devoted to his works.

The Festival Chorus sang *Dona Nobis Pacem* and *Job A Masque for Dancing*, a ballet score which Vaughan Williams based on Blake's *Illustrations of the Book of Job* and which is dedicated to Boult, made up the rest of the programme.

The two Polish composers featured were the 59-year-old Witold Lutoslawski and his 20-years-younger compatriot, Krzysztof Penderecki, both considered *avant-garde* at some time in their careers. Lutoslwaski's *avantgardisme* was Bartok-related – by even 1972 considered rather old hat – whereas Penderecki's was more way out and tended to go in for sounds difficult to make with conventional musical instruments such as wood sawing, mechanised screeching and the clacking of typewriters. However, the purpose of music is the communication of emotions and ideas and the younger man certainly seemed to get through to people notably in his *St Luke Passion*.

A powerful performance of a recent work *Utrenja* depicting in two parts the entombment and the resurrection of Christ, given by the Cracow Philharmonic under Jerzy Natlewicz in the High Kirk of St Giles made a searing impression. This dynamic interweave of archaic and dissonantly modern sounds at extremes of range varying from a bass snarl to the tenor G above high C was tense and high drama which seemed to justify Peter Heyworth's description:

> *Unencumbered by either Stalinism or serialism, he has established himself as a composer who seems to have dissolved the barriers between avant-garde music and the ordinary concert-goer.*

Lutoslawski conducted a section of the Scottish National Orchestra and the Festival Chorus in his percussive *Three Poems by Henri Michaud*; the Royal Philharmonic gave a bold concert under Lawrence Foster which included Charles Ives alongside two Polish composers with a fine-spun ecstatic account of the Szymanowski First Violin Concerto and a brilliantly spiky interpretation of Penderecki's Violin Capriccio from the young Polish soloist, Wanda Wilkomirska. A concert in which Rudolf Kempe conducted the same orchestra introduced us to a thrilling new young singer with a voice of remarkable beauty and character, the black soprano Jessye Norman singing Mahler and Schumann, Brahms, Strauss and Ravel in another recital, 'bitter-sweet poignancy without a trace of sentimentality'.

There were divisions of opinion as to whether the greatest excitement was in the opera or the drama. To the King's, which had a brand new lighting board and a newly excavated orchestra pit, the Deutsche Opera am Rhein from Dusseldorf brought Bernd-Alois Zimmermann's 'unperformable' *Die Soldaten* based on a play by Jakob Michael Reinhold Lenz, friend to Goethe and a founder of the *sturm und drang*, the storm and stress philosophy of the German 18th-century romantic movement, which pleaded for human rights and a return to the direct influences of nature. Zimmermann interprets this comparatively simple message in the heart-cry of a middle-class girl: 'Must those who suffer live in fear? Can only the wrong-doers be glad?' when she is destroyed by the heartless philandering of well-born young officers of a military garrison – with pluralistic opera. A concentration of all available media, light and movement, tapes and cinema projection, sub-divided stages operating together, dance, speech and every form of music from lyric theatre to jazz and *musique concrete*, it was undeniably a remarkable piece of theatre set to music of a high emotional strike rate which you might not instantly whistle in your bath but whose sheer weight of dramatic impact went far beyond the 'good tune' concept into a wholeness of operatic *force de frappe* which was highly memorable.

'*Die Soldaten* is a triumph for Dusseldorf and a triumph for modern opera,' said the critics.

> *The Dusseldorf production is a simplification of his (Zimmermann's) aims,* wrote Peter Heyworth, *but highly impressive and ingenious in its telling of the bourgeois tragedy and powerfully rams home the universal message about war and man's inhumanity to man. From the pounding tread of its prelude right through to the closing minutes when the two cinema screens show boots tramping across the*

centuries it casts a powerful spell. The strong, moving and finally shattering production by Georg Reinhardt and the designs by Heinrich Wendel incorporating three cine screens, a revolve, sliding tracks and a corps de ballet dominated by a red-head with a whip, are backed by a magnificent cast with Catherine Gayer tackling her formidable vocal leaps while degenerating from middle-class miss to regimental whore. Die Soldaten *packs a punch I would hardly have credited to a serial opera.*

Some pointed out the score's indebtedness to Alban Berg's *Wozzeck*. No-one mentioned the influence which J. M. R. Lenz's play had on *Wozzeck's* original creator Georg Buchner. There was, however, no argument about the noble origins of the *magnum opus* which Scottish Opera brought to the 1972 Festival. Although Gounod said of Hector Berlioz: 'Like his heroic namesake he perished on the walls of Troy', Berlioz's monumental operatic version of Virgil's *Aeneid* had since been reclaimed as a masterpiece not least when in 1969 Scottish Opera had given the first uncut performance of the work in Glasgow.

Berlioz had such travails with *The Trojans* that he never saw a complete production. *The Trojans at Carthage* the second half of this epic work was played at the Théâtre Lyrique in Paris on 4 November 1863 in a truncated form after endless battles about cuts, scenery, instrumentation and costumes vividly and bitterly delineated by Berlioz in his *Memoirs*.

The full score was not in fact published until 1969, the centenary of his death and Scottish Opera's performance in that year was the first complete version ever staged. However, as Berlioz had written the libretto as well as the music, royalties from the 1863 performance at least brought him some relief. He was able to give up his work as a music critic! I quote from the brilliant translation of the *Memoirs* by David Cairns published by Victor Gollancz in 1969:

> *To my unutterable joy I perceived that the interest from these combined sums would just about equal my annual income from the* Journal des débats *and I at once resigned from my post as critic. At last, at long last, after 30 years of slavery I was free. Free – with no more feuilletons to write, no more platitudes to condone, no more mediocrities to praise, no more rage to repress, no more lies, no more make-believe, no more ignoble time-serving. I need not set foot in an opera house again, I need never speak of an opera house or listen to anyone speak of an opera house, nor even have to laugh at the messes they concoct in these great stew-pots.* Gloria in excelsis Deo, et in terra pax hominibus bonae voluntatis!

Although Berlioz cannot have been the easiest of composers to work with it seems one of musical history's real tragedies that he could not have seen the splendid production and the zestful and inspired performance his six-hour work was given at the Edinburgh Festival. Helga Dernesch as Cassandra and Janet Baker as Dido were truly magnificent, Gregory Dempsey made a handsome and clear voiced Aeneas, the lavish presentation and the savage pagan Trojan horse gave visual and barbaric grandeur to the settings. Alexander Gibson's invocation of the subtle rhythms and the lyrical pulsing splendour of the vast score moving from

Sir Alexander Gibson

111

tenderness to pomp and celebration to tragedy and loss from the SNO was one of his greatest operatic achievements.

After all this innovation, incisive and glorious sound and spectacle, the opera from Sicily, the Teatro Massimo in Palermo, was something of an anti-climax. The programme was interesting enough: Verdi's *Attila*, Rossini's *Elisabetta, Regina d'Inghilterra* and Bellini's *La Straniera*. The native Sicilian Bellini wrote some ravishing music for *La Straniera* but the plot by Felice Romani is of such tortuous and fatuous complexity that it is easy to grow intolerant of its unravelling and the Teatro Massimo production did little to help. *Elisabetta* is not one of Rossini's best operas. Written when he was 23 and involving two of Mary Queen of Scots' non-existent children, its score was heavily mined of the better numbers for later works (including the overture which is virtually identical to that of *The Barber of Seville* and was originally cannibalised from *Aureliano in Palmira!*): 23 years later Rossini wrote to the impresario of the Pergola Theatre in Florence, Andrea Bandini suggesting – apropos of *Elisabetta* – 'Such operas ought to be left in peace.'

Attila is quite a different matter. It was one of Verdi's progress operas in which he was feeling his way towards future, more profound musical characterisation. Rossini ironically christened Verdi *The Composer in the Helmet* and this was one of his works which aroused nationalistic fervour and what to Venice's Austrian masters were unseemly scenes in the theatre when it was premiered at La Fenice in 1846. It is one of the strangest official oversights that the Roman general Ezio's *Avrai tu l'universo, resti l'Italia a me!* (To you the universe but leave Italy to me!) in his duet with Attila in the prologue ever passed the censors who caused Verdi so much trouble with many other operas. There is a lot of stirring and tuneful music in *Attila* but the Palermo production was rather stilted and old-fashioned and although there was a fine central performance from Ruggero Raimondi, a great bass in thrilling voice as Attila, Renato Bruson as Ezio was disappointing and Luisa Maragliano as the vengeful but seductive Odabella was rather too forceful and strident to be convincing.

One other opera experience however was outstanding. Peter Williams wrote:

> *I don't see how anything in the whole Festival can be more beautiful than certain moments of Cavalieri's* Representation of the Soul and Body *in Deutsche Oper's production in St Mary's Cathedral – no wonder the work created such a stir in 1600 – its beauty is direct and affecting. That Deutsche Oper can mount both this and* Die Soldaten *within a few days of each other is not the least striking thing of the evening. The Soul is personified by Rachel Yakar, Body as Man by Peter-Christophe Runge – so movingly told nobody knew at the end whether to clap or not.*

In the Royal Lyceum there were Noh plays from Japan, long ceremonial rituals with impassive-faced actors gliding across a fixed screen backdrop of a painted tree, voices tuned like instruments accompanied by a chorus changing to a high-pitched flute and drums. The Kyogen comic interludes in between plays were more lively and better appreciated, but most of the audience looked fairly baffled. There was also the newly formed Actors Company (everything done by discussion including casting and production, no stars, one for all and all for one) which had Ian McKellen playing a walk-on spotty page boy in a Feydeau farce; and a tedious bit of theatrical questing after *Moby Dick* from the Gruppo Sperimentazione Teatrale from Rome at the Church Hill Theatre. The long slow search for the white whale was largely unobserved and unappreciated in the audience's uncomprehending and unfeeling flight into the street.

Frank Dunlop added to the repeat of *The Comedy of Errors* at the Haymarket Ice Rink a striking half-hit *Bible One*. Allen Wright wrote:

> *Frank Dunlop conjures up the happiest half-hour of the Festival. His production of* Joseph and the Amazing Technicoloured Dreamcoat *bubbles with joy but is so brief one would like to see it performed in triplicate.*

Encores of this Pop oratorio would be more enjoyable than the series of Wakefield Mystery Plays which form the first part of this theatrical presentation of Genesis.
The Assembly Hall housed blood and thunder on an epic scale in a massive and sensational production by Glasgow Citizens' Theatre of Marlowe's *Tamburlaine the Great* directed with vivacity and boundless panache by Keith Hack. The forecourt of the Assembly Hall beneath the disapproving gaze of the minatory statue of John Knox warned of the pagan barbarity to come as audiences were greeted by a fire-eater, a boa-constrictor and a kilted monkey. To the accompaniment of anachronistic organ music the blood-drenched saga of conquest swept across the pews of the Kirk's parliament as 'The scourge of God and the terror of the world' pursued his relentless way played by three actors, Rupert Frazer as the young conqueror, Jeffrey Kissoon as the sullen ruthless monster and Mike Gwilym as the mellowed master of the world.

Harold Hobson loved it: 'An adornment to the Festival,' he wrote, 'I have never seen the resources of the sombre Assembly Hall so richly or imaginatively exploited.'

PETER DIAMAND 1966-78
Diamand Years II: The Phantom of the Opera House

XVIII

In his introduction to the Souvenir Programme for the 1973 Festival Edinburgh's first Labour Lord Provost Jack Kane struck an optimistic note:

Those who come to Edinburgh year by year at Festival time – and they are a growing number – know that no Edinburgh Festival is quite like any other. Each has its own special individual quality that fixes it in the mind and makes it easier to recall with pleasure. One seldom knows in advance what the quality will be, and indeed it will be different for different individuals. This year too each will find his own intangibles. But there are tangible things too that will set 1973 apart as a memorable year. The Festival has had a few 'firsts' but surely few more notable than the Festival Society's own first opera production. Still more significant for the Festival's future are the decisions now finally taken to build a new theatre that will provide a fitting setting for Festival Opera and to reconstruct the Lyceum as a home for drama.

In material terms the completion of these projects will remove the limitations that have inhibited Festival productions in the past and give vastly greater scope to artists and directors. To audiences they will bring higher standards of comfort and convenience.

But they have a deeper meaning too. They are a firm expression of our confidence in the future of the Festival and our determination to encourage and develop the arts not only at Festival time but throughout the year. We hope that we are creating places of pilgrimage not only for our welcome visitors from abroad but for the Scots as well. The realisation of these dreams still lies a little way to the future. In the meantime let us enjoy together the riches of 1973.

Brave words and I am sure that Jack Kane, a fine honest man and an excellent Lord Provost, meant and believed every one of them but time and Edinburgh were to prove him an ill prophet.

The development of its own opera production company had long been one of Peter Diamand's plans for the Festival. He had mentioned it at his very first press conference in 1965 when he took over from Lord Harewood. There had been previous co-productions with other festivals – Holland for *Don Giovanni* in 1965 and the Maggio Musicale Fiorentino for *La Cenerentola* in 1971 – but the idea that Edinburgh should choose its own opera and take on the task of hiring the singers, the director, the orchestra, the conductor, the set and costume designers and all the other responsibilities inherent in such a venture was a daunting prospect.

It was planned as a long-term venture. The chosen opera was to be given at the Festival for two consecutive years and plans were already in the pipeline for a six year programme covering three operas. The choice for 1973/74 was Mozart's *Don Giovanni*. The English Chamber Orchestra was in the pit, Scottish Opera Chorus, which had appeared before with visiting companies, played their part, the producer and designer was Peter Ustinov and the conductor Daniel Barenboim. As Ustinov was better known as an actor, comedian and playwright than as an opera director and designer and Barenboim had never conducted an opera before, there were some doubting off-stage mutterings but Gerald Larner, the *Guardian* music critic did not share them:

The Edinburgh Festival has staked a lot in mounting its own production of Don Giovanni *– a lot of money and a lot of reputation too. Peter Diamand and his colleagues would* *look rather silly, if, after all the controversial years of buying operatic productions from elsewhere, they themselves could do no better at far greater expense.*

Was the festival director wise in appointing Daniel Barenboim, who has never worked in opera before, as conductor? And was it commercial or artistic instinct that led him to engage Peter Ustinov as director and designer?

At the first performance on Monday the musical events can only have enhanced Edinburgh's reputation. In fact there has rarely been such a well-prepared musical performance in the King's Theatre.

Daniel Barenboim

Not all of Peter Ustinov's theories about the theatrical side of *Don Giovanni* were as well received as Roger Soyer's suave handsome Don, Geraint Evans's jolly round-cheeked Leporello and Barenboim's pointed and accomplished handling of the score.

The ending of the opera when the statue of the Commendatore comes to dinner on Giovanni's invitation and delivers the Don to Hell has always been controversial. There have been productions in which Giovanni's dramatic descent to eternal doom has been the ending and the final moralizing sextet *Questo il fin di chi fa mal* (this is the end of evil-doers) is dropped. Mozart himself changed several things including the ending between the première in Prague in December 1787 and the first performance in Vienna six months later. Ustinov caused a furore when he added an extra touch, as he recounts in his memoirs, *Dear Me*:

> *Oh, you should have heard the outcry from the purists when I brought two policemen on at the end, late as ever, to measure the hole through which Don Giovanni had disappeared in preparation for a long-winded report to Madrid! What was the justification for such a facetious conceit? Quite simply signori miei, that they are in the text if you only bother to look. Don Ottavio, frustrated in his attempt to rid the world of Don Giovanni (largely owing to the influence of the women who can't bear to see their tormentor dispatched), has recourse to Madrid with a formal charge which he waves about as he swears revenge, and he returns finally, when it's too late to matter, with due ufficiali.*

And of course it is exactly the kind of thing that the rather wimpish Don Ottavio (who allows himself endlessly to be fobbed off by Donna Anna) would do and if you look at the introduction to his second act solo *Il mio tesoro*, there he is saying he is going off to inform 'the proper authorities' as soon as he's finished his aria.

There were five *Don Giovannis* that year and the rest of the programme at the King's Theatre was occupied by two performances of Britten's latest opera *Death in Venice* by The English Opera Group and a mixed programme of opera and ballet from the Hungarian State Opera.

Death in Venice had had its première at Aldeburgh just two months earlier. I had listened to it on the radio without really catching on to the ambience and mood of the piece which Gillian Widdicombe of *The Financial Times* called Britten's 'most painful resourceful expression of sophisticated passion and many-layered surrender' but in the theatre the experience was quite different. The story from Thomas Mann's novella of an eminent and highly intelligent man tortured by the guilt and lust of being mesmerised by the beauty of a boy he sees on the beach of the Venice Lido is a delicate and complex one which Britten set with great skill and intensity and it was given a performance wholly worthy of its quality.

In her review Miss Widdicombe bemoaned its brief showing:

A shame that only two (performances) were feasible, for Death in Venice *is one of those superficially ambiguous, complex operas demanding and deserving time and thought for just appreciation. It does not seek to stun, as did the* War Requiem *or shock, as Tippett did in* The Knot Garden *and has nothing at all in common with the shallow pretty-picture world of Visconti's film of the same name: its theatrical power is far removed from the world of grand climax, finger-tip lyricism, blatant emotions. But that ironic restrained theatrical power is enhanced, if anything by the transfer of the English Opera Group's excellent production from the open stage of The Maltings to the intimate surroundings of the King's Theatre. The small theatre allows the singers to communicate without strain those passages of half-knowing, half-innocent suggestion, led by a truly great performance by Peter Pears as Aschenbach, haunting ones of his many sinister roles by John Shirley Quirk and fine playing by the English Chamber Orchestra conducted by Steuart Bedford.*

From the Hungarians came Sandor Szokolay's *Blood Wedding*, tensely introspective and based on the play by the Spanish poet Federico Garcia Lorca and Bartok's only opera *Duke Bluebeard's Castle* a grim and highly charged symbolic examination of the Bluebeard story in one act. Set in a gloomy Gothic windowless castle with seven doors behind each of which lies the terrible blood-spattered secrets of Bluebeard's murderous past, this two-character unveiling had great power and atmosphere if very little action. It made an impressive evening in the theatre in combination with the mysterious decadence and barbaric fury of the composer's most famous ballet score, *The Miraculous Mandarin* brilliantly danced by the Hungarian Ballet with a marvellous central performance by Vera Szumrák as the girl. By contrast the Hungarian dancers' other performance, the three-act *Spartacus* to the music of Khatchaturian, although full of vigour and spectacle, seemed curiously lacking in depth and characterisation.

In the Usher Hall a concert by the London Symphony Orchestra under Giulini offered a rarity which did not seem to be able to decide whether it was oratorio or opera, Schumann's *Das Paradies und die Peri* – the forerunner of many Festival concert performances of opera. It had its origin in the best-selling poem *Lalla Rookh*, a series of oriental verse-tales with prose links which made Irish poet Thomas Moore a European reputation in the early years of the 19th century.

Schumann considered it one of his greatest works 'a poem made for music', this tale of the Peri, a fallen angel who, as the price of her return to Paradise, must scour the world for 'the gift that is most dear to Heaven'. With a strong cast which included Edith Mathis, Birgit Finnila, Peter Pears, Wolfgang Brendel, Sheila Armstrong, Thomas Allen, Anthony Rolfe-Johnson and the Edinburgh Festival Chorus it proved to be work of genuine enchantment full of wonderfully lyrical and atmospheric music which seemed to invite strongly a spectacular operatic production on a less bloodthirsty scenario than the oriental excursions of Puccini and Delibes.

There was also a fine bouncingly energetic and impassioned account of Mahler's Second Symphony from Leonard Bernstein with the LSO and André Previn's interpretation with the same orchestra of Shostakovich's war-torn brutal and desolate Eighth Symphony – written at the time of the battle for Stalingrad – was a starkly moving experience. A new young Italian conductor 32-year old Riccardo Muti made a good impression with the New Philharmonia in works ranging from Vivaldi and Cherubini to Prokoviev. Boulez conducting the BBC Symphony in a concert which included one of his own works *ee cummings ist der dichter* as well as a piece by the great Swiss oboeist Heinz Holliger ensured that *avant-garde* music had an Usher Hall showing and there was a spirited largely French programme in two concerts from the Orchestre de Paris including a new piece by Boulez pupil Gilbert Amy and a wildly pagan performance of *Le Sacré du Printemps* under the baton of Georg Solti. Altogether a fascinatingly varied and star-studded series of concerts.

As usual the immensely popular chamber music concerts were a kaleidoscope of styles, periods and ideas. Martha Argerich and the Amadeus with Cecil Aronowitz played Mozart piano sonatas and three of the great quintets; Cathy Berberian with Bruno Canino provided two evenings of skilful and very funny musical satire in *A la Recherche de la Musique perdue*, Peter Williams with Les Clavecinistes francais played Couperin and Rameau in St Cecilia's Hall and Holliger was everywhere.

Gillian Widdicombe thought that Holliger's performances ranged from the fascinating to the silly and cited as an example the long-winded late-night concert in the Assembly Hall full of improvisations and schoolboyish musical jokes which continued long after most of the audience had departed, 'bored blue' as she tersely put it. Of the rest of the chamber music she said:

> *This year Edinburgh has made a deliberate assault on the musical avant-garde. A high-powered hand-picked assault of international calibre, far removed from the kind of play-school prattling that seems to get sheltered by impressive initials. From Stuttgart the unrivalled Schola Cantorum came: 16 singers as skilled in the arts and invention of contemporary vocalising as the inimitable sorceress Cathy Berberian. And the original Miss Berberian came too, for two performances of her nostalgic* A la Recherche de la Musique perdue. *There were two concerts by Les Percussions de Strasbourg and several featuring the Swiss Heinz Holliger. So Peter Diamand has added at last, a contemporary link to the Lord Provost's musical chain.*

Unfortunately the same interest was not provided by the 1973 drama. Because of the expense of mounting the special Festival opera production, despite protests from the Festival Director, there was less money available for the theatre and it showed.

A fifth revival of *The Thrie Estaites* at the Assembly Hall by the Royal Lyceum Company used a new adaptation of the text by Tom Wright and Bill Bryden was the director. But such changes only underlined the proven virtues of Robert Kemp's version of Lyndsay's play and the brilliance with which Tyrone Guthrie (who had died in 1971) had directed it. It was an unfortunate year for Edinburgh's most original venue in which Guthrie had pioneered the thrust stage, for Georg Buchner's *Woyzeck* of which the Young Lyceum Company gave seven matinee performances at the Assembly Hall was also a disappointment.

There were divided opinions about the early Chekhov *The Wood Demon* which was later re-written as *Uncle Vanya*. With intricate text and character analysis, Robert Cushman in *The Observer* managed to find in it the seed-bed of not only *Vanya* but also of *The Seagull, The Three Sisters* and *The Cherry Orchard!* The Actors' Company production by David Giles in the Royal Lyceum was well received and a wistful success with Ian McKellen an appealing Khruschov but there was always the feeling that it was not a very good play and that this talented company of actors was wasting its time on it.

The reverse was true of the David Williams's production of Congreve's *The Way of the World*, undoubtedly a good play but thrown out of focus by being perversely set in the Edwardian period to which neither its language nor its manners could adapt successfully.

Whether or not *Pericles* is a good play is as open to question as whether or not it is by Shakespeare. Scholars agree that it is certainly not all by Shakespeare and the plot is so convoluted that it seems very likely that it is not all by any one writer. Beginning with incest and moving through brothel-keepers to reconciliation, it takes some accepting, particularly as much of the verse is more reminiscent of McGonagall than the Bard of Avon. But Toby Robertson and the Prospect Theatre made the most of it in vigour, bawdiness, fisherman's comedy and ironic noble sentiment by setting the whole play to music by Carl Davis in the brothel at Mytilene rather than on an anguished Cook's Tour of the Levant. 'The complete whorehouse divertissement,' Robert Cushman called it. Harold Innocent brilliantly upstaged everyone in leering decadence and bored debauchery in his double corrupt and sleazy roles as Antiochus and the Bawd and Derek Jacobi struggled nobly for purity as the puzzled and much put upon Pericles. Played for all it was worth – probably more.

It was at this Festival that I made my first appearance as a member of the Festival staff. Apparently there had been protests from the Critics' Circle about the recent handling of press facilities by The Scottish Tourist Board which had been responsible for Festival press and publicity matters ever since its inception in 1947.

As a result the Festival Society decided to appoint its own publicity officer and when the post was advertised I applied. First I was summoned to an interview with Peter Diamand in the Festival's gloomy London office in St James's Street.

It was a curious interview, with Diamand, austere and unblinking behind a modest desk, being tensely inquisitorial about the range of my cultural interests but saying rather wistfully at one point 'I hope, Mr Crawford, if you are appointed, you will be able to find time to attend some of the performances.' But the biggest surprise was the language – or rather languages. I had said in my application that I spoke French and Italian and suddenly in mid-interview without warning Diamand switched the questioning first into French and then to Italian. Fortunately my linguistic claims were not mere window-dressing (as they might well have been) and as one possibly spurious qualification was dispatched, Peter Diamand relaxed visibly although I was sent off at the end with the usual bromide about 'getting in touch'.

Rather to my surprise I had a letter a few days later summoning me to Edinburgh to confront the whole majesty of the Festival Council. After spending about 45 minutes in an ante-room of the City Chambers in the company of several other postulants whose attitudes varied between staring at the wall behind me about two feet above my head with nervous hostility and making fractured Ionescu-like pseudo-flippant conversation, I was summoned to face a row of distinguished faces behind a long table who asked a series of polite but rather disinterested questions, none of which I can remember. Eventually I received a letter of appointment and arrived in Edinburgh for the 1973 Festival in time to pick up the rumour that one of the postulants was spreading the story that I had got the job because I had been at one time a golf correspondent!

It was not a very clearly defined job but as well as relations with the press I was supposed to be responsible for the festival brochures, posters and newspaper advertising and the general image of the event. I attended meetings of the Festival Council and various sub-committees and gradually came to discover that Bill Thomley, Diamand's assistant whose principal field of endeavour was the drama side of the programme also considered he had a brief which embraced brochures and design.

An owl-eyed, nervous and secretive young man whose chief relaxation was playing bridge he seemed distrustful of journalists even when employed by the Festival Society and my pretty spurious athletic reputation obviously increased his suspicions of my cultural viability. At length we got on pretty well in a kind of neurotic way because behind the oversensitive facade he had a splendidly caustic sense of humour. Peter Diamand, despite his rather awesome remoteness, I liked from the first because he was always sure of what he wanted. Relationships were not helped because Diamand and Thomley spent most of their time in the London office or beyond it searching for programme material for the next or future festivals and you were lucky if you saw either of them more than once a month outside Festival time.

One of the first things I had to do after the 1973 Festival was to inform the press that Diamand was going to stay on for another five years. Negotiations on the renewal of his contract had been going on for some months in the usual interminable municipal fashion of haggling over the bawbees.

But before anyone could light a bonfire on Arthur's Seat at this news (that was to come later) there were ominous political rumbles along the skyline when Councillor Peter Wilson, prospective leader of the new Regional authority due to be set up in 1974, objected to the Festival grant being tied to a half-penny rate and the complaints about the 1973 drama programme rose from a mutter to a whine.

Being not only chronically short of money but kept in ignorance about where it was coming from, when and how much, made the Festival Director's job a planning nightmare. Pressures for adventurous programme-making came from all sides, the issue of the use of native resources was also a keen social and political issue but a large section of the regular Festival audience from home and abroad did not want endless innovation and parochial choice but great performances of well-loved dramatic, musical and dance works by world-famous names to form the bulk of the Edinburgh summer offerings.

Adventure is expensive and world famous names do not come cheaply either but ironically, parochial choice often costs more. British-based theatre, the London orchestras and dance companies do not receive large subsidies to appear at the Edinburgh Festival. They have to be employed at the full going rate. The admirable Scottish Opera, the Scottish National Orchestra, the National Theatre and other 'local' companies can be a bigger drain on the Festival budget than a subsidised unit from France, Germany, the United States or Eastern Europe. So, spend a substantial part of your perhaps-we-are-going-to-get-enough allocation on a new project and something has to suffer. The word 'elitism' is flown like a banner over all the vociferous and enraged protesters. But 'elitism' simply means choice and in planning there always has to be choice. Even in the world's most comprehensive festival you can't have everything.

So for 1974 bigger and better drama was promised. It was distinctively international. Theatre fare came from France, Greece, Sweden, India, the United States, Switzerland, Israel and Ireland. One of the Irish contributions had a Greek Cypriot director and the other a Scottish director. There were 102 theatre performances and 61 musical performances a ratio of five to three. But in 1973 there had been 84 speech and drama performances to 53 musical performances – a ratio of eight to five. Not so very different. Clearly what agitated the dramaphiles could not just be attributed to numbers.

At the Assembly Hall the Actors Company gave two very different classical plays. Euripides's *The Bacchae*, a terrifying blood-boltered account of the imposition of an alien religion from the East, the orgiastic worship of Dionysius, on Athenian society was done with much passion and vibrant conviction by the whole company dominated by Mark McManus as the god of growth and decay himself. By contrast Molière's *Tartuffe* was more even-paced, almost cool, with a fine sinister central performance by Charles Kay in the title role.

The foreign visitors were at the Lyceum from opposite ends of the world and very diverse poles of the theatre. Kathakali from Kerala in Southern India were used to performing in the open air and the accompanying music on drums and cymbals proved deafeningly oppressive in the confines of the Lyceum but the resplendent scarlet and gold, blue and silver costumes helped to make their graceful and subtle dance and voiced chorus representations of the Hindu epics of conflicts between gods and demons easy on the eye without rendering them any more comprehensible.

The Gothenburg City Theatre brought to Edinburgh one of August Strindberg's most remarkable plays *Gustav III*, not performed until after his death in 1912 and having its first showing in Britain. Strindberg, although best known as a virulent misogynist, wrote several historical plays and *Gustav* suggests that he should have written more. In his introduction to the play in the Souvenir Programme, the eminent translator of Scandinavian drama, Michael Meyer, describes its central character:

> *Gustav III was a remarkable figure – a gifted dramatist and essayist (at least one of his plays was acted at the Comedie Francaise), founder of the Swedish Academy and a liberal reformer who, among other things, proclaimed religious tolerance and the abolition of torture as a means of legal investigation. Anxious to remove power from*

the aristocracy, he became (in the classical manner of reformers) disillusioned with democracy.

He decided that the only way to achieve full reform was through a benevolent absolutism, and was finally murdered as a result of an aristocratic conspiracy at a midnight masquerade at the Stockholm opera house in 1792 at the age of 46.

This is of course a familiar tale. It is the plot of one of Verdi's best operas *Un Ballo in Maschera* based on a libretto by Scribe for an opera by Daniel Auber written 70 years before Strindberg's play. But Strindberg gets much nearer to the real Gustav, who like his uncle Frederick the Great was homosexual and much more likely to make a pass at the page Oscar than sing an impassioned love duet with his friend's wife as he does in Verdi's opera. However Verdi had quite enough trouble with the censors over the libretto of *Ballo* without introducing homosexuality as an aspect of the plot and Strindberg only touches on it in his strangely wrought play through the king's cynical relationship with his queen. It was a fine production with an elegant enigmatic performance by Sven Wollter as the actor king who never knew when he was playing a part or living reality and who saw the coming of revolution and decided he would not be the object of its policy of overthrow but its leader.

An event, wrote *The Scotsman's* Allen Wright, *of which the Festival could be proud, but the fact that so few people paid to see it would suggest that all the clamour about the Festival drama needing to be more international is just so much cant.*

Haymarket Ice Rink was pressed into service again, having established its reputation as a place of popular entertainment largely under the regime of Frank Dunlop. The Young Lyceum Company's attempt to take over this mantle was not really a success. *The Fantastical Feats of Finn MacCool* by Irish playwright Sean McCarthy portrayed some of the Celtic legends surrounding the epic figure of Finn McCool, the Gaelic hero and father of Ossian, central to the pre-Christian mystery of the Celts.

Finn met the criteria of adventurous programme-making and the use of local talent but tried too assiduously to follow the Haymarket tradition of spectacular comedy. Finn himself, as played by Tony Haygarth a fine actor, was simply not large enough in any sense to fill out the magic of the giant hero and the production, set to the haunting music of uillean pipes, bodhran, mandolin and hurdy-gurdy played live by Planxty, stumbled uneasily between moments of visual entrancement and farce.

W. B. Yeats's version of Sophocles's *King Oedipus* in the Abbey Theatre Dublin's production by Michael Cacoyannis had the virtue of a strong central performance as the King from Desmond Cave but stylistically it wobbled between ancient ritual and demotic tragedy. *The Tooth of Crime* from the Performance Group of New York, and directed by the shaman of ritual theatre Richard Schechner, was about the rise and fall of a modern idol, a rock singer, and offered little but feet of clay and brass dust.

The most outstanding theatre of the Festival came from one large company and one very small group. At the Lyceum the Royal Shakespeare Company gave Marlowe's *Dr Faustus* in a weird but striking production by John Barton, quite heavily cut and interpolated with extracts from earlier versions of the Faust story, but illuminated by a brilliant performance by Ian McKellen, wonderfully arrogant and lustful for new learning and the heady reek of unique sensation in the first part and most morally debauched and anguished in the second.

The small group was the Mummenschanz, three mummers from Switzerland who at the Church Hill Theatre made and reassembled themselves in silent faceless shapes of quite breathtaking pliancy in what was neither mime, drama nor dance but sheer theatrical endearing and funny sorcery. Marcel Marceau defined mime as 'the form of dramatic expression closest to Man'. Andres Bossard, Bernie Schurch and Floriana Frassetto of Mummenschanz offered what is possibly the form of amoebic expression closest to creation. Until you see it, inexplicable. Also at the Church Hill Theatre was the Bat Dor Dance Company from Israel, athletic and graceful in two programmes mostly to original music by Israeli composers although

Ligeti and Samuel Barber also figured. The dancing, fluent and expressive , was rather academic although there was more emotion in *And After* ..., created in memory of a soldier killed on the Golan Heights and *Requiem for Sounds* danced to a score composed of animal noises and bird calls, both made by black Israeli choreographer, Gene Hill Sagan. An incident at rehearsal when a revolver fell from the stage manager's handbag underlined the tense reality under which Israeli artists lived just a few months after the uneasily brokered peace with Syria.

The Greek theme was repeated in the operas. Gluck's *Alceste*, taken from Euripides by the great 18th-century opera reformer, was given by Scottish Opera. Although sometimes regarded as a rather statuesque composer of the old school where opera was too often simply a procession of arias and duets by costumed singers, in fact Gluck led the way into the music drama so successfully exploited by later composers like Mozart, Rossini, Verdi and Wagner by dramatising the recitative between numbers so that the drama flowed as an integral part of the musical construction, simply and effectively between the emotional outbursts of the set pieces. Originally Janet Baker had been cast in the title role and her withdrawal caused some disappointment but that was totally dissipated on the first night when the young Romanian soprano Julia Varady scored a triumph as Alceste, the queen who offers herself as a sacrifice so that her husband King Admetus may live. Musically and dramatically she made all Gluck's music drama points in a performance of great visual and vocal beauty, admirably backed by Robert Tear as Admetus, Peter van der Bilt as Apollo in the role of *deus ex machina*, a rather bulky Hercules from Delme Bryn Jones, an elegantly simple production from Anthony Besch and with Alex Gibson and the SNO in their most precise and inspiring form. It was an evening to be savoured and cherished.

Nor was that all. The King's Theatre, although eminently more suitable for 18th-century opera than for Strauss or Janacek, had its problems brushed aside in two productions by the only visiting opera company, the Royal Opera Stockholm. In *Elektra* the great angular bronze doors cramped the stage, the orchestra looked as if they were sandpapering elbows in the pit but the scale of human passion projected by Birgit Nilsson, Barbro Ericson and Berit Lindholm dwarfed mere presentation and sounded through the theatre in a great litany of doomed tragedy of heroic dimensions. Nilsson was not just magnificent she was immense, stunning, wonderful – the adjectives putter out in verbal inadequacy.

When we had our post-performance conference the next day, some earnest desecrator of the King's asked the vexed question of what she thought of the house and its facilities for opera. She put down her pint of beer and said gravely: 'It is a very small theatre so I only have to use one of my vocal chords' and turned to me and winked prodigiously with a sly and immensely gratified grin. Some lady.

Götz Friedrich overcame some of the problems of Janacek's *Jenufa* in the King's with a thrust stage projecting over the orchestra pit on which Elisabeth Söderström agonised over her lost lover and dead child. The first Janacek opera to make an impact outside his homeland, it is a powerful drama with highly contemporary overtones – domestic violence, single parenthood even drugs – and in Edinburgh being given in Swedish rather than Czech was not a serious drawback. The production, the fine ensemble work and the two central performances from Söderström as Jenufa and Kerstin Meyer

Birgit Nilsson and Berit Lindholm (1974)

121

as her foster-mother Kostelnicka brought opera back from legend to reality, movingly sung and splendidly played by the Royal Stockholm Orchestra under Berislav Klobucar. Handel's *Il Pastor Fido* a jewelled production from Drottingholm, the 18th-century theatre which Gustavus III bought from his mother, was conducted and arranged by Charles Farncombe with great elegance and charm.

At the same time it reminded us of the musical/dramatic problems of operatic reform to which Gluck addressed himself so effectively later in that century. The second year of the Barenboim/Ustinov *Don Giovanni* won even more acclaim than the first with Antigone Sgourda's Donna Anna much more assured and definitive, a warm and human portrayal of what is often an exceptionally bossy role. The only cast change was Daniéle Perriers as Zerlina in place of Helen Donath.

The Scottish National Orchestra opened the concert programme with Beethoven, a Mozart Piano Concerto played by Clifford Curzon and Tippett's Third Symphony conducted by the composer. Composer participation was continued in their second concert in the last week of the Festival when Thea Musgrave conducted her own Horn Concerto with Barry Tuckwell as soloist in a programme which also included a Nielsen overture, Liszt's Second Piano Concerto played by John Ogdon and the Sibelius Second Symphony.

There was a lot of singing in the concert halls, Margaret Kingsley was the soprano soloist in Tippett's symphony, Heather Harper, Helen Watts, Luigi Alva and Peter Lagger sang the Bruckner *Te Deum* with Barenboim, the Festival Chorus and the London Philharmonic, Dietrich Fischer Dieskau was the soloist in the orchestral setting of Mahler's *Lieder eines fahrenden Gesellen* (Songs of a Wayfarer) with Barenboim and in a couple of other recitals. Schoenberg was strongly represented in almost all of his facets from Anja Silja's searing *Erwartung* with Haitink through Heather Harper's contributions in Quartet no 2 to Cathy Gayer's *Brettl Lieder* and Cleo Laine's *Pierrot Lunaire*.

The Festival Chorus had one of its most demanding years. In addition to the Bruckner *Te Deum* and Hugo Wolf's rarely heard *Der Feuerreiter* (The Fire-rider), to mark the 100th anniversary of its first performance in Milan there were two performances of the Verdi *Requiem* with the London Philharmonic and Giulini.

The second of these was smitten by one of those back-stage Festival crises which enliven the lives of the administration in Market Street. The two performances were on Tuesday and Wednesday of the first week. The soloists were the American soprano, Martina Arroyo, two Italians, mezzo-soprano Fiorenza Cossotto and the tenor Luciano Pavarotti and Bulgarian bass Raphael Arie.

On the Tuesday, although the performance was compellingly shaped by Giulini and sung with tremendous attack, power and finesse by the Festival Chorus and three of the soloists, Miss Arroyo was clearly under some strain. Unfortunately when she decided she could not sing on Wednesday she did not tell Peter Diamand until lunch-time. This initiated a frantic telephonic search through major sopranos known to have sung the role within easy – or even difficult – reach of Edinburgh. which went on half the afternoon. At 3.45 pm Rita Hunter, the English National Opera star who had just returned from singing the Requiem on the continent, was persuaded to fly to the rescue. She caught the 5.25 pm plane from Heathrow, was met by a police escort at Turnhouse airport and taken at full siren through the city to her hotel, where she changed into her concert finery and was rushed across to the Usher Hall so that Giulini, who had never heard her sing, could be persuaded that she should assume the soprano role.

In mid-afternoon I was summoned from my press bureau in the Mount Royal Hotel on Princes Street to the Director's office. As well as putting out the necessary press release, Peter Diamand told me I was to go on stage immediately before the concert and announce the change to the audience. I demurred mildly that I thought that was usually the task of the Festival Director. Mr Diamand fixed me with a beady but twinkling eye. 'Mr Crawford,' he said, 'I do not wear the kilt so you are more conspicuous than me. You are also much bigger than me and have a much louder voice.' So that is how I came to share a stage with Pavarotti.

There was a sequel to this rather nerve-wracking incident, which I had thought to have carried off with reasonable aplomb. The distinguished BBC producer, Archie Lee, was sitting in the Circle that night behind a group of eagerly prattling Morningside ladies. One of them was insistently calling to the attention of her friends her niece in the Festival Chorus. 'There,' she said her voice ringing with family pride, 'that's Maisie, the tall blonde in blue in the second row.'

And then, as I made my entrance, her voice dropped an octave and a few social rungs with 'Aw Christ! Here comes bad news!' So fragile a thing is even the two-minute limelight.

I am happy to say, however, that I was anything but bad news. Rita Hunter, in sonorous trumpet-like voice slimmed to a soft woodwind whisper in the closing 'Libera me', was superb. The other three soloists, the chorus, Giulini and the orchestra rose to yet greater heights as I listened to Verdi's monumental music for the second time in 24 hours. The audience, knowing nothing of the frantic telephone calls, the rush to the plane, the ululating police cars through the city, rose simply and spontaneously to a great performance. Crisis resolved into triumph, real festival material.

Earlier I had a small personal success to add to the Festival spirit. In an attempt to cheer up the beginning of the Festival I organised a bonfire on Arthur's Seat, Edinburgh's 800-foot-high domestic mountain, for the opening Sunday. With the untiring and enthusiastic assistance of the temporary press bureau staff, the Scottish Amateur Athletic Association, the Territorial Army, the Royal Navy, Edinburgh Corporation Cleansing Department, the Scottish Gas Board, the British Caledonian Airways Pipe Band, the Actors' Company, the police and the prisoners in Saughton Jail, we put the whole thing together as a spectacle. The Cleansing Department supplied combustible rubbish to make the bonfire, the Royal Navy, the Territorials and countless others got it up to the peak of Arthur's Seat.

The Scottish Amateur Athletic Association provided teams of runners to carry four torches from Edinburgh Castle to the bonfire; the prisoners at Saughton made the torches, the Gas Board supplied gas cylinders to fuel them, Scottish Command allowed a team of actors to lurk within the Castle Gate waiting for their entrance. It was a dramatic occasion.

People thronged into the stands built for the Tattoo on the esplanade of the Castle, to see a new Festival spectacle. In one corner of the dark parade ground the British Caledonian Airways band formed up and began to play. There were stirrings and movement and shadowy figures in the great bowl of the esplanade. The pipes and drums skirled and beat.

On a drum roll from the band the gates of the Castle were suddenly flung open and across the drawbridge, to the stately pace of a slow pipe march, came four 18th-century figures, bewigged and cockaded, silk-jacketed and hoop-skirted, players from The Actors' Company production of *Tartuffe*, Sheila Reid, Robert Eddison, Windsor Davies and Mark McManus in full magnificent fig, bearing aloft flaming torches.

Robert, one of the Festival's most recurring and most welcome figures, told me afterwards: 'It was the greatest entrance of my life'. The roar that greeted them echoed round the ancient battlements like a broadside of cannon. 'I didn't know,' said Windsor Davies, 'whether I'd just scored a try at Cardiff Arms Park or Prince Charlie had won!'

Halfway down the esplanade the actors handed over their torches to the first four in a relay of noted Scottish athletes from Edinburgh Athletic Club and Edinburgh Southern Harriers. The runners, among them several British and Scottish champions, carried the torches in relays down the Royal Mile, out into Holyrood Park and up the hill to light the bonfire. Thousands crowded the route to watch, the bonfire was seen over most of east central Scotland and Fife. Back at the press bureau on the top floor of the Mount Royal Hotel we had a party at midnight for all the volunteers who had made it possible.

Before it broke up in the early hours of the morning there was a little local difficulty with a well-drammed piper who monopolised one of the lifts, going up and down from the basement to the seventh floor playing his pipes in a splendid Celtic resonance throughout the hotel.

In the morning I apologised to the hotel duty manager and asked nervously if the lift-shaft pibroch had occasioned any complaints. He came from Lewis in the Outer Hebrides. 'Och a few people mentioned it,' he said dismissively. 'But I chust told them it wass the ghost of Bonnie Prince Charlie.'

IX

My attempt to launch the Festival with some kind of public spectacle which would be freely available to as many citizens and visitors as possible and not have the opening ceremonies confined to a strictly ticketed church service in St Giles and the equally restricted opening concert seemed to have met with general approval and been a success. However I had reckoned without *particular* disapproval.

Although it is visited by many thousands of people every year, some of whom even have the temerity and the hardihood to climb to the summit of Arthur's Seat, there were dark mutterings about encroachment on the environment of Holyrood Park. Too many people had wanted to watch the torchlight run from the Castle to the summit I was told by the police. So permission would not be given for the bonfire run to be repeated next year. Having too large an audience at a festival event seemed a very odd reason for banning it. It still does.

The following year I attempted to organise a cavalcade in procession along Princes Street to get the Festival off the mark. This proved to be a more acceptable and enduring idea although in 1975 it was something of a shambles. As at the outset of the Festival we were already deeply immersed in the myriad problems of dealing with the hundreds of journalists who come to Edinburgh from all over the world for the occasion, I realised that such a parade was beyond the organisational scope of the press bureau. So I arranged to delegate the cavalcade. Tragically, the man to whom I delegated it, Robin Richardson, a former BBC producer, became fatally ill shortly before the Festival began.

Unfortunately, the Tattoo had refused to join in this initial parade so we did not even have the assistance that military discipline might have provided.

So in a frantic last-minute scramble with the help of the Fringe Administrator, John Milligan (who also had more than enough on his plate at this time), we cobbled together from the elements which Robin had arranged, a sort of tatterdemalion band of mummers and drummers, pipers and hikers, local youth groups, a few bands making brave if not exactly synchronised music and launched them along Princes Street waving banners and making an approximation to a joyful noise. Fortunately this function has now been taken over by the *Evening News* and the well-ordered, tuneful and colourful display you see nowadays on the first Sunday of the Festival is all their own work – and mighty glad I was to see them take it on.

But starting the Festival with a colourful splash was by no means the only problem of 1975. Before the 1974 Festival was over there were further rumbles on the contentious subject of the opera house. When after fourteen years of vacillation by the Corporation, William Ross, Secretary of State for Scotland announced in 1973 that the Government would pay half the cost of the project, he stipulated that the plans must be approved by the Royal Fine Art Commission.

In August 1974 the Commission said they thought the plans were bold, ingenious and of high architectural quality but unacceptable. The sheer size of the building they claimed would have a damaging visual impact. So a new firm of architects were called in, Sir Robert Matthew, Johnson Marshall & Partners. The Government warned sternly that there should be no more delay. New plans suggested reducing the size of the fly tower. It was objected that this would militate against speedy scene changes and although only slightly reducing the scale of the building would greatly reduce its scope. The project was delayed.

During the 1974 Festival Hank Putsch, Executive Director of the Greater Philadelphia Cultural Alliance, came to see me. Philadelphia had plans for a festival and he wanted to assess the economic impact a cultural festival had on a city like Edinburgh.

The Philadelphia Festival was planned for 1976, the 200th anniversary of the American Declaration of Independence which had been signed in Philadelphia on 4 July 1776. This particular celebration was assured but Mr Putsch was collecting evidence as to whether or not an annual festival in the American city would be a worth-while project for which 1976 might prove to be the launch-pad. In pursuit of this information he interviewed key policy-making, business and administrative people, banks and finance houses and studied the financial reports of the Festival, the Film Festival, the Fringe and the Military Tattoo for the previous five years, as well as the history and development of the Edinburgh Festival since its inception.

There was quite a lot of subsequent correspondence and three months later one of his staff, Palmer Reed came to Edinburgh and conducted more interviews and research. In February 1975 I was invited to Philadelphia for further discussions with the Cultural Alliance on the advantages of Festival as a civic ingredient – an enjoyable but intensive six days, apart from the breakfast conferences at which I was the principal speaker, a role in which I never feel at my best at 7.30 am.

The report which Mr Putsch and his colleagues produced as a result of their survey emphasised the significant economic effect which the Edinburgh Festival has on the city and the region.

The Philadelphia report stated:

1) The Edinburgh Festival has an annual positive economic impact of more than $38,435,125 dollars (£16,485,799).

2) It achieves up $5 million dollars (£2,150,000) annually in the value of world-wide press and media coverage for the city and Scotland.

3) As a result Edinburgh has become a leading international tourist attraction and its annual tourist season has increased from three to six months in duration.

4) The economic benefits of the Festival provide significant direct and indirect economic benefit for a majority of citizens in the region.

This report underlined the notable tourist effect which the Festival has on Scotland, bringing people from all over the world who may have come in the first instance to see the Festival programmes or been drawn to visit at other times by the publicity engendered by the Festival, but who then 'discovered' Scotland and Edinburgh as places immensely worth visiting in their own right.

The first reaction to the publication of the Philadelphia report in Edinburgh was a fervid desire by the local authorities to prove it wrong. The culmination of this came in 1977 in a report prepared by the Department of Economics at Heriot-Watt University and sponsored by The Scottish Tourist Board and Lothian Regional Council called *The Economic Impact of the Edinburgh Festival.*

Using entirely different criteria such as how often money earned during the Edinburgh Festival changed hands within Edinburgh and the Lothians and how much it cost to import from outside the Region the food and other commodities required to sustain Festival visitors, nevertheless it estimated that visitors to the Festival in 1976 spent £3.7 million and that £1 million remained in the city as income for local people in pay packets, rents and profits. This survey took no account of the publicity value of the Festival to the city and the brief was a narrow one but even so the impact on the economic life of the city was very positive – a return of £3.7 million for a civic investment of £190,000 in 1976.

The reasoning behind this fortunately did not go so far as slaying the goose but there was considerable tramping on the golden eggs.

In 1974-75 the battle for who should control the Festival was joined between the newly constituted local authorities, Lothian Region and Edinburgh City and District. Peter Wilson, elected Convener of

Lothian Region, announced that local authority representatives should form the majority on the Festival Council. 'I threw my hat right into the arena he said by stating the number of seats we were prepared to buy. If there were to be 11 seats (out of 21) for the local authorities, Lothian would want seven and four would go to Edinburgh District.' He also made the eminently sensible suggestion that the Festival should have a fixed grant for the next three or four years, with a built-in allowance for inflation and growth thus saving the Festival from applying for an increase every year and enabling forward planning to be done on a more realistic basis.

Later he explained that what he meant by 'buying' seats was that each local authority's grant would be related to the number of representatives it had on the Festival Council.

This was deeply resented and bitterly opposed by the City and District. A letter to *The Scotsman* from Councillor Magnus Williamson stated their position:

> *It has certainly not been agreed that the number of seats on the future Council will be determined only by financial support. That may be the view held by Councillor Wilson who has some very grandiose ideas about his own status and a Regional take-over. I can however assure the Convener after consultation with some of my senior colleagues in the District who have had to listen to his often derogatory remarks about the Festival in past years that we are in no mood to accept the casual way in which he proposes to dismiss us from the Festival scene.*

This wrangle continued over some months to the great detriment of the actual work supposed to be done by the Festival Council. In January suggestions that the Festival was in danger because of the row between the two local authorities were dismissed as 'totally unfounded' said the Edinburgh *Evening News*.

> *Councillor Peter Wilson, Convener of Lothian Region, reacting to reports that because neither authority could resolve who should be in charge of the Edinburgh Festival, denied that the question of future grants could not be decided and the Festival programme for 1975 was in jeopardy. 'We will be discussing,' he said, 'how much each of us should give and indeed if only one of us should assume the task entirely'.*
>
> *Councillor Wilson said the final decision over financing the Festival depended on which of the two authorities was given larger representation on the Council of the Festival Society. 'We are not prepared to pay a share unless we can help call the tune through our representation. However the issue is about to be resolved one way or another.'*

Later the dispute degenerated into a squabble about who should be chairman. Peter Wilson refused to accept the District proposal that the chairman should be the Lord Provost of Edinburgh, a title still held after the municipal re-shuffle by the chairman of the District Council. Disclaiming any wish to take over the office, Wilson suggested an independent chairman. Lord Provost Jack Kane pointed out that the Lord Provost had been chairman since the Festival began 28 years before. 'I see no reason for changing this arrangement,' he said.

This seemed to be resolved by the District taking over the whole matter and undertaking to finance the 1976 Festival to the tune of £180,000 in return for 12 seats and the chair on the Festival Council.

No sooner had the Articles of Association of the Festival Society been altered by the lawyers to accommodate this situation than Lothian Region changed its mind and decided to settle for six seats in return for a grant of £90,000 and another meeting of the Society had to be called and the Articles changed again. In the meantime we were trying to get the 1975 Festival on the road.

Edinburgh Festival Opera made its third appearance with a new production of Mozart's *Le Nozze di Figaro* by Geraint Evans, very strongly cast with Ileana Cotrubas as Susanna, Heather Harper as the

Countess, Teresa Berganza as Cherubino, Fischer Dieskau as the Count and Evans himself in the title role. As with the *Don Giovanni* it was conducted by Daniel Barenboim. It lacked the originality of Ustinov's direction apart from an extraordinarily arch not to say camp performance by the Count (not a quality I have ever associated with either Almaviva or Fischer-Dieskau) but I remember that Edward Heath, paying one of his lone visits to the Festival, was dismissive of this facile analysis when we chatted at the interval.

There were three other operas. Deutsche Oper Berlin wallowed in depravity with two works featuring a brace of opera's most licentious ladies – Wieland Wagner's production of Strauss's *Salome* with Ursula Schröder-Feinen as the necrophilic Princess and a splendid new realisation by Gustav Rudolf Sellner in stunning sets by Filippo Sanjust of Berg's *Lulu*. The Festival had seen Wieland Wagner's production of this opera in Peter Diamand's first year as Festival Director in 1966 when it was brought by Stuttgart with Anja Silja as Lulu in a striking and original performance. Catherine Gayer, America's gift to modern German opera, was equally unforgettable, a more vulnerable, less consciously knowing seductress caught in a web beyond anything but her sensuality's comprehension. As the infatuated lesbian Countess Geschwitz, Patricia Johnson was movingly effective and Hans Günter Nöcker as the luckless Dr Schön combined cynicism, jealousy and fatalism most convincingly in a finely imaginative production.

Perhaps the most important 1975 performance was the world première of *Hermiston*, the first opera by a Scottish composer given at the Festival. Bill Bryden provided the libretto taken from Robert Louis Stevenson's last unfinished novel *Weir of Hermiston*, and set by Robin Orr to music which powerfully and poignantly evoked the terrible dilemma faced by the implacable Lord Justice-Clerk and his son Archie, accused of murder. Toby Robertson's production for Scottish Opera opened with the body of the beggar, Duncan Jopp hanging mid-stage as the curtain rose, the execution from which the motif of the plot begins. Michael Langdon was rigorously sonorous as the harsh and tortured Lord Hermiston, Lenus Carlson sang the rebellious Archie with grace and style, Cathy Gayer filled her second, more innocent role of the Festival with charm and anguish as Christina and the grim tale was fleshed out with some evocative singing by Scottish Opera Chorus and the playing of the Scottish Chamber Orchestra conducted by Alexander Gibson.

There was almost bloodshed too at Sunday's opening concert, which contained another work by Robin Orr, his *Second Symphony* as well as Prokoviev's *Romeo and Juliet Suite*. Claudio Arrau was to have been the soloist in Beethoven's Fifth Piano Concerto but called off at the last moment. His place was taken by Daniel Barenboim, in Edinburgh to conduct *Figaro*, despite an accident suffered that morning when a mirror before which he was shaving fell from the wall and severely gashed his hand. Rushed to hospital, he refused to have it stitched because it would have prevented him playing the piano and despite the wound gave a brilliant performance with Alex Gibson, as he told me afterwards, 'palpitating on the podium', apprehensively waiting for the keyboard to be covered in blood when Barenboim attacked the Emperor Concerto with his usual bravura.

It was an unusual concert programme for two concerts were repeated. Giulini with the London Philharmonic gave the Beethoven Ninth Symphony twice preceded once by Mozart's E flat major Sinfonia Concertante and once by Haydn's Sinfonia Concertante for violin, cello, oboe and bassoon.

On the final Friday and Saturday, Bernstein with the Orchestre National de France gave an all-Ravel programme which included the conductor as soloist in the G major Piano Concerto, Marilyn Horne singing the orchestral version of *Schéhérazade* and the young American violinist, Boris Belkin in Tzigane. There was a delightful concert of Mozart and Johann Strauss at their most Viennese given by Gibson and the SNO with the SNO Chorus and Gundula Janowitz; an all-Russian evening from the London Philharmonic with Rostropovich conducting, a great deal of Russian music – Mussorgsky, Tchaikovsky, Shostakovich, Rachmaninov, Stravinsky and Prokoviev in various forms; three concerts by the Israel Philharmonic under Zubin Mehta including an exquisitely wrought Mozart *E flat major Concerto* from Alfred Brendel and a

127

wonderfully exhilarating account of Berlioz's too little played *Harold in Italy* symphony which made us all realise just why Paganini went into such raptures when he first heard it.

Rich and heady fare: but for me the most memorable evenings came in the last week when Abbado and the London Symphony gave two one-composer concerts, devoted to Prokoviev and Brahms. I have never heard a more brilliantly structured Brahms's Fourth Symphony and to have it preceded by a performance of the Second Piano Concerto played with such fire and power by Rafael Orozco and the LSO was true musical intoxication. But the Prokoviev was even better.

It began with the Sinfonia Concertante in E minor for cello and orchestra played with lyric passion and sonority by its dedicatee, Mstislav Rostropovich and accompanied by the LSO with the delicate purity of a chamber music group. At the interval it seemed hard to believe that the quality of rapt and masterful performance could be sustained by music from a film score.

But the Alexander Nevsky Cantata which followed was instantly breathtaking and must rank as one of the finest performances the Edinburgh Festival Chorus has ever given.

From the slow desolation of the opening through the folk song hymn in praise of Nevsky, the 12th-century hero who defeated the invading Teutonic Knights on the banks of the Neva. The passionate invocation to combat, the thrilling virtuosity of the orchestra in the Battle on the Ice, and the harrowing despair of the Lament, movingly sung by Galina Vishnevskaya, to the cry for freedom and triumph at the end. This was a hair-raising performance of fine-spun dramatic tension, noble and nerve-searing sounds of such dazzling accomplishment that it was not just memorable but unforgettable. It is a stunning piece of music, one of the great choral works of the 20th century, which never fails to impress with its colourful and inspirational pugnacity, but this performance was fused together into something uniquely splendid beyond words.

It was the first good year for ballet for some time. The problem of finding an appropriate theatre for dance since the defection of the Empire to Bingo was a recurring difficulty and it had not been resolved by getting it back into harness for the Festival period only, a project which had proved both costly and unsatisfactory when it was tried. So the 1975 dance programme, which contrasted two very different styles, found Rudolf Nureyev and the Royal Ballet in the second week at the King's and the Nikolais Dance Theatre USA for the final week at the Royal Lyceum.

Nureyev danced in all three of the Royal Ballet programmes in a series of contemporary classical roles in *Romeo and Juliet*, *Giselle* and *The Dream* with his usual athleticism and panache but he was pretty tiresome off stage, agreeing to times and places for photo calls and press interviews and then calling off or sardonically hiding in the King's Theatre for no other seeming purpose than to make life difficult for as many people as possible. But the public adored him and he and the very distinguished Royal Ballet company which included Lynn Seymour, Margaret Barbieri, Marion Tait and Alan Dubreuil played to packed houses.

The Nikolais company were much less celebrated on this side of the Atlantic but highly original, vividly talented and superbly entertaining. This was a new world of dance, a kind of total theatre with hallmarks of genius, dazzling stuff. Alwin Nikolais, a charming, witty 63-year-old, the sole progenitor of this unique style, said:

> *I cannot be content only as a choreographer. As such my dominant concern should be motion; yet I cannot forego my attraction to the shapes and forms of things. Therefore I do not hesitate to stress the sculptural form to the exclusion of motional excitement. Nor can I divorce myself from strong passions for sound and colour, so I invade the fields of the composer and painter as well. In truth then, I am not a devoted husband to dance. for I choose to marry the lot of my innamoratas rather than swearing fixed fidelity to one.*

There was something of the Mummenschanz concept in the Nikolais dances. People became things, shapes expressive of abstract ideas, expressed theatrically with inventive lighting in strangely compelling patterns, sometimes humorous but often stressful and emotive, always evocative and elegant theatrical wizardry.

Unfortunately there was not much theatrical magic in the drama that year. A bold attempt by Prospect Theatre directed by Toby Robertson to make a musical out of a morality play based on John Bunyan's *Pilgrim's Progress* never really gelled. The music for *Pilgrim* by Carl Davis, one of the most accomplished of theatrical composers, was somehow neither operatic nor popular and although there were good performances from Paul Jones in the title role, Peter Straker as Appolyon and Paul Nicholas as Worldly Wiseman, it failed adequately to fill the Assembly Hall with the kind of dramatic excitement and vivid action which suited it best as a venue.

How Mad Tulloch Was Taken Away, a new play by John Morris at the Royal Lyceum was a worthy, angry army drama which in the end was curiously lacking in impact, although it introduced the idea of male nudity to the Festival. Luca Ronconi's return to the scene of his 1970 triumph with *Orlando Furioso* at the Haymarket Ice Rink with a modern overall view of Aristophanes's preoccupation with comic idealism called *Utopia*, ran into trouble with the Customs and Excise who could not understand why the Edinburgh Festival wanted to import battered old cars and a wrecked aeroplane. Attempts at the ice rink to link them with manic acting to evoke even the most cynical ideas of the perfect state never really caught on.

There was brisk production by Peter Gill for the Nottingham Playhouse at the Royal Lyceum of *As You Like* It with a spirited performance by Jane Lapotaire as Rosalind but the whole presentation was rather lacking in woodland magic and seemed to have no other concept to put in its place.

Athol Fugard, the most admired dramatist of protest to battle in words against South Africa's apartheid policy, wrote a new play for the 1975 Festival. In an introductory article in the souvenir programme he attributed the inspiration for it to an entry in Albert Camus notebooks which he had read 14 years before:

> *Dimetos had a guilty love for his niece, who hanged herself. One day the little waves carried on to the fine sand of the beach the body of a marvellously beautiful young woman. Seeing her Dimetos fell on his knees, stricken with love. But he was forced to watch the decay of this magnificent body, and went mad. This was his niece's vengeance, and the symbol of a condition we must try to define.*

Unfortunately in abandoning his brave fight against apartheid for the wilder shores of dramatic philosophy, Fugard seemed rather to have lost his way in unfamiliar territory – an accusation levelled once more against the whole drama programme by those with short memories.

In compensation it was a year of particularly interesting exhibitions. The 350th anniversary of the death of the first King of Great Britain, James VI of Scotland and I of England was marked with the showing of a fascinating collection of paintings, prints, documents, manuscripts, books, jewellery and artefacts organised by Basil Skinner and designed by Geoffrey Scott in the Royal Scottish Museum. If it emphasised the King's interest in literature and his patronage of the arts rather than his quirky and contentious character and his weakness for attractive and feckless young men, then that was a side of his historical portrait not as often delineated as some others and most suited to the occasion of an anniversary. 'In lapidary inscription,' as Dr Johnson said, 'no man is upon oath.'

There was also a fine show of pictures by the Welsh artist Ceri Richards at the Royal Scottish Academy. Many of them were inspired by music and poetry, such as his paintings of Debussy's *Cathédrale Engloutie* and the powerful evocation of Dylan Thomas's poem 'The force that through the green fuse drives the flower'. Kandinsky, with his revolutionary concepts of visual order outside the direct images of the visible environment, was on show in more than 30 paintings at the Scottish National Gallery of Modern Art; there was a delightful exhibition of Elizabethan miniatures by Nicholas Hilliard and Isaac Oliver at the

Scottish Arts Council Gallery in Charlotte Square and some striking examples of the critical realism and post-surrealism in landscape, portrait and stark fantasy in *Eight From Berlin* at the Fruit Market Gallery There was plenty of drama and colour in the browsing that year.

XX

Festivals are – or should be – about excitement and for the 30th Festival in 1976 Peter Diamand compiled a programme which mixed a certain amount of nostalgia with innovation, the introduction of new artists and challenging original performances. Thirty is not perhaps the most thrilling age in the calendar with its nuances of the end of an era, the faint concern with the spreading waistline, the gradual evolvement of definitions like 'middle age' into 'maturity' as the vocabulary also broadens.

There was certainly not much sign of middle-aged spread about the 1976 Festival. Demands for economy in programming saw to that. In comparison with the previous few years, the Festival was slightly smaller although just as varied in scope. Perhaps the most remarkable thing, looking back over those 30 years, was how little it had changed in concept since it began in 1947 and how that had solidified into a strength rather than a weakness. The initial plan from 1947 was so bold that the years had served to fill it out rather than alter it.

Two years after World War II ended, when food and clothes and furniture were still rationed, the creation of the Edinburgh Festival was regarded either as a shining good deed in a gloomy world or a piece of municipal cultural insanity, according to your viewpoint. What Edinburgh did from the very beginning was to 'go for broke' as the Americans say, by setting itself the immodest target of being the most comprehensive and largest scale festival in the world. In support of this laudable but wildly ambitious idea there came to the Scottish capital in that bright hot summer of 1947, Italians, Germans, French, Americans, Australians, Hungarians, Austrians and Czechs to augment the performers from Britain who offered us opera, ballet, concerts, chamber music and international theatre.

The sturdy total of 30 years on the boards in Edinburgh proved that Rudolf Bing's original grand design had worked, even triumphed.

In commemoration of that first programme, two of the operas given at the first Festival, Verdi's *Macbeth* and Mozart's *Le Nozze di Figaro* were repeated. The Vienna Philharmonic, one of the two foreign orchestras which appeared in 1947, returned. The policy of having visiting companies giving plays in other languages was maintained by Bunraku from Japan, the Gruppo Teatro Libero from Rome, La Mama Company from New York and The Clowns, Carlo and Alberto Colombaioni. Amazingly there was also one singer who had appeared in the first Festival, the tenor Peter Pears.

Although the number of performances and the number of companies taking part had increased down the years, the pattern set in 1947 remained remarkably consistent. There were still national and international orchestras and opera companies, still chamber music at the Freemasons' Hall in the mornings, still theatre groups from Britain and elsewhere, still ballet, still rarities and classical war-horses. A comforting but far from complacent feeling of permanence had settled over the whole affair. Relations with Edinburgh's mixed bag of City Fathers allowed no room for complacency.

Earlier in the year the dream of an opera house had been effectively and officially killed off by the Government's withdrawal of its offer to pay half the cost of such a venture. This was partly due to the economic crisis in the country but the offer could have been taken up much earlier if it had been pursued with true enthusiasm and vigour. The proposed site had been cleared but there had been squabbling over design as well as funding and in the end Edinburgh finished by paying as much for not having an opera house as the original cost of the scheme when it was first planned. Edinburgh's long saga of civic inaction was about to acquire another symbol. In 1822 a subscription of £20,000 was raised to build a

'Temple of Minerva' on Calton Hill in commemoration of the part Scottish soldiers had played in the victory over Napoleon. George IV laid the foundation stone in 1822. Twelve columns were built in 1823 then the money ran out and it was never finished.

It was to be called the National Monument but soon became known locally as 'Scotland's Disgrace'. The 'Hole in the Ground' in Castle Terrace was to have the same shameful civic significance for the next 20 years.

One result of the decision to abandon the opera house project was a scheme for adapting the Playhouse, a large dual purpose cinema-theatre in Leith Walk set into the hill rising from the valley below 'Scotland's Disgrace' so that it falls away from the entrance level on Leith Walk and you enter the circle from the ground floor. Designed in 1927, it originally held 3,048 and was part of a scheme for building Playhouses in Glasgow, Edinburgh and Dundee. A pretty graceless building, its one recommendation was size but it offered none of the facilities of a modern theatre backstage. Nevertheless, it attracted a considerable body of support headed by the ubiquitous Convener of Lothian Region, Peter Wilson.

Wilson, despite his often virulent criticism of the Festival over a number of years, is a man of determination with a strong sense of civic purpose. Despite being regarded by dewy-eyed Festival supporters as an apostle of philistinism with horns and a forked tail in his municipal briefcase, he had made several sensible proposals about Festival support, among them a four-year inflation-related subsidy and a plan for the Chamber of Commerce to raise a levy from its members to boost finances. He persuaded Lothian Region Council to back in principle a £4 million grant to redevelop the Playhouse. When the Festival Director dissented from the view of the Edinburgh Theatres Working Party Wilson had set up that The Playhouse could provide first-class facilities for the presentation of large scale opera and ballet, he launched a personal attack.

He told the Policy and Resources Committee:

> *I am getting a bit annoyed about a certain gentleman who keeps knocking the great amount of work done on this – and that is a gentlemen by the name of Diamand.*
>
> *He is making statements which are completely incorrect. He says, for instance, that visiting opera companies have complained about the King's Theatre and its lack of facilities – but what he doesn't say is that the working party have recommended that the King's be comprehensively adapted.*
>
> *On the Playhouse he tells complete lies by saying the Playhouse would not meet the technical stage requirements necessary. This is simply not true. Anyone who reads the excellent report on feasibility will realise that what he is saying is just a lot of hooey. Again he tells an untruth when he says that the renovated Playhouse would have a lesser depth of stage than the King's. That is quite untrue.*

There were two elements to Diamand's opposition to the Playhouse scheme. First he found the theatre unattractive and he genuinely did not think it could be successfully adapted to serve the purposes for which the Festival required it. Secondly, he believed that if he accepted the Playhouse plan, Edinburgh would never get the purpose-built opera house which had been so long promised and which was desperately needed and that the Festival would be left with a botched and unhappy compromise. The Playhouse has been used for both opera and ballet at the Festival since it has been modernised but it has never been totally satisfactory in either of these roles.

Diamand's antipathy to the Playhouse never waned. I remember four of us having lunch in the Cafe Royal after the main programme press conference in 1977 and discussing the première of the South African composer Priaulx Rainier's *Violin Concerto* which was to be given with the Royal Philharmonic by Yehudi Menuhin.

'He rang me, you know,' Diamond told us thoughtfully, 'to ask whether he should publicly give his support to the Playhouse project.' He looked at us all beadily through his glasses. 'You may imagine,' he added tersely, 'what I told him.'

George Bain, the administration manager said that of course Menuhin would always back what he saw as a good cause and Bill Thomley chipped in with something laudatory about the support he always offered to human rights, musical development and similar charities.

'Yes,' agreed Diamond rather reluctantly. 'He is a very charitable man. But there are those of us who wish,' he said, drawing fervently on his cigarette in a God-give-me-patience sort of way, 'that he spent more time practising the violin.'

So the euphoria of the 30th Festival was not exactly undimmed by controversy. But the programme was a success. In addition to the commemorative items relating to the Festival itself there were anniversary performances of works by Carl Maria von Weber (died 150 years earlier) and Manuel de Falla (born 1876) and, spread like a majorette's sash across the broad bosom of the Festival was a series of programmes celebrating the Bicentennial of the foundation of the United States of America. In the first week it was led off by a new production of *Pal Joey*, the first really great example of the new wave of American musicals which hit the theatre like liquid gold in the 1940s. Naturally all the major American orchestras were busily engaged celebrating the Bicentennial in the United States but we had the Vermeer Quartet giving morning concerts at the Freemasons' Hall and the unusual combination of the American Brass Quintet playing a range of works by American composers as well as pieces by Bach, Poulenc and Gabrieli. In the Moray House College gymnasium just off the Royal Mile, La Mama – the famous experimental theatre company from New York – gave Euripides and Sophocles in Greek and three performances of Brecht's *The Good Woman of Setzuan*.

Other American artists included two greatly talented and extremely good-looking singers in Judith Blegen who sang Susanna in *Figaro* and Frederica von Stade who was the mezzo-soprano soloist in the Mahler Fourth with the Vienna Philharmonic and gave a morning recital of songs by Mahler, Ives, Poulenc and Britten. But the undoubted top of the American beauty and celebrity parade was Princess Grace of Monaco, making her first public appearance on the international performance scene since she ceased being film-star Grace Kelly on marrying Prince Rainier. In the third week of the Festival she gave three recitals, with Richard Kiley and Richard Pasco, of *An American Heritage*, a prose and poetry programme devised by John Carroll, in the smallest of the Festival venues, the 18th-century St Cecilia's Hall in the Cowgate.

The announcement of Princess Grace's participation in the Festival sent the press into a frenzy. Demands for tickets, interviews, photo sessions and other forms of access to Her Serene Highness were so strident and demanding that it was clear something would have to be done about the publicity angle of her visit to Edinburgh if there was not going to be some kind of press riot.

As it so happened, my wife and I had arranged to go to the Italian Riviera on a golfing holiday to Garlenda near Alassio in the month before the Festival and I set up a meeting in Monaco to discuss the Edinburgh arrangements. We flew to Genoa and hired a small white Renault Five to transport us to Verona for the opera and back across Italy and through the endless tunnels of the Riviera coast to Garlenda. On the appointed day (my wife having elected to spend it by the swimming pool) I drove alone along the Riviera coast in my now rather travel-stained Renault for my rendezvous with the Princess's secretary at the Hotel de Paris. I was followed from the Corniche down the narrow winding road into Monte Carlo by a gleamingly opulent bronze Lamborghini driven by a heavily moustached man of imposing appearance garlanded with a slinky blonde, who hooted imperiously at my little car every time I slowed down to take my bearings.

His impatience became most noisily manifest as we entered the Place du Casino and I drew up outside the Hotel de Paris, to consult a tall and noble figure arrayed in what seemed to be the full panoply of a Monegasque admiral, embellished with gold epaulettes, aiguilettes and a chestful of medals. The Lamborghini stood on his horn with indignation. When I informed the admiral whom I had come to see, a barrier was instantly lifted and the driver behind raised both arms in a wonderful gesture of uncomprehending derisive despair to his glamorous companion. With ceremonial deference I and my little Renault were ushered to a prime parking place in front of the hotel while the Lamborghini was summarily halted by the magnificently attired *chef du parking*. When I was safely installed and the other car imperiously waved on, he practically ripped the synchromesh out of the Lamborghini's gear box and almost accelerated up the steps of the Casino. The expression on the face of the Lamborghini driver remains fondly as one of my happiest memories of the Riviera.

Fortunately the single Festival press conference arranged for the Princess of Monaco was also a pleasurable experience. So that everyone could have an equal opportunity, it was arranged in one of the ante-rooms off the ballroom in the Assembly Rooms. When Princess Grace, looking suitably radiant in a cream dress and a necklace of gold shamrocks, Peter Diamand and I made our appearance we had to struggle through a dense crowd, fortunately in a happy mood, mellowed by the splendid champagne Moët & Chandon had given me for the occasion. When we settled behind the table at the end of the long narrow room, it was wall to wall press and I had to ask the phalanx of photographers who were standing up and blocking the view of everyone behind them to struggle to the side. Diamand had no

The author with Princess Grace and Peter Diamand (1976)

sooner performed the rather superfluous introductions when he was summoned away by a message passed from the back and had to crawl out on his hands and knees to deal with some incipient Festival crisis.

That left Her Serene Highness and myself sharing a table and a bottle of champagne and the avid attention of about 300 members of the Fourth Estate.

She was magnificent, completely relaxed and totally unruffled, charming, articulate and delightful. She gave every impression of enjoying herself exchanging quips and observations with her tight-packed audience. The only problem was getting away. The sole exit was blocked by serried ranks of newspapermen and women, gawping unashamedly. Fortunately, they had deadlines to meet, so we just sat there until they melted away on what I think was only our second bottle of champagne. If only all press confrontations were so effortless.

Although the Princess Grace recital was the publicity highlight of the Festival there was plenty of life and controversy in the rest of the programme. David Pountney's production of *Macbeth* for Scottish Opera was a spectacularly weird and off-beat but strikingly effective setting of one of Verdi's greatest operas in powerfully imagined sets by Ralph Koltai and with fine performances as the tortured demonic hero and his queen by Norman Bailey and Galina Vishnevskaya – although there were complaints about sightlines in the King's when Lady Macbeth's Act I aria was sung on a high rostrum which allowed audiences in the upper circle to see only her feet!

The *Figaro* repeated from the year before was as mellifluous as ever with Fischer-Dieskau's Count being described as 'dandified and ripe for the tumbrils'. Deutsch Oper am Rhein brought from Düsseldorf the Festival's first *Parsifal* with a heroic performance in the title role by Sven Eliasson, a sparkling Rossini *L'Italiana in Algeri* directed and designed by Jean Pierre Ponnelle and two performances of Schoenberg's unfinished masterpiece *Moses und Aron*. For most people it seemed to come into the category of Rossini's brisk verdict on Tannhauser 'Not the sort of opera you can judge on only one hearing and I've certainly no intention of hearing it again.' As I had seen it before I was rather more charitably disposed.

It is not the sort of work you can say you 'enjoy' because there is not much joy in Moses's inarticulate struggle to make his conception of God heard against Aron's insistence on comprehensible public relations imagery. But there is genuine excitement and thrill in the clash of two fundamental principles of the receiving of faith and the musical means to delineate it. In the orgy scene it is difficult to sustain the high emotional and spiritual tension because producers tend to wallow in it as did Georg Reinhardt in the Düsseldorf production and the ending can seem a moral and dramatic anti-climax. But a good performance of *Moses und Aron* is never less than a great experience.

To mark his 150th anniversary there was also a concert performance of Weber's *Die drei Pintos* with Sona Ghazarian, Bernadette Greevy. Sarah Walker, Michael Cousins, Ian Wallace and the BBC Scottish Symphony Orchestra and Singers conducted by Alberto Erede. This musical curiousity was abandoned by Weber in favour of *Euryanthe*, passed by his widow to Meyerbeer, tried out on Wagner and finally knocked into shape by Mahler. A hybrid with a preposterous plot concerning suitors who pass on the task of wooing the heroine Clarissa to each other in succession, it has some pleasing melodies but lacks both true comedy and dramatic tension.

There was a fine tension about the Birmingham Repertory playing of Shakespeare's *Measure for Measure* at the Assembly Hall with David Burke slimily sinister as Angelo and Anna Calder Marshall gently vulnerable as the virtuous Isabella. La Mama's tearaway productions of bits of two Greek tragedies *Trojan Women* and *Electra* were billed as 'environmental', which apparently meant that the audience was on the floor with the actors, getting pushed around to give them the impression of being physically involved with the drama. In the comparatively crowded space of the Moray House Gymnasium the involvement became rather complex with naked actors struggling through milling crowds of tweed jackets and anoraks but there were some high dramatic moments in Andrei Serban's productions of both plays.

At the same venue and using the same techniques (which the Italians had pioneered at the Festival with *Orlando Furioso*), the Gruppo Teatro Libero, setting most of the action on a mobile raised stage, made a clearer and less confused impression with Armando Pugliese's *Masaniello*, a spirited account with music of the rebellion led by an Amalfi fisherman against the Spanish Bourbon rulers of Naples in 1647. At the Lyceum was the almost motionless allure of Japanese puppets with Bunraku and the amazing Twyla Tharp dancers in seeming perpetual motion on their first European tour in a highly original series of programmes.

In the concert hall we had the three most distinguished Italian conductors of the day, Giulini, Abbado and Riccardo Muti conducting three different orchestras, plus Kurt Masur with Germany's oldest orchestra founded by Bach and Telemann and conducted by Mendelssohn, the Gewandhaus: Mark Elder with the London Sinfonietta, Gibson with the Scottish National, Barenboim with the Orchestre de Paris and John Eliot Gardiner with the Monteverdi Orchestra and Choir in Handel's *Jeptha* in which Peter Pears sang the tenor role.

It was a real United Nations of a programme with the Italians being very un-nationalistic – Giulini and the London Philharmonic with Haydn, Mahler and Beethoven's *Missa Solemnis*; Abbado with the Vienna

Philharmonic with Schubert, Mahler, Webern, Schoenberg and Brahms; Muti with the New Philharmonia in Weber, Beethoven, Bartok, Stravinsky, Schumann and Beethoven. Due chauvinism was provided by Raphael Frühbeck de Burgos with Alicia de Larrocha in a de Falla programme, the 82-year-old Karl Böhm in a memorable interpretation of Mozart's three last symphonies, Kurt Masur with the Gewandhaus from Leipzig in Beethoven and Schumann as well as the then politically affiliated Shostakovich and Szymanowski, and the Orchestre de Paris under Barenboim filling their programmes with Ravel, Boulez and Berlioz.

The power and authority of the Gewandhaus under Masur, the evening when Abbado played Schoenberg's moving *Survivor from Warsaw* twice ('to stick it into their heads,' he said afterwards) with a glittering virtuoso performance of Brahms's First Piano Concerto from Pollini to follow and the delicate lingering affection and pride with which Böhm led the Vienna Philharmonic into Mozart are the outstanding concert memories of 1976.

Even a truncated Festival has its triumphs. Although pressurised by rising costs and inflation (the Edinburgh Festival had been diminishing in size – in terms of the number of programme items it had shrunk by 30 performances since 1974) quality and innovation were still high. It was to face this problem yet again in 1977.

The opera chosen as the Festival's 'in house' production for 1977 was Bizet's *Carmen*. The conductor, Claudio Abbado and the producer Piero Faggioni wanted at least two weeks rehearsal in the King's Theatre before the Festival. The cast which included Teresa Berganza singing her first Carmen, Placido Domingo as Don José and Mirella Freni as Micaela was world class but expensive; the sets and costumes designed by Ezio Frigerio were to be made in Rome: the financial logistics were horrifying.

Although there had been many donations given in financial support to the Edinburgh Festival down the years (nominally in return for advertisements in the souvenir programme) and companies and orchestras of various kinds had come to the Festival with backing from specific governments, firms and bodies (in 1976 IBM had supported the visit of the Vienna Philharmonic) there had been no direct commercial sponsorship in the sense we know it today and the whole idea was thought rather downmarket and unworthy of high-flown artistic endeavour. Peter Diamand, in particular, was very wary of the impositions of choice and taste which could be exerted by sponsors.

> *But facts are chiels that winna ding*
> *An' downa be disputed*

as Robert Burns says in his poem *A Dream*. I don't think Peter Diamand was familiar with the poem but anyone who has directed as many festivals as he had could not but be familiar with the situation. Reluctantly, he agreed to let me make some approaches about direct sponsorship, initially and specifically for *Carmen*.

Two years earlier I had brokered a deal with British Caledonian Airways whereby in exchange for an advertisement in the souvenir programme and calling themselves 'The Festival Airline', they provided the Festival with airline tickets to a value of several thousand pounds a year, so I was already 'contaminated' by commercial contact. For 1977 I targeted the oil companies operating in the North Sea which had displayed some anxiety to have an identification with Scotland. The war-cry of the Scottish nationalist's 'It's Scotland's oil!' had been heard between the first flow of North Sea oil to BP's Isle of Grain refinery in June 1975 and the announcement by the new Labour Prime Minister James Callaghan in 1976 of plans to give Scotland its own parliament.

Connection with Scotland seemed to be an important part of a North Sea oil company's image I thought and fortunately, when I had discussed it several times with top officials at BP, they agreed. On a dark and cold morning in December 1976 in the Central Hotel in Glasgow my principal BP contact Bob Mennie and his colleague Paul Stafford offered to sponsor *Carmen* with £35,000. Later Total Oil Marine, Elf Aquitaine, British Airports Authority, Tennent Caledonian, An Comunn Gaidhealach, Scottish Widows,

Marks and Spencer, Scottish Provident, Citibank, Midland Bank, Laskys, The Highlands and Islands Development Board and Scottish Life provided hundreds of thousands of pounds of sponsorship over five Festivals before a professional sponsorship management company was appointed in 1982.

The sponsorship was welcome of course but not enough to prevent further cuts in the programme. From 134 performances in 1976 we had shrunk to 119 planned for 1977 – three of which never took place because Melina Mercouri and the State Theatre of Northern Greece, in a modern Greek version of Euripides's *Medea,* never reached Edinburgh because of Miss Mercouri's illness.

Despite these cramps on lavishness and content, 1977 was a Festival to cherish and remember and proof, if proof be needed, that quantity is nothing and quality is all.

The only other opera was a world première from a Scottish composer, Thea Musgrave's *Mary, Queen of Scots.* In every way different from most other operas and plays about Mary, it was not derived from Schiller and so did not feature the dramatic but completely unhistorical meeting between Mary and Elizabeth; nor was the religious confrontation with John Knox central to the plot. Knox did not appear.

The text by the composer herself was based on a play by Amalia Elguera, the librettist for Miss Musgrave's previous opera *The Voice of Ariadne.* Entitled *Moray* it focused on the character of Mary's half-brother, James Stewart, Earl of Moray, an illegitimate son of James V, but in her adaptation of it Thea Musgrave focused the dramatic attention on Mary. The character and the tragedy of the tempestuous Mary was well developed musically from the vivacity of her flirtation with Darnley and the reel danced with Bothwell's soldiers, through tenderness, anger and the final obstinacy which leads to her execution. It was an impressive production by Scottish Opera directed by Colin Graham and conducted by Miss Musgrave. As Mary, Catherine Wilson gave one of her finest performances, touching and imperious, vivacious and bitterly lonely and she was admirably supported by Jake Gardner as Moray, Gregory Dempsey as Bothwell and Stafford Dean in a couple of cameo roles. One of the most distinguished of Scottish opera premières.

Theatre offered what was cunningly designed to seem a plethora of riches although most of it involved just two companies, Prospect and the Nottingham Theatre. At the Assembly Hall were two plays about 'a pair so famous' as Octavius Caesar has it in his epitaph, two of the world's most impassioned lovers in Shakespeare's *Antony and Cleopatra* and Dryden's *All for Love* and one of the Bard's most disillusioned swains in *Hamlet.* In addition Prospect offered an adaptation by Christopher Logue of Homer's *Iliad* in *War Music* and an arrangement by Gordon Honeycombe of Milton's *Paradise Lost.*

Not content with this comprehensive repertoire, distinguished actors from the company gave prose and verse recitals in St Cecilia's Hall – Dorothy Tutin and Alec McCowen with Frank Muir in *He and She,* Timothy West as *Sydney Smith* as well as Ian McKellen in *Words, Words, Words* and Rex Harrison reading theatre criticisms from George Bernard Shaw. It was like a star-studded Honours course in Eng. Lit.

Nottingham Theatre were not quite so swashbuckling. Adrian Mitchell's *White Suit Blues* was a celebration of Mark Twain, and Stephen Lowe's *Touched* a new play, a war play without weapons about the women who stayed at home, set in the curious period of almost unbelieving euphoria between VE Day and VJ Day 1945. From Germany, two centuries after the playwright's birth, came the Württembergische Staatstheater with Heinrich von Kleist's *Das Kätchen von Heilbronn,* a stylised production of a pseudo-medieval comedy in which four parts were played by a young actor who two decades later was to play both Shakespeare's Antonys in German at the Festival, Gert Voss.

America contributed the British stage debut of Julie Harris in a one-woman show *The Belle of Amherst* about the reclusive 19th-century poet Emily Dickinson and there was a British tribute to Hollywood in Max Wall's impersonation of Buster Keaton in *Buster* late-night at the Lyceum in the third week following Spanish guitarist Paco Peña and his flamenco dancers.

Again the theme was America in the two exhibitions presented at the Royal Scottish Academy and the Scottish National Gallery of Modern Art. *The Modern Spirit* covered the years of American painting from

1908 to 1935, the paintings of the Ash Can School, the photographs of Stieglitz, the influence of Rodin and Matisse and the breakaway towards abstraction from social realism and project realism. *America America* began approximately where *The Modern Spirit* left off with a group of paintings and sculptures spread from 1940s Jackson Pollock and Willem de Kooning via Claes Oldenburg, Andy Warhol and Robert Rauschenberg to 1960s Frank Stella, exuberance in various eye-catching post-war styles ranging from abstract expressionism to Pop.

The Dryden and Shakespeare versions of the Antony and Cleopatra drama were both very un-Egyptian and not very Roman, locked in the periods of their writing 70 years apart. Shakespeare's lovers as played by Alec McCowen and Dorothy Tutin were rather low key but passionate and eloquent while Dryden's as interpreted by John Turner and Barbara Jefford were imperious and sensuous, a deft contrast although the Shakespeare seemed a shade lacking in Antonine recklessness. There was a superbly positive, vigorous and beautifully spoken Hamlet from Derek Jacobi with a chillingly deranged Ophelia by Suzanne Bertish. *War Music*, the *Iliad* story retold by Christopher Logue was imaginatively directed by Toby Robertson and spectacularly choreographed by William Louther. All the Prospect productions had great sweep and pace, feasting the eyes if not always the ears and very much what Festival theatre should be in excitement and passion. Even when an interpretation quarrelled with your view of the character or the text you left the theatre invigorated and stimulated to discussion well into the small hours.

Derek Jacobi Hamlet *(1977)*

Scottish Ballet, who shared the King's Theatre with the two operas, also offered Shakespeare in *Othello* as well as *La Sylphide* and *Les Sylphides*, enlivened by two star guests, Natalia Makarova and the superbly athletic 22-year-old Cuban-American, Fernando Bujones.

Savings on the main concert programmes in the Usher Hall were achieved by cutting the number of orchestral concerts and having five celebrity solo recitals, two by Barenboim and one each by Annie Fischer and Maurizio Pollini and with the Yehudi Menuhin/Louis Kentner duo playing Beethoven sonatas. There was a lot of Beethoven, 30 works in all, plus an entire song recital by Hermann Prey. Five orchestras appeared, only one of them foreign and only one (oddly enough the Scottish National) for a single concert. The foreign orchestra was the Concertgebouw from The Netherlands in four concerts with two conductors, Kyril Kondrashin and Bernard Haitink with whom Pollini gave a stunning performance of the Beethoven Fifth after the exotica of Debussy and a first hearing of Lutoslawski's *Mi Parti*. From London came the New Philharmonia with Giulini, the Royal Philharmonic with Charles Groves and Antal Dorati and London Symphony with Erich Leinsdorf and Abbado.

If ever an orchestra was on a three week high, it was the LSO that year. They played in the pit at the King's Theatre for seven electrifying evenings of *Carmen* and gave four concerts, eleven full-scale performances, nine of them conducted by Abbado, with a virtuosity and élan which I have never heard equalled in sustained musicianship. They played Wagner with Jessye Norman singing the *Liebestod* from *Tristan und Isolde,* they played Mahler with Janet Baker singing the *Ruckert Lieder,* Richard Strauss, Ligeti, Schumann, Mozart, Beethoven, Tchaikovsky and Stravinsky but mostly and superlatively, they played Bizet.

After all the complaints about the King's Theatre, at last it had a meticulously tailored success. Piero Faggioni's production caught the dark side of Mérimée's tense passionate drama of *Carmen* from the start with the curtain rising each act as the fate theme sounds in the orchestra, on José in prison awaiting his fate. Only then did the tale of the taunting gypsy fierceness of the girl's independence, the terrible infatuation of José, the seedy vigour of Lillas Pastia's tavern and the tumult, danger and drama of the final tragedy unroll.

Berganza had her own particular vision of Carmen, safely free in the libertarian creed of the gypsy mind and very much her own woman; Domingo made José a disorientated man stumbling into passion,

Peter Diamand, Teresa Berganza, Placido Domingo

struggling in the coils of fate he hardly understood and could not escape, unable to accept the gentle refuge of Micaela from his fever of obsession. The piece flowed from the almost pastoral opening in the plaza outside the cigarette factory to the tension of the bullring and the last fatal confrontation between the lovers with a taut and sure touch. Everything from the spitfire zest of Carmen to the final pitiful anger of José was brilliantly done, superlatively delineated dramatically and musically.

Having been involved in finding some of the money to help mount the production and having got to know the company while they rehearsed – hearing and seeing snatches here and there and wondering what was going to be served up to satisfy the sponsors – I felt very personally committed to *Carmen*. I remember vividly the first heady moment when I realised that is was going to be better than all right – that here was a genuine 22-carat triumph.

It came right at the beginning of the dress rehearsal on the first Sunday of the Festival, the moment when Abbado raised his baton and launched the orchestra into the overture with such electrifying impact that everyone in the house was half-off their seats in the first two seconds. And that supreme lyrical and dramatic tension never faltered. This was a great production with superb performances but the architect of the triumph was Abbado. Fortunately, it can still be heard on the Deutsche Grammophon recording made in conjunction with the Festival performances. Listen to the brilliant orchestral and choral scene-setting outside the bullring at the beginning of the final scene. Opera does not come any more dazzling than that.

But, inevitably, not all was undiluted rapture. In *The Guardian* Gerald Larner's review was entitled 'Berganza's Unseductive Flop':

> Tickets for Edinburgh's Carmen *have been changing hands for £50 each – which, as the Festival management has no doubt noted, makes the official £20 top price look cheap.*
>
> *The roars of approval at the King's Theatre indicate that for the most part, it actually was good value.*
>
> *Eventually, I would have been happy to pay £10 for Mirella Freni's Micaela, £5 for Placido Domingo's José and for Teresa Berganza's Carmen and Tom Krause's Escamillio, £2.50 the pair. Since, out of the £20 printed on my ticket that leaves £2.50 for the mainly well-presented smaller parts, the brisk precision of Claudio Abbado's conducting, some beautiful playing by the London Symphony Orchestra and excellent*

singing from the Scottish Theatre Chorus, I should be happy. Ezio Frigerio's designs and Piero Faggioni's production and Mariemma's obviously authentic choreography – not to mention the rich variety of foreign accents applied to the French texts – have not been reckoned in at all. But frankly I was not happy to come away from a Carmen *in which Micaela is more seductive that Carmen herself and in which so much of the visual aspect is embarrassing. Faggioni seems to have had endless trouble in getting the demure little Berganza even to walk interestingly and his efforts to make her provocative – daringly putting on Escamillo's toreador hat and kicking her foot behind her when she kisses José – are distressing. In much of the last act, in her final encounter with José she just stands there, which is not what dignified means.*

Berganza sings well with much subtlety but not superlatively. Her Habenera was a little breathless on the first night, her gypsy song too subdued, and it was only in her dance with castanets that she seemed positively to enjoy Bizet's marvellously coloured vocal writing.

The superlative singing in the production came from Freni, Tu lui diras *has never sounded more beautiful and certainly she inspired the best in Domingo's always lyrical but not always committed singing. His acting has incidentally the additional strain of a little and not easily explicable mimed vignette of helplessness in the prelude and each of the entractes. The additional music, which is to say several standard cuts happily restored, is nothing but welcome. It compensates in a way for the unconvincing economy in setting, where three stuccoed walls must represent a street in Seville, Lillas Pastia's, a mountain and the outside of a bull ring.*

This review, unsurprisingly, enraged Berganza and scornfully she sent Gerald Larner a Scottish £5 note. Somewhat embarrassed, and thinking sardonically that one day he might frame it, Gerald stuck it in his wallet, dismissing it as one of those slings and arrows that beat about the critic's head. But one day, removing his car from the car park, he found he had no money, only the vengeful £5 note. So he paid his parking fee with it. There ought to be a moral to this somewhere.

Carmen tickets created other problems. At the beginning of the second week there was a *Carmen* performance on a Sunday. During the first week, Andrew Porter, then music critic of one of the world's leading magazines, *The New Yorker,* telephoned me. 'I hear the *Carmen* is wonderful,' he said (obviously not being a loyal reader of Gerald Larner). 'If you can get me a ticket for Sunday night I will fly over specially to see it.'

I, of course, pointed out that we had told him it was going to be wonderful a couple of months before; that tickets were like gold dust, but I said I would see what I could do and phone him back. I tried George Bain, the Administrative Manager, the financial officer James Sibbald, explaining to them carefully the importance and prestige of Mr Porter. I tried Peter Diamand and Piero Faggioni who knew all about the eminence of Mr Porter – nothing.

Then Claudio Abbado's wife, Gabriella, told me she had managed to get a returned ticket from the box office the previous day. I got on to the box office and asked about returned tickets. 'I have one returned ticket for Sunday,' said the formidable lady in charge of the box office, 'but you can't have it.' In vain I explained the eminence of Mr Porter, the prestige of *The New Yorker* and I may even have pointed out the effect it could have on the National Debt. 'My instructions from Mr Sibbald,' said the box-office manager grimly, 'are that the tickets must be sold.'

'Hold on to it, don't let it out of your sight,' I told her. 'Someone from my office will be over with the money in ten minutes.'

I sent Alan, our most speedy leg-man, hotfoot from the press bureau in the Assembly Rooms in George Street across to the Festival Office, clutching the notes as if his life depended on it. When he arrived back with the ticket, I telephoned Andrew Porter, he flew across the Atlantic to see *Carmen* and wrote a four-page rave review about it in *The New Yorker*. However Mr Sibbald was adamant. I wrote to him; I sent him a copy of the review.

'You have your press ticket allocation, Mr Crawford,' he told me. 'If you want to buy additional tickets for your friends that is another matter and entirely your affair.'

I never got my £20 back.

XXI

1978 was to be Peter Diamand's last year as Director of the Edinburgh Festival. Although the 1977 Festival had been a triumph artistically, pared to the bone financially but setting in many respects a benchmark for the quality which Diamand believed should always be the prime aim in constructing programmes, the squabbling on the Council and among city and regional politicians would not go away and was reaching intolerable levels of pettiness and invective.

Just before Christmas in 1976 Lothian Region had voted to renege on the £90,000 grant which it had agreed to contribute to the Festival budget and Edinburgh City and District Council had added £100,000 to their grant and taken on the full responsibility of being the major civic source of Festival funding.

The situation was summed up by Councillor Brian Meek, chairman of the Leisure and Recreation Committee:

> *The Festival Council and other Region and District boards have proved a disaster – a squabbling match between one authority and the other, with the only sufferers the ratepayers.*

Peter Diamand said cryptically that he would be surprised if the Festival Council would wish to continue to have Lothian Region represented on it. 'I cannot say that the expertise which the Region brought to the Festival would be missed if the money did not accompany it,' he added.

At the time when the Region withdrew its financial support, Diamand had said he would resign if the Edinburgh Festival's international status declined because of falling cash support. He criticised the Region's decision to axe the £90,000 grant for 1977.

> *Two years ago at the time of local government reform, I understood that the Region was very anxious to be involved in the Festival. If the quality of the Festival were in serious jeopardy, I would have to consider whether this was the correct Festival for me to work for. For two years the scale of the Festival has been reduced but we have maintained the quality. But any further cuts by the subscribing authorities could put the Festival's world-wide reputation at stake. There are no miracles. Without an increase, the quantity of the Festival will have to be reduced. To say that Edinburgh gets a world-class Festival on the cheap is an understatement. There is no doubt that the Festival brings to Edinburgh and Scotland an enormous amount of money every year.*

In addition to the proposed reduction in grant, rentals for halls, theatres and offices used by the Festival had been trebled and now totalled more than £25,000. There were moves to close the London office and pressure for a complete freeze on local authority funding until after 1978. In vain it was pointed out that it cost about 30% more each year to maintain the Festival at the same standard; that despite steeply rising costs it had balanced its books in the previous year. A probe into Festival finances was ordered by the Policy and Resources Committee of Lothian Regional Council.

In the autumn of 1977 it was announced that Peter Diamand, whose contract as Festival Director ran out in autumn 1978, would be resigning and that a new Director would be appointed to take over after the 32nd Festival. In fact the new director was chosen in October 1977 and joined the Festival staff almost immediately.

John Drummond came from BBC Television where he was Assistant Head of Music and Arts Programmes and although keenly interested in a wide spectrum of the arts, he had no hands-on experience of running a Festival when he became the heir to Edinburgh's barbed cultural throne

For just under a year he sat – literally – in the corridor of power in the Festival's St James's Street offices in London, learning the ropes and the routines of how the Festival was put together and run and formulating his own ideas. On his frequent visits to Edinburgh we saw a lot of him. By nature more sociable than Peter Diamand, he was a frequent guest at our Bruntsfield Place flat where we had long conversations about Festival matters and where we held a special party to introduce him to influential Edinburgh figures such as Lord Cameron, MPs, luminaries from the Scottish Office and the editors of local newspapers.

John Drummond (now Sir John) is a tall handsome, intellectually brilliant, lonely man who is always talking about his friends. Tense as a violin string, watchful for grievance he can by turns be uncomfortable or delightful company. His taste, intelligence and flair had a great influence on the Edinburgh Festival as it did later on his running of the BBC Proms. Extrovert yet intensely private, articulate at machine-gun pace and witty yet probingly analytical with a widespread rebelliousness of interests; over six-foot in height and conspicuous he was very much the opposite of Peter Diamand. Through 1977-8 he prowled the corridors of power waiting for the doors to swing fully open while Diamand got on with compiling and presenting his last festival.

It was very much the end of an era. Diamand had been Festival Director for 13 years and with his experience of the Holland Festival before he came to Edinburgh in 1966, he was the most experienced festival director in the world. Musically his final festival spanned the range of his interests with opera from its beginnings with Monteverdi in the 16th century, through Berlioz, Bizet, Debussy, Stravinsky and Janácek to the British première of a work by Luigi Nono written in 1974. There was a lavish choice of orchestras including the International Youth Orchestra, the Staatskapelle from Dresden and the Chicago Symphony Orchestra and some of Diamand's favourite conductors in Abbado, Barenboim Gibson and Giulini.

Although the theatre, as he always admitted, depended more truly on the choice and the contacts of his Artistic Assistant, Bill Thomley, it also reflected the Diamand years – wall-to-wall Shakespeare and classics from the Russian theatre. Dance, never the most prominent of the arts in the Diamand regime, was however powerfully represented by the Tanztheater Wuppertal with three ballets by Pina Bausch to music by Stravinsky, *West Wind, The Second Spring* and a wonderfully pagan *Rite of Spring*.

Nor was the Festival as truncated as in 1977. With four opera companies offering seven operas and eight orchestras, four drama companies and a dance company together with all the music, prose and poetry recitals in the Freemasons Hall, Leith Theatre, St Mary's Cathedral, St Cecilia's Hall and the new venue of Daniel Stewart's and Melville College, the performance count was up to 131.

The great 1977 *Carmen* was repeated although with some cast changes. The previous year José was sung at the first six performances by Placido Domingo with Peyo Garazzi taking over for the final night. In 1978 José was sung by Pedro Lavirgen and the role of Micaela was shared between Ileana Cotrubas and Yvonne Kenny. It was not quite the same without Domingo's powerful lyrical presence but Berganza in the title role remained brilliantly original, the production still sparkled, Lavirgen was more than adequate and the thrilling ensemble and orchestral playing under Abbado were as compelling as ever.

Scottish Opera brought a Colin Graham production of Debussy's only completed opera, *Pelléas et Melisande* with Thomas Allen and Anne Howells in the title roles and Joseph Rouleau as Arkel. The newly knighted Alexander Gibson handled the subtle and evocative score with great skill. It is unusual for Pelléas to be sung by a baritone but Tom Allen had done it at Covent Garden and in Edinburgh the additional warmth of his voice gave the role a more human and less ethereal dimension and its delicate and fine-veined passion was conveyed with true mastery.

Pelléas et Melisande has been called the French *Tristan* and indeed there is something Wagnerian about the orchestration but its passion is a much more fragile flower in the shadowed twilight world of Maeterlinck's play. The fey childlike character of Melisande is one of the most difficult to convey but Anne Howells was both distractedly innocent and naively passionate as the mysterious star-crossed heroine. It was a fine performance of this strange unique masterpiece.

The Monteverdi operas came from Zurich in the performing editions of the German conductor and musicologist Nikolaus Harnoncourt whose long fascination with early music had led him back to Monteverdi's original scores. Following directions from the composer in prefaces and recorded observations, he made new arrangements for the instruments on which the music was originally played – baroque violins and violas, cembalo, chitarroni, lutes, flutes, harp, cornetts, dulcians and trombones. By thus returning to the first principles of opera he not only made an important contribution to musical history but created – or re-created – performing versions which bring out the latent dramatic qualities of the earliest truly blended musical works for the theatre.

Opera, as we know it, was born in Mantua at the lavish court of the Gonzagas in whose rambling palace *L'Orfeo*, the first great opera was staged. The fusion of words and music had, of course, been going on for a very long time but the conception of them linked together as a single dramatic entity was very *avant-garde* in the 16th century. Peri, Caccini and Cavalieri in Florence had created entertainments which may have claims to being the first operas although unfortunately Peri's *Dafne*, first presented in 1597, is lost and Cavalieri's *La rappresentazione di Anima e di Corpo*, performed in Rome in 1600 and given at the 1972 Festival by the Dusseldorf Opera is often referred to as the first oratorio. Two versions of *Euridice* by Peri and Caccini also pre-date Monteverdi but the quality of the music both for voices and instruments and its relation to the text make *L'Orfeo* unquestionably the most important early opera.

Monteverdi may well have seen some of these early works by Peri and Caccini as he learned his theory from Marcantonio Ingegneri, director of music at the Cathedral in his birthplace Cremona and probably from the writings of the first Baroque music theorist, Vincenzo Galileo, father of the astronomer, who taught that the aim of composers should be 'to express the conceptions of the mind and to impress them with the greatest possible effectiveness on the minds of the listener'. His reputation was firmly established by the production of *L'Orfeo* at Mantua in 1607.

Here was an opera which went far beyond the stilted conventions of Peri and Caccini, a combination of elaborate Renaissance entertainment with a simple pastoral classical

Il Ritorno d'Ulisse in Patria *(1978)*

142

tale told in recitative, where the orchestra played a very real part in the dramatic narrative by associating particular instruments with characters and situations. The trombones which dominate the overture to the third act set in The Underworld retained their infernal associations as is clear from their use in the last act of Mozart's *Don Giovanni*. It was this opera together with two others composed in Venice in his 70s for the water city's first opera house, *Il Ritorno d'Ulisse in Patria* and *L'Incoronazione di Poppea*, which Zurich Opera brought to Edinburgh.

The result was three evenings of sheer delight unrolled in splendid Renaissance sets designed by Jean-Pierre Ponelle and directed by him with elegance and style. Under Harnoncourt's sensitive baton the tale of Orpheus and Euridice, Ulysses and Penelope and the infatuations of Nero and Poppea were played out to glorious music, formal and antique up to a point but in no way lacking in lyricism. *Orfeo* and *Il Ritorno di Ulisse* are the stuff of legend from which such cantata entertainments had always been made up to that time but *Poppea* is the first true modern opera, the 17th-century *Traviata*. The importance and charm and theatrical impact of these operas lies not only in their musical sophistication but in their emphasis on dramatic development and the range and scope of their characterisation.

Here for the first time on the musical stage are human beings in recognisably real situations, expressing their feelings and intentions not only with great musical beauty but with astonishing emotional accuracy – most effectively perhaps in *Poppea's* last great duet *Pur ti miro*.

In contrast to the radiant flourishes of Monteverdi there was passion torn to shreds in Janacek's *Katya Kabanova* from Frankfurt Opera. Based on Alexander Nikolayevish Ostrovsky's play *The Storm*, a tale of intrigue and tempestuous passion on the banks of the Volga, it introduced a new European star to the Festival in Hildegard Behrens who had been chosen as Karajan's Salome and had recently made a sensational debut at Covent Garden as Leonora in *Fidelio*. She made an appealing Katya, vivid vocally and convincing dramatically in what was a rather muddled and lumpish production by Volker Schloendorff, not otherwise strongly cast apart from Sona Cervena as Kabanicha but orchestrally impressive under Michael Gielen.

I must confess I went to the concert performance in the King's Theatre of Luigi Nono's *Al Gran Sole Carico d'Amore* (To the Great Sun Burdened with Love) out of a sense of self-educating duty with the firm intention of going on to Solti's concert with the Chicago Symphony in the Usher Hall for the second half. But I found this curious musical expostulation of the place of women in society from texts drawn from sources as varied as Fidel Castro, Gramsci, Marx and Rimbaud so fascinating as set to Nono's spiky and implacable music that I stayed. I am far from sure that I am very clear what it all means but it had its own sentimental and polemical allure. As far as I know this was its British première and dernière.

Following Diamand's opera example, the company bringing Shakespeare to the open stage of the Assembly Hall that year was called Edinburgh Festival Productions.

Directed by David Giles, who had been responsible for two earlier Festival plays with The Actors Company but was probably best known for his production of the BBC TV series *The Forsyte Saga*, it gave *The Tempest* with Alan Dobie as Prospero, Janet Maw as Miranda and Richard Easton as Caliban and *A Midsummer Night's Dream* with Marilyn Taylerson as Titania, Jack Galloway as Puck and Dobie as Bottom. If they were a little lacking in the high innovative style which some former Shakespearean performances had brought to Edinburgh and a bit bereft of star names and vivid performances, they were worthy enough and audiences enjoyed them.

The Royal Shakespeare Company appeared in one of the Festival's off-beat venues, Daniel Stewart's and Melville College, one of Edinburgh's hospital schools, built by philanthropists' money and endowed for the education of the less privileged, always an important Scottish concern. This resulted in the 19th century in a profligate variety of architectural scholastic styles of marvellous eccentricity, ranging from the classical Athenian of Thomas Hamilton's splendidly sited Royal High School on the south slope of

Calton Hill through the baronial extravagance of David Bryce's French-Gothic Fettes College to David Rhind's Stewart's College, a scaled-down version of a plan which won second prize in a competition for the new Houses of Parliament in London which had to be built after the fire of 1834.

The RSC offered *Twelfth Night*, rather improbably as an Edwardian comedy but with a wonderful foxy Sir Toby from Ian McKellen and Emily Richard as a touching and spirited Viola. Trevor Nunn made *Three Sisters* less mocking than it can sometimes seem although perhaps that was because sighing for the fleshpots of the capital in a culturally over-stuffed Edinburgh might have been more than obviously ironic. It was a stylish performance but the venue was rather incongruous and has only been used once since. The Royal Lyceum offered more Chekhov with *Ivanov* and the Moscow Drama Company from the Malaya Bronnaya Theatre in Gogol's *The Marriage* and Turgenev's *A Month in the Country*.

Prospect, following the Festival trend of offering early Chekhov plays which had flopped on their first appearance (*The Wood Demon* in 1973 was the other), gave us *Ivanov*. But no-one was complaining when what was offered was a production of such endearing pace and passion as Toby Robertson's interpretation with the title role brilliantly played by Derek Jacobi with strong support from Jane Wymark, Louise Purnell, Michael Denison and Oz Clarke. It was the Russians in their own language with the Gogol and the Turgenev who were disappointing. The passing competitive romantic flutter between Natalia and her god-daughter in the manner of *Rosenkavalier* was much too heavy-handed and doom-laden and 'the absolutely incredible event in two acts' of *The Marriage* hardly lived up to the necessary 'willing suspension of disbelief' in presentation.

But if the drama was something of a curate's egg the music in the Usher Hall was splendid. The International Youth Orchestra and Chorus and Isaac Stern under Giulini gave a memorable opening concert with Mozart's Third violin concerto and Beethoven's Ninth symphony – made the more remarkable when the young Japanese basses from the chorus formed up on the hall steps facing on to Lothian Road as we left and sang the *Song of Joy* as an *a cappella* encore with great resonance and exuberance.

There was a fine *Damnation de Faust* from Daniel Barenboim and the London Philharmonic with Jessye Norman, Stuart Burrows, Jules Bastin and Don Garrad as soloists and our own Festival Chorus. The Chorus appeared again with Giulini and the same orchestra, Ileana Cotrubas and Dietrich Fischer-Dieskau in the Brahms's Requiem. As well as playing for *Carmen* at the King's, Abbado and the London Symphony with Stern gave the Sibelius violin concerto in a programme which included a wonderfully detailed but powerful

LSO and Abbado in the Usher Hall (1978)

account of Janacek's *Sinfonietta*. Their second concert had a novel programme of Mozart arias sung by Teresa Berganza, Ryland Davies and Fischer-Dieskau, plus Schubert's Eighth symphony and a glittering celebration of two Stravinsky ballet suites, the pungent *Firebird* and the Pergolesi-derived *Pulcinella*.

Under Yevgeny Svetlanov the LSO played the rousing Shostakovich Fifth in tandem with a sensitive romantic performance of Chopin's First piano concerto by the young Polish pianist, Krystian Zimerman and accompanied a strikingly authoritative Beethoven Third from Alfred Brendel, set rather incongruously in the middle of a Rimsky-Korsakov evening. There was Vivaldi and Schubert from Pinchas Zuckerman and the English Chamber Orchestra; Boulez with the BBC Symphony in Mahler and Schoenberg, his own *Rituel* and Stravinsky's near-opera *Le Rossignol* and more Mahler and Beethoven from Sir Georg Solti and the Chicago Symphony who finished their stint in the Usher Hall with Brahms's two last symphonies, massively rendered. The Scottish National Orchestra with the two newest musical knights, Alexander Gibson and Clifford Curzon provided the closing concert in no less monumental a fashion with Dvorak's *Te Deum* and Janacek's *Glagolitic Mass* sandwiching an elegant and lyrically expressive performance of Mozart most radiant piano concerto, the C major K467. It was a Festival full of memorable music, definitively performed with grace, passion and affection for the man who spent the previous decade and a half underscoring and refusing to devalue the high standards which he believed were the most central tenets of its existence.

For him on the Friday of the first week, after Giulini had conducted the German Requiem, in the Usher Hall there was a special concert, *Festival Garland*, which I was conscripted to introduce. It was a somewhat embarrassing honour, thrust upon me at the last minute by Bill Thomley who seemed to have no very clear idea of what was happening and was intimidated by the dazzling distinction of the cast. I had to play it by ear, taking the running order from a slip in the programme and in some cases scrabbling around backstage to find out exactly what everybody was going to offer in tribute to *le grand Diamand*. Fortunately, I think I got most of it right or if I didn't, no-one was brutal enough to point it out afterwards.

It certainly was a starry line-up. Jessye Norman and Fischer-Dieskau sang Schubert; Cathy Gayer gave Schoenberg cabaret songs, Giulini conducted *Eine Kliene Nachtmusik*, Isaac Stern and Barenboim played a Mozart sonata. Cotrubas sang with the orchestra with Barenboim conducting, Teresa Berganza sang with Abbado conducting, Gibson took over the orchestra for a sarabande from Britten, the Festival Chorus had an item, Barenboim played for the singers and soloists with Abbado turning the pages and everything was rounded off with the Mozart B flat piano concerto.

The tributes were many and deservedly fulsome. Fortunately they appeared in print in the *Festival Garland* programme, the souvenir programme and the press. There were no embarrassing speeches after the music had spoken its gratitude. Just 'Thank you Peter!'

Alexander Gibson called him 'one of the world's virtuoso administrators'. Harold Rosenthal, editor of *Opera* magazine, said: 'his contribution to opera in this country cannot be too highly praised'. After listing some of the programmes of his Festival years, *The Times* music critic William Mann wrote:

> *Any Edinburgh Festival artistic director might have put on some of these events. I doubt whether any other but Peter Diamand would have contemplated choosing all of them. Not just Edinburgh, or Scotland, but the world is the richer for what he has done here.*

I talked to Peter Diamand again eight years later at the 1986 Festival when he returned to Edinburgh for the 40th Festival Gala Concert. I had been asked to write the programme introduction, (once again at the last minute) and, having attended this pathetic celebration and felt aggrieved at being associated with something which in its general slapdash standard and air of having been casually thrown together did not match my idea of a worthy commemoration of 40 Edinburgh Festivals, I was not surprised to find Diamand agreeing with me.

I was invited by Frank Dunlop to come here for a few days and take in some of the programmes. But I looked at the brochure and to tell the truth, I could not find anything that interested me enough to make me feel I wanted to spend two or three days attending events in Edinburgh.

Recalling his own ideas about the Festival when he first arrived in 1965, he said:

I tell you two things I wanted to do. One was, where artistically justifiable, to involve Scottish elements – which up till then was hardly the case. I mean, there was a sort of obligation to have one concert with the BBC Scottish Symphony Orchestra and one concert with the Scottish National Orchestra – to have it and get rid of it as quickly as possible, more or less – and I wanted to involve, if at all possible, Scottish Opera.

And to involve other Scottish elements not only at the Festival but so that their appearance in the Festival would be of such importance to them that it would be reflected in their annual work. And I wanted, in addition to the policy of bringing the most prominent artists to the Festival, to open the Festival to young artists.

I found that when I came here the Festival was a sort of oasis in a complete artistic desert. I think – I may be wrong – but I think that the standards of the SNO in their winter seasons improved greatly. Because they were given responsible tasks in the Festival they have now become a superb international orchestra.

On the problems he encountered during his long reign as Festival Director, he said:

Well, in the first place the difficulty was lack of funds, lack of an opera house, and the general weight of the Festival Council being dominated by the Town Council and the many philistines among them who were looking at the box-office rather than any kind of artistic innovation or risk.

In the end I did succeed in realising most of the things I wanted to do – all in opposition from town councillors and the diplomatic game which had to be played. I mean, if I very much wanted to succeed in one thing and not so much in others, I had in the end to give priority to the one in which I was most interested, and to make a sort of gesture to the Council and say 'all right I give up this other one' – a ritual sacrifice. Yes, he added with a wry smile, *but there were also gains, hidden charms.*

When I asked how he saw the future of the Festival, he said:

I'm worried about it. I am worried about the hypocrisy, that basic hypocrisy which I encountered first in Holland has greatly increased, and by that I mean this. The Festival is made more and more to attract an undiscriminating public where the quantity matters. And I think this is sheer nonsense, I am convinced. I know that such statements have been attacked often enough – and will be attacked at the Festival. But what I consider as the Edinburgh Festival is addressed to a limited audience and even if you made the admission price very very low you could gain little more. Without any doubt you would not gain all the people here nor the people who are passing by. The idea that the Festival should cater for everyone is just plain nonsense.

Since we live in a democracy with elected councillors and whatever they are who want to be popular with the masses, it must be open to the masses and the Festival events must then be brought to the whole of Edinburgh, into the suburbs.

Without knowledge about the content of the Festival you cannot expect to attract a mass audience. I am convinced of it. I watched last week on three consecutive nights the programme Russell Harty comes to the Festival. *If I didn't know anything about the Festival, this – the Edinburgh Festival which I saw on this programme – I would stay away from it. I mean, it was principally the Fringe and every allusion to 'serious' programmes was carefully avoided. Because obviously the producers and Mr Harty were afraid that if they were to go into the more serious parts of the Festival, people would switch off their television sets. Well, let them switch off their television sets. You can't have it all ways. You must choose what your ambition is and my ambition has never been to play to the greatest numbers of audiences. I knew this and constantly did programmes which I knew would appeal only to a limited number. Unless you fix a very definite line, I think you risk falling between two stools, instead of just sitting on one.*

And all this stuff about people being afraid to go to cultural events – they're afraid to go to the Usher Hall and afraid to go into the King's Theatre – and you must make it easy for them. It's all nonsense. They're not afraid – they're just bloody well not interested. And why shouldn't they be? I am uninterested in many things.

As an example of the high standards which Diamand demanded of Festival performances and performers, we talked about the 1977 *Carmen:*

Yes, and that Carmen went from here to Hamburg, to Paris, to La Scala – but it never came off as well in any of these places as here, for we in Edinburgh worked under Festival conditions with enough rehearsal time. We created – and God knows with how many difficulties – the conditions in which artists could work for a Festival performance.

I went to the first night at La Scala, Milan and all of the people who had seen it in Edinburgh came to me afterwards and said 'What a pity it was not as well-prepared as in Edinburgh.'

He cited an occasion when one conductor demanded very considerable and expensive rehearsal time for him and his orchestra in Edinburgh:

They got it. And then shortly before they were due to come they said: 'Oh, we will come two or three days later, and we give up our first rehearsals'. I said, 'Thank you but no. If you want me to take you seriously, I must assume that the rehearsals you asked for are what you need and now you have no engagement in the meantime you can use this time to have as little rehearsal as some of your colleagues do. No. Come another year.'

You have to set standards to remind audiences what art is like at its best. One of the tasks of a Festival Director is to create the conditions for it to be as good as possible.

SIR JOHN DRUMMOND 1979-83
Diaghilev to Vienna

XXII

Although John Drummond had come as Festival Director somewhat shackled by a promise to stick to a budget, there was none of the austerity of the last Diamand years about his first Festival in 1979. As a dance enthusiast he was determined to restore ballet to its due prominence in the programme and as the opening day of the 33rd Festival, 19 August was the 50th anniversary of the death of the greatest ballet impresario of them all, Sergei Diaghilev, the occasion was ready-made for dance to take centre stage.

Sir John Drummond

In the introduction he wrote to the 1979 Souvenir Programme, Drummond set out his theme:

It is hard to find one word to describe Diaghilev. Nijinsky in his Diary noted that Diaghilev hated to be called an impresario. He felt it smacked too much of the commercial world and too little of the creative. Creative is certainly the adjective that must be applied to Diaghilev and his career. In an age before governments had policies for the arts, before the existence of Arts Councils, for nearly 30 years Diaghilev caused things to happen, from editing magazines to mounting exhibitions, to organising concerts and opera, as well as touring ballet throughout Western Europe and the Americas. He discovered talent everywhere and harnessed it to his ambitions. He changed the whole way in which people looked at design. He gave a new dimension to dance. Some of his work was inevitably ephemeral, much of it more lasting than even he can have realised.

His central belief was in the interdependence of all the arts. It is a profound belief that still needs restating, and where better to reaffirm it than in the context of a festival?

Especially one like Edinburgh which since the beginning has concerned itself with all the arts and whose readiness to continue that policy is one of its principal justifications.

In a world changed radically since the Festival began in 1947, let alone since Diaghilev's death in 1929, the need for festivals is sometimes questioned. Apart from sheer excellence of performance, the main criterion, the justification must also be that, through the concentration of time effort and money, they can do things that would not otherwise happen, and surprise as well as satisfy. Just as Diaghilev, improbably, turned the reactionary world of late 19th-century ballet into a fulcrum for new ideas for the 20th century, so festivals can place even the familiar in a new context giving it new life and new relevance. There must also be a continuing commitment to innovation. If any festival achieves even a portion of Diaghilev's impact then it is still serving its purpose.

Having set out his creed, John Drummond set out his stall. So there were concerts, opera and ballet programmes, exhibitions and lectures and theatre associated with Diaghilev. Unlike the Diamand and Harewood pursuit of the theme, it could hardly be said that it was perfectly possible to attend many events at the Edinburgh Festival and be unaware of its devotion to Diaghilev in 1979.

The opening concert, 50 years to the day from Diaghilev's death in Venice, had a Russian-Scottish accent in celebration of the great *maestro*, with Gennadi Rozhdestvensky conducting the BBC Symphony in two of the great ballet scores which Diaghilev had presented, Stravinsky's *Rite of Spring* and Prokoviev's *Chout*, with Scots actor Andrew Cruikshank as narrator. Two of the operas had Diaghilev associations – he had known Tchaikovsky and helped to popularise his music in the West and he had studied with Rimsky-Korsakov. So Scottish Opera's productions of *Eugene Onegin* and *The Golden Cockerel* fitted the celebration bill.

The Golden Cockerel, Rimsky-Korsakov's last work is based on a satirical fairy-tale by Pushkin, mocking government incompetence, and it was given a gilded and colourful pantomimic production by David Pountney which included a trapeze artist as the Cockerel and an excellent performance by one of Scottish Opera's stalwarts, William McCue as the bumbling King Dondon.

But for all the spectacle and entertainment value of *The Golden Cockerel*, it was still the music that mattered, Sergei Rachmaninov wrote:

In Rimsky-Korsakov's scores there is never the slightest doubt about the 'meteorological picture' the music is meant to convey. When there is a snowstorm the flakes seem to dance and drift from the woodwinds and the sound holes of the violins; when the sun is high, all the instruments shine with an almost fiery glare; when there is water, the waves ripple and dance audibly through the orchestra and this effect is not achieved by the comparatively cheap means of a harp glissando. The sound is cool and glassy when he describes a calm winter's night with a glittering starlit sky. He was a master of great orchestral sound-painting and one can still learn from him.

As did Glazunov, Prokoviev and Stravinsky, all of whom were his pupils. Henry Lewis, America's first black conductor, conjured all the colour and sound perfumes of the Orient from the rich score with the BBC Scottish Symphony Orchestra. It matched almost perfectly Dr Johnson's definition of opera as 'an exotic and irrational entertainment'.

There was less glitter and more substance to *Onegin*, Tchaikovsky's finest achievement on the operatic stage. Not even David Pountney and Alexander Gibson could do much with the galumphing peasants in the first act, but things got better with Tatiana's letter, one of the great solo scenes in opera, sung with touching sentiment and innocent passion by Canadian soprano, Lilian Sukis.

Anthony Rolf-Johnson voiced his duel aria with an exquisite sense of doom, Stafford Dean made a sonorous Prince Gremin, and John Shirley-Quirk, more than adequately Byronic, managed the transition from the dismissive, caddish dandy of the early acts to the impassioned lover of the last with considerable musicianship and skill.

Anthony Besch's fine production of *The Turn of the Screw*, most admirably conducted by Roderick Bryden also came from Glasgow to the Festival with Catherine Wilson as the tormented governess, George Shirley the sinister Quint and Peter Pears as Prologue. In all, a programme which gave a splendid impression of Scottish Opera's maturity and range.

Almost every concert contained music from Russia or Eastern Europe, Shostakovich, Rachmaninov, Tchaikovsky, Mussorgsky, Penderecki, Bartok, Scriabin, Stravinsky, Prokoviev or scores from which Diaghilev had presented ballets – Debussy, Ravel, Falla, Poulenc, Rossini, Schumann, Weber and Chopin. The Glasgow Citizens' Theatre managed to do a theatrical double on Diaghilev with a play by Robert

David Macdonald about the *maestro* himself, *Chinchilla*, and Goldoni's comedy *The Good-Humoured Ladies*, best known as a Massine ballet.

Opening the theatre programme at the Royal Lyceum was a company from Russia – or rather Georgia. (I got the distinct impression from Robert Sturua, its brilliant director, that he was about as fond of being called 'Russian' as I am of being designated 'English'.) At all events, the Rustaveli Company which John Drummond had discovered on a visit to Tbilisi (among his linguistic accomplishments are fluent Russian and French) turned out to be one of the most powerfully exciting theatre events which the Festival had staged. As usual, no amount of advance hype would persuade people to fill the theatre for a play in an obscure language on the first night, but word soon got around via the mysterious Edinburgh galley wireless and, by the end of the week, the Rustaveli could have filled the place for the rest of the Festival.

The plays they brought were familiar; Brecht's *The Caucasian Chalk Circle* and Shakespeare's *Richard III* but the direction and the acting had a power and virtuosity all too rarely seen. Ramez Chkhikvadze, described by Michael Coveney in his programme note as 'the Laurence Olivier of the Caucasus' fully lived up to his billing, a player of great physical and vocal resource, wonderfully over-the-top, dominant and compelling, not only as Shakespeare's evil king but also as Azdak, the wildly eccentric rabbit-stealer who becomes a judge in *The Caucasian Chalk Circle*.

There was *Parade*, an exhibition of dance costumes covering three centuries, in Edinburgh College of Art, scene of Dicky Buckle's great Diaghilev exhibition of 25 years before.

On show, set simply against black backgrounds, was an array of dance costumes, from the formal elegance of the 18th-century Tuscan theatre to the stretch synthetics of Alwin Nikolais, exhibited on sculptured dummies and in glass cases and given the illusion of movement by the inter-play of light. Designed by John Paterson with the costumes arranged by Philip Dyer, among the particular treasures on view were costumes worn by Pavlova, Nijinsky and Massine in Diaghilev ballets. Many of them came from The Theatre Museum in

Ramaz Chkhikvadze (1979)

London for which Buckle had obtained some of its most valued items.

At the National Gallery there was an exhibition of paintings, pastels, drawings, prints and sculpture by the supreme painter of dancers, Edgar Degas. *Degas 1879* was so titled because in that year he exhibited at the Fourth Impressionist Exhibition and three of his most important pictures, *Miss Lala at the Cirque Fernando*, *Portrait of Duranty* and *Portrait of Diego Martelli* were painted. More than half the works at the 1879 exhibition featured dancers or the musicians who played for them and in Edinburgh 35 of the 124 exhibits had the same theatrical provenance.

Many of them were sketches and preliminary drawings for finished paintings, but they included such famous works as *The Green Dancer*, *The Ballet Class*, *The Rehearsal* and sketches and maquettes for *The Little Dancer of 14 Years* as well as the final bronze sculpture. There were also some vivid racecourse pictures and several fine portraits. Five lectures in St Cecilia's Hall given by Moira Shearer, Anton Dolin, Noel Goodwin, Richard Buckle and John Drummond, illuminated the myriad aspects of Diaghilev's creative talents.

And then of course there were the dance companies.

The lack of a theatre in which effectively to present dance was daringly overcome by putting two of them in a circus tent on The Meadows, Edinburgh's green space tucked away between the University in George Square, the King's Theatre at Tollcross, the Queen's Hall and Morningside where the first golf clubs had been formed in the 18th century and where James IV's army assembled in 1513 to march to its doom at Flodden.

Sadler's Wells Royal Ballet brought to The Tent in the first week an intriguing mix of the classical and the innovative, including the Chopin arrangements made by Glazunov and others for the Ballets Russe, *Les Sylphides* and Prokoviev's *The Prodigal Son* as well as two works having their world premières, *Punch and the Street Party* to music by Lord Berners (another Diaghilev protégé) and choreography by David Bintley and *Playground*, choreographed by Kenneth Macmillan to a score by Gordon Crosse.

Although The Tent was not an ideal venue – passing traffic dulled some of the terspischorean magic and a very long thin orchestral pit made the music a little ragged at times – the dancing rose to the occasion and there were some sparkling performances by principals like Margaret Barbieri and Desmond Kelly and the splendid *corps de ballet*.

The second week brought the National Ballet of Cuba with the amazing Alicia Alonso. Alonso, born in Havana, had first appeared at the Edinburgh Festival in 1950 and again in 1953 with the New York Ballet Theatre and in 1959, on the personal request of Fidel Castro, she founded the National Ballet of Cuba. Her age was something of a mystery – the most gallant calculations in 1979 suggested she was then 58. She had suffered for some time with her eyesight but when she came to the conference arranged for her in the press bureau at the Assembly Rooms in George Street, she had to be carried upstairs to the first floor!

However this seemed to be more of a precaution than an ailment, for, miraculously, she still danced, a trifle stiffly and with a couple of muscular young men in constant hovering support, but with a kind of imperious grace which was impressive artistically as well as courageous.

Her company were splendid, a brilliantly, vigorous athletic troupe bursting with enthusiasm and *joie de vivre* who danced a variegated programme of short ballets, many of them Hispanic in origin but including two full-length *Gisells* and the second act of *Swan Lake*.

The dance spectrum in the third week shifted close to the royal Palace of Holyroodhouse, to Moray House Gymnasium in Holyrood Road. But despite the regal associations down the road, with American veteran dancer Merce Cunningham and his company there were no elaborate Diaghilevian trappings of exotic fabrics and startling sets but something nearer the pure essence of dance itself. Forswearing narrative, psychological characterisation and the resources of both allusion and illusion, the company performed in a kind of aleatory dance was 'the art of the inexplicable' as one of his admirers in the United States called it.

Up for praise and almost worship were the multifarious resources and the grace and dignity of the human body and its relationship to space.

The series of what Cunningham called *Events* were compilations of pieces woven together into a continuous dance sequence, an ever-changing, uniquely expressive library of dance ideas, investigations and possibilities. With the performed *Events* there were *Open Rehearsals, Technique Classes, Discussions* and a *Composition Workshop* taking dance into different dimensions and areas of experience. It was as if the ancient art was casting off its fetters and making a new beginning.

Although it did sometimes seem that about the only place you were likely to escape the Mitsouko-perfumed air of Diaghilev was at the Military Tattoo (but even here there was a link for his father was a major-general!), there were other diversions.

The Bristol Old Vic occupied the Assembly Hall with a lively *Troilus and Cressida* directed by Richard Cottrell in which the lovers were played by Jonathan Kent and Meg Davies and a gangly young man called

Daniel Day-Lewis literally carried a spear. At the same venue was a fine lusty production by Adrian Noble of a rather neglected 18th-century comedy by Irishman George Farquhar (although it did achieve the distinction in 1789 of being the first play ever presented in Australia!). Bristol Old Vic's version of *The Recruiting Officer* was very lively, very funny and played with great panache by all and with a bravura performance by Neil Stacy as Captain Brazen.

The Traverse, elevated (or as some would have it 'shanghaied') into the 'Official Festival' was at its most self-consciously domestic with two original plays, Billy Connolly's prison comedy, *The Red Runner* and Tom McGrath's *Animal*. Neither Connolly's comedy nor McGrath's animal analogy was a big hit although the actors being animals received a lot of praise without anyone finding that the play itself added up to very much.

In fact, the animal impersonation field was rather hijacked by a piece about an English cat presented by an Argentinian group from Paris, the TSE, which occupied the Lyceum for the final week. *Peines de Coeur d'une Chatte Anglaise* (Heartaches of an English Pussycat), in spite of sounding desperately twee, done in wonderfully realistic masks inspired by the drawings of J. J. Granville in *Scenes de la vie privée et publique des animaux*, had been a smash-hit in Paris for over a year.

Geneviève Serreau's stage adaptation of the ironical Balzac tale, Alfredo Rodriguez Arias's masterly direction and the extraordinary masks by Rostislav Doboujinsky (creator of masks for the film *The Tales of Beatrix Potter*) and the comic and touching performances were an unembarrassing delight. The satire on the mores and manners of 19th-century London and the insight into the pangs of females (cats or human) who marry for money and dream of romance gave a pleasingly lemony edge to the sugary costumes and decor.

The opera programme was augmented by a company new to the Festival, Kent Opera. Founded by Norman Platt ten years before and conducted by Roger Norrington, this young company was well-used to performing in small theatres and had established a reputation for lively productions of wit and vigour, making a virtue out of necessity in the belief that smaller houses offer opportunities to experience opera more directly than in more grandiose theatres. They proved this, year after year, in their tours through southern England from Norfolk to Devon and at the Bath, Schwetzingen, Cheltenham and City of London Festivals.

To Edinburgh they brought a new production of Verdi's *La Traviata* by Jonathan Miller with Jill Gomez as Violetta and Keith Lewis as Alfredo and Gluck's *Iphigenia in Tauris*, directed by Norman Platt with Eiddwenn Harrhy as Iphigenia and Jonathan Summers as Orestes. Both operas were sung in specially commissioned English translations and both were conducted by Roger Norrington. Although Jonathan Miller's direction of the Festival's first *Traviata* contrived to be somewhat anti-romantic, Jill Gomez made a wistfully emotional Violetta and Keith Lewis was naively ardent as Alfredo.

Iphigenia was another matter. Gluck has the reputation of being an opera reformer and in his preface to *Alceste* (written for him by his principal librettist, Ranieri da Calzabigi) he said that opera 'should be devoted to seeking a beautiful simplicity' purged of the exaggerations and ornaments imposed by singers. The Kent production by Norman Platt underlined these virtues and was conducted by Norrington with great sensitivity and style in a manner which offered a link and counterpoint to the realism of *Traviata*, itself a pattern-breaker in operatic history. So although Gluck was hardly the Diaghilev of his day (he married a rich wife and could afford to be arrogant with the gorgons of baroque opera), there was a sense of artistic innovation which matched the Festival theme.

There were other important innovations. The conversion of Newington St Leonard's Church into the Queen's Hall provided the Festival with an important new venue.

Initially looked upon as the most risky items in the Festival structure, the morning concerts of small instrumental and vocal groups and recitalists, given first in the Freemasons' Hall and later spreading to

Leith Town Hall, had become one of the most readily sold-out sections of the Festival programme. The Freemasons' Hall with its rather swimming-pool acoustic had never been totally satisfactory and for many concerts it had proved too small.

Leith Town Hall (which at one time also went under the name of the Citadel Theatre) is bigger than the 400-seater Freemasons' but rather off the beaten track, so for a considerable time there had been a need for a hall holding between 800 and 1,000, not only for the Festival but for music-making and other activities all the year round.

The Scottish Philharmonic Society bought the Georgian building from the Church of Scotland and, with a contribution from Lothian Regional Council, transformed it into a medium-size concert hall suitable as a home for such groups as the Edinburgh-based Scottish Chamber Orchestra and the Scottish Baroque Ensemble both of which had established international reputations. It was opened by Her Majesty the Queen on 6 July 1979, who had earlier given permission for the hall to use her title in its name. As well as providing a much more satisfactory venue for smaller scale concerts, it also has an agreeable restaurant and bar and has proved an excellent centre for Festival and Fringe performances as well as a year-long cultural asset to the city.

In its first year it housed a dozen Festival performances by the Scottish Chamber Orchestra, the Scottish Baroque Ensemble, the Polish Chamber Orchestra, the Schütz Choir with Roger Norrington and the London Baroque Players and the Netherlands Wind Ensemble as well as a number of distinguished solo recitals by Peter Schrier, Elizabeth Söderström and a group of Chinese musicians playing on traditional instruments.

Another programme breakthrough was Mike Westbrook's *The Cortège*, an original composition for voices and jazz orchestra, the first part of the trilogy of a large scale work on a Life/Death/Life theme based on the classic format of the New Orleans jazz funeral, performed at the Moray House Gymnasium. There were also Artists in Residence, James Galway, the Netherlands Wind Ensemble and Richard Rodney Bennett who as well as appearing in regular Festival events and late-night shows played in parks, housing estates, outside and indoor venues. Le Contrade di Cori, 20 young Italians with banners, trumpets and drums, dressed in medieval costumes were out and about with their spectacularly acrobatic flag-waving displays not only in the squares, streets and parks of Edinburgh but also in Livingston, Haddington, Dunbar and Portobello. Austerity was banished.

Appropriately the 1979 Festival ended with a flourish of Diaghileviana. After the BBC Symphony with Rozhdestvensky, the Scottish National with Gibson, the London Symphony with Abbado and Riccardo Chailly, the Philharmonia with Muti, the 23-year-old Simon Rattle and Jesus Lopez-Cobos had all paid their tributes, Japanese conductor Seiji Ozawa, the Boston Symphony Orchestra and the Festival Chorus brought the celebrations to a rapturous close with the complete *Daphnis and Chloë*, one of the most stunningly colourful scores of the century, commissioned by Diaghilev from Maurice Ravel as a ballet, but always a greater success in the concert hall than the theatre.

Including exhibitions of Kandinsky paintings, Lehmbruck sculptures, Finnish Art Nouveau and two major Polish painters, Stanislaw Ignacy Witkiewicz and

Sir Simon Rattle

153

Henryk Stazewski, this was the biggest Festival of them all, with almost 200 events from 23 different countries.

Before the first Drummond-inspired Festival began, there had been several other innovations. I persuaded the Director that the Festival should have a new logo, a fresh design identity to go with what was clearly going to be a fresh era. This was not just change for change's sake for there was strong community pressure to locate the Festival more firmly in Scotland. At one time John Drummond had talked himself of moving to Edinburgh but eventually he decided against it.

The central design for Festival material had been done in London since the earliest Peter Diamand days by Hans Schleger and his wife Pat and the splendid doves and the castle logo had served us well for 12 years. However I suggested that there were good designers in Edinburgh and that it was time we had another Festival image and with John Drummond's agreement, I set out to find one. There were quite an number of submissions and after a lot of discussion, the choice fell on John Martin of Forth Studios who had designed and produced programmes for individual events for some years and who knew the work well.

I practically had to drag John Martin into the bid to be the Festival's new designer but eventually he produced the familiar EF tri-coloured ribbon design. Despite the Festival Society's depute chairman, Ronald Mavor complaining that it looked too like a & sign (other Councillors were less worried about that) it gave good service and lasted for 14 years.

Having the designer in Edinburgh also enabled me at last to establish proper editorial control over the souvenir programme, which had irritated me for years by the manner in which the text was totally dominated by design concepts. One result of this was the tiresomely off-putting lay-out of having to turn to pages at the back of the book (sometimes more than once) to finish an article begun at the front. By proper editing, confining contributors to specific lengths and consultation with the designer, the 1979 souvenir programme had more than 50 articles to none of which there were tag-ends at the back.

To extend the field of early publicity three editions of *Festival 79,* a tabloid newspaper, written, edited, subbed and laid out by the publicity department, were produced in June, July and August. These contained articles, pictures and information about Festival artists and programmes and were distributed free to the press, radio and TV, tourist offices, shops, banks, hotels etc. One of the stories they carried was about Festival souvenirs which I had initiated in 1978, this year featuring the new logo and a much extended range of items – T-shirts, sweat shirts, a shopping bag, cook's apron, tea towel and a pack containing a Festival poster and car sticker, all produced in Edinburgh.

All this activity helped to offset unique problems in the media as *The Times* newspaper group (*The Times, The Sunday Times* and its magazine, *The Times Literary Supplement*, both the *Educational Supplements*) and all the ITV networks on strike. Despite this, the number of journalists attending the Festival was again a record, 436 from 34 countries, 137 of them from overseas.

The last press conference before the 1979 Festival was to announce the most enterprising piece of sponsorship, negotiated with the brewers Tennent Caledonian. This established the Tennent Caledonian Award of £20,000 per year, to go towards commissioning and paying for the production and presentation of a new work created especially for the Festival each year, beginning in 1980.

> *New works are essential to the continuing vigour of a major festival,* said John Drummond. *I am particularly happy that this Award will not only take in commission fees in more than one field but that it will also make a substantial contribution to the cost of production, something much harder to achieve. This is just the sort of forward-looking idea that we hoped for from those who support us.*

The thematic content of John Drummond's second festival in 1980 was less pervasive and less manic, at least partly, it could be argued, because its influence was less significant than that of Diaghilev. This was unlikely to be widely disputed because the dominant colour of the programmes was a kind of faded red, reminiscent of the place the British Empire had once occupied on the world map, and featured programmes from the Commonwealth countries, particularly the second largest country in the world, Canada and the biggest island, Australia. Unjustly perhaps, neither of them would have leapt immediately to mind as headings for a discussion on the world's leading cultural states but just to redress the balance of ill-informed opinion, there was also to be a grand discussion full of starry names and lasting five days under the intriguing title *Whose Language is it, anyway ... ?*

Unfortunately, only one of the writers taking part in these literary symposia came from either of the featured Commonwealth countries: Elizabeth Smart, author of *By Grand Central Station I Sat Down and Wept.*

There were 28 Canadian performances or events plus Ms Smart, seven Australian nights at the Royal Lyceum Theatre plus Master of the Queen's Music, Australian composer Malcolm Williamson in a rather curious concert of Royal Music at Hopetoun House, where his *Ode for the Queen Mother's 80th Birthday* was given for the first time in public. Pianists Roger Woodward and Geoffrey Parsons from 'down under' were also prominent, Kiri Te Kanawa represented New Zealand in Strauss's *Four Last Songs*, Zubin Mehta conducted the New York Philharmonic, there were two concerts of Indian music by Ravi Shankar and Alla Rakha and a dance recital by Ritha Devi in the Queen's Hall and New Zealand and Canada sent pipe bands to the Military Tattoo. So the Commonwealth theme was well represented.

The most impressive were the Canadians who sent not only an excellent retrospective show of paintings and drawings of one of Canada's most important 20th-century artists, Jack Bush to the Talbot Rice Gallery in the Old College of the University and *The Legacy*, a fascinating and visually seductive exhibition of the arts and crafts of the North-West Coast Indians to the City Art Centre, but also made important contributions to the music and theatre programmes. Among the traditional masks, highly ornamented boxes, pottery, jewellery and contemporary artefacts from eight different tribal groups, there were some strikingly original and very beautiful objects, carved in a very distinctive style. During the three weeks of the exhibition, Richard Hunt, an Indian artist on the staff of the Provincial Museum of British Columbia carved a totem pole in the Art Centre foyer.

The major theatre company was the National Arts Centre, Ottawa, a remarkable group who, following an almost Japanese tradition, presented two plays, Büchner's *Woyzeck* and Strindberg's *Dream Play* using both actors and half-life-size puppets, and, representing the bilingualism of Canada, gave the Büchner in English and the Strindberg in French. The second Canadian theatre company came from Edinburgh's twin city, Vancouver.

The East Cultural Center brought *Billy Bishop Goes to War*, a two-handed play with music which had already proved a coast-to-coast hit on tour in Canada and in Washington and New York. Billy Bishop was the most decorated and successful Allied air ace in World War I, and the play is a probing,

Eric Peterson Billy Bishop Goes to War *(1980)*

moving and satirical analysis of what it was like for a country boy from Owen Sound, Ontario to be a colonial hero in 1914-18 Britain. It was written by John Gray who played the piano and sang in the show and Billy and the other 17 parts were played with dazzling virtuosity by Eric Peterson. A remarkable evening in the theatre, funny, musically effective, touching and important.

Other music of a rather different kind from John Gray's ('ranging in tone from the bitter irony of Brecht to the patriotic fervour of Kipling,' as one critic put it) was provided by the great jazz pianist Oscar Peterson in a late night concert and by the 180-strong Toronto Mendelssohn Choir who sang Delius's *Sea Drift* with the Philharmonia and Thomas Allen in the Usher Hall. The Choir also sang with the lively and talented Canadian Brass, five gifted musicians who could play anything from Gabrieli to Fats Waller, in a concert in St Mary's Cathedral under their conductor Elmer Iseler, the programme of which spread across the centuries from Gabrieli through Handel and various Canadian composers to Harry Stewart Somers who wrote an interesting Canadian opera, *Louis Riel* which would have made an intriguing Festival item. Canadian Brass also gave a Queen's Hall concert and a late-night show in the Festival Club as well as playing around the city as the Netherlands Wind Ensemble had done in the previous year.

Australia's main contribution was in dance. Australian Dance Theatre from Adelaide made its debut with six new works never seen in Europe, five more or less within the established traditions of modern dance and the sixth, *Wildstars*, a piece of total theatre with dance as a main element. An Everyman story pursued man from life to death. 'A whammo night of fun and dance theatre', with more than 3,000 lighting cues.

This kind of show is of course hideously difficult to transfer and not everything worked quite to plan. Many sequences were impressive in rather brash visual show biz terms rather than as dance, perhaps because the collaboration between whizz-kid theatre director Nigel Triffit and ex-Ballet Rambert Jonathan Taylor, director of the Australian Dance theatre, did not seem to gel successfully, although it did produce moments of genuine dramatic excitement.

The other ballets were fine, showing off the company's high qualities of athleticism and interpretation, satirical and broadly comic in *Incident at Bull Creek* and ethereally romantic to the music of Schoenberg's *Transfigured Night*.

Beyond the Commonwealth, there was Cologne Opera with two rather similar operas from 18th-century Vienna, premièred in the same theatre within two years of each other, Domenico Cimarosa's *Il Matrimonio Segreto* and Mozart's *Così Fan Tutte*. In defiance of the judgement of history, the more popular of the two in its day was the Cimarosa. *Matrimonio* was commissioned by the Emperor Leopold II and when it was performed he was so enchanted by it, he invited the entire cast to dinner and to perform it again afterwards, thus establishing *Matrimonio* in history as the only opera to have its first two performances on the same night.

Leopold's predecessor Joseph II had a part in the creation of *Così Fan Tutte*, passing on to Mozart's librettist, Lorenzo da Ponte, a piece of court gossip he thought might make a good opera plot. He never showed as much enthusiasm for the result as his brother Leopold did for the Cimarosa piece and opinions of *Così* have varied down the years from 'exquisite music to a fatuous libretto' to 'the most subtle and profound of Mozart's comedies'. This clearly leaves a lot of interpretative latitude. Ponnelle's production for Cologne kept the comedy rather too simple, although Julia Varady and Ann Murray as the sisters were more involved, and John Pritchard handled the score with finesse.

With fewer emotional undertones in the plot, Michael Hampe's direction of *Matrimonio* played the comedy with style and Barbara Daniels and Krisztina Laki as Cimarosa's pair of sisters and Claudio Nicolai as the English milord on the Grand Tour were splendid, without quite eliminating the memory of Strehler's superb 1957 production for La Piccola Scala for those who had seen it.

Scottish Opera brought Janacek's *The Cunning Little Vixen* in an English translation and a charming and sensitive production by David Pountney, done in co-operation with Welsh National Opera and conducted by the Cardiff company's musical director, Richard Armstrong. The brutal contrast of Berg's

Wozzeck conducted with much fine-spun detail by Alex Gibson was produced by David Alden and proved a powerful vehicle for the talent and emotional range of Benjamin Luxon and an agonisingly troubled Marie from Elise Ross.

Arguably the most important Festival event was *The Lighthouse,* a chamber opera in a prologue and one act by Peter Maxwell Davies, the first recipient of the Tennent Caledonian Award instituted to commission a new work for the Edinburgh Festival each year. Based on a real incident – the disappearance of three lighthouse keepers from the uninhabited Flannan Isles off the Hebrides in 1900 – Maxwell Davies described it as a piece of psychological music drama.

Played in a stark, symbolic set and written for three male voices, playing both the vanished and the searchers, sung by Neil Mackie, David Wilson-Johnson and Michael Rippon, all with their own motif songs – a music-hall ditty, a love ballad, and a revivalist hymn – it made a weird and gripping piece with sinister and disturbing undertones of depravity and terror, stirred by the endless heartless rhythms of the winds and the sea – and the unsolved mystery of the fate of the three men kept in memory down the years by Wilfred Gibson's poem.

> *Aye, though we hunted high and low*
> *And hunted everywhere*
> *Of the three men's fate we found no trace*
> *Of any kind in any place*
> *But a door ajar, and an untouched meal*
> *And an overtoppled chair.*

The Lighthouse subsequently went on to play successfully at various other European festivals.

In a strong drama programme the impact of the National Theatre, paying its first visit to the Festival, with *The Passion,* a two-part adaptation of the York Mystery Plays in the Assembly Hall, was astonishing. Directed by Bill Bryden with great imagination and earthy forcefulness, this cycle of 15th-century plays ranging from the Creation where the naked Adam and Eve emerge from the dust of the earth to the Cruxificion of Jesus Christ were done with such narrative power, rough humour and genuine emotion as to rapidly become a sell-out.

The two parts were *Creation to Nativity* and *Nativity to Judgement.* They were presented with frighteningly realistic simplicity in the Yorkshire accents and dialogue, crafted in rough verse from the handed-down medieval texts by Tony Harrison, members of the National Theatre's Cottesloe Company and other writers and brilliantly acted with tough and passionate sincerity and great visual flair.

By comparison the National's Lyttelton Company at the Royal Lyceum in *Watch on the Rhine,* Lillian Hellman's war-time play about a German refugee family in America just before Pearl Harbour, seemed rather tame and slick – even with Peggy Ashcroft playing Mrs Farrelly. There was two-part drama too from the Royal Shakespeare Company at Daniel Stewart's and Melville College in Shakespeare's most lavish historical tapestry, *Henry IV* Parts One and Two.

Directed with crisp pace and character insight by the young Bill Alexander, they were highly enjoyable with sharp and mellow performances from David Rintoul as Hal and Alfred Marks as Falstaff but did not stay in the mind and senses like *The Passion.*

Four years before an unknown Polish painter had been lured to the Edinburgh Festival Fringe by the indefatigable Richard Demarco and had presented his own play, *The Dead Class.* In 1980 Tadeusz Kantor returned, now famous as the result of *The Dead Class,* which had since played all over Europe and even reached Australia. His new play *Wielopole Wielopole* appeared under 'official Festival' auspices at Moray House. The title means 'Many Fields', and these were ploughed, harrowed and turned over in relentless reminiscence in a mournful and grotesque portrait of family times past on the fringes of the old Austro-Hungarian Empire; an exhumation of old dreams and horrors and images of war, confusing and at times incomprehensible but undeniably dripping with atmosphere.

There were some fine concerts in the Usher Hall, Beethoven and Schubert with the Philharmonia and Riccardo Muti, with a dazzling account of the Brahms's Second piano concerto from the Russian Emil Gilels in the second concert; the SNO with Gibson and the Festival Chorus contributed a notable *Child of Our Time* as a 75th birthday tribute to Sir Michael Tippett; the Scottish Chamber Orchestra under Raymond Leppard offered a little more Cimarosa with the overture to a forgotten opera *I Traci Amanti* in a delightful programme of Mozart, Mendelssohn and Strauss with Scottish soprano Margaret Marshall; the European Community Youth Orchestra with Abbado, Salvatore Accardo and Shlomo Mintz superb in Bach's Concerto for two violins, also gave a sizzling performance of Bartok's *Miraculous Mandarin* suite and a noble Brahms's Second Symphony. Mehta with the New York Philharmonic played the European première of Penderecki's Second Symphony, a highly impressive *Eroica* and followed with a splendid concert with Jessye Norman singing Mahler's *Ruckert Lieder*.

John Currie, the second Chorus Master of the Festival Chorus

There was Masur with the Gewandhaus and Claudio Arrau and a brilliant Prokoviev *Sinfonia Concertante* from the Russian cellist, Natalia Gutman; the LSO with Previn in more birthday celebrations for living composers – American Aaron Copeland's 80th – with two pieces including the Clarinet Concerto played by Richard Stolzman: Carl Orff's 85th was marked by his extraordinary setting for chorus, orchestra and soloists of medieval Latin songs on love and drink, *Carmina Burana*.

The 1980 Festival closed with Abbado, Philip Langridge, the London Symphony Orchestra, the SNO Junior Chorus, the Festival Chorus and organist Gillian Weir in what is perhaps the greatest of the Berlioz 'gigantic' works, the *Te Deum*. The programme for that evening contained a note by John Drummond. *Tonight's concert has involved taking something of a risk. Unfortunately the organ in the Usher Hall is not in a fit condition to be used for a large-scale work like Berlioz's* Te Deum. *It was necessary to find another solution. Through the co-operation of the BBC, radio and television will link the Usher Hall with St Mary's Cathedral a mile away. In St Mary's Gillian Weir will perform on a recently restored organ. The audience in the Usher Hall will be able to hear the organ through loudspeakers. Television viewers will of course be able to see her as well. We are grateful to Maestro Abbado and Miss Weir for accepting the challenge. I have the suspicion Berlioz would have enjoyed it too.*

In the Festival of the hook-up – flawlessly accomplished with a taxi delivering Miss Weir to the Usher Hall in time to take her bow – I had become unhooked before the Festival. There had been differences of opinion on various matters with the new Festival Director and in a close-knit working group like the Festival staff, it is not possible to work with someone who does not want to work with you. So I left before the Festival began.

An announcement made on 5 September, the day before the 1980 Festival ended, appointed three people in my place, Roger Witts as publicity officer in Edinburgh, David Palmer as press officer in London and Sheila Colvin, Drummond's dynamic executive assistant, responsible for sponsorship.

XXIII

The 34th Festival in 1980 was adjudged by the media as 'an enjoyable Festival if not a particularly distinguished one' which I thought rather unfair because it seemed to me both then and now to have been a good deal better than that.

The Canadian contribution was interesting and workmanlike rather than brilliant, apart from the excellent *Legacy* exhibition of the art of the North-West Coast Indians and the *tour de force* of Eric Peterson's riveting solo performance in *Billy Bishop Goes to War*. The National Theatre's *Passion* was a triumph; Merce Cunningham's dance 'Events' were fascinating; Peter Maxwell Davies's *Lighthouse* an eerie and disturbing experience.

There were some superb concerts including Mehta's Penderecki première with the New York Philharmonic and Abbado's tremendous *Te Deum* to finish. Alastair Cooke talked about *American Humor* one afternoon in the Queen's Hall and was a big hit. The Writers' Conference *Whose language is it anyway ...?* in the Music Hall of the George Street Assembly Rooms was vibrant with sparkle and thrust and occasional contentious wisdom: everything you might have expected from a star-spangled and divergent line-up which included Frank Muir, John Mortimer, Sir Victor Pritchett, John Wells, Fay Weldon, Melvyn Bragg, Gore Vidal, Anthony Burgess, a gaggle of Scots and English playwrights and directors, a posy of Scots poets, and Seamus Heaney and Kingsley Amis. For the most part, it avoided being too earnest and academic and without being overtly flashy was highly entertaining and most amiably chaired by Frank Delaney, the BBC's resident literary *cathedra*.

The exhibitions included Joseph Beuys being devastatingly *avant-garde* with doors at the Demarco Gallery, the Royal Scottish Academy showing some of the colourful tapestries woven by the Dovecot Studios at Corstorphine from designs by Eduardo Paolozzi, Graham Sutherland, Henry Moore, Stanley Spencer and David Hockney; there were Lion Rugs from Iran and contemporary art from New Mexico which maintained the Drummond average of almost 200 events.

Although the programming style was generally acclaimed, already there had been the usual moaning about money. In February 1980 John Drummond complained that the Government made absolute nonsense of their financial dealings with the Festival.

It is really quite impossible he said to expect us to be cost-effective and to budget accurately, when they don't tell us how much money we're getting. Everything has to be booked before we know whether we can afford it.

His first Festival in 1979 had a deficit of just £2,500 on a turnover of £1.4 million and although more people than ever attended the 1980 Festival there was still a deficit, the principal problems being identified as audience reluctance about foreign language theatre, poor attendances at Scottish Ballet performances and, although Scottish Opera was judged an artistic success, numbers were disappointing. There was also concern about the Festival Club in the Assembly Rooms.

When it opened in 1947 the Festival Club in the handsome 18th-century Assembly Rooms in George Street was created as the social centre of the Festival, open as such for the three weeks but with the exceptional provision in those days of having a license to serve food and drink until 1 am on every Festival day except Sunday. In 1977, after many protests from thirsty visitors, a table license was granted for serving drinks with meals on Sundays. By 1978 it was fully licensed seven days a week.

However these measures proved too little and too late. In 1947 the Club had not only been a novelty, but had the considerable advantage of being the only place in Edinburgh where you could get a drink after 10 pm and one of the few where it was possible to have a meal after a Festival performance.

This advantage was considerably eroded in the mid 1970s when the licensing laws in Scotland changed, permitting restaurants and bars to stay open much later. Despite various innovations in the Club, including cabaret, concerts in the Music Hall and using part of the building for events like the Writers' Conference, membership declined in 1980 to 5,000, one-third of what it had been ten years before. The Club's position was not helped by the City Council's decision to increase the rental for the Assembly Rooms from £600 to £6,500.

So in 1981 the Festival Club abandoned the Assembly Rooms and moved to the University Staff Club in Chambers Street on a temporary lease for the Festival period. Instead of providing a place to relax and socialise, the new 'Club' rapidly became just another Festival venue housing continuous mini-performances and putting on up to 14 shows daily. The Assembly Rooms passed to the upmarket end of the Fringe.

The 1981 programme was as lavish in numbers as its predecessors but there was a certain look of sameness about it. Cologne Opera returned, Oscar Peterson was back, as were Scottish Opera and the National Theatre, the London Symphony Orchestra, the BBC Symphony, the London Philharmonic, the Philharmonia, the Scottish Chamber Orchestra and the SNO. Many of the conductors and the artists were the same – Abbado, Salvatore Accardo, Tom Allen, Peter Frankl, Philip Langridge, Raymond Leppard, Maxwell-Davies, Muti, Jessye Norman, John Pritchard, Rozhdestvensky and Peter Schrier etc. Even the names from the previous year's Writers' Conference tended to crop up again in the six-day *Television and the Arts* speak-fest in St Cecilia's Hall – Melvyn Bragg, John Mortimer, Owen Dudley Edwards and John Drummond among them.

There were tell-tale signs of fiscal panic in the seven small-scale or solo (i.e. inexpensive) evening recitals in the Usher Hall plus a concert for the five-strong Equale Brass and the (unpaid) Festival Chorus under their conductor, John Currie and only nine performances of three operas at the King's.

The main innovation was in theatre where, in bold defiance of warnings about the penchant of audiences for staying away in droves from plays in strange languages, there were three companies from Europe. The Théâtre de la Salamandre from Lille did Racine in Moray House Gymnasium, the National Theatre of Romania at the same venue put on a 2,000 year-old Latin play in Romanian and the Amphi-Theatre from Athens offered a curious piece of theatrical recreation *Iphigenia in Lixiourion*, directed by Spyros Evangelatos. This pseudo-classical romp was by Petros Katsaitis, an 18th-century Greek amateur tragedian who wanted his account of the tragically sacrificed Iphigenia to end happily, so he had most of the characters married off to each other by the final curtain. Not surprisingly he could find no professional company to perform this unlikely piece so he had it staged by the villagers of Lixourion in his home island of Cephalonia. Evangelatos's production 'as played in Lixourion', in 18th-century costume and demotic Greek, made a fair bid to the title of Hellenic ancestor of *Carry On Up Euripides*.

By contrast, Racine's vengeful and plot-infested tragedy about Nero's half-brother *Britannicus*, although set in Versailles at the time of Louis XIV rather than in imperial Rome, had a savage contemporary political edge. It was acted with great verve and brilliance by the young company of the Théâtre de la Salamandre directed by Gildas Bourdet. *The Girl from Andros* by the Romanian National Theatre was another semi-classical romp by the Roman slave-playwright Publius Terentius Afer, played in a series of styles from the pantomimic to the acrobatic, in which pace and invention gave zip to the complex story of two pairs of star-crossed lovers.

Some critics found it 'inspired clowning', and *The Sunday Times* called it 'A frolic for a feast day, full of gentle charm and energetic clowning, comedy that genuinely transcends the language barrier.'

Unfortunately that barrier was not always surmounted. Two Americans attending the superb *Britannicus*, turned to each other in horror as the play began, loudly chanting *a cappella* 'My Gawd! It's in French!' and noisily clattered out.

The Assembly Hall was, as it often has been, a scene for what Kipling called these two impostors, 'triumph and disaster'. The 'disaster' was not due to a bad play or indifferent acting nor even especially quirky direction but rather because Shakespeare's sparkling sylvan comedy *As You Like It* got lost in the lavish extravagance of its setting. Over-dressed and performed in over-complex sets, the romantic ardour of Lyn Dearth's winsome Rosalind and David Rintoul's manly Orlando sadly drowned.

Having laid the Forest of Arden to waste, the Birmingham Repertory Theatre made more than amends with a joyfully exuberant account of Voltaire's great satire on believing that 'all is for the best in the best of all possible worlds', *Candide*. To the light-hearted and entertainingly pointed music of Leonard Bernstein, an inspired pastiche of romantic opera and musical comedy, the whole piece swept along in a lively and imaginative production by Peter Farago, who provided an intriguing Edinburgh link between *Candide* and the Scottish capital.

In the 1960s as a schoolboy at George Watson's College, a leading Edinburgh Merchant Company school, Farago got a summer job through his music master, Richard Telfer, as a kind of general dogsbody in the Assembly Hall. While he watched rehearsals for various 1960s plays, he often wondered what would be the ideal show for the unusual space of the Assembly Hall. In *Candide*, he found it.

Having done so, curiously enough, he was back where he started, because Dick Telfer, who had given him his first contact with theatre and had encouraged him to pursue a career as a director after taking a degree at Edinburgh University, was still managing the Hall.

Dick, who died early in 1996, was one of the great characters of the Festival scene. In 1947, using his fluent French, he worked as a tourist guide for a travel firm, helping visitors get the best out of the city during its first Festival. A 'musician to trade', as they say in Scotland, he became professionally involved with the Festival and the Assembly Hall in 1956 when he organised the chorus for *The Pleasure of Scotland* 'a kind of hotch-potch' as he described it 'put together by George Scott Moncrieff and Anthony Besch'.

Earlier in 1952 when the first foreign opera company came to the Festival, Hamburg Opera needed 40 singers for the chorus in *Fidelio*. Dick Telfer trained and provided them. In 1953 it was an extra chorus for Glyndebourne's *Idomeneo*; in 1954 singers for the Lully music in the Comédie Francaise's brilliant *Bourgeois Gentilhomme*. In 1959 he was inveigled into management when the appointed manager for the Assembly Hall broke his leg – just a temporary appointment which lasted more than 20 years – before he went on to manage St Cecilia's Hall and the Reid Hall. In the 1976 he had an especial pleasure. On Saturday of the first week in that Festival, Scottish Opera, the company of which he had been a founder, gave its 1,000th performance and he was there. I am only sorry he did not live to see his 50th Festival.

There were two other important theatre contributions. The National Theatre returned in a very different mood with a new play by Tom Stoppard, *On the Razzle*. It was not strictly speaking a 'new' play, not even to the Festival. In 1954 we had seen Thornton Wilder's version of 19th-century Viennese dramatist, Johann Nestroy's use of the same plot.

Nestroy, who had in turn borrowed it from a play by John Oxenford – *The Times* drama critic who was the librettist for Julius Benedict's *The Lily of Killarney* – called it *Einen Jux will er sich machen* (You can't keep a good joke down). It should have been called 'You can't keep a good plot down', because Wilder made two versions of it, *The Merchant of Yonkers* in 1938 and *The Matchmaker* in 1954, and in 1964 it was turned into the successful musical *Hello Dolly!* – and there is some suspicion that Oxenford borrowed it from *commedia del arte*.

In what had to qualify as one of the main Festival's more unlikely venues, cramped in the basement of the Freemasons' Hall – used in early days as the Festival press bureau – Richard Crane and Brighton Theatre succeeded in reducing Dostoyevsky's last novel *The Brothers Karamazov* to less than two hours in a penetrating production by Faynia Williams which reached great heights of power and pity, wrung from the Russian text as a lament for the shadows cast by heredity. It contained a superlative performance by Alan Rickman, wonderfully extracting terrifying drama from the fable of the Grand Inquisitor and the visitation of the Devil as a devastating sardonic commentary on nihilism. It deserved a much bigger venue.

The music came in for some critical knocks. In *The Observer* Stephen Walsh wrote:

> *Though any excuse to visit Edinburgh is better than none, this year's Festival is, at least musically, shorter on absolute compulsion than John Drummond's previous efforts. Money, misfortune and Mr Drummond's regrettable passion for ballet are probably about equally to blame. But a few genuinely strong and original events have come through, of which the first was Thursday's premiere in an Usher Hall concert of John Tavener's Akhmatova: Requiem. This latest product of Tavener's enthusiasm for the Orthodox Church shifts emphasis back to an authentically Russian large-scale subject for the first time since his opera A Gentle Spirit of four years ago.*
>
> *The actual construction of the work for soprano, bass and a typical orchestra of strings, heavy brass and percussion (including a lot of bells) is extremely artificial. Tavener remains obsessed with palindromes, 12-note canons, cantus firmus, refrain forms and other superficially mechanical devices refined from his studies of Messiaen and late Stravinsky, yet the feeling of the music in performance is unique.*

The Scotsman's Conrad Wilson was waspish, designating performances as 'heavy-handed' and attacking Claudio Abbado's opening concert of Bach's St Matthew Passion as being 'too big even with the cut chorus' (about which there had been an unholy row resulting in the resignation of several members of the Festival Chorus when the Italian conductor decided 48 hours before the first performance to reduce the chorus to less than half of its usual 280).

It was about this time that *The Scotsman* critic adopted a rather relaxed style of dress for attending concerts which included a large brightly coloured ball-point pen, dangling on a cord against his chest. Someone in the group chatting to the Festival Director at the interval of an Usher Hall concert commented on this: 'What on earth is Conrad wearing round his neck?'

'His hearing aid, I assume,' Drummond said crisply.

There were a number of smaller musical groups giving major concerts; Capricorn with Janacek, Bartok and Beethoven and a new work *Landscapes and Magic Words* by Simon Bainbridge; the London Sinfonietta with Henze in an all-Henze programme and Stravinsky and Weill in the Queen's Hall; Anthony Rooley's Consort of Musicke with Emma Kirkby and David Thomas in four programmes of music from the Stuart Court in the Canongate Kirk and the Polish Chamber Orchestra, the King's Singers and the Camerata Lysy, Gstaad with Menuhin dodging about between the Usher Hall and the Queen's.

The opera programme was sparse, only three works in the King's, one of them not truly an opera and one newish work, Thea Musgrave's *The Voice of Ariadne* premiered at Aldeburgh in 1974 and being given its first performance in Scotland. Based on a Henry James story *The Last of the Valerii* about a statue-obsessed Italian count who seeks happiness by digging up an antique in the garden of his villa, it was a brilliantly crafted and fascinating piece but unfortunately its two performances at the Royal Lyceum did not pull in the audiences.

Scottish Opera's production of Gay's 18th-century *The Beggar's Opera* is not only the ancestor of such diverse forms as the American musical and *verismo* operas like *Cavalleria Rusticana* and *I Pagliacci*, but could claim to be one of the most successful musical satires ever written. In fact satirically it was so apt in lampooning politicians, social snobbery and hypocrisy in general that its sequel *Polly* was banned from the London stage for almost 50 years.

But this new edition adapted and conducted by Guy Woolfenden and directed by David William just did not gel. Despite a fine robust performance from Tom Allen as a baritone Captain MacHeath and a fetching Polly from Kate Flowers, it never captured the raucous and defiant spirit of the original, somehow lacking the gutter warmth and vibrant vulgarity that drives the piece.

Cologne brought a truly vivacious *Barbiere di Siviglia* directed by Michael Hampe, conducted by John Pritchard and sung with that precisely elegant wit and bravura which Rossini needs, by a cast including a lovely and adroit Rosina from Alicia Nafe, an experienced Almaviva in Luigi Alva and as opera's original Mr Fixit, a fine bouncing free-voiced Figaro in Leo Nucci. Unfortunately the German company's other offering, Mozart's *La Clemenza di Tito* was excessively staid. Like Rossini's *Barbiere* (13 days) *Tito* was written at speed.

The commission from Prague for a work to celebrate the coronation of Leopold II as King of Bohemia arrived just four weeks before the first performance on 6 September 1791, just three months before Mozart's death.

Although it contains some fine music it has always seemed to me that *Tito* does not really work as an opera. The leading characters have no dimensions. They are just puppets representing attitudes – magnanimity, revenge, unrequited love and so on – rather than people. Although I have seen the opera several times, it has always failed to be dramatically convincing. Cologne's production by Jean-Pierre Ponnelle was no exception.

Even what Stephen Walsh called 'Mr Drummond's regrettable passion for ballet' did not win too many plaudits. The 1981 Tennent Caledonian Award went to the London Contemporary Dance Theatre for *Dances of Love and Death*, a new full-length work created by Robert Cohan, the company's artistic director, to music by Carl Davis and Conlon Nancarrow. But even choreographing one of the interludes for roller-skates between *scenas* for Tristan and Isolde, the Sleeping Beauty, Cathy and Heathcliff and Marilyn Monroe failed to rouse the critics to rapturous acclaim, although it must be said that the audiences at Moray House loved it. The San Francisco Ballet at the much larger (3,000 seats) Playhouse Theatre was less impressive.

San Francisco is the oldest classical ballet company in the United States with a style derived through very strong early links from the Maryinsky and Diaghilev companies and Fokine's Ballet Russe de Monte Carlo. The claim was that this had evolved from the pure classicism of 19th-century Russian ballet with American physique and temperament into the open large and lucid dance developed by Balanchine (under whom director Lew Christiansen had studied) and contemporary American choreographers.

But in performance there was a general feeling that the choreography did not relate too well to the music. *Romeo and Juliet* to Prokoviev's score was found 'eclectic and anonymous'.

Audiences sigh, said *The Observer* critic, *for a truer reflection of Shakespeare's vivid mix of animal passion and spiritual ecstasy.*

The second programme to music by Stravinsky and Glazunov was praised for speed and precision but was accused of lacking character and style and it was only *A Song for Dead Warriors* on the life and death of a young Red Indian that aroused real enthusiasm for the exceptional dancing of Antonio Lopez.

Dan Wagoner and his small flexible troupe at the Royal Lyceum brought a programme of dances to poems and songs and silence as well as instrumental music but the critics were again hard to please:

Dan Wagoner and Dancers made me think less of dance than of the games staff at some college where a firm hand was needed for compulsory sports, wrote Noel Goodwin in *The Observer.*

163

The exhibitions too had a kind of ritual savagery. The focus was on America once more with the Fruit Market Gallery housing a major exhibition of *Abstract Expressionists* from New York's Museum of Modern Art – puzzling primitive images from Jackson Pollock derived from Indian sand painters, brooding sex-symbolic canvases from Robert Motherwell, metaphysical 'tragedy, ecstasy and doom' from Mark Rothko. In the City Art Centre American photographers chronicled their often-gloomy observations of the previous 20 years.

The Royal Scottish Academy put on show Dr Armand Hammer's extraordinary collection of works by Honoré Daumier, including paintings, drawings, water-colours and portrait bronzes as well as the famous lithographs, biting political and social jibes at 19th-century contemporaries and events, mingled with merciless portraits in bronze of the great and the good of the era of Louis-Phillipe.

At the Lyceum Little Gallery in Cambridge Street, *Scotch Myths*, an exhibition devised by Murray and Barbara Grigor, had a go at Scotland in its self-appointed year of International Gathering.

An outrageously funny exhibition, said *Scotsman* art critic Edward Gage, *it contains elements of real scholarship and food for serious thought in its process of computing the sum of how others see us, the image of ourselves we Scots have projected over the years. Fingal's Cave is a central theme in this multi-media satire, its hexagonal columns of basalt a formal source for the screens and pillars that carry the broad river of post-cards which provide the running commentary throughout the show.*

Their substance leaves no chuckie-stane unturned in this field of popular description or caricature and positively inundates the mind with Highland lochs, glens, cattle, stags. games, whiskies, tartans, thistles, bag-pipes, soldiers, comic singers and simultaneous dancers.

Scotch Myths was funny and brilliantly contrived but some of the laughter it provoked was a little hollow. It was of course terribly un-British not to laugh at the savagely satirical portraits it painted, but its hilarious worship of tartan and kailyard kitsch made most Scots slightly shame-faced, uncomfortable and tetchy, good for the soul but uncertain for the temper.

Perhaps that was what made John Drummond so testy at the end of the 1981 Festival. First he had a go at the Government for their proposal to cut the BBC Transcription Service which enabled items from the Festival to be broadcast to 50 different countries, calling it 'a pathetic and fatuous economy'. Then he criticised Edinburgh District Council for failing to invest in the city's theatrical assets:

I suggest Edinburgh District Council hold its next meeting in the bandrooom of the King's Theatre, he said. *It is constantly amazing to me that artists don't walk out, because they are being made to work under such deplorable conditions.*

The 1982 Festival started to go wrong early on. Designed as an Italian festival and with the whirling EIF ribbon of the Festival symbol appropriately resplendent in red white and green splashed over the preliminary brochure, the main ingredients proved singularly difficult to put together. 'I seemed to spend most of last winter at Milan airport,' said John Drummond. A lot of last minute rearranging had to be done.

There was no major Italian orchestra in the concert hall; there was no major Italian theatre company, there was no Italian ballet but the Italian theme was boldly maintained by a visit from La Piccola Scala, Carlo Colla et Figli, a marionette troupe from Milan, the Cooperativa Teatromusica from Rome doing an opera without music, Akroama, a small company from Cagliari with Hans Andersen to Sardinian folk tunes, three Italian conductors, a clutch of Italian soloists and singers, a group of flag-wavers from Gubbio and a couple of exhibitions.

The Geneva Ballet, announced in the preliminary programme, did not appear; the new play backed by the Tennent Caledonian Award to be commissioned from the Scottish Theatre Company failed to materialise and the number of performances in the Festival excluding exhibitions dwindled to 128.

The Tennent Caledonian Award was applied not to a new work specially created for the Festival but to the visit of La Piccola Scala which brought two oddly contrasting operas, *La Pietra del Paragone* by Rossini and Handel's *Ariodante*.

La Pietra del Paragone (The Touchstone) was the 20-year-old Rossini's seventh opera and amazingly the fifth to be performed in the incredibly prolific year of 1812. It was also his first for La Scala, Milan, then as now the most important house in Italy, and written as a vehicle for the beautiful Marietta Marcolini, Rossini's mistress, undoubtedly a star and probably responsible for getting Rossini the Milanese commission.

In two previous Rossini operas in which she appeared, the *risqué* comedy *L'Equivoco Stravagante* (The Eccentric Mistake: taken off by the censors after three performances; the heroine was accused of being a castrato in drag!), and *Ciro in Babilonia*, La Marcolini had great success displaying her shapely legs in *travesti* parts. This clearly became an obsession. Her involvement in *La Pietra del Paragone* resulted in what was originally conceived as a one-act piece being extended so that in the second act she could come on disguised as her brother, a hussar, with the chance to strut around in tights.

This makes the second act somewhat artificially repetitious because the hero disguises himself as a Turk in the first act to prove that he can be loved for himself alone and not just for his money. Despite these convolutions, *Pietra* was a great hit when first performed at La Scala where it ran for 53 performances in its first season, a record surpassed only by Verdi's *Nabucco* 30 years later.

The music is sprightly and inventive and although the stagy characterisations of the venal pompous journalist Macrobio and the fatuous literary critic Pacuvio are not as striking now as they must have been in 1812, the principal characters are ardent and romantic, and the comedy is well pointed and genuinely funny. I liked Eduardo de Filippo's production very much, and enjoyed the way Roberto Abbado (Claudio's nephew) handled the lively and witty score, sung with elegant passion by Julia Hamari and Justino Diaz as the lovers and with hilarious and lugubrious *brio* by Claudio Desderi as the appalling Macrobio.

But the critics who, it often seems to me have never taken Rossini to their hearts, did not agree and reserved their praises for *Ariodante*, a Handel *opera seria* about a Scottish princess, taken from Ariosto's *Orlando Furioso*. It was directed with great style and invention by Pier Luigi Pizzi, each main character being shadowed by a dancer in a very directorish production which rather got in the way of the music, beautifully sung as it was by Carolyn Watkinson as Ariodante (it was a great festival for 'pants' parts) and Leila Cuberli as Princess Ginevra and conducted with an exact sense of period by Roger Norrington.

Other opera came from Dresden in a feebly sung *Ariadne auf Naxos* and an undistinguished *Die Entführung aus dem Serail*. There was also the first full-length Puccini opera ever performed at the Festival, *Manon Lescaut* from Scottish Opera. Although it was Puccini's first success, it is some way from being his most popular opera and many people feel

Ariodante Piccola Scala (1982)

165

that Massenet's *Manon* (written ten years earlier) is a more appealing portrait of Abbé Prévost's tragic if tarty heroine. However, although in essence a moral tale on the theme that loose-living brings you to a bad end, I have never seen a performance so lacking in the albeit transient joys of pursuing pleasure and the fleeting delights of love. The orchestra made the most of the symphonic aspects of the score but the singers played out their tattered romance with a grim and doom-laden fatalism which contrasted bizarrely with the lyrical qualities of their music.

It took a second Handel work to restore the operatic balance sheet to something like credit. Welsh National Opera's production of *Tamburlane*, the work largely of the highly successful theatre team from the Citizens' Theatre in Glasgow, was sung in a new English translation by Robert David Macdonald and directed and designed by Philip Prowse.

Although archaic in form and musical structure it was both good to look at and excellent on the ear, creating a genuine touch of festival in both quality and performance with Eiddwen Harrhy as the vengeful Asteria scoring a notable triumph – 'putting last week's German sopranos to shame,' said one critic – and a finely sung Bajazet from Anthony Rolfe-Johnson.

Genuine Italian musical excitement came in the Usher Hall at the opening concert:

By starting these three weeks with the Last Trump, *said* The Scotsman's *Christopher Grier,* you could be tempting fate. But the full radiant splendour of what we in the Usher Hall and listeners and viewers beyond were to experience defied superstition. It was a performance of such awesome potency that it soared into a different dimension from high-class professionalism at full stretch. Even the stoutest heart must sometimes have quailed, have been directed to ponder anew man's latter end and hoped most earnestly that Margaret Price would be available to offer comfort and consolation at the last.*

Abbado brought pace, high drama, tension and passion to the score but also a rare tenderness and devotionalism, knitting these ingredients together with a unswerving sense of direction and perspective.

There have been many fine performances of Verdi's Requiem at the Edinburgh Festival for it is a work which can be approached and interpreted in many ways. Abbado's 1982 realisation, played as the opening concert and repeated two days later with the London Symphony Orchestra, Margaret Price, Jessye Norman, José Carreras, Ruggero Raimondi and the Festival Chorus was one of the most moving and most memorable – and that is high praise indeed.

The LSO's other concert was also acclaimed for a Symphonie Fantastique of 'sensational verve and brilliance' and a superlative account of Beethoven's Second Piano Concerto from Maurizio Pollini.

Cuban pianist Jorge Bolet, looking exactly like a character from a Mack Sennett comedy, played Liszt with dazzling virtuosity with Gibson and the SNO and at a morning recital in the Freemasons' Hall. In the Queen's Hall with equal brilliance Salvatore Accardo celebrated the bi-centenary of the birth of Paganini with the 24 Caprices. Another anniversary commemorated Percy Grainger. There were a number of cancellations. Pascal Rogé replaced Alicia de Larrocha, *L'Olimpiade* mislaid an actress en route from Rome and Festival Administrator Richard Jarman had 24 hours in which

Jorge Bolet (1982)

to find a beautiful, talented actress who was also a lovely mover; one of the Dresden Opera's sopranos went to Glasgow instead of Edinburgh for the Festival; the scores for Albinoni's Concerto Grosso in A for I Musici's concert vanished in transit and they had to play Mozart instead: Maxim Shostakovich stood in at almost the last moment for the ailing Rozhdestvensky and the Usher Hall exhibition arranged by Gillian Widdicombe on the life and works of Sir William Walton to mark his 80th birthday was made rather *de trop* when the Russian conductor cancelled the Walton performances in his second concert because he did not know the music. He substituted his father's Second Piano Concerto played by Peter Donahoe.

Opera being the great Italian musical invention it was proper that it should be examined at an Italianate festival but the scrutiny seemed rather to be focused rather on 'When is an opera not an opera?' The 1982 answer seemed to be 'When it's a play'.

First we had *L'Olimpiade* from the Cooperativa Teatromusica, by the doyen of 18th-century librettists, Pietro Metastasio. Set as an opera more than 30 times, it was performed in Edinburgh as something halfway between a verse recital and a ballet with interpolations in English from Irene Worth.

There was also the American Repertory Theatre in Lee Breuer's controversial production of Wedekind's *Lulu*, best-known as an opera by Alban Berg and then we had theatrical all-rounder Peter Ustinov in what the Festival brochure described as 'a hilarious new play around an opera in rehearsal' which he wrote, directed and acted.

> *It shouldn't really be considered as a play*, Ustinov told me. The Marriage *was commissioned by an opera house, La Scala, Milan and it's really an envelope for the opera. I've tried to explain in the part that is a play why Mussorgsky's opera was incomplete and why in Russia in these days practically everything was incomplete – and if it wasn't incomplete, it was late. It's all very much in the style of Gogol – who wrote the play on which Mussorgsky based his opera – and I suppose they could have done it by singing the first part and acting the second but that would have been very different. It's an explanation – they've been rehearsing for six years in some terrible provincial theatre, deep in snow with packs of wolves running around outside and they're still waiting for the second act.*

Unfortunately Ustinov's explanation turned out to be a lot funnier than the play/opera which induced 'a fatal attack of tedium' in one critic and was reviewed under headlines such as 'Unhappy Marriage'. The American Repertory Theatre attached to Harvard University fared no better. Their first production at the Royal Lyceum *Sganarelle: An Evening of Four Molière Farces* was condemned as 'too boisterous commedia del arte cross-bred with slapstick, creating a fairly coarse hybrid' and *Lulu* was savaged as 'swollen with pretentiousness and dismal dialogue, up-date, the way in which it is presented is appalling'. Even *L'Olimpiade* which had some style and elegance was dismissed as 'a faint experience and a complicated tangle of lost children and courtly love, like *Oedipus* crossed with *Two Gentlemen of Verona*'.

The wolves had a great time. However, while the diminished drama programme of the official Festival was reeling in the aisles, the Fringe was flourishing.

XXIV

The flourishing rather than simply the burgeoning of the Fringe had many causes. For several years, disgruntled drama critics had trawled the idea that the Fringe provided more interesting, exciting and inventive theatre than the official Festival and there were as many opinions about that as there were fish suppers in Leith Walk. The splendid sense of outrage which helped to make the Edinburgh Fringe's reputation of nakedly embracing every vibrant loud-mouthed cause from alternative androgyny to Zen among zebras got acres of media coverage. Tickets for Fringe shows were cheaper than opera at the

King's Theatre and concerts at the Usher Hall, and being a Fringe groupie for a mixture of democratic, diverted snobby and protesting artistic reasons had become a trendy way of Festival life.

Most importantly, in recent years the Fringe had increasingly shed its amateur and dilettante guise and attracted professional groups who looked on it as a serious venue at which to display their as-yet-unrecognised talents as playwrights, directors, actors and image-makers. The critics a-prowl in the wings excited them and they intrigued the critics and from this unholy alliance had come success, transfers to London and other pastures greener, even fame and modest fortune.

In the 1980s two new and important players came into the alternative act, William Burdett Coutts, a tall pale-faced black-bearded Zimbabwean actor-manager-impresario and John Drummond. Looking for a space in which to stage a play at the 1981 Festival, Bill Burdett-Coutts was pointed in the direction of the historical Assembly Rooms in George Street by the then Fringe Administrator, Alistair Moffat. The original Festival, which had used the building for 34 years as the Festival Club, had been driven out by the steeply rising rent demanded by the City and District Council and the falling away of trade as Edinburgh pubs and restaurants, basking in the euphoric moonlight of the amended licensing laws, stayed open later and later.

He decided that instead of booking just one space for his play, he would lease the whole building and try to fill it with performers. Of course, Rikki Demarco had been doing something similar for years. But Bill, a shrewd character who, unlike most Fringe companies had a firm grasp of financial realities (perhaps due to his family connection with Coutts Bank), rented out the other spaces to carefully selected Fringe groups clamouring for somewhere to perform.

Drummond had always been enthusiastic about the Fringe and had often stressed the important part it played in the Edinburgh Festival concept but this was the first time there had been any actual collaboration between the Festival and the Fringe except for the Festival including information about the Fringe in its preliminary leaflet and the Souvenir Programme. Not everyone was happy about the merger and the spending of a substantial sum from Festival funds on the adaptation of the Assembly Rooms Music Hall as a theatre, although 1982 was the first year since 1948 that the Assembly Hall in the Church of Scotland building on the Mound (another expensive adaptation) was not used.

The Sankai Juku, a virtually naked male group, gave a drama/dance performance of brilliantly athletic and graceful movement co-starring with a peacock and interpreting a baffling Japanese legend. In their spare time they hung about – literally – in various places around the city including dangling 50 feet up and upside down from the roof of Lothian Region Council Chambers. Antonio Gades's *Flamenco Suite* was accomplished touristy kitsch but *Blood Wedding*, a dance version of the Lorca play, had more dark vitality and tense personal drama.

There were 51 other shows housed in the Assembly Rooms

Sankai Juku *(1982)*

in the four weeks to which the Fringe elongated itself in 1982. *We will put more people through here in that time than the whole International Festival has audiences. Around 150,000,* boasted Burdett-Coutts.

Other fairly arrogant noises were being made on the Fringe. The Circuit, another large-scale company, appeared to rival Burdett-Coutts's Assembly Rooms. Located in Castle Terrace in the notorious 'Hole in the Ground' once earmarked to be the site of the Edinburgh Opera House recently abandoned as the site for a new hotel it took a leaf out of John Drummond's 1979 book with a 500-seat theatre tent and a four-venue complex.

We may be getting to a stage where there will be three festivals, said Anne Bonnar of Glasgow Citizens' Theatre, spokeswoman for The Circuit, *the official Festival, the professional Fringe and the amateur Fringe.*

For the first time there are more professional than amateur companies on the Fringe, said Burdett-Coutts.

This seemed to pose a threat of some substance to the official Festival. With 5,000 performances of 830 shows, the Fringe had for several years held the edge on numbers and before he left to go to Scottish Television, the previous Fringe Administrator Alistair Moffat had boldly claimed that the Fringe did not need the International Festival and could exist on its own.

But the experiment in 1982 of the Fringe getting ahead of itself and beginning a week before the official Festival did not prove a success. Week Zero (rapidly christened 'Week Naught' by one acerbic columnist) proved to be something well short of a sell-out.

There were mutterings by companies persuaded to open early about demanding their Fringe deposits back. Michael Dale, the new Fringe Administrator had never seemed too keen and although the idea of the extra week lingered on for a year or two, the extra days gradually atrophied and dropped off until the Fringe came back to running roughly in tandem with the International Festival. As Bill Burdett-Coutts said at the beginning of his bold entrepreneurial venture

People are always going to come to a venue where it is possible to arrive at almost any hour of the day and find something going on. Talking with companies, it is the sort of thing they want. It is simple economics – the strength of clubbing together so that the shows spin off on one another.

By becoming in effect an impresario, he was breaking with a hallowed tenet of Fringe belief – the idea that there should be no quality control other than the power of the box-office itself. Burdett-Coutts carried the financial can (to the extent of £110,000 and a rent of £15,000 to the City and District Council, nearly three times their final demand for the Festival Club) and felt that he was entitled to make quality control judgements on the companies who paid to use his venue. In 1982 he said:

I have seen half of what's on here. Some 30% I know about through trusted friends and on about 20% I take a risk. Risk is something that was missing when this venue was in the hands of the official Festival.

In fact Burdett-Coutts only achieved just over half the target he had claimed for the Assembly Rooms in his second year – 83,500 tickets sold; but his stated policy of converting the George Street venue into a lively Arts Centre for the Festival period was an undoubted success and set a new pattern.

At the beginning of the 1982 Festival, it was announced that John Drummond's contract as Director was being extended for three years.

I know it is worth going on with, he said, *and I know how much this city and region depends on the Festival economically. I have not in recent years seen any figure under £12 million quoted as being its economic value to the region.* He even made some comments about his plans for European Music Year in 1985, 'also my last year'. But disillusion for the charismatic Drummond was already setting in.

When I talked with him several years later he was typically candid about it.

I can't honestly say that I had a great deal of difficulty – in the sense that people talk about – with the City Fathers in the way that I think Robert did and perhaps George did. But I did have a constant feeling of apathy. People say to me, what really got you out of it, why did you really leave? I didn't just walk out in a sulk of anything like that. I left the job because I was no longer enjoying it. It's so difficult and physically taxing that you can't do it unless you are really enjoying it. And I got to the stage where I'd stopped enjoying it.

The actual straw that broke the camel's back was when they re-drafted my contract for the second period. I asked quietly whether the contract could express in some way that the fund-raising role was not exclusively the responsibility of the Director but that some responsibility for fund-raising should be accepted by the Council. And they refused it. They absolutely categorically, point blank refused to say in my contract that there was any kind of shared responsibility for fund-raising. And I left the meeting and thought to myself 'That's it'.

And three or four days later they put out a press statement saying what they were going to spend on the Commonwealth Games. And I thought to myself 'It won't do. It just simply won't do'. I'd said to myself I'd stay on a bit longer but I think I was wrong to do that.

And I got to the stage where I actually do think if you get disenchanted with something as I was, you can actively damage it by staying. And I think if I'd stayed on another couple of years, with the transition to the Labour group, things might have got much rougher. And ultimately the beneficiary would not have been the Festival.

Because if you're not on good terms with the people you're working with – the authorities – then things are tricky. In fact from that moment in my third year when I said to them "Well, you think things are going well but I'll tell you what went wrong last night in the Usher Hall or the King's Theatre, what went wrong at the Lyceum, what went wrong at the Queen's Hall, what went wrong in the Freemasons' Hall and ran through various lists of why things didn't work and one of the members of the Council started laughing. I said "I', glad you find it funny. I'm trying to carry one of the world's great arts festivals and you think it's a joke". And from that moment they never trusted me because I'd done the unforgivable thing. I criticised them. You're not allowed to criticise them.

Earlier we talked about when he first took over the Festival:

It was an exceptional thing. My position when I took over was unlike any other director, because of the length of Peter Diamand's tenure of the job. I remember – for I was around in Edinburgh for quite a lot of the time – a curious sense of deja vu about his programmes. I mean they were at the very highest level, his music programmes. He had the absolute top level you could get in terms of artists and orchestras and yet I remember feeling every year about his programmes, thinking "Oh God, them again". It was a very odd feeling but I felt I had to do something different. I had to change the pack of cards.

So I wanted to change things. I wanted to change the personnel and in my first year we had nine conductors who'd never been to Edinburgh before including Simon Rattle, Klaus Tennstedt and Riccardo Chailly – people like that. A bit of changing the pack was what I wanted to do but most of all I wanted to reanimate some areas which I thought were a bit sleepy. And to do some unpredictable things. The Tent in the Meadows was one of the things in the first year and the Degas exhibition. And of course I was terribly lucky with the Rustaveli Theatre. It was the first foreign company that I brought in and of course it was the biggest success we ever had. I was very lucky in that way and the way I did it was by deliberately – absolutely deliberately – downgrading opera.

I mean I'd just come in after that Carmen *had cost a third of the Festival's budget – for five performances or something. And it didn't seem to me we should do that every year. I shall go to my grave defending doing* Carmen *but not every year with that percentage of budget. I mean one year we'd spend an awful lot on theatre, one year we'd spend an awful lot on opera, an awful lot on an exhibition – and I wanted to move things around in that way. And it's funny, looking back on it, the way the two festivals I did that I really liked – I mean as a whole – were my first and my last. It was very odd. No-one thought the first was mine. Everybody thought I inherited it from Peter – when it was in many ways the most strictly personal of them all. I inherited absolutely nothing from Peter you know – the tour of the Boston Symphony Orchestra, that was the only thing. Of course because I was a new broom, I had an enormous amount of co-operation. I never got the co-operation of the National Gallery again after the first year.*

And we did the Degas exhibition at 14 months notice, put 100,000 people through the National Gallery and the Gallery staff were too exhausted ever to do it again. I remember the Keeper of Painting at the National Gallery saying "Oh we can't ever do that again in August. It's so tiring".

It's odd, the relations between Edinburgh and the Festival. one has argued about it and talked about it and said some highly controversial things about it. I, in fact, don't complain a great deal about the central thing people complain about, which is the size of the grant from the City to the Festival. I never thought that was disproportionate. For a city of that size a grant of about £1 per head seems to me pretty good. I never thought that was the one to complain about.

One thing which happened in my time which is dangerous was the politicisation of the Festival Council. The fact was that the Council when I arrived had roughly proportional representation of the party strengths, but during that time, because of the party opposition from the Labour group, the Tories took virtually all the seats – you'll remember nine out of the eleven Festival councillors were Tories. That meant of course that when Labour got back in, they wanted to reverse everything and it became a political football in much the same way as it had been before my time with the two Councils.

My complaints about Edinburgh were two-fold. One was the sheer laziness of getting on and doing things about the buildings. I mean it's absolutely indefensible, Edinburgh's record in terms of buildings. Before these buildings were owned by the District Council, the Howard and Wyndham record was lamentable. Not just Edinburgh's Council. But once they did inherit the Lyceum and the King's, there was this extraordinary attitude that one did up the foyer, one did up the bar, put in new carpets or something but one didn't think about the stage. In fact, it took until the 39th Festival to get an orchestra pit in the King's.

It used to make Edinburgh a laughing stock going round the world showing people the plans. They would say 'All right, now show me the plans of your real theatre'. You know, they'd just shout with laughter when you explained to them that the Lyceum still had handlines not counterweights.

The Usher Hall is a good hall but Tennstedt said to me once that it was the only concert hall in the world where the female soloists had to share a changing room with the conductor. It's preposterous for a city with any pride. What really angered me about Edinburgh is that it has immense grandeur but absolutely no pride at all. I mean how could it allow itself to be laughed at by the world in this way? It's been told often enough but it just doesn't believe anyone from outside. The key moment of my time in Edinburgh came when I told the Council what I thought of this side of things. Halfway through my third Festival when the Council were congratulating themselves on how well they'd done in running the Festival, I'm afraid I just flipped and told them exactly what had gone wrong that week and to what extent it had almost brought the Festival to a standstill by the incompetence of the management in every building we worked in. You see, what absolutely shocked me most when I went to Edinburgh was the absolute total amateurishness of the way in which the Festival was run. I couldn't believe it. I couldn't believe the administration. I couldn't believe the way the finance side was handled. I couldn't believe the way the halls, the theatres and the adaptation of them was handled. The sort of loose arrangement with the City Architect's Department that someone might do it part-time if he was sober enough. You know. It really isn't on. So what I tried to do with the Festival on that side was to professionalise it. To get to that stage with a Festival which had been going for 30 years and had an Administrator who'd never seen an artist's contract! Let alone be able to go out and negotiate with someone. They'd left it running along in that curiously amateur, rather sloppy kind of way. I couldn't believe the things we didn't have. The box office was absolutely hopeless. And symptomatic of the whole attitude somehow or other, was that it was just like a temporary picnic and not a permanent feature. And it was that sense of impermanence which I reproach.

But when you come to the Edinburgh people, the ordinary people of Edinburgh who benefit from the Festival, – I mean the taxi drivers, bar keepers, whatever it is, know the Festival is important. The class of people who want the benefit of the Festival without contributing are in fact the Edinburgh professional classes, particularly industry and commerce. All these people sitting around St Andrew's Square and up and down George Street and banks and insurance companies think it's jolly nice to have a Festival, but actually do very little for it.

Every year we'd have a meeting with the Chamber of Commerce, with the major firms of the City. Even by the time I left, when we'd got the sponsorship up from £25,000 to £185,000 or something like that, practically all the sponsorship came from outside Scotland. It came from London and the international conglomerates. And when we did get something specifically Scottish like the Tennent Caledonian Award, the moment I left, it lapsed, which made me very disappointed.

So the disappointed John Drummond determined to leave but not before he had followed the great tradition of departing Festival Directors by staging the finest Festival at his command. In his last year the Festival Director does not have to worry to anything like the same niggling extent about his budget because he knows that the next Director will be given an easy run-in during the honeymoon period of his first year. Even extra money can miraculously be found to give him a good start.

The theme of the 1983 Festival was Vienna 1900, the dying days of the Austro-Hungarian Empire and the extraordinary outbursts of radical thinking, theorising and endeavour in science, art, music, social and philosophic theory which accelerated its demise.

There were also two musical anniversaries. 100 years since the death of Wagner and the birth of Anton von Webern, whose music was banned by the Nazis but who became a casualty of World War II.

The content of the 37th Festival was rather overshadowed when John Drummond announced at the end of March 1983 that he was resigning two years early from his contract because he had been told there were insufficient funds to fulfil the plans he had made.

The Scotsman reported:

He said yesterday that the Festival faced 'massive problems' but it could not reduce its standards. Emphasising that he did not have another job in prospect, Mr Drummond said he was prepared to risk unemployment rather than betray 'certain principles'. While declining to discuss his departure, Mr Drummond said there was no point in being secretive about the Festival's financial position. He had drawn attention to the problems when he gave evidence to a House of Commons Select Committee on the Arts last year. Since then, he had been involved in a series of discussions about ways of raising funds but all these talks had achieved very little. 'It would seem to me that the Festival is not wanted,' said Mr Drummond. 'We are not arguing about art or the price of tickets for an opera. What's at stake is the economic health and vitality of the city and the business which the Festival brings to the shops, hotels, pubs and others.'

To make things worse, Mr Drummond had just released the preliminary programme to the Press when he learned the level of the Council's grant. 'I had to make three cuts in what I had announced. The East Berlin Ballet, a contemporary music group and events at the Royal Lyceum. Now the Festival won't be using the Lyceum in the first week though the Lyceum Company will put something on there at that time.'

Unless another £30,000 could be found within the next few weeks, there would have to be further cuts in the programme, he said. It would be necessary to drop an orchestra, a theatre company and a dance company. 'I am mandated by the Festival Council not to exceed the cash we have in the bank. The programme as it stands is £30,000 over that level'.

Last year, the Festival had made a small surplus but the number of performances had been reduced. He said: 'Year after year, I have balanced the books and have been penalised for it. We don't run a deficit. But generally speaking, I have got less from the Scottish Arts Council than companies which have run up deficits.' Mr Drummond said that he wished people would realise that the Festival was not adjustable in size, cost and weight. It could not be reduced from three weeks to two without losing revenue, both in grants and from the box-office, and the range would also be limited. The Festival had to live in the top league or not at all.

The programme presented in August was not as threadbare as Drummond's angry denunciation had inferred it might be. The preliminary brochure had announced 169 performances; eventually there were 184. However, almost half of them were small scale, involving anything from a couple to a handful of performers and little or nothing in the way of expensive settings. The second theme of the Festival, 'Man and Music' lent itself to that kind of economy. An exhibition in the Royal Scottish Museum reflected man's need to make music ritually and for enjoyment and human ingenuity in contriving instruments throughout the ages and across the world – everything from conch shell trumpets and bone flutes to complex harps, fiddles, drums, xylophones, bagpipes and tuned oil drums. Musicians and dancers from many countries performed in the Assembly Rooms and in streets, squares and courtyards all over town, in an endearing and colourful perspective of the function, practice and focus of music internationally.

There was gamelan music from Indonesia, street musicians from Mexico, a steel band from the West Indies. West African praise singers, trance singers from Morocco, Rajasthani singers making weird ornamental harmonies to three-string viols and tamburas and pipers from Serbia, Northumberland and Scotland.

The main Vienna 1900 theme was grander and more expensive. Presumably the financial curbs prevented the presence of a Viennese orchestra, but there were plenty of compositions from the turn of the century as well as earlier music with claims to Viennese connections. Thus the Philharmonia under Andrew Davis played Berg and Beethoven, the Academy of St Martin in the Fields, gave us Schubert, Mozart and Richard Strauss, the LSO in two concerts did Webern, Schoenberg and Mahler, the SNO with the Festival Chorus under Gibson gave a massive performance of Schoenberg's *Gurrelieder*, Bruckner with Jesus Lopez-Cobus and all the jolly Strausses plus Franz Lehar with Neeme Jarvi. The Czech Philharmonic played Zemlinsky, Smetana and Dvorak and The Songmakers' Almanac in a delightful song biography, explored the diaries and memoirs of the beautiful, highly articulate and capricious Alma Mahler. She would only sleep with men of genius – her lovers included composers Mahler and Zemlinsky, architect Walter Gropius, painters Kokoschka and Klimt, writer Franz Werfel – and in her 80s she proposed marriage to Benjamin Britten!

Wagner, the greatest centenary celebrant only got three outings; a couple of overtures, the five songs of the *Wesendonck Lieder* and Act II of *Lohengrin* in the Usher Hall. I remember complaining at the time that it seemed rather parsimonious on his centenary only to offer a bit of a Wagner opera but much as I disapprove of snippetism I am now prepared to blame it on underfunding again for a very simple reason.

I had gone to the concert with a very beautiful girl who was not a great fan of classical music and fidgeted rather through the first half – Wagner's *Faust* Overture and Webern's *Five Pieces for Orchestra*. An interval glass at the pub across the road which keeps changing its name restored her good humour. The second half was *Lohengrin* which Abbado had recently conducted at La Scala for the first time. With Rosalind Plowright as Elsa, Eva Randova as Ortrud, Hartmut Welker as Telramund and Siegfried Jerusalem as Lohengrin, the London Symphony Orchestra and the Festival Chorus. Abbado wove the sublime music of faith and betrayal into a seamless tapestry of splendour, drawing passion and wonderful sound from orchestra and singers in a performance which I have never heard equalled.

When it ended I walked out of the Usher Hall, the music blazing in my head in a transported daze. My companion caught up with me in the street and reminded me somewhat tersely that I had also invited her to dinner. It was not a very comfortable meal, nor a relationship that prospered, but I have never forgotten that *Lohengrin* and I am almost glad it was only one act; at that level of intensity, three acts might have been unbearable.

Less emotionally demanding were the two one-act operas by Alexander von Zemlinsky which Hamburg Opera presented at the king's *Eine Florentinische Tragodie (A Florentine Tragedy)* and *Der Geburtstag der Infantin (The Birthday of the Infanta)*. Both are taken from Oscar Wilde. *The Birthday of the Infanta* from a story published in Paris in 1889, one of Wilde's semi-fables. The story is about a spoilt Princess who adopts a dwarf who amuses her, then when she is told he will sing no longer because his heart is broken says 'In future let those who play with me have no hearts'. *A Florentine Tragedy* is from an unfinished play, in which only in the killing of her lover does a wife recognise her husband's strength and he his wife's beauty. From this quirky material, Zemlinsky fashioned two delightful short operas, set with music which is more romantic than the later atonal and serialistic compositions of his star pupils Schoenberg and Webern, but with shrewd and telling undertones of horror and sadness.

Hamburg did them with a fine sense of *fin de siècle* decadence, a kind of glitter undermined by artifice and cruelty. It made you regret that Wilde never had the chance to see them (they were first played in 1916 and 1921, 16 and 21 years after his death) for they catch something of his ironic and slightly macabre spirit and would surely not have provoked his aphorism about music enthusiasts – 'So absurdly unreasonable. They always want one to be perfectly dumb at the very moment when one is longing to be absolutely deaf.'

The most brilliant exposition of the Viennese theme was in the exhibition *Vienna 1900* in the National Museum of Antiquities in Queen Street, devised by Peter Vergo, lecturer in Fine Arts at Essex University and author of *Art in Vienna 1898 – 1918*, a distinguished book on the period.

With the Austro-Hungarian Empire falling apart around them – the assassination in Geneva of Empress Elizabeth by an anarchist in 1898 and the election of a socialist mayor the year before – society in Vienna was crumbling. The artists of the period in all disciplines reflected their times in rebellion against established forms of painting, music, writing and theatre, many of them adept in more than one branch of expression. Schoenberg painted stage designs and portraits, Kokoschka wrote plays and poems. Paintings and designs, photographs, posters and newspapers, documents, books and plans for new architecture illuminated the period and revealed its links with Scotland through Charles Rennie Mackintosh and others, leading to the final destructive tragedy of 1914.

Ballet Rambert with the assistance of the Tennent Caledonian Award presented the world premiere of *Murderer Hope of Women*, a remarkable dance version of Oskar Kokoschka's bizarre and violent play about lust, destruction and betrayal in the search for spiritual regeneration, choreographed by Glen Tetley and set to music from Schoenberg's Chamber Symphony, in a strong ballet programme which included two other new works *Colour Moves* by Robert North and *Concertino* by Christopher Bruce.

Vienna seldom suggests the epic even in the revolutionary period around 1900 but Drummond and the Citizens' Theatre from Glasgow found one for the 1983 Festival. This was *The Last Days of Mankind* by Karl Kraus, one of the most controversial and combative figures of early 20th-century Vienna, a title not lightly earned in a city where strife and intellectual eccentricity were the stuff of *frustuck*, the first of the many Viennese meals of the day. Kraus, a man of private means, founded a magazine *Die Fackel* (The Torch) in which he satirised and critically demolished journalism, corruption, sexual hypocrisy, militarism and propaganda. He wrote this epic play about war and its causes, quoting extensively from speeches and writings of war's perpetrators and victims in a documentary drama which is a damning indictment of the World War I in a constantly changing stream of episodes without plot, a kind of theatrical impressionism. It was brilliantly captured in the translation/adaptation by the Citizens' resident *dramaturg* Robert David Macdonald who also directed what proved to be a memorable and disturbing evening in the theatre, light on structure but heavy and compelling in emotional impact. Also at the Assembly Hall, in a translation by Macdonald, was the play Hugo von Hofmannsthal wrote as the first draft for the libretto of Richard Strauss's most famous opera *Der Rosenkavalier*. The polished production by Philip Prowse of pantomimic comedy and sexual innuendo was good fun but underlined firmly how much Strauss and Hofmannstahl had improved upon it when it came to be set to music.

There were lectures about the Vienna effect on art and society, literature and theatre, aspects of Schoenberg and other subjects; a powerful play from Israel about the last hours of an anti-Semitic anti-feminist Jewish Viennese philosopher who killed himself because he could not come to terms with his Jewish identity and the move towards Zionism.There was Britten's opera *Death in Venice* ably done by Scottish Opera under Roderick Brydon, with its Viennese links through the identification of Aschenbach with Mahler. There was Chekhov and Nuria Espert in Lorca and John McGrath succumbing to the seemingly irresistible Scottish temptation to mess about with Aristophanes in the theatre.

It was a farewell which perfectly expressed the Drummond Festival philosophy:

> *I think what we have created in the 20th century are ghettos for the arts. We've created film festivals, theatre festivals, contemporary music, early music festivals – specialist festivals. It seems to me to do very little good except for people who live in that particular ghetto. The function of Edinburgh as I see it, of absolutely paramount importance, is its multi-disciplinary aspects. In fact, it's like a pin-table and you ricochet around from one art form to another and you see their relationship to each other. And if you can put them in a relationship – thematically or something like that – then you really are able to demonstrate what culture is rather than what individual art forms are. And that to me is what matters. But if it ever decides to become only a theatre festival or only a music festival, I would not then be interested in it. The breadth is what gives it its importance and its uniqueness now. I wouldn't for a moment not have done it. No way in which I would not have done that job. It did me a great deal of good.*

FRANK DUNLOP 1984-91
The World Drama Highway

XXV

After Drummond's resignation in March, the post of Festival Director was immediately advertised and within a month or so, it was announced that the next Director would be a familiar face on the Festival scene, the innovative and talented theatre producer, Frank Dunlop.

Dunlop had been coming to the Festival for 30 years as a theatre director beginning with an Oxford Theatre Group production of *Miss Julie* and continuing with his creation Pop Theatre, the Young Vic and other companies right up to 1983 when he had a play on the Fringe. So there was no question of familiarisation but his reputation as a maverick and irreverent character and the appointment of a man of theatre to the top Festival job aroused quite a few tremors among the faithful.

Although the Edinburgh International Festival of Music and Drama had often been called upon to defend itself against the charge of being purely, mainly or largely a music festival, there was a feeling that this accusation, always rebutted with a spirited defence of its catholicity of taste, in fact tended to muddy the waters and obscure what had always been a salient virtue in its programming.

As has been noted before, Edinburgh had regularly pioneered theatrical innovation although it *had* always been primarily a music festival. The idea that, with this new appointment, music should somehow be made to take a back seat was deeply worrying to some of the Festival's most perfervid supporters.

Dunlop talked about reducing the Festival's dependence on the London orchestras. It was easy enough to see where that temptation lay in fiscal terms. The London orchestras were often as expensive if not more so to the Festival than visiting foreign orchestras. Scotland does not qualify for a subsidy from London in the way that orchestras from abroad are often backed substantially by their own governments or their equivalents of the Arts Council.

But increasingly in recent years, the programmes offered by foreign orchestras had been circumscribed by the limited repertoire these bands were prepared to take with them on tour. Too often the Festival had become a stopping-off point for such visitors with programmes subsequently performed at the Proms in London or elsewhere. For performances of unusual or rarely-heard works, Festival Directors had often relied on the London orchestras or the Scottish National Orchestra – such as in the SNO's magnificent 1983 *Gurrelieder*, a work you are lucky to hear more than once in a decade. There was also the simple but inescapable fact that London happened to have more good orchestras then any other city in the world and that to ignore this profusion of talent, virtually on Edinburgh's doorstep, seemed very foolish indeed.

Of course, orchestras are reluctant to rehearse massive and expensive works for performance in only one place and Festival planning had somehow to encompass this difficult problem. But it had been done in the past and it seemed important that the principle it enshrined should not be lightly abandoned. Another temptation which needed to be resisted was to opt only for lesser-known, smaller-scale works.

Festival programming had always made room for such pieces but Edinburgh had also been renowned for superb performances of the great works in the classical repertory by the kind of forces rarely assembled for that purpose. The Edinburgh Festival, it was felt, was not just for music critics.

The presence of major critics is important to its international reputation and if there are no interesting works or performances or they can be heard soon afterwards elsewhere, they will not come. But Edinburgh had built up a large and loyal audience, who, while accepting new and unfamiliar works with an enthusiasm which would have seemed impossible a few years before, still wanted great performances of the standard classical war-horses.

I outlined several of these forebodings in an article I wrote at the time:

There are still plenty of marvellously appealing works which have never or rarely been performed at the Usher Hall – Rossini's Stabat Mater *has only been done once, Delius's* A Mass of Life, *Bernstein's* Kaddish Symphony *never – and the list could be much extended. What applies to the concert hall also affects opera programming. I know all about the inadequacies of the King's Theatre and the shortcomings of the much-maligned Playhouse and I agree most whole-heartedly with everyone who thinks that a hole-in-the-ground filled with Fringe tents is no substitute for the opera house Edinburgh should have built 20 years ago. That the city has failed in 37 years to put one brick on top of another to create any kind of building for the Festival which is its best advertisement throughout the world is a lasting disgrace.*

Why is there so little Wagner opera at the Festival? This year we had a riveting performance of the second act of Lohengrin *in the Usher Hall from Claudio Abbado. Why wasn't he conducting the whole work in the King's?*

Why has Scottish Opera's universally praised and beautifully produced and sung Die Meistersinger *never appeared at the Festival? Why have three of the greatest Verdi operas,* Otello, Aida *and* Don Carlos *never featured on a Festival bill? They cannot be done in the available theatres is the standard answer but I remember a long and enthusiastic conversation with Piero Faggioni, who directed the famous Festival* Carmen *about how* Aida *could be presented in Edinburgh. Not everyone thinks it is impossible. Now that Scottish Opera have Puccini's* Turandot *in their repertoire, can we have it at the Festival? Puccini is not exactly an over-represented composer in Edinburgh, having one and one-third operas presented in 37 years. And there is Rossini's* William Tell *and Mussorgsky's* Boris Godunov *etc. etc. The big things are what the International Festival has always done best. It can safely leave the smaller programme items to the increasingly professional Fringe.*

Please Mr Dunlop, despite your understandable devotion to the theatre, can you keep in mind that Edinburgh is one of the greatest musical festivals in the world, which in its day has commissioned important musical as well as dramatic works and initiated its own superb productions of opera. The money is a problem, I know. But then since 1947, when hasn't it bean?

I never had any reason to believe that Frank Dunlop was a great fan of my writings on the Festival (and quite some evidence to the contrary) but Rossini's *Stabat Mater* and Delius's *A Mass of Life* both appeared in 1984 and an extremely impressive mini-*Aida* introduced the Folkopera of Stockholm in 1986. However, I am still waiting for *Otello, Don Carlos* and Bernstein's *Kaddish Symphony*.

The other problems which Dunlop faced immediately were the Scottish Arts Council's manifesto *The Next Five Years* which announced a three-year freeze (effectively a cut) in Festival funding and the dominant Labour group on the Council which demanded that the Festival be 'taken to the people'. This led to Frank Dunlop making cheerful noises about making the Festival 'more fun'.

'Fun' is a jolly, up-beat word but when used in conjunction with an event like the Edinburgh Festival, there is a sore temptation to reach for the cultural Kalashnikov. Of course festivals should be enjoyable but a call for 'fun' makes the heart sink. In the mouths of such potentates as Festival Directors, it acquires a red-nose, banana-skin, fall-about connotation which fills the hearts and souls of genuine Festival devotees with nameless dread.

There was a time when the Fringe stood largely for fun. In the early days on the frayed edges of the Festival, the Fringe preferred the snicker, the sly dig in the ribs, the chuckle and the occasional belly-laugh at the pomposities of official culture. Although no-one wished to deny the alternative theatre its right to social awareness, black protest, anti nuclear polemic, gay and women's lib and the odd bit of full-frontal revelation, there was always been a little bit of nostalgia for when it was – or did it just seem? – funnier. There had always been plenty of irreverence but where were the laughs?

There was an element of making a plea for the Fringe to become again the fall-about faction of the Festival in this attitude. A gut feeling that a little soul-searing protest was good for us all but did we have to have so much of it? And the incestuous commingling of Festival and Fringe seemed to many people not only confusing but positively wasteful. After all, everyone was always complaining about how much money they didn't have. Everyone was constantly talking about 'doing their own thing'. Why, it was wondered, didn't they do it?

There was acknowledgement that impresarios like Bill Burdett-Coutts had undoubtedly achieved new standards of professionalism on the Fringe. But it was also felt that instead of trying to get in on the small-scale act, the international Festival should spend its money, little enough as it was, on the big items, the kinds of programmes on which the Festival was founded and leave the small-scale programmes to the increasing enterprise and excellence of the Fringe. The different facets of the Festival programme should not be nakedly competing with one another. Together they made up the most remarkable cultural three weeks in the world and each should concentrate on the things it did best.

Yet for some reason, while making heartfelt statements about economy, Festival directors seemed to have gone out of their way to enlarge the programmes – as if being seen to offer fewer items than the last man would earn black marks. Diamand had recognised the validity of austerity in 1977 when in order to do *Carmen* for 12 performances over two years with as starry a cast as he could assemble and to present a new commissioned opera, he had smothered his unease about sponsorship and cut the size of the programme to preserve the quality.

In an article welcoming Frank Dunlop, Allen Wright, arts editor of *The Scotsman* wrote:

> *Look forward to a Festival when major drama and dance productions and great international exhibitions will be surrounded not only by operas and concerts of classical music but by the best rock bands in the world, by spectacular shows for children, by top-class fashion shows of clothes created from Scottish fabrics by international designers, with pavilions all over Edinburgh where various countries will present their national food and drink as well as projecting their national culture. This vision of the future is a collection of just a few of the ideas which are bouncing around the exceedingly fertile brain of Frank Dunlop.*

I was not the only one who did not like the sound of that. Fun, fashion shows, gourmet pavilions and hot air balloons do not make a festival of Edinburgh's stature. It was all beginning to sound like a fairground. Although the most regular threat to the Festival is financial tinkering and civic meanness, the most insidious is doctrinal and sociological – the 'take it to the people' philosophy which had imbued left-wing protest about it. Thunder from the left always contained much talk about the Festival being 'elitist', a word which always carries ominous overtones of privilege and intellectual snobbery but which simply means having the right to make a choice. An omni-choice Festival dilutes support just as a mini-choice one confines interest to too small a group. No-one suggests that it is 'elitist' to favour a particular football team although more people in the country go to concerts and theatres than attend football matches. If people want to experience the arts which the Edinburgh Festival has successfully offered over its lifetime then that is a valid choice and there is no need to dress up the appearance of the Festival with gee-gaws to pull in a wider and less appreciative audience in order to embrace some kind of statistical political correctness. The structure of the Festival had proved itself over 37 years, the structure of the Fringe had begun to prove itself after 35 years. Both had their own scale but the International Festival was in danger of losing the concept of its scale. The two Festivals needed each other but they also needed to be distinct. To be extinct could be the alternative.

Considering all the forebodings, when the programme for the first Dunlop festival in 1984 was announced, he seemed to be doing pretty well. Not too much pusillanimous kow-towing to the Council's social conscience but there were ominous signs. The first was that the Festival was pulled forward a week in the calendar. Traditionally it had started on the third Sunday in August and the matter of having it earlier had often been discussed before but dismissed principally on account of its then clashing with the Salzburg Festival with which Edinburgh shared many artists.

In 1984 it cost Edinburgh the Vienna Philharmonic Orchestra. Unable to come in the year celebrating *Vienna 1900* it had promised to appear the following year but was prevented from doing so because the dates were moved, so that the Viennese orchestra was still playing in Salzburg when it should have been in Edinburgh.

This did nothing to dispel the impression that the new Director was not too interested in the music programme. Other indications could be found if searched for. The major musical performers were presumably the choice of John Drummond but the selection of programmes seemed largely to have been left to the convenience of the orchestras, most of whom were moving on to the BBC Proms in London, now organised by ex-Festival Director Robert Ponsonby, immediately after Edinburgh.

There were only two foreign orchestras, one of them the Boston Symphony (oddly enough left as a programming legacy from Peter Diamand to John Drummond when he took over the Festival) and the Australian Youth Orchestra – and just two Scottish premieres among the 200-plus items on the Festival programme.

Somehow the musical items lacked the sense of occasion they had so often had in the past. The Boston Symphony under its graceful and dynamic conductor Seiji Ozawa gave a vividly articulated and exciting account of the Shostakovich Tenth Symphony, the strings like steel, the horns war-like cries of despair, swept together in the final movement to a shattering emotional climax. But there was the feeling that Ozawa had not quite made up his mind about the fervid anti-Stalinism of the piece; he could and did produce the dynamics but there was some faltering in the interpretation. In their other concert they played Dvorak's New World Symphony, the ultimate American orchestra programme piece which one imagines the Boston orchestra could have played in its sleep. There was no native American music.

The rest of the programmes were rather like that. Muti conducted the Rossini Stabat Mater with spirit but the tenor cracked on the famous D flat in the *Cujus animam;* Prokofiev's Alexander Nevsky Cantata is one of the great sure-fire concert hall pieces with the triumphant final section as the conquering Alexander enters Pskov to the heart-felt acclaim of the Russian people guaranteed to bring audiences to their feet applauding wildly, but under Yuri Termirkanov it took until the solo in the second-last movement to get everything together properly; the other big choral piece, Delius's *A Mass of Life* written by an egotistical English atheist in German to a text based on Nietzsche's Night Song of Zarathrustra was pagan, momentarily magnificent but remote, diffuse and unsympathetic. There were cancellations, substitutions, programme alterations and an absence of big-time music critics at concerts and recitals. The Modern Jazz Quartet, Sweet Honey in the Rock, Cleo Laine, the Royal Thai Band, Cajun Dance and John Williams vied for space in the halls with the Smithsonian Chamber Players, the Brodsky Quartet, Zimerman, Accardo, the magnificent Yo Yo Ma, the Moscow Virtuosi, the Ensemble of the 20th Century and Dietrich Fischer-Dieskau.

Modern Jazz Quartert (1984)

Unfortunately half the opera programme was cancelled too late to be replaced by anything else when Welsh National Opera withdrew their productions of Wagner's *Parsifal* and Bohuslav Martinu's *The Greek Passion* from the Playhouse. The Washington Opera gave five performances of Gian Carlo Menotti's *The Telephone* and *The Medium*, a double bill which had opened on Broadway in 1947 facing musical hits like *Oklahoma, Annie Get Your Gun, Finian's Rainbow* and *Brigadoon*. It had almost gone to the wall when Arturo Toscanini came to see it three times and his acclaim launched it into a run of 200 performances, proving that opera could compete on the Broadway scene and making Menotti the most famous living opera composer. The additional reason for presenting his work at the Edinburgh Festival – that he is a local resident with a house in East Lothian – had not had a great appeal for previous Festival directors.

However, this ingenious programme *melange* rode gallantly to the rescue of the beleaguered music programme. *The Telephone*, a skilfully wrought wry comedy, was used as a curtain-raiser to *The Medium* a tense and powerful psychological drama of the fake clairvoyant who finds herself in the tragic grip of powers she does not know she possesses. Written and directed by Menotti himself, in a manner incisive, elegant and sinister by turns, to music of a strange and evocative lyricism, it made a memorable evening in the opera tradition of the Festival.

Scottish Opera's contribution lacked the immediate dramatic power of the main Menotti piece. What was claimed to be the first performance of Cavalli's *Orion* since the 17th century, was another baroque-around-the-clock confection by conductor and adapter Raymond Leppard, a specialist in the field whose versions of 17th-18th century gems sometimes seem glossed up to the point of caricature. Given that this was his intention, it was quite successful, adroitly directed by Peter Wood and colourfully set and costumed to make a period romp out of the usual baroque plot of gods squabbling among themselves and messing up the lives of humans.

The music is pretty trivial and the production verged on the 'cute' with Cupid coming up and down like a yo-yo from the flies on a pink silken chair and a collection of monsters attendant on Vulcan who could have come straight out of the Muppets. Orion himself, musically and as a character, was rather a bore but at least you could understand his infatuation with the goddess of the moon, Diana; Anne Howells looking charmingly un-chaste in an eye-catching low-cut dress, especially when egged on by the irrepressible Ann Howard as the campest Venus in the business.

Of course not everything was a disaster or a disappointment. In a line-up such as Edinburgh always assembles, it never is.

There were two excellent concerts from the Philharmonia under the 26-year-old Finnish conductor Esa-Pekka Salonen (who looked about 16), the great Chinese cellist Yo Yo Ma played Bach's six Cello Suites with a glory which invited awe and admiration and there was a stunning concert of Berg, Bartok, Debussy and Boulez by the BBC Symphony Orchestra conducted by Boulez with Jessye Norman as soloist in the *Altenberglieder* and *Trois Ballades de Francois Villon*.

Esa-Pekka Salonen (1984)

It seemed hardly fair to judge the new Festival Director by his music programme anyway because most of it had undoubtedly been inherited and had to be implemented 'as best possible' by the indefatigable team of planning manager Sheila Colvin and administrator Richard Jarman, both of whom had stayed on after Drummond (although Jarman announced his resignation in the middle of the 1984 Festival). So there was no-one to blame for what felt like a rather undistinguished list of concerts and – Menotti excepted – a very un-scintillating opera programme. Frank Dunlop was quoted as saying rather plaintively: 'I thought I was walking into a much more organised musical side. There was much more to do than I had supposed.'

The Dunlop *forte* – theatre – however, was well to the fore. For the first time, the King's Theatre, the Festival's sacred if much maligned citadel of opera, was being used for drama, offering more performances than the Washington Opera and Scottish Opera combined from a two-handed American company of Anne Jackson and Eli Wallach in what was described as 'an evening of fun and frolic' and the heavy-weights of the European theatrical scene, the Berliner Ensemble from the German Democratic Republic. Even in the hands of two of American theatre's most gifted comedians, Murray Shisgal's *Twice around the Park* , a couple of lightweight one-acters, hardly seemed adequate Festival material.

Why should anyone bother to cross Edinburgh, let alone the Channel or the Atlantic to see the kind of pleasant but harmless pap they can watch on their own TV every night? Cliches fail me said *The Sunday Times*.

However, there could be no complaints about lack of originality or theatrical frippery in the rest of the drama menu. There was something of a *souffle* in the first week at the Royal Lyceum in John Murrel's *Sarah et le Cri de la Langouste,* another two-hander but of quite a different mood, texture and dramatic power. At the age of 77, the great Sarah Bernhardt is trying to write her memoirs with the assistance of her devoted secretary of 20 years, the submissive, dedicated, martyred but far from spineless Georges Pitou, who – under her instruction – writes down fragments from her past, assumes characters real and theatrical to jog her recollection, part nurse, part parent to the still wilful, still fascinating one-legged diva. Sarah is moody, sulky, triumphant in her resumption of the great roles – Racine's *Phedre,* Dumas's *La Dame aux Camelias,* Wilde's *Salome,* her mind confused, her strength waning towards death. Delphine Seyrig and adaptor-director Georges Wilson handled the delicate and sensitive text with rare feeling and skill for its comedy and nostalgia, in a fine, fragile and subtle piece of theatre.

Later at the Lyceum came the Black Light Theatre of Prague in *A Week of Dreams*. A brilliantly represented series of live cartoon images with actors, puppets and startling stage effects of the fantastic adventures of a taxi-driver ranging from delivering a letter, through undersea diving to Shakespeare and *The Doors*, relating the company's amazing presentational techniques to *commedia dell' arte*. The final week saw more black theatre, this time from the Negro Ensemble Company in Charles Fuller's tense and strongly portrayed army thriller *A Soldier's Play*, about the murder of a black career sergeant at an army base in Louisiana, whose agonised last words were 'They still hate you'.

Black Light Theatre of Prague (1984)

Rather more than murder and service morale in World War II America came under the spotlight in this tightly written drama. After O'Neill and James Baldwin, it was another reminder of the qualities of passion, conviction and expressiveness which black Americans bring to their own genre of theatre.

From the company he founded, the Berliner Ensemble, naturally there was Brecht, lavishly directed by his pupil Manfred Wekwerth, against stark grey black and bleached woodwork sets in *Galileo Galilei* with a wonderful central performance in the title role from Ekkehard Schall. Brecht's dramatic vision, named with numbing falseness 'alienation' by some critics, that a play must show the emotions from which its action derives, is particularly suited to the rebellious, hedonistic mulishly truthful astronomer.

Ur Faust (Scenes from Faust) by Goethe leaned, on the other hand, towards German romanticism. After a rather confusing prologue (not helped by the breakdown of the simultaneous translation machine) it moved from the perplexing to the inspired. Although Hermann Beyer's Faust seemed more tempted by carnal than scientific opportunities, this gave the production a certain lecherous reality beyond the elaborate use of gauze to convey the mystery and febrile detail of temptation, an expressive and beautiful performance by Corinna Harfouch as Margrete matched the haunting music and wove a complete Gothic contrast to Galileo and the devious pursuit of reason, demonstrating the company's extraordinary range.

The small and technically ill-resourced Church Hill Theatre in the depths of Miss-Jean-Brodie-land Morningside, became a surprising temple to another kind of drama, the minimalist theatre of Samuel Beckett. Over two weeks, five of his plays offered the most sustained homage the Festival had ever paid to one writer. They were performed by The Harold Clurman Theatre from New York, tantalising fragments of drama suspended in time and space.

Backing up the performances were readings of poetry and prose including Max Wall giving what amounted to a performance of the best-known of Beckett's novels, *Malone Dies,* the death-bed of an old man seeking articulate meaning in truth before the light finally goes out. There were talks, discussions, films, analyses, poems, largely organised by Beckett's publisher in English, John Calder, the most extraordinary symposium about one writer ever mounted in Britain. Only for the arch-enthusiast was attendance at all the events possible – or even tolerable. But from them emerged a new concept of one of the most astonishing writers in the history of the craft, a man who reached the point of almost abandoning words to make the search for what they say and what they conceal more compulsive and, despite the darkness of some of the text and the silences, more illuminating. John Calder in his article in the programme book quoted one of Beckett's poems which summarised the writer's quest as succinctly as anything

Who may tell the tale of the old man?
weigh absence in a scale?
mete want with a span?
the sum assess of the world's woes?
nothingness in words enclose?

There was also Marius Goring being Coleridge's *Ancient Mariner* at St Cecilia's Hall; a magnificent exhibition from the National Museum of the United States of America, the Smithsonian Institution in Washington, which included items ranging across American history from handmade quilts to the Apollo Lunar Roving Vehicle which explored the Moon; and 16 other exhibitions encompassing artistic manifestations from Edinburgh's own Eduardo Paolozzi to Padua's Andrea Palladio.

There were German dancers from the Komische Oper Ballet doing *Swan Lake* to the music arranged as Tchaikovsky intended it in The Playhouse and the Paris Opera Ballet doing *Commedia dell'Arte* with Rudolf Nureyev as Harlequin – although Nureyev gave his most dramatic performance off-stage when he seized and tore up my friend and colleague Emilio Coia's sketch-book during rehearsal. There was also a new production of the Robert Kemp text of *The Thrie Estaites* by Tom Fleming in the Assembly Hall.

Despite all this dramatic enrichment there were still complaints. One came from as far away as Salzburg to which *Observer* music critic Peter Heyworth had taken himself instead of Edinburgh. His despatch from Mozart's birthplace compared the two festivals:

> *To anyone who knew Salzburg in the immediate post-war years, the booming festival city of today seems a miracle. In 1946 a room was hard to come by, food was short, even access to the American-occupied zone of Austria difficult. And at a time when the burgeoning young Edinburgh Festival could assemble a glittering roll-call of international stars, Salzburg was still largely dependent on Austrian artists. Today the boot is on the other foot. For all Edinburgh's brave PR front, its festival has failed to retain the international audiences who flock to Salzburg. Foreign critics have long since shrugged it off as a festival of music. That is hardly surprising. In the intervening years, Edinburgh has failed to provide itself with a theatre capable of housing opera. Its major concert hall lacks air-conditioning and alcoholic refreshment. Above all, its predominantly run-of-the-mill offerings are not calculated to attract those who seek at festivals what they do not find at home.*
>
> *Salzburg is blessed with unmatchable artistic assets. It is Mozart's birthplace. It has the services of the Vienna Philharmonic Orchestra. In Karajan it has a conductor who provides an unrivalled magnet for* tout Dusseldorf.
>
> *But the fact that it already boasted two opera houses as well as an open-air auditorium has not prevented it from building a huge new theatre. Countless hotels and restaurants have sprung into existence. Vast car parks have been carved out of solid rock. The city centre sparkles with new paint and fresh stucco. The smell of success lies heavy on the air. The crowded inner city, the packed restaurants, the astronomic prices (over £50 for a single seat in the Grosses Festspielhaus for a performance conducted by Karajan, £4-odd for an evening's parking, £8 for the Festival almanac) and the spectacle of hundreds of natives lining the streets to gape at the arrival of assertively over-dressed audiences are not, as it happens, greatly to my taste. But before we wrinkle our noses in puritanical disdain, we should perhaps reflect that it is precisely Salzburg's ability to attract the rich that gives it the artistic elbow-room which the wretched director of the Edinburgh Festival notoriously lacks. Thirty, even 20 years ago, Edinburgh had the ball at its feet. It too has, after all unique assets. Neither the*

city's beauty nor the appeal of the surrounding countryside needs emphasis here. But by adopting penny-pinching policies, the city fathers have failed to exploit their potential. by regarding the issue as one of art versus cash, they have failed to see how art can make cash as it so conspicuously does in Salzburg.

Only last week I read of the difficulty Edinburgh now finds in affording the fees demanded by top-line artists. That does not surprise me in view of the modest prices that are all it is able to charge for most of the events it presents. To judge from this year's programme, Edinburgh is going down-market in an operation that grows increasingly conventional and gives increasing emphasis to populist sideshows. That has the merit of attracting a wider social mix than one finds in Salzburg. But such policies will not attract spending visitors. The Scots have a reputation as shrewd investors. But they have a thing or two to learn from the Austrians when it comes to exploiting the potential of an international festival as Edinburgh still claims to be.

Nor was this an isolated cry in the wilderness. David Cairns, *The Sunday Times* music critic actually came to Edinburgh and was more generous, but his opinion on the Festival's condition was not very different:

No music festival that offers an experience as powerfully satisfying as the concert given by the BBC Symphony Orchestra under Pierre Boulez at the Usher Hall last Wednesday can be written off as no longer of serious account. But it is a measure of Edinburgh's lack this year of a distinct musical personality of its own that the second week at its best has suggested a footnote to the stirring events of 1983, the year of Vienna 1900 *when the festival had a theme and the component items were planned in accordance with it. Boulez and the BBC orchestra in electrifying form played Berg – the* Three Pieces for Orchestra *and with Jessye Norman as the majestic, intensely evocative soloist, the* Altenberglieder *(the whole programme comprising the Berg works, Debussy's* Villon Ballades, *Boulez's* Notations *and Bartok's* Miraculous Mandarin *is being repeated at the Proms tomorrow and simply must not be missed) and at a morning concert, the Ensemble of the 20th Century from Vienna under Peter Burwick, gave us Webern's* Six Pieces op Six *in the rarefied haunting desolate version for chamber orchestra and ended with Schrecker's rarely performed Chamber Symphony. But these were isolated examples of imaginative planning. The concert programmes as a whole revealed little flair and no consistent idea beyond a vaguely Eastern European flavour – nothing to match the well thought out and thorough exploration of Beckett's works on the dramatic side.*

Perhaps I am letting my disappointment with the operatic side colour my judgement. In opera this has been the feeblest Festival I can remember.

Later in his review he tackled other aspects of Festival planning:

It is tempting to relate this year's operative distempers to the arrival of a Labour district council whose leader Alex Wood disapproves of spending a lot of the budget on so elitist an art form. But apart from the cancellation of Welsh National opera's visit, the programmes were fixed before the present council came to power. They reflect, if anything, the fact that the new Festival Director, Frank Dunlop, comes from the theatre and is not primarily interested in music.

Indeed, if we are talking of politics and parties, what has happened this year is the logical consequence of the past 20 or 30 years of Tory councils with their selfishly uncomprehending attitude to the arts, their consistently grudging subsidies and their hopeless mismanagement of the opera-house issue. Were Labour really to 'pull the plug on the festival' (a most unlikely eventuality) it would bring poetic retribution on the narrow profiteering interests which for so long have starved the festival which benefiting hugely from the trade it attracts. But that would be equally short-sighted. The answer to the uneven distribution of wealth is to distribute it evenly, not to cut the supply.

In the same way the answer to the restricted middle-class orientation of the cultural events associated with the Festival is not to abolish them but to extend them to all parts of the community, as Alex Wood apparently intends to do. The idea however must include opera, about which Mr Wood is supposed to have made threatening noises, but which is not inherently any more elitist than any other medium.

To make classical music available to people who have till now never dreamt of listening to it, is of course only half of what is required ('Gie us something cheerie-like – no thaat stuff' was the indignant cry of a lady from Stockbridge who found herself listening to the New World Symphony at one of Jack Payne's LPO concerts in the Empire Theatre during the war).

The rest is a matter of education, if not of a fundamentally reordered society in which activities like the Festival's are no longer alien and irrelevant but meaningful, necessary and eagerly sought. Pending such changes, there is plenty that can be done in small and gradual ways. The 'outreach' of orchestras and opera companies into places where they had not been before is a phenomenon of the times and need not involve lowering of sights and compromising of standards.

On Thursday afternoon at Waverley Station, Jessye Norman ceremonially unveiled a new 125 locomotive, 'Edinburgh International Festival'. I trust it is symbolic. The arrival of a council leader with populist ideas should not be assumed to be inimical to the international status and general well-being of a festival which has had to struggle for years against the greater menace of indifference and cultural conservatism. It could give the dear old institution a vital stimulus – and a proper subsidy. But Mr Dunlop will need to develop a sharper nose for what makes a music festival memorable.

The distant approach and the reasoned analysis did not approve. If further emphasis was needed, Rodney Milnes in *The Spectator* simply fumed:

What may happen in Edinburgh has less to do with socialism than with John Knoxery, xenophobia and foam-flecked prurient hatred of quality and pleasure, all British characteristics from time immemorial but seen at their most virulent in the Scottish capital. There will be little prospect of largesse in the future unless the Festival programme is limited to ethnic street theatre (and Scottish ethnic at that) and wholly innocent of militaristic obscenities like the Tattoo and foreign elitist filth like opera and ballet.

On the final Friday of Frank Dunlop's first Festival, he announced record box-office figures – more than half a million people had attended Festival events. The Fringe also announced record figures – an increase of 20%.

'A triumph over hysterical controversy,' said Mr Dunlop.

XXVI

In the announcement of the 1985 programme Dunlop firmly nailed his programmatic colours to the mast. The predominance of music was swept aside and for four years the first items in the programme brochures were always drama, with the immodest exception of 1986 when the brochure began with the concert hall version of Weber's *Oberon* – directed by Frank Dunlop!

Otherwise it was wall-to-wall international theatre, an idea which Dunlop had picked up from Peter Daubeny's London World Theatre Season from 1964-1973 and whose name he borrowed in subsequent years. In 1985, designated a year of celebration of the Auld Alliance between Scotland and France, it was appropriate enough because the original idea of a season of international theatre (which the Festival had been offering in a modest way for 39 years) had come from Paris where the Government-subsidised Théâtre des Nations season began in 1954.

Edinburgh 1985 offered a repeat of the previous year's *Thrie Estaites* sharing the Assembly Hall with a new production of Sydney Goodsir Smith's 1960 Festival-commissioned historical drama *The Wallace*. Tucked away in the Assembly Rooms in George Street was France's most distinguished actor, Jean-Louis Barrault in his production of Victor Hugo's *Angelo, Tyran de Padoue* . At the Royal Lyceum was the Théâtre National de Belgique in a sumptuous, Louis XIV period staging of Molière's *Le Misanthrope*. At Church Hill, Scotland's contribution to the Auld Alliance was Rikki Fulton in Denise Coffey's Scots version of another Molière masterpiece *Le Bourgeois Gentilhomme* entitled *A Wee Touch of Class*. The Lyceum also staged a first play by Scots actress Sharman Macdonald, *When I was a Girl, I used to Scream and Shout*, a pungent contemporary social comedy which had won a London *Evening Standard* play writing award. *Greater Tuna* a slick, folksy two-handed portrait of the third smallest town in Texas, occupied the Ballroom in the Assembly Rooms before Jean Louis Barrault.

Another French connection was at the King's where Feydeau's hotel bedroom farce *Le Dindon* was transmogrified into English for the Theatre of Comedy by John Wells. South Africa brought a version of Frank Dunlop's original Festival production *Miss Julie* to the Lyceum with a race-conscious interpretation from the Baxter Theatre of Cape Town. The Toho Company of Japan, in the same theatre, presented the most striking piece of foreign drama in the Festival in Yukio Ninagawa's production of Shakespeare's *Macbeth* in Japanese, transferred with astounding virtuosity and complete success from 11th-century Scotland to 16th-century Samurai feudalism.

This astonishing production in an incomprehensible language related very directly to Shakespeare's play and was stunningly evoked in Ninagawa's brilliant stage imagery, binding together spiritual and earthly values and the medieval necromancy of disordered ritual; its cherry blossom Dunsinane linking beauty and danger in the most extraordinary way to make an unforgettable theatrical experience. This, the beginning of Frank Dunlop's long love affair with the Japanese theatre, was a hallmark that was to give his drama programmes an overall dignity and triumph not always achieved in other disciplines.

At least there was a theme. Quite why the Auld Alliance was being celebrated in 1985 remains something of a mystery. By my calculations it marked the 689th anniversary of a union which has always been more celebrated by the Scots than the French. The Auld Alliance had begun at the end of the 13th century when Scotland's weak-kneed puppet king John Balliol was driven by a committee of bishops, barons and earls at Scone to defy Edward I of England and form an alliance with Philip IV of France. It did not do him any good because Philip ditched the Scots when he married off his sister to Edward.

But the Alliance staggered on down the centuries, fuelled by claret, whisky, rizzared herring and the predilection of the Stewarts for marrying French ladies; Ronsard writing sonnets to Mary, Queen of Scots and a number of highly ineffectual half-hearted attempts by the French to involve themselves in Scottish politics. Perhaps with a track record like this, 689 was as good an anniversary to celebrate as any. However there were a number of other candidates for 1985. Bach's tercentenary was remembered, Victor Hugo's 100 was encapsulated within the 689th spectrum but there was very little Handel, also 300 that year and Domenico Scarlatti, also born in 1685, did not get a tinkle. One would have thought that with 550 harpsichord sonatas on offer, one might just have been squeezed into the programme.

However there was certainly no lack of enthusiasm for the French. In addition to the theatrical contributions, the Opera de Lyon brought Chabrier's *L'Etoile* and Debussy's *Pelleas et Melisande* to the King's, and Les Arts Florissants with two 18th-century operas, Charpentier's *Acteon* and Rameau's *Anacréon,* decorated the Lyceum.

Peter Darrell unveiled a new Scottish Ballet production of *Carmen* as well as Nurevev in the Auld Ballet Alliance of *La Sylphide,* plus the Choreographic Research Group of Paris Opera Ballet in The Playhouse. L'Orchestre National de France, L'Orchestre Opéra de Lyon and L'Orchestre de Paris played at the Usher Hall and a host of French soloists such as Jean-Phillipe Collard, Helène Delavault, Michel Beroff and Nicolas Rivenq also contributed a great deal of French music and 13 out of the 26 featured exhibitions were French.

Despite the prose bias, the French connection was for the most part more elegant on the musical side of the programme than in the theatre. It might have been forecast from the brochure.

Angelo, Tyran de Padoue was described as Victor Hugo's 'James Bond play'; the Belgian National Theatre's blurb for *Le Misanthrope* got the hero's name wrong; the selling point for Chabrier's *L'Etoile* was that it resembled the Marx Brothers; Lorin Maazel was billed as TV director, raconteur, writer and administrator, which might have made some readers wonder why he was conducting the Pittsburgh Symphony Orchestra. Reading on, you wondered if Rameau's *Anacréon* would be hailed as an 18th-century template for Walt Disney.

At the opening concert in the Usher Hall, given by the Orchestre National under Charles Dutoit, the fully Frenchifying effect of Berlioz's powerful arrangement of *La Marsellaise* as a start to the Festival, vanished in a clomping display of insensitive chauvinism. The Festival Chorus had learned the lot and all the words had been printed in the programme, but it was decided only three verses of the Berlioz arrangement made for six, should be sung, so as not to fatigue the distinguished audience by keeping them on their feet for too long! What could well have been cut from the opening concert was Debussy's scrappy and disdainful *Marche Ecossaise* and the anti-climax of the bouncy encore played after impressive second-half performances of *La Mer* and the full version of Ravel's *Daphnis and Chloë*

There was more Ravel under Thomas Fulton when both Piano Concertos were played by Michel Beroff and Martha Argerich – Beroff sparkling and percussive in the Left Hand Concerto and a simply superb account of the jazzy concerto in G by Argerich, flying black hair and the kind of electrifying fingering that sends shivers up and down your spine. Unfortunately as time wore on there was more Ravel – and more and more. I remember saying in a radio broadcast that I had played truant from the Orchestre de Paris's top-of the-classical-pops concert of Beethoven's Pastoral Symphony, Rapsodie Espagnole and *Bolero* because I felt if I had to listen to any more Ravel, I might be found roaming wild-eyed in the streets tearing up New Town cobblestones to hurl at the Festival Director.

However the truancy was worth it, because I went to Jean-Louis Barrault's production of *Angelo, Tyran de Padoue* in the Assembly Rooms, which was not in the least like James Bond but a wonderful concerted performance by actors who managed to take the emotions right up to the edge of absurdity without ever over-stepping, creating a powerful sense of theatre more reminiscent of Webster than Fleming. Barrault himself had a small part, a kind of ghoulish Hunchback of Padua, but his touch was on everything, the sure sense of style and pace, the text played flat out for all it was worth with acting creating its own dimension, shedding canons of belief like confetti to make a splendidly theatrical evening which made the hideously uncomfortable seat in the Assembly Rooms almost unnoticeable. It was a last glimpse of a great master, worth a hundred *Boleros.*

The opera was a mixed bag. John Eliot Gardiner unearthed Debussy's first version of that most enigmatic of operas *Pelléas et Mélisande*, made before the composer was obliged to plump it up with orchestral interludes for its première at the Opéra Comique in 1902. He directed his fine orchestra with inspiration and grace to give a notably persuasive account of the iridescent and haunting score, on a scale ideally suited to a small theatre like the King's.

It was well cast and sung – a moving Mélisande from Diana Montague, a fine Pelléas from Francois Le Roux and a brilliantly disintegrating Golaud from José van Dam – but Pierre Strosser's production, allegedly set in the 1920s in an aristocratic country house, seemed to want to turn it into a mixture of Ibsen and Simenon. Against the music, this invoked the kind of pedestrian atmosphere which made you feel that the next man in a raincoat might turn out to be Inspector Maigret. A million miles from the ambience for the most introspective romantic opera ever written

Emmanuel Chabrier's L'*Etoile*, on the other hand, was a delight.

One of those works which no-one seems to know whether to classify as opera, operetta or *opéra comique*, in this Opéra de Lyon production it most gloriously did not matter. It was genuinely funny, outstandingly melodic and sung with such verve and charm that it won all hearts. For once it was possible to read the programme note afterwards and just nod with charmed approval:

> *Most importantly,* wrote Roger Savage, *the piece is singular in the sense that its sheer musical quality sets it apart from most other* opéra bouffe *of the time. It is no derogation of the catchiness, energy, charm and fizz of the best Offenbach, Lecoq and Sullivan to say that Chabrier's music for* L'Etoile *has a dimension the other composers lack. It allows more room among his high jinx for pathos, wistfulness, regret. It is more highly wrought melodically, more demanding chorally, more daring harmonically and subtler in its orchestration. (There are stories of the pit-band at the Bouffes-Parisiens threatening a walk-out at the first rehearsals because the music was not formulaic enough for them. There were even accusations of creeping Wagnerism, which would not have worried the perfect Wagnerian Chabrier at all!) And yet, by some miracle of tact and affection, none of the score's subtleties and sophistication clog the action or give any sense that the traditional bouffe form is being patronised or subverted.*
>
> L'Etoile *presents itself as just another diverting night out, but it is in fact an* opéra-bouffe *for connoisseurs.*

The performances of Colette Alliot-Lugas as Lazuli, Georges Gautier as King Ouf and Jules Bastin as the Court Astologer raise a reminiscent smile to this day and Eliot Gardiner's masterly handling of the wit and vivacity as well as the more poignant and romantic moments, brilliantly underlined his versatility.

The other French operas were also stylish although stylised would be a more accurate description. Les Arts Florissants specialise in French 17th- and 18th-century opera and that period is firmly where their presentation rests. Their double bill of Rameau's *Anacréon* and Marc-Antoine Charpentier's *Actéon* was decorative and tuneful courtly entertainment with a discreetly classical element of titillation.

Thus *Anacréon* faces the difficult social decision between wine and love as the principal elements of his life-style. While caressing the fairly certain possibilities of love in the delectable form of the fair Lycoris, he is invaded by the minions of Bacchus insisting that his criminal worship of L'Amour be banished and that the rites of Bacchus should have his undivided attention. This dilemma was neatly resolved in favour of both and the *Anacréon* cast of singers and dancers dissolved to the sidelines to become the courtly audience for Actéon, a slightly less languorous piece.

Wearied by bear-hunting, *Acteon* drops out of the chase and finds himself inadvertently – well almost – observing the naked goddess Diana, looking extremely fetching in nothing, bathing in a woodland pool. Detected in this Peeping Tom exercise, he is doused with well-water which turns him into a stag as which he is then pursued and torn to pieces by the hounds of his hunting party. If you can imagine all this being sung with eloquent drama and danced with sinuous provocation, you have got the picture of top people's entertainment in the 17th century. Hedonistic or divinely vengeful, as you choose.

There was also another form of ancient musical show-biz: *Zarzuela* at The Playhouse. It is said to date back to the Armada and to that amazingly prolific playwright Lope de Vega, who served in that fleet and wrote 1,500 plays, probably not at sea.

In spite of the definitions offered by various Festival spokespersons, it was *not* like musical comedy but more like opera – a word Festival spokespersons were avoiding that year as if it were some kind of virulent plague to which exposure could be malignantly deforming. Which was strange when you consider that down the years some of the Festival's biggest hits have been operas.

Anyway, the *Zarzuela* excerpts we heard had lots of good operatic-type tunes, some of them with folk-melody overlays, musically enticing, spectacular and colourful, requiring real voices and not miked-up moaners and they were intermingled with a good deal of vigorous, leaping, foot-stamping Spanish dancing, making a vivid mix and an entertaining evening of earthy musical and dance action. Not very subtle perhaps but it fairly lit up the vast unprepossessing barn of The Playhouse.

Nor were elegance and finesse the characteristics of the two attempts to render French drama into the tongues of the British Isles. The adaptation of *Le Bourgeois Gentilhomme* by Denise Coffey into *A Wee Touch of Class*, designed as a vehicle for the talents of Scots comic Rikki Fulton, was heavy-handed in a broad pantomimic fashion and hardly reflected the intricate pretensions of nouveau-riche Mr Jenner's attempts to make progress up the Edinburgh social ladder. But at least it was funny if you had no affection for (or knowledge of) the Molière original.

John Wells's version of Feydeau's *Le Dindon*, renamed *Women All Over* was a travesty in every sense of the term. In this hotel bedroom farce the plot was turned on its head by the women being the lechers, aggressors and arrogant bullies and the performances by a very distinguished cast somehow just made the whole thing more awful. What a talented director like Adrian Noble and actresses of the calibre of Caroline Blakiston, Eileen Atkins and Faith Brook were doing getting involved in this shoddy affair remains a mystery.

Any bit of programme planning can go awry, but the King's had just been refurbished and supplied with a long-needed orchestra pit. Thus the real disgrace was that while this unfunny and tasteless piece of demi-semi-vaudeville occupied the King's Theatre for the best part of two weeks, Menotti's *The Consul* a splendid and important opera on a highly emotive contemporary theme by the composer of 1984's only Festival operatic success was relegated to four showings in the totally inadequate and out-of-the-way Leith Theatre.

Despite the cheerless and badly-equipped venue *The Consul* was given a superlative performance by the composer's production with The Connecticut Grand Opera and the Scottish Chamber Orchestra conducted by Laurence Gilgore. The anguished tale of the wife of a freedom fighter in an oppressed Eastern European country, who seeks escape from persecution and worse but is endlessly frustrated by the mindless and chilling bureaucracy of the consular office of a Western power which is supposed to enshrine the very values she and her husband stand for, is a powerful piece of musical theatre.

In Menotti's dramatic score, spiky and painful at times but capable of rising to great heights of lyricism at the big emotional moments, this highly topical tale was told with great power and the composer's incisive production made its points tellingly. This is a great modern opera, valid, dramatic and important, and it swept along the enthusiastic audience in Leith Theatre from the first crashing entrance of the

189

wounded John Sorel to the final act curtain. It was easy to understand why *The Consul* had won Menotti the first of his two Pulitzer Prizes and the New York Critic's Circle Award when it appeared on Broadway. In the central role of Magda, Susan Hinshaw gave a striking performance of great intensity and passion in a highly demanding role, using her splendid voice to great effect in the most telling moments, particularly in the trio at the end of the first scene and the wonderful outburst against bureaucracy in Act Two.

When *The Consul* hit the Broadway stage in March 1950. Gian Carlo Menotti was already a celebrity. His first opera *Amelia al Ballo* was part of the repertoire of the Metropolitan Opera in 1938, a year after its première: *The Old Maid and the Thief* became the first opera written specifically for radio in 1939 when it was broadcast by NBC and *The Medium* with *The Telephone* as a curtain-raiser were the first contemporary operas to have a long run on Broadway (212 performances) when they appeared in 1947.

Yet Menotti, then as now, was a controversial composer, described as 'the Puccini of the Poor' (better, he said, than 'the Boulez of the Rich') because he refused to fit into any contemporary musical category, as he still does. The programme note set out his views:

Modern music is an unnecessary chronological separation which implies that there is something fashionable about art, making the work of the past ridiculous and old-fashioned. First, I don't believe there is progress in art. I believe art is constant and the only thing that is important about art is its performance. That means that pre-Columbian sculpture is not any better or any worse than a sculpture by Henry Moore; they are just two different things. The values come only from what you say. What is a contemporary work? It is like saying there is a contemporary way of speaking. Think about the fact that James Joyce, Thomas Mann and Lorca lived at the same time. In literature people don't care what style you use. You use the language that suits your inspiration, that matches what you have to say.

The operatic tradition is important to him, as is obvious in his music from the supreme importance he attaches to the human voice.

There is a certain indolence he says towards the use of the voice today, a tendency to treat the voice instrumentally as if composers feared that its texture is too expressive, too human.

Also, in destroying tonality, we have destroyed one of the most useful dramatic elements; tonality may not be necessary but its dramatic role has not yet been replaced with an equivalent device. For these reasons, I prefer to write in a simple, recognisable language. I do not feel the need for Esperanto, nor do I find obscurity or complexity a virtue. I have run the risk of sounding unfashionable in the hope that my music will appeal to open minds and untutored hearts.

The preference for badly translated farce to Menotti in the choice of venue cast serious doubts on the standards of Frank Dunlop's artistic judgement. The introduction to the programme of Moscow State Circus, jugglers, hot-air balloons and a football match also raised questions about how the much-disputed-over Festival funds were being spent.

The constant bickering about funding had not done the situation any good. When, at the beginning of the Festival, Councillor Mark Lazarowicz, chairman of the District Council recreation committee, had accused the Festival Director of not working with the city's Labour administration 'in a constructive fashion' and added: 'We would like to work closely with Mr Frank Dunlop but obviously if he is unhappy, we would not want to keep him here against his will' it looked as if the writing was on the wall. Part of the dispute was about funding the Leith Theatre, interpreted by Dunlop as a fulfilment of the Council's vigorously expressed wish to create events outside the city centre, and it was tempting to assume that the District Council did not consider an opera highly critical of the incompetence of bureaucracy to be suitable material for the citizens of city fringes.

Too tempting perhaps: but it would have been interesting to see what would have been the civic reaction if French farce in English had been sent to the suburbs instead of contemporary opera. At all events in 1986 Dunlop approached the programming with a wary eye.

The brochure trumpeted theatre with 18 companies from 11 countries performing in eight languages and no less than six theatrical entertainments in Scots, two of them in the suburbs. Opera was provided by a company to which no socialist administration could seriously object, the Maly Theatre of Leningrad, a folk-opera group from Stockholm and three not too operatic performances of Weber's *Oberon* in the Usher Hall, directed by the well-known theatrical populist, Frank Dunlop.

There was also dance from France in the form of Lyon Opéra Ballet, the Ballet of the Great Theatre, Warsaw, London Festival Ballet's second company and some dancers from the National Ballet of Canada in the Toronto Symphony Orchestra's *The Soldier's Tale* in the Usher Hall. Dunlop seems to have developed quite an obsession about the Usher Hall as a theatrical venue. The King's Theatre, refurbished to be more of an opera house, had only a week of opera. Other than the Maly Theatre, above its empty orchestra pit there were the jugglers, The Flying Karamazov Brothers, Ibsen's *John Gabriel Borkman*, Cleo Laine and John Dankworth and yet another four performances of Strindberg's *Miss Julie*.

Gerald Larner summed it up in a *Guardian* preview:

> *Not very long ago Edinburgh could offer as much music in three weeks as the BBC Proms in two months, and – though the Proms boasted a reputation as 'the greatest music festival in the world' – the Edinburgh programme was at least equal on quality and certainly more varied in content.*

> *Frank Dunlop has changed all that.*

> *After all, until Dunlop appeared on the scene, we concert-goers had always had the best of it and there was a strong case for favouring a different public at last. It was arguable that there was too much music going on anyway and that judicious pruning might well improve the quality of the concerts.*

> *There is nothing judicious however in Dunlop's arrangements for the Usher Hall and the Queen's Hall this year, If he had spent less and bought more purposefully and imaginatively one could have some respect for his programme. But, on the contrary, it seems to have been compiled from concert agents' special offers – with, moreover, little taste or discrimination, little knowledge of the repertoire, little flair for the coming sensation, and sadly little ambition for the reputation of his Festival as something special.*

> *An exception, he might argue, is the item he has billed as Composer's Choice – a series of seven programmes of modern music chosen by Alexander Goehr. True, these concerts did not come from an agent's list. But to entrust the choice of all but a fraction of the Festival's provision of contemporary music to one outside personality and to cram that into one weekend in the Queen's Hall is not so much unenterprising as irresponsible and, bearing in mind the spurious excuse it offers for playing safe in the Usher Hall, not a little cynical.*

> *So Vladimir Spivakov is bringing the Moscow Virtuosi from Harrogate to the Usher Hall to play Viennese polkas. Two orchestras (the Oslo Philharmonic and the Hallé) are playing three Tchaikovsky symphonies, two soloists are playing romantic concertos (including Tchaikovsky's in B flat minor), two pianists are playing Beethoven concertos, two orchestras are playing Beethoven symphonies and the Academy of St Martin-in-*

the-Fields, also fresh from Harrogate, is giving not a Mozart programme but an 'Amadeus Concert'. The Chamber Orchestra of Europe is coming by way of Lichfield, Harrogate and the Proms and the BBC Symphony Orchestra is repeating Strauss's Alpine Symphony in the Proms two days later.

Some of these things are worth doing of course, even in Edinburgh. But for programmes really worthy of the Festival we have to turn to Neeme Jarvi and the Scottish National Orchestra concert of rarities (mysteriously billed as 'a popular concert') inspired by Scott and Ossian, to Andrew Davis and the Toronto Symphony Orchestra's pairing of The Soldier's Tale *and* Oedipus Rex *and to Simon Rattle and the City of Birmingham Symphony Orchestra's combination of Berio's* Sinfonia*, Mahler's Second Symphony (which latter, however, they have performed just about everywhere else). And, except for the Alexander Goehr weekend, there is not much point in looking at the Queen's Hall programmes for unconventional consolation.*

Happily Dunlop's passion for the theatre has inspired him to resist the pressure to exclude imported opera and he has invited the Maly Theatre of Leningrad to give two performances each of Tchaikovsky's Queen of Spades *and* Eugene Onegin *and Sergei Slonimsky's* Maria Stuart *– which is very much an unknown quantity but all the more fascinating for that.*

*The Folk Opera of Stockholm is presenting a mini-*Aida *at the so-called Leith Theatre and, most interesting of all, the Festival Director himself has accepted the ultimate challenge of producing the unproduceable in the unimaginable. If the prospect of a staged performance of Weber's* Oberon *in the Usher Hall fills you with a feeling of impending doom, you have less courage than he has.*

Surprisingly this somewhat harsh look at the 40th Festival proved merciful rather than savage. There was a distinct feeling of lack of enterprise about much of the programming and there were serious disappointments. There was criticism of the repetition of *Miss Julie*, Mahler's Second Symphony and the Rikki Fulton venture into Molière *A Wee Touch of Class* and the major opera contribution by the Maly Theatre of Leningrad proved a sad disappointment.

The two Tchaikovsky operas *Queen of Spades* and *Eugene Onegin* were made to look almost tolerable by the total worthlessness of Slonimsky's *Maria Stuart*, described by one critic as 'a collector's piece ... surely the worst production of the worst opera ever brought to the Edinburgh Festival'. But in truth the Tchaikovsky productions were muddled, the acting, by and large, was appalling, the sets uninspired and the lighting erratic and incompetent. The voices were usually large enough but many of them were ill-focused and only the orchestra, conducted with a kind of despairing ardour by Valentin Kozhin, conveyed any real sense of the beauty, passion and drama of Tchaikovsky's music.

Frank Dunlop's direction of Weber's last opera, *Oberon*, on the other hand, was a distinct bonus. The Usher Hall is not the ideal place to stage opera but there is a widespread school of thought which claims there is no ideal place to stage *Oberon*. With an ingenious set and vivid costumes by Carl Toms and an inventive use of amusing and colourful props to point the way, Dunlop's production surmounted the absurdities of the plot and gave it the ethereal fairy-tale dimension it required, to gentle and pleasing comic effect. In the centre of the whirling set of steps, catwalks and circular platforms, Seiji Osawa and the Junge Deutsche Philharmoni played the score with charm and elegant incisiveness. Elizabeth Connell as Reiza, Philip Langridge as the questing Oberon and Benjamin Luxon in the Papageno-like role of Sherasmin sang with a fine sense of style, and the disembodied faces of the Festival Chorus, emerging from time to time behind the gauze in which they were framed, became tuneful fairies, sea nymphs, pirates, slaves and members of the harem on command. It was as colourful an opening to the Festival as it has ever had.

The impact, however, was theatrical rather than musical. This was also true of the remarkable *Aida* brought by the Folkopera of Stockholm.

Aida is not, of course, a folk opera but neither is the Folkopera a company devoted to rural music. With its headquarters in a converted cinema in the Swedish capital, it made its reputation with a kind of half-size version of spectacular operas. Verdi's Egyptian masterpiece, commissioned for the new Cairo opera two years after the opening of the Suez Canal, is always regarded as one of the grandest of grand operas and in arenas and immense theatres all over the world this impression has been reinforced by lavish productions centred around the triumphal procession of the second scene of Act II. In fact, *Aida* is in many ways the most intimate of grand operas and it is quite unnecessary to have elephants, camels, zebras and half the Italian army welcoming the victorious Radames back to Thebes.

In Leith Theatre the Swedes thrust *Aida* at the people. You were met in the foyer by a half-naked dancing girl. There was a pool in which the scantily clad heroine bathed. It opened with a sexy quasi-Egyptian striptease. The 21-piece orchestra sat on top of the temple back-drop, and instead of elephants in the procession scene there were baskets of severed hands. Visually it was a knock-out and you would have sworn it could not be done in the space. Synthesizers and wooden tone-boards helped out the orchestral effects.

(Incidentally, Verdi would have approved of having the band at the back. In a letter to his publisher Giulio Ricordi at the time of the negotiations about *Aida* he wrote:

> *Another improvement would be to make the orchestra invisible. The idea is not mine but Wagner's, and is an excellent one. It is absurd today that we should tolerate horrid white ties and tails against Egyptian, Assyrian and Druid costumes, to set the orchestra, which should be part of an imaginary world, almost in the middle of the stalls among the crowd as it applauds or hisses. Add to this the annoyance of having the tops of harps* 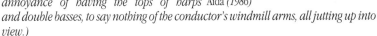 Aida *(1986)* *and double basses, to say nothing of the conductor's windmill arms, all jutting up into view.)*

Some purists may doubt if he would have been as enthusiastic about the synthesizers but they worked very well in Leith and Verdi was essentially a practical man of the theatre. He would certainly have been pretty leery about the elephants.

The only thing that was not entirely satisfactory was the music. A reduction of the score was made by Folkopera's musical director, Kerstin Nerbe, a woman conductor who is also a composer and musicologist, to suit the size and instrumentation of the orchestra. In general this worked well although inevitably there was some lack of richness and range in what is one of the most enchanting melodic scores, a miracle of lyrical beauty and inspired orchestration, that Verdi ever wrote. There was some seriously indifferent singing, although Margareta Edström as Aida and Anne-Marie Muehle as Amneris were both excellent and comely to behold but the men were disappointing and often clumsy and strained and the chorus inadequate and ragged. Still it was a remarkable piece of theatre, brilliantly and imaginatively conceived and directed by Claes Fellbom, a marvel in the space, if not quite what I had imagined as the first production of Verdi's masterpiece at the Edinburgh Festival. It also did not seem to have too much to do with the 40th year's theme, the Scottish Enlightenment. An enlightened Scotland, one would have thought, would have put *Aida* in the King's in place of the jugglers, the sequence of Scandinavian plays and Cleo Laine. Or even, dare one suggest, have built an opera house.

Prose theatre not only got the best venues but generally the best productions and performances. Both Scandinavian plays at the King's were directed by the great Swedish director, Ingmar Bergman. The first by the Bavarian State Theatre in German, Ibsen's *John Gabriel Borkman*, a chill psychological study of disintegration and aridity, presented in an almost cinematic emphasis of focus in close-up and long-shot in a half-frame dried blood interior and a bleak mountainside, had a towering central performance as Borkman by Hans Michael Rehberg.

From the disgraced self-lacerating bank manager and his tortured loves Bergman moved less successfully to the convoluted social patterns of lust in a grey, misogynistic production of Strindberg's *Miss Julie* in the original Swedish from the Royal Dramatic Theatre, Stockholm, underlining extraordinary depths of humiliation and bitterness in the characterisation and the clashes of sensual emotion. There was a double tribute to Federico Garcia Lorca on the 50th anniversary of his execution by the Falangists at the beginning of the Spanish Civil War, by the Spanish companies of Nuria Espert and José Luis Gomez. In an extraordinary production of *Yerma*, Espert in her interpretation of the childless woman, taunted for barrenness and barred by the rigid code of Spanish honour from taking a lover, combined passion and delicacy with a rare and intense grace.

Michael Radcliffe in *The Observer* was very enthusiastic about the Spaniards:

> *The late Victor Garcia's celebrated 1972 production of* Yerma, *re-staged by Nuria Espert with herself still in the leading role of the childless wife, wears its age well (so does she). Garcia turned Lorca's tragedy into the kind of choreographic dance play for actors whose influence has been felt in European theatre ever since, right down to* The Great Hunger *from Dublin, seen on the Edinburgh Fringe in the first week.*
>
> *The astounding design – an enormous grey trampoline slung inside a pentagonal steel ramp that thrusts out over the front stalls – is pulled up by hawsers into a rolling landscape through which the fertile women of the village tread in triumph like horses or into a steep precipice of the writhing damned.*
>
> *At the end of the play it collapses and withers into a dark sleeve of oblivion which pulls Yerma and the husband she has strangled into the earth like trash. Garcia and Espert take Lorca far beyond the confines of Spain, linking him with his precursors in the north and west, and Yerma herself with the wasted unlived lives in* Hedda Gabler *and* The Playboy of the Western World.
>
> *José Luis Gomez is post-Garcia and virtually unknown here. His magnificent production of* Blood Wedding *from the Teatro de la Plaza in Madrid uses innumerable small gestures of conviviality and self-containment where Garcia's were pagan and bold; no sudden shifts of gravity here. He creates a rustic society whose rhythms are both formalised and spontaneous, gentle and fierce, in which speech song and natural sound move in and out of one another without a break. Manfred Dittrich's designs suggest the achievement of brief privacy in the turning of a chair and the claims of male lust in the casual lifting of a woman's empty shoe. The acting is both fastidious and impulsive and I hope there isn't an empty seat in the house tonight. What a play!*

There were three plays from the Market Theatre of Johannesburg which had brought the award-winning *Woza Albert* to the Fringe in 1983. Like almost everything which came out of South Africa at that period, they were about apartheid. *Asinamali*, set in a prison cell with five shaven-headed actors, was a frontal attack on the injustice of their incarceration, stomped and shouted at the audience, a raucous assault on persecution, belief full of raw anger, punctuated with dancing and singing of an astonishing violent power. *Born in the RSA* was static and documentary, a less exciting delineation of the intimidation and betrayal of apartheid, and, despite its strong emotive content, tended to get monotonous. *BOPHA (Arrest)* at the Traverse, a relentless satire on black policemen warring against their own kind was both funny and horrifying, a scarifying lampoon of the abuse of political power, brilliantly done by the multi-talented cast, choreographed to rebellion against cruel authority.

Not everything was as compelling. The Théâtre de la Salamandre, which provided a superb *Britannicus* in 1981, was baffling rather than entertaining in a pretentious nonsense language farce by its director, Gildas Bourdet.

The Oxford Playhouse's *Hamlet* with David Threlfall as a deranged and whimpering prince, was eccentric, 18th century and camp; the Scottish contributions John Home's *Douglas* and Allan Ramsay's *The Gentle Shepherd*, both in the gorgeous setting of the Signet Library – one of the most beautiful interiors in Edinburgh – were meant to represent the Scottish Enlightenment but seemed hardly adequate to reflect the period being celebrated with two pieces of pastiche, an overblown, ill-structured drama and a tame ballad opera. There certainly was not much that was enlightening about *A Wee Touch of Class*, such a crowd-puller in 1985 that it was recalled to Leith Theatre, where it seemed more pantomimic than ever.

The most distinguished Scottish contribution came from Jimmy Logan in *Lauder* at the Town Hall, Portobello, Sir Harry Lauder's birthplace. There is a very real sense in which Lauder represents everything that is kitsch about Scotland in the theatre and therefore to be remembered only with a cultural sneer as a kind of betrayal. But he was an artist of international repute in a day when Scotland was making very little impact on the boards. For years Jimmy had immersed himself in the Lauder legend and with great skill he compiled a one-man play about the man and his work. There could be no question of impersonation for Logan looks nothing like Lauder – tall and robust with a wry cutting humour, completely unlike the wee pawky terrier of the kailyard that was Scotland's first theatrical knight. But this was a performance of formidable technical virtuosity, brilliantly conceived and put together with all the songs and the treacly sentiment but, as the scene moved from the Valhalla Hippodrome to a Band of Hope concert, a behind-the-lines World War I troop show, America, Australia and receiving the Freedom of Edinburgh in the Usher Hall, there were glimpses of the real man as well as the show-biz king. It was a masterly and affectionate performance.

To add to the linguistic complication in the theatre there was also Polish and Japanese. Poland's most famous film director Andrzej Wajda, before an audience restricted to 100, put the watchers and listeners as well as Raskolnikov on trial in a searing examination of Dostoyevsky's *Crime and Punishment* in the gloomy vault-like space of St Bride's Centre. One of the curious effects of foreign-language theatre is that in a strange tongue plays become more like opera and critics sitting there seeking understanding constantly reached for phrases like: 'As the text rumbles musically past the uncomprehending ear, the production emerges as a kind of opera-ballet where the nuances of interpretation rely on the actors facility with gesture or vocal inflection, illuminating the spoken word through the use of behavioural tics.'

There was lots of this in the confrontational analysis of Wajda's *Crime and Punishment* with the leading actor Jerzy Radziwilowic delineating Raskolnikov's tortured philosophy that murder can be justified by greatness of spirit while Jerzy Stuhr as the lawyer Porhpiry goads and probes him towards confession while the prostitute Sonia provides a gentle obbligato of divine forgiveness.

It was increasingly hard to see what all this had to do with the principles and aims of the Scottish Enlightenment, a good deal of whose celebration seemed to be centred around the not-exactly-hallowed figure of James Macpherson, the 18th-century creator of the Ossian poem. Credited as the inspiration of *Oberon*, Schubert, Mendelssohn and Brahms as well as Goethe, Schiller, Georges Sand, Lessing and a number of minor Napoleonic composers featured in a concert given by the Scottish National Orchestra, he was given an adulatory paragraph all to himself in the programme brochure which conveniently omitted to mention that the epics by an ancient Gaelic bard which he foisted on the literary world were forgeries and that in his own lifetime he was exposed as a fraud. What the writers, architects, poets, philosophers, doctors, sociologists, geologists, economists and engineers of the Scottish Enlightenment did in the 18th century was to release the minds of men and women from the shackles of feudal and religious conformity. Their insistence on clarity of thought – tempered by a compassionate interpretation of humanity – was badly needed after centuries raddled with imposed prejudice from Church and State. They sought to tell people it was NOT heresy to challenge established beliefs and practices; that knowledge and wisdom were NOT finite but capable of enlargement and development. To them, and to the many others who trumpeted the challenges of the 18th century, we owe our current modern freedom of thought and action, our attitude of challenge which has pushed back the frontiers of human knowledge. Within this conception of the best of 18th-century Scotland, the Ossianic fakes of Macpherson should have had no major part.

The source of Yukio Ninagawa's Toho Company production, Euripides, commanded greater respect. Scots have always fancied themselves as Greek scholars. But it was the manner rather than the matter of the Toho *Medea* which drew wonder. Set after nightfall in the open air within the 18th-century courtyard of the Old College of Edinburgh University, designed by the Greek-inspired Robert Adam, it made of the tragic and horrifying sequel to the story of Jason and the Golden Fleece a spectacle of powerful magic and wonderful drama. Even seen in an Edinburgh downpour with rain lashing past the old pillars on to the brightly costumed actors and the damp but mesmerised audience, it remains one of the most outstanding memories of any festival, a triumph from the opening wail of the Nurse to the brilliant and daring climax when Medea and her murdered children were flown high above the roofs of the Old College in a chariot drawn by a dragon.

Ossian should have been so lucky.

Medea *(1986)*

196

For some years in spite of fervent annual protests about the inadequacy and parsimony of the Festival budget, it seemed to have been the practice of Festival directors to succumb to hot flushes of *folie des grandeurs* and plan their programmes on the assumption that 'More is better'. In 1986 for the 40th anniversary there were 278 performances. In 1987 Frank Dunlop managed to turn 'more is better' into 'much is unreachable' by creating (including the 14 performances per day announced for the Festival Club) a total of 551. A strange growth of parsimony indeed.

The range of the fare on display became so rich and strange that it turned festival attendance into a kind of cultural Olympics. The complexity of the many-itemed programme structure meant that there were so few performances of most things that the punter of multi-faceted interests, at whom every Edinburgh Festival had been directed since 1947, could not get to a representative selection of performances to slake the very thirsts they encouraged.

For example there was no way you could hear the Bolshoi Orchestra, see the Leningrad Gorky Theatre in *Uncle Vanya* and *The History of a Horse* and also catch one of Ireland's greatest theatre companies, the Gate, in Sean O'Casey's finest play *Juno and the Paycock*. And if you attempted to perm any two from three or three from four of that lot you were going to miss the Leith Spectacular, the Folkopera of Stockholm in *The Magic Flute*, Black Ballet Jazz and most of the pidgin English plays from the Raun Raun Theatre from Papua, New Guinea. All this in pursuance of the theory that a World Theatre Season was OK provided you did not perform in the same language more than twice running. Just why this should apply particularly to performances in Russian, German, South Sea dialect, Hebrew, Japanese, German and Chinese was never made clear. A triumph for technology as the whine of simultaneous translation earached through the stalls.

However there was no trouble catching Frank Dunlop's production of Schiller's *Mary Stuart* with Hannah Gordon as Mary, (the Festival was getting seriously obsessed with Mary Stuart and her various continental interpreters) because it ran throughout the Festival at the Assembly Hall. A Festival Director has to have some privileges, after all.

But you had to make an incision in your World Theatre programme if you were to get to the Cameri Theatre from Tel Aviv's *Michael Kohlhaas*, yet another tribute to Diaghilev featuring Nureyev and *Descent of the Brutes*. Taking in the Papua, New Guinea Theatre or Juno and the Paycock meant you had to miss hearing the Festival Chorus sing Berlioz's *Damnation de Faust* with Neeme Jarvi and the Scottish National Orchestra. Berlioz's *Damnation* has been said to be 'like reading Goethe by flashes of lightning'. Festival-going in 1987 would have fitted that description to a D.

The same problems faced the eager multi-culturalist all through the three weeks. Even the alleged first-ever resident orchestra, in a week of the Pittsburgh under Lorin Maazel and Michael Tilson-Thomas, clashed with such opera as there was at the King's, the Finnish National Opera in *Rigoletto* and Aarre Merikanto's *Juha*. The resident orchestra claim was just unprincipled hype. The Vienna Philharmonic, the New York Philharmonic and the

Frank Dunlop and Hannah Gordon

Boston Symphony had all spent weeks at the Festival with more or as many as the Pittsburgh's five concerts and in 1977 the London Symphony Orchestra was in Edinburgh for three weeks, playing in the pit for seven performances of *Carmen* at the King's and giving five concerts in the Usher Hall. How resident can you get?

The 1987 Japanese epic *Descent of the Brutes* from the Yume no Yuminsha Company featured astronauts on a voyage to the Moon which they found inhabited by a Playboy Bunny. 'A completely different experience from last year's Toho *Medea*' said the programme brochure – and there was no disputing that.

With his penchant for odd anniversaries, Dunlop elected to celebrate the 70th anniversary of the Revolution of 1917 which led to the creation of the Soviet Union. It was a time of more openness, *glasnost*, *perestroika* and messages from Gorbachev.

Artists from the Soviet Union were a good buy that year. There were two old-style traditional productions from the Gorky Theatre of Leningrad, the Tbilisi State Puppet Theatre from Georgia, folk-dancers from Archangel, four concerts from the Orchestra of the Bolshoi Theatre from Moscow conducted by Mark Ermler and Alexander Lazarev, the superb Shostakovich Quartet, exhibitions of contemporary Soviet painting and of Decorative Arts from Soviet Asia at the Royal Scottish Museum. This was also one of the venues for *USSR Now*, a conference of delegates from the USSR and Britain discussing literature, theatre and the media which included the Vice-Minister of Culture V. I. Kazenin and the poet Yevgeny Yevtushenko. With Nigel Hawthorne reading English translations of some of the poems, Yevtushenko also gave two recitals at the King's.

The music was consigned to the back of the programme brochure as had become customary in the Dunlop regime and once again most of the opera was given at Leith Theatre. Only the Finnish National Opera was allowed into the King's in the last week, the other two being allocated to the Gorky Theatre and the Berliner Ensemble's *Troilus and Cressida* and *The Caucasian Chalk Circle*.

Although music had been even further side-lined, in this year the theatre hardly offered the quality which had redeemed Dunlop's planning in previous years. *A Wholly Healthy Glasgow* by Iain Heggie was a genuinely funny, foul-mouthed contemporary comedy set in a Glasgow massage parlour; *Mary Stuart* was competent enough romantic pseudo-historical pageantry but hardly the best contribution to the Festival's cult of Mariolatry.

Tom Fleming's St Cecilia's Hall programmes, *Edwin Muir and Willa* devised by Henry Donald and *Guthrie on Guthrie* devised by Margaret Dale, were affectionate and percipient tributes and reminders of how well such small-scale things could be done. But there was no single great event, no eminently memorable performance which gave the Festival the lift it needed.

The Berliner Ensemble is never less than impressive and Manfred Wekwerth's production of Shakespeare's *Troilus and Cressida* emphasised the arrogance, violence and cruelty but lacked the magic of the language even with a series of cameo appearances by Ekkehart Schall as the 'deformed and scurrilous Grecian', Thersites. Brecht's *Caucasian Chalk Circus* seemed haunted by oppression and guilt and even Brecht's son-in-law did not eclipse the memory of the genial villainy of the Rustaveli's great star, Ramaz Chkikvadze, as Azdak at the 1979 Festival.

Folkopera of Stockholm's *Magic Flute* at Leith Theatre was more successful musically than the 1986 *Aida*. The plot of *The Magic Flute* never makes much sense anyway with its mix of pantomime and masonic symbolism, so producer Claes Fellbom's idea of making the Queen of the Night some kind of freedom fighter dressed in turquoise and feathers combating the evil misogynistic racist Sarastro in hounds-tooth tweed did not particularly matter. Some of the costumes were even odder and I never understood why the orchestra was dressed like coal-miners from a harem thus abandoning the previous year's excellent Verdian idea of being as invisible as possible. But it was well-sung and played, acted with style and spirit and in a bizarre kind of way pleasing on the eye.

Hans Werner Henze's *The English Cat*, an operatic adaptation of Balzac's *Peines de Coeur d'une Chatte Anglaise* done at Leith by the Alte Oper, Frankfurt was interesting and well performed but it lacked the elegance, wit and pathos of the Alfredo Arias production of the play seen at the 1979 Festival.

The Shanghai Kunju Theatre at Leith in *The Woman Warrior* and *The Kunju Macbeth* was full of graceful traditional gesturing and martial arts jumping about at impressively dangerous speeds, while the 350-year-old opera *The Peony Pavilion* was a-twitter with high-pitched brightly costumed human starlings doing very little. Curiously enough, the best Chinese performance on view was in the Finnish Opera *Rigoletto* at the King's where Gilda was sung by Dilber, a sweet-voiced soprano from Beijing with considerable charm who brightened up an otherwise pedestrian production.

Juha, the company's other opera was more interesting as an unknown innately Finnish 20th-century work, a kind of Baltic *Jenufa* with a tensely written score by Aarre Merikanto which moved along the plot of domestic conflict in the remote wastelands of Finland with some passion and urgency. Jorma Hynninen (who had sung Rigoletto) was an impressively anguished betrayed husband but like the Verdi opera, *Juha* would have benefited from a more inspired and imaginative production.

Indeed lack of inspiration seemed to be the hallmark of 1987. The Pittsburgh, the Scottish Chamber and the Bolshoi orchestras all had their moments as far as execution was concerned but the choice of programmes lacked flair and originality. The Scottish National with Jarvi gave a fine account of *The Damnation of Faust* with the Festival Chorus back under the control of its original maestro, Arthur Oldham. But it was only the Swedish Radio Orchestra at the end of the Festival under its youthful conductor Esa-Pekka Salonen, which offered programmes outside the standard repertoire, as Salonen himself did with various smaller groups in a Weekend of 20th-century Music in the Queen's Hall.

1988 was announced as the year of Italy and Naples but the star attraction, the San Carlo Opera, pulled out because there was not enough money and another Neapolitan company *Peppe e Barra*, a mother and son team compared to the Crazy Gang, also failed to appear, perhaps because they had taken a good look at their venue, Leith Theatre.

Whether 1988 was another of Frank Dunlop's peculiar anniversaries (128 years since Garibaldi ended the Neapolitan kingdom in 1860?) was never made clear but the territory of southern Italy certainly had the potential to provide a wide and generous source of Festival material.

The Kingdom of the Two Sicilies was one of the most confused, complex and undisciplined areas of European history. Squabbled over for centuries by pontifical power politics, a *stupor mundi* of Hohenstaufens, Angevins of France and Aragons of Spain, falling into the hands of the Spanish Bourbons – about as nasty a lot as even the blood-boltered history of the Mediterranean has to offer – it was ruled by two members of Napoleon's family before finally falling to Garibaldi and becoming part of the Kingdom of Italy.

The programming possibilities were vast, a weird and strange mixture of people whose ancestors included Greeks, Carthaginians, Romans, Spaniards, Arabs and Normans and whose kingdom stretched from south of Rome almost to the coast of Africa, embracing Italy from north of Naples to the southern tip of Sicily.

There were typical contributions from Naples, a royal city full of imperial buildings, dominated by smoke-crowned Vesuvius, in whose back vennels passion, family life and conspiracy had run for centuries in a viscous and faintly malodorous stream.

From the theatre *Miseria e Nobilta* (Poverty to Riches) proved to be not an angry social document of teeth-gritting protest but a farce. Written by Eduardo Scarpetta, father of the great Neapolitan comedian and playwright, Eduardo De Fillipo (of *Saturday, Sunday, Monday* and *Filomena* fame and director of *La Pietra del Paragone* at the 1982 Festival), it carried the winning-the-lottery device to improbably ludicrous heights with a poor family transported to temporary aristocracy in an attempt by a young nobleman to win the hand of a ballerina.

It was played, frozen in the conventions of the 19th century, with lots of burlesque but almost no sense of social irony, except from a gloriously farcical performance by Lello Serao as the potential bride's father, himself a *parvenu* who had come to fortune via the kitchen. Quite fun but not really one of the glories of Italian theatre.

However *La Gatta Cenerentola* (The Cat Cinderella) won high praise and splendidly redressed the balance. Written and brilliantly directed by Roberto de Simone, former artistic director of the absent San Carlo, it was neither an opera nor an operetta nor exactly a folk opera. Fusing different aspects of the Cinderella story with Neapolitan life both in its street-based immediacy and the ceremonial of its grand buildings, it had enormous vitality and visual appeal and a real enchantment all its own..

> *An utterly individual, unpredictable piece,* said *The Scotsman's* Conrad Wilson, *embracing the entire history of Italian music theatre. Elements of Monteverdi madrigal mingle with Rossini and Donizetti. Bel canto mixes with smoky Neapolitan song. Opera, in its structure, was never so free as when Italy invented it in the 16th century, and it is the freedom of this modern Italian Cinderella which is one of its most attractive features.*
>
> *Layers of history also contribute to the way the story is presented. Cinderella as ritual, as sexual symbol, as erotic comedy, as oedipal fantasy, as commedia dell'arte, played against a background of church, ballroom and dream, takes us some distance from the Perrault fairy-tale we know and love.*

The exhibitions associated with Naples also offered interesting curiosities. In the time of the Bourbons, in intervals between assassination and plot, the court of Naples inspired a good deal of fine painting and collected avidly.

At the City Art Centre *Reality and Imagination* offered the fruits of Neapolitan acquisition and inspiration from the 17th, 18th and 19th centuries. It was in the final years of the 18th century that Sir William Hamilton, elderly husband of Nelson's mistress, Emma, took part in the excavations of Pompeii and Herculaneum and became a celebrated collector of antiquities, some of which he presented to the British Museum. *In the Shadow of Vesuvius* at the Royal Museum of Scotland displayed a collection of such relics of the lava-buried cities of the Bay of Naples, among them some never seen before outside Italy.

The other contribution from the Kingdom of the Two Sicilies was the Opera dei Pupi, Sicilian puppets, gorgeously caparisoned in armour, battling against wicked Saracen ravishers in the Church Hill Theatre and rescuing pale-skinned damsels from fates worse than death.

All this was very splendid, but despite the turbulent histories of both the Kingdom and the Festival, I felt that the Two Sicilies could well have provided Edinburgh with a more exciting programme than this. Scarpetta was all very well but what about Pirandello, one of the greatest European dramatists of this century and a crucial influence on modern theatre?

Pirandello is international but he is also Sicilian and only two of his plays had ever been given at the Edinburgh Festival, most memorably in 1956 when the companion to Giorgio Strehler's scintillating production of Goldoni's *Arlecchino* for Il Piccolo Teatro was *Questa Sera si recita a Soggeto*.

Other Italian contributions were Aterballetto, a dance company from the Teatro Municipale in Reggio Emilia which offered mixed classical and contemporary pieces at the King's, and works from more than 20 Italian composers, only one of whom, de Simone, hailed from the Two Sicilies.

In case anyone should think this was a barren area for compositional talent, imagine the attractions of a programme featuring the music of Pergolesi, Paisiello, who wrote the original *Barber of Seville*, Bellini,

Alessandro Scarlatti, founding father of modern opera, Cilea, Cimarosa, Leoncavallo and Spontini, to name but a few.

And, in a year from Naples and the south, would it not have been a good idea to have a recital of Neapolitan songs? And a few Italian conductors? The admirable Claudio Scimone with just one morning concert with his I Soloisti Veneti, was the only one. But where was the Neapolitan-born Riccardo Muti – or Abbado, Chailly, Giulini and Sinopoli, all erstwhile regular attendees?

However although there were grouses about not satisfactorily using the opportunity of an Italian season to the full, it has to be said that 1988 was the most balanced Festival Frank Dunlop had produced to date.

Despite being relegated as usual to the back of the book, there was a genuinely interesting opera programme, although inevitably the focus of interest was on the direction rather than the music. However there could be no complaints about imagination and innovation with a line-up which offered in addition to *La Gatta Cenerentola*, two new operas in Mark Anthony Turnage's *Greek* and John Adams's *Nixon in China*, *The Little Rats* from the National Youth Music Theatre and Stockholm's Folkopera in *Turandot*. The fact you could actually get to see all of them in the course of the three weeks without sprint training was also a bonus.

In offering a stark contrast in styles, the two new operas underlined the problems facing modern opera composers.

Greek, from a play by Steven Berkoff, with its reworking of the Oedipus legend in the setting of London East End violence, a *singspiel* speckled with Cockney obscenities, family banalities and romantic verse/ prose, harked back to the legend-based works before Mozart.*Nixon in China*, a firmly contemporary modern spectacular in the style of *Aida* or *Don Carlos*, was a reflection of big-scale 19th-century works. Not that the music sounded very like either Cavalli or Verdi although both works had their lyrical moments. The inadequacies of Leith Theatre did nothing to help the devious unrolling of the plot of *Greek* as the orchestra without a pit frequently drowned the singers.*Nixon* fared better. It was presented in the 2,500-seater Playhouse (presumably because even Frank Dunlop's theatrical ingenuity could not fit half a Boeing 707 onto the stage of Leith Theatre) in a vivid and inventive grand-scale production by Peter Sellars, who had first suggested the subject to the composer John Adams. Adams conducted the Scottish Chamber Orchestra and although the rhythmic pulsating repeated figures of the orchestral part were in the best minimalist tradition, the vocal parts were written with much more melodic structure, individual characterisation and warmth. James Maddelena as Nixon, Carolann Page as his wife and Trudy Ellen Craney as Madame Mao all had striking arias to sing and despite the use of accident-prone amplification increasing the impression of puppetry in some places, there were several moments of vital drama. Not least of them was a marvellous Rossinian storm in the middle of the second act ballet, Pat Nixon's compassionate lament for the abused heroine of The Red Detachment of Women and Madame Mao's brilliant coloratura aria. A breakthrough in modern opera and an evening of theatrical brilliance and musical excitement to remember.

There was one other piece of musical theatre in Jacques Offenbach's *La Perichole*. 'The Schiller Theatre chose to present *Perichole* to break the image of the company's heavy dramatic reputation' said the programme brochure and the Festival never produced a better instance of the need for the cobbler to stick to his last.

The charm and sparkle of Offenbach's music was completely absent, the production was clumsy and vulgar, the singers were out of tune and feeble and what should have been a delightful if light-weight musical evening was an affront to the composer and an insult to the musical taste of the audience. The National Youth Music Theatre's *The Little Rats*, an original piece by Jeremy James Taylor and David Scott with music by Peter Allwood, about the children of the Paris Opera's dance school in the 1840s, was more professional, better sung and much more appealing than the Schiller Theatre's travesty of Offenbach.

The Folkopera's *Turandot* was a different matter. Although designed to be compressed into a small untheatrical space, it managed to give an impression of ruthless splendour and cruel mystery, avoided making political comparisons between the rules of Turandot and Chairman Mao or offering profound psychological interpretations outside the rather pretentious programme notes. In general it was better sung than previous Folkopera offerings and the attenuated score was played well although sometimes it lacked thrilling edge and impact. The weakness again lay in failing to find a tenor to sustain the leading role, but Pia-Marie Nilsson's Liu was affectingly done and the steely-voiced Anne-Lise Bernsten made an impressive heroine/monster.

Even *The Scotsman's* critic, still slightly foaming at the typewriter after his ritualistic evisceration of *Carmina Burana* at the opening concert, liked it. Part of his praise was due to its not being anything like the recent Scottish Opera production which had played it as a kind of Puccini autobiography featuring the Doria Manfredi affair, with the composer as Calaf, Signora Puccini as Turandot and poor besotted Doria as the luckless Liu. 'Turandot,' he said, 'may be a sick opera, but in this performance it is rarely a dull one.'

Fortunately not everyone shares Mr Wilson's detestation of *Carmina Burana* and its performance was enhanced by one of those last-minute dramas so dear to the that curious piece of offal, the media's heart.

When the soprano Deborah Rees developed a viral infection during rehearsal, there was a hectic search for a replacement and Juliet Booth flew in at a few hours' notice. The result for the musically non-dyspeptic was a lively and exhilarating evening. Michael Tumelty in *The Herald* wrote:

> Only the most intransigent could have remained entirely unaffected by last night's monumental performance. This was the Jarvi/SNO chemistry on full display – fronted by the incomparable Edinburgh Festival Chorus. Jarvi drew blood with this performance. He was at his wicked best. He pummelled it, he teased it. He drew out its pastoral sections to a languorous length and degree that must have had the intractable opponents of the work demented,.
>
> The chorus was raw, subtle, supple in articulation, and consistently compelling in characterisation. Less strong on characterisation though impeccably lyrical was the Russian baritone Sergei Leiferkus. Tenor Neill Archer was magnificently agonised as a roasted swan. Award of the night however, to the beautifully lyrical soprano, Juliet Booth who was called in at the last moment, and who, less than 12 hours earlier, had been looking forward to a quiet Sunday. This will have done her career no harm.

Festival Director Frank Dunlop said: 'I have never felt an audience to be so joyful.'

The concert programme hinted at hidden treasures with the State Orchestra of the USSR under Yevgeny Svetlanov playing largely unfamiliar pieces by their most celebrated native composers, most of which except from the hardly unfamiliar Prokoviev's *Classical Symphony* and Tchaikovsky's Symphonic Fantasy *The Tempest*, although played with style and skill, seemed well worth their obscurity. Of the two Youth Orchestras on view, the Scottish one played more Italian music than the Italians; the programme of the Royal Philharmonic – Brahms, Dvorak, Mozart, Tchaikovsky, Sibelius and Shostakovich – hardly broke new ground.

Although the same could have been said of the Gewandhaus under Kurt Masur, the Leipzig orchestra's shining qualities of interpretation made up for lack of programme enterprise. The two Verdi Requiems from the Orchestra of the Maggio Musicale, Florence under James Conlon were marred by a last-minute tenor who lacked finesse, beauty of tone and the ability to sing below mezzo-forte, and their other concert made a curious mixture of lollipops and Liszt's *Dante Symphony*.

The best music of the Festival came from the Shostakovich Quartet who, in six unforgettable concerts, played all 15 quartets by the great Russian composer whose name they took. It was a profoundly emotional experience. sharp, agonised, disturbing and very occasionally optimistic and tender, played with sustained brilliance by four remarkable musicians Andrei Shislov, Sergei Pishchugin, Alexander Galkovsky and Alexander Korchagin.

Dance always took rather a back seat in Dunlop's planning (although it appeared in the brochure ahead of music) and although the Scottish *primo ballerino* Michael Clark had some ingenious and testing dance ideas in his *I am Curious, Orange*, a celebration of the 300th anniversary of William of Orange which managed to meld football and bombs; the Japanese company Matsuyama, a classical group in the European balletic mode were colourful rather than highly skilled although their *Giselle* with the lovely Yoko Morishita won some praise. The Italian Aterballetto failed to arouse any enthusiasm.

Four Wonderful Plays in English, trumpeted as part of the 1987 World Theatre Season, certainly sounded an innovation if only as a relief from the whine of simultaneous translators. Unfortunately although the plays were undoubtedly in English and one of them was by William Shakespeare and another by James Bridie none of them, at the point of viewing, was at all wonderful. The Royal Exchange Theatre's *Midsummer Night's Dream* (not the third Festival production as claimed in the brochure but the fourth) ran for three weeks at the Assembly Hall and was lavish but uninspired.

On the centenary of the birth of Dr Osbert Mavor better known as the playwright, James Bridie it was presumably mandatory to present one of his plays. Bridie had been a member of the original Festival planning group and a good theatrical craftsman and as Scotland's leading playwright of his day was worth celebrating. Just why it was decided to present *The Holy Isle*, one of his most dated and most boring plays, to mark the occasion is another facet of the Dunlop enigma. There were plenty of alternatives – *Mr Bolfry, A Sleeping Clergyman, The Anatomist* and, supremely perhaps, *The Queen's Comedy*, his Trojan horse of a play commissioned for the 1950 Edinburgh Festival, a brilliant denunciation of the follies of war with a dramatic sweep and breadth of vision which he achieved fully in no other play. All the great Bridie virtues are there, the imaginative gleam of the language, the shrewd and witty characterisation, the pithy comedy; but, above all, there is a superb dramatic idea, and something profound and moving to say which transcends the witty lines and the confrontations between soldiers and the Olympian gods, to make great theatre. *The Holy Isle*, indifferently presented by Charles Nowosielski and the Brunton Theatre Company, gave a poor idea of Bridie's power, wit and genius.

The two Canadian contributions, *The Rez Sisters* and *B-Movie: the play* were exceedingly odd. I expected a play about living in a Rez, a native Indian reservation in Canada, to be angry, sad, dramatic, significant. It spent most of its time trying to be funny with women whose lifetime and daily hopes are linked to bingo, haunted by a Puck-like mythological demon of many shapes who dances through their lives, their gossip and the hopes and fears aroused by the world's biggest bingo game arriving in Toronto. It was hard to laugh because it made you feel guilty.

At *B-Movie: the play* however, it was not in the least difficult to laugh because in its deeply trivial way, it was really very funny. The only problem was that it should have been fast-moving and funny, a kind of sparkling tinsel ball of every Hollywood cliché you could dream up.

Unfortunately it moved so slowly that you caught yourself inventing the next gag before anyone on stage did it.

On the comedy side the best the rest of the World Theatre Season could do was a sentimental musical lament for Cape Town's *District Six*, the multi-ethnic tradesmen's district of the port under Table Mountain, demolished in 1966 and designated under the Group Areas Act as a residential area for whites only. It was rather soft on the tyranny behind the Act but perhaps that was a condition of performance. But there was real warmth and lots of vitality in the dancing by the 'sexy boys' and their friends and the reinvention of life in the cosmopolitan District Six made its point with vivacity and charm. *Trafford Tanzi*, featured an all-conquering woman wrestler and her new-invented hold 'The Venus Flytrap', came from Belgium and was performed totally charmlessly in a mixture of Flemish snort, English grunt and French *mugissement*. A lot of people laughed in a rather nervous sort of way.

There was more nervous laughter at Rainer Fassbinder's *Blood on the Neck of the Cat* subtitled *Marilyn Monroe Against the Vampires*, a highly weird piece from the late, strange (mad?) German film director presented by the Schiller Theatre. There was no plot but the efforts of a visitor from the great beyond trying to find out about communication, sex, desire, perversity and power in a twisted world where contact is concluded with a vampire bite was somehow summed up by the fact that the extra-terrestrial visitor was called Phoebe Zeitgeist. A sort of Hammer Films version of *Carry on Outa Space*.

The blend of sheer inventive stage lunacy and old time music hall nostalgia which Jerome Deschamps brought to *Les Petits Pas* was equally devoid of plot but its setting in a singularly under-furnished home for retired vaudeville artistes suggested a kind of protest piece on behalf of the maltreated elderly against their indifferent minders, but in fact turned out to be hilarious and warm-hearted.

The elaborate production of Marivaux's *Le Jeu de L'Amour et du Hasard* (The Game of Love and Chance) by the Argentinian director Alfredo Arias and his Groupe TSE from Paris was set against a romantic ruin and played in monkey masks and 18th-century costumes. It could have been rather twee but was done with such skill and elegance that it was never less than a pleasure. The tangled social skirmishings of Dorante and Silvia exchanging places with their servants in order better to study the person to whom they are betrothed has echoes of da Ponte's plot for Mozart's *Così Fan Tutte* (although written 60 years earlier) but it had its own tensions and twists and the idea of masks upon masks as a kind of social protection against love was cunningly played out, although the more obvious animal antics were, of course, confined to the servant class. After the company's brilliant presentation of *Peines de Coeur d'une Chatte Anglaise* in 1979 however I felt it would be have been interesting to see Senor Arias's talented company perform with their own faces.

Once again the Dunlop theatre programme was a triumph for the Japanese. The Toho Company felt they were unable to bear the touring cost of such a large production as Yukio Ninagawa's *The Tempest*, so Ninagawa formed his own company and brought it to The Playhouse in Edinburgh. No Shakespearean play offers a talented and imaginative director such scope in staging as *The Tempest* and Ninagawa seized the chance with avidity in one of the most memorable spectacles the Festival has ever staged. Anne Smith in the newly created *Scotland on Sunday* wrote:

> *One of the secrets of Ninagawa's genius is the way in which he manages, quite deliberately, to evoke subconscious memories in his audiences, 'Not recent memories, generational memories – atavistic memories even. The audience partakes in the play through these memories. Between the play itself and the memories of the audience the work of art is created. I stir up my actors to go very far in their performances. I want to make the theatre for the eyes rather than the ears.'*

Theatre for the eyes was underlined as part of the Ninagawa technique not only by the lavish scenery, brilliant lighting and dramatic staging but by using sur-titles above the stage for the text, a welcome respite from the intrusive buzz of simultaneous translation.

Reflecting on his 'unique festival' at the final press conference, Frank Dunlop had a go at the critics. Allen Wright reported:

> *He suggested that the 'golden glow of yesteryear' seems to be blinding critics to the facts. For instance, they went on about the Usher Hall always being full in Lord Harewood's time when, in fact, many concerts in those days had attendances of 40 per cent. Indulging in a little nostalgia himself, Frank Dunlop recalled working on*

the Fringe with the Oxford Theatre Group in 1953 when 'we were the darling of the critics' while the stuffy old Festival bored the Press with Richard Burton's Hamlet *at the Assembly Hall and a new play by T. S. Eliot.*

It would seem that the golden glow of yester-Fringe had blinded Mr Dunlop because I cannot recall nor trace any critics who were bored by Burton's thrilling *Hamlet* with Claire Bloom as Ophelia or less than intrigued by Eliot's *The Confidential Clerk*. The slings and arrows of outrageous misfortune were hurled at critics all through this final 1988 meeting with the media:

They used to accuse the Festival of being elitist but they had to change that to complaining that the Festival was just a touring date on the way to London. We are not getting that criticism any more because we are putting on things that are unique – like a season of three operas all of which are new to Britain and not being done anywhere else.

He said he resented the tendency of London-based critics to assess the Festival when it was at the half-way stage:

They seem to want everything to be presented for their benefit at the beginning, all the highlights on an hors d'oeuvre plate. But the Festival is not designed for a handful of people and many of the best things come in the final week.

Whether all this lashing around at the media was a product of the difficulties he was experiencing with finance and future programming problems or was just an incautious reaction to bickering, it seemed to be recklessly tactless and unjustified. The London papers had covered *Nixon in China* extensively at the end of the final week and it was simply not true to say that the operas had not been done elsewhere. *La Gatta Cenerentola* had toured in Europe, *Turandot* had run for several months in Sweden before coming to Edinburgh, *Greek* appeared in the Munich Neue Musik Theater Festival earlier in the year and *Nixon* had several previous performances in the United States. There had been a considerable amount of media support for Dunlop's World Theatre Seasons and positive response to the more enterprising approach to music programming when it was announced. Biting the hands which wrote your publicity seemed ungracious and was made the more strange by Mr Dunlop's statement at the end of the second week when he declared 'It is the happiest atmosphere Festival I have known. People are much more relaxed about it and the artists feel the same way. There is now a warm feeling about the Festival.' Truly, a week is a long time in Festival.

Before the 42nd Festival came to an end the perennial mirage of an Edinburgh Opera House had reappeared in a new guise. Perhaps it had been stimulated – or goaded – by an illustrated exhibition held at Nine Atholl Crescent during the three weeks of Festival entitled *The Hole in the Ground* which cast a reflective and sardonic eye over the most significant schemes launched since 1959 including the 1965 Castle Terrace demolition which wiped out Poole's Synod Hall Cinema and the Festival office, to create a still-vacant space for the phantom of the opera.

The sorry story of the 30 years in which this vision had remained unfulfilled had suffered its latest blow when it was announced in 1988 that a plan had been formulated to build a financial centre on the site which might possibly incorporate a small theatre. Exit once more trailing clouds of misery and frustration stage left (aka abandoned), the Edinburgh Opera House. But in mid-Festival, rising like a phoenix from the ashes, came a new scheme for a £25 million development incorporating the misty outlines of an opera house along with apartments, offices, shops, restaurants and public houses in Leith. This had hardly drawn breath as a proposal when it was blown away by the owners of the site denying that they had ever given permission for such a scheme.

The mournful obbligato of teeth-grinding had barely died away however when there was some good news for the Festival. On September 2 1988, on the day before the Festival ended, Edinburgh District

Council's Labour administration suddenly announced a new attitude of wholehearted support for the Festival. It was proposed to give the Festival financial stability by assembling a funding package over three years. The Council hoped to give an increased grant and to announce it before the end of the year, instead of when festival plans were already in place in April or May, and to indicate likely sums offered for 1990 and 1991. Other means of raising money were to be pursued including an approach to Lothian Region, the Scottish Arts Council, foundation trusts, endowment funds and a development of sponsorship.

This Damascene conversion had been prompted, one councillor admitted, by the success of the *The Scotsman* campaign after last year's funding shortfall, which had demonstrated public support for the Festival by raising £90,000. It could also have been brought on by the Policy Studies Institute's report on Glasgow which had found the arts to be a good buy and that tourism generated by arts attractions sustained more than 4,000 jobs in Glasgow and that every arts job had helped create 2.74 other jobs in the wider economy and enhanced the tourist beds figures.

So it was in a state of comparative euphoria that Frank Dunlop marched forward towards 1989.

XXVIII

In 1989 Frank Dunlop elected to celebrate the anniversary of the French Revolution's Declaration of the Rights of Man on 26 August 1789, and, although he had missed the 400th anniversary of the Armada by one year, he decided to throw Spain in as well, perhaps in memory of the joyous looting of the wrecks of the Spanish galleons which went on through 1589 along the west coasts of Scotland and Ireland. At all events the Spanish contribution was the most significant and, shattering observed Dunlop tradition, music dance and opera headed the programme brochure.

Stranger and more ground-breaking still was the twinning.

Double, double toil and trouble
Fire burn and cauldron bubble

The witches' incantation at the beginning of the apparitions scene in 'The Scottish Play', as theatrical superstition nervously calls it, began to sound rather like the minutes of an Edinburgh Festival planning meeting, because out of the cauldron of that year Frank Dunlop plucked not one but two doubles. One of them inevitably was *Macbeth*

The previous year that irrepressible impresario Richard Demarco had brought over a weird and sometimes wonderful company from Sicily which mingled with Scottish actors and scenery to present *A Prologue to Macbeth*. This took the elements of Shakespeare's play, plus a somewhat bemused audience wrapped in blankets from the Demarco Gallery just off Edinburgh's Royal Mile by bus to South Queensferry, entertaining them with taped excerpts from Verdi's opera *Macbeth* on the way, and by boat to Inchcolm, an island in the middle of the Firth of Forth.

Another thrilling instalment was planned for 1989, backed by Demarco and the Italian Institute, when the same Sicilian company, La Zattera di Babele directed by Carlo Quartucci, were to present a version of the complete play on Inchcolm.

'La Zattera di Babele' means 'the raft of Babel': Inchcolm has long been associated with Scottish kings and is mentioned in the first act of Shakespeare's play when the Thane of Ross reports Macbeth's victories to Duncan:

Sweno, the Norway's king craves composition
Nor would we deign him burial of his men
Till he disbursed at Saint-Colme's-Inch
Ten thousand dollars to our general use.

The Demarco *Macbeth* was included in the original 1989 official Festival programme but when Carlo Quartucci and Carla Tato, principals of the Sicilian company, faxed Rikki Demarco just ten days before the first night on Inchcolm, to say they were suffering from nervous exhaustion and under doctor's orders not to travel from Sicily to Edinburgh, the curse of 'the Scottish Play' seemed to have struck again. But Rikki Demarco does not know what nervous exhaustion means, and with producer and adapter John Bett, he proceeded to reconstruct the Inchcolm *Macbeth*. Bett made a new adaptation of the text; a new company of actors was hastily gathered and rehearsed. In the programme note, Bett set out his ideas.

It is a threnody of loss that sounds deep in our national psyche, and whose echoes resound in our cultural and political life of today. In Shakespeare's play, Macbeth loses everything – his king, his best friend, his wife, the respect of his peers, his peace of mind, his own self-respect and finally the crown and temporal power he so much desired. Each life he touches is irredeemably tainted. His tragedy becomes their tragedy, their tragedy becomes inextricably woven with his. In our production the tragedy has already happened, and Shakespeare's play too has been swallowed up into myth. Here on St Colme's Inch, in the precincts of a ruined abbey, over this ancient burial ground of kings, the main protagonists, the ghosts of the tragedy, the 'walking shadows' tell us something of their own individual story.

They sing their own song of pain and loss, give whispers of their close acquaintance with horror and evil and recall for us briefly their rare moments of joy. Theirs is an old story but in these 'cruel times' in which greed has acquired a new respectability, and loss of all kinds has become a commonplace experience, it is a tale whose moral and spiritual gracenotes cannot be easily ignored.

Although John Bett's text did not quite achieve all this, the Inchcolm *Macbeth* was a landmark in Scottish theatre experience. Hideous witch cackles rose from the bilges of the boat ferrying the audience to Inchcolm. From a headland on the island shore the pipes wailed a ghostly lament, kilted figures clashed claymores on the beach, a Gaelic soothsayer sang doom by the lapping sea. Figures silhouetted against the ragged sky ululated the mournful keening of loss among the wheeling harsh screaming gulls. Somewhere among the old stones there was a weird of singing voices as tattered clansmen guided the audience in their blanket cloaks around and into the sinister abbey cloisters. The watchers shifted to meet each new cameo scene or ringing declamation from the battlements. John Cairney's was a Macbeth of the reeling mind, searching for lost valour, tormented by self treachery and indignity. Gerda Stevenson's Lady hissed with fraught ambition, John Bett as Custodian of the Memory savaged the huddled followers as he led them on tragedy's circuit. Aonghas MacNeacail wailed lyrically in Gaelic coronach. Of course, not all of it worked perfectly and there was more than some sacrifice of poetry to polemic but the atmosphere was wonderful, electric and trailing clouds of nostalgic Celtic glory.

There was, however, no glory for Dunlop and the official Festival. When the Sicilians pulled out they abandoned the whole enterprise, causing endless confusion by returning the tickets they had already sold, withdrawing their support for Inchcolm and doing their best to make a disaster out of a misfortune. So much for supporting Scottish theatre and programming for courage and enterprise.

Whatever the deviations from the text found at Inchcolm, the end result was a lot nearer Shakespeare's play than the other 1989 *Macbeth* at the King's Theatre, a brutal ballet devised by one of Europe's most original choreographers, Johann Kresnik for the Bremer Theatre company from Bremen. The *Macbeth* story was used as a means of examining the motives, methods and purposes of political assassination and Kresnik's no-holds-barred talent for the macabre filled the stage with blood-boltered savage images of sado-masochism and violence. Not an evening for the squeamish but impressive in the range of Kresnik's talent and the athletic qualities of his team of virtuoso dancers.

By the time you had seen both *Macbeths* you might well feel with Shakespeare's hero ...
I am in blood
Stepp'd in so far, that, should I wade no more,
Returning were as tedious as go o'er
... which took you, neatly if gorily, to the other double, the two *Salomés* also presented in the first week.

Both the play from the Gate Theatre, Dublin in a production by Steven Berkoff at the Royal Lyceum and the opera by Richard Strauss done by the Festival Folkopera at Leith Theatre were more securely based on the original text than the Shakespeares.

Oscar Wilde wrote the play in French, specifically for Sarah Bernhardt but, although she had already taken a theatre in London for its performance, it was banned by the Lord Chamberlain on the somewhat flimsy grounds that the law forbade the portrayal of Biblical characters on the stage. (Rossini's *Moise in Egitto* and Verdi's *Nabucco* evaded censorship in 1822 and 1846 respectively by changing the name of the work and as *Salomé* is not actually named in the Bible it is difficult to see how the ban was justified). Oscar's account of the making of the play is itself highly dramatic.

The subject of Salomé, the decadent daughter of Herodiade, who demanded the head of John the Baptist as the price of dancing for her lecherous stepfather, has fascinated writers and painters for centuries. Titian, Guido Reni, Rubens and Gustave Moreau were among the artists who evoked the sensual and sinister confrontation between Salomé, the lustful king and the unyielding prophet. Heine, Flaubert, Anatole France and Mallarmé have all written about her. In fact, the most popular in-joke of literary Paris in 1891 was that Mallarmé's Herodiade, begun in 1864, was 'the best-known unfinished poem since Kubla Khan', Coleridge's never-completed oriental fragment.

In its original draft, the play was written in one night. Wilde had been lunching with a group of young French writers, including André Gide, and had been elaborating on the *Salomé* theme. When he returned to his lodgings in the Boulevard des Capucines, he found a blank notebook, which he had bought earlier, lying on the table. He began writing there and then.

Later in the night, hungry and exhausted, he went out to the Grand Cafe on the corner for something to eat.

> *That fellow Rigo*, he wrote later, *who ran away with the Princesse de Chimay, Clara Ward, was then the leader of the orchestra of Tziganes. I called him over to my table and said 'I am writing a play about a woman dancing with her bare feet in the blood of a man she has craved for and slain. I want you to play something in harmony with my thoughts.' And Rigo played such wild and terrible music that those who were there stopped talking and looked at each other with blanched faces. Then I went back and finished* Salomé.

Few plays have been received with such outraged protest or caused such public and private quarrels as *Salomé*. Reviewing the publication of the French edition in 1893, *The Times* wrote:

> *An arrangement in blood and ferocity, morbid, bizarre and very offensive in its adaptation of scriptural phraseology to situations the reverse of sacred.*

Wilde never saw the play performed. He was in Reading Jail when it was premièred in Paris in 1896, and dead by the time Max Reinhardt performed it in Berlin in 1902. Steven Berkoff's production in modern dress was all choreography and visual grace with Jokanaan's captivity portrayed as rather a sick cabaret act at a decadent dinner party and Salomé lacking the vocal rhythm and emotive stress to go with the slinky movement and outrageous demand. It moved rather slowly like a kind of underwater ballet and seemed steeped in ritual rather than passion. Only Joe Savino's Jokanaan in his outbursts of righteous wrath had true dramatic authority although Alan Sandford's Herod was also a finely spoken performance, particularly in the scene when he attempts to bribe Salomé away from her terrible dance-price. But if sensuous decadence can be reverential, then this subdued elegant performance made it so with its simpering sycophantic guests merely a chorus to Herod's vanity, Herodias's vengeance and Salomé's carefully gestured lust.

At its first performances, as noted already in connection with the 1956 Hamburg presentation, Strauss's opera caused as big a scandal as the play. In the end, however, the public, captivated by the bizarre drama and the power and excitement of the music, spurned the verdict of the first narrow-minded critics.

At Edinburgh the opera was performed by Festival Folkopera, a company specially formed by Frank Dunlop for the Festival, which aped the structure of the Stockholm Folkopera and their successes.

Indeed it employed the Stockholm director designer and conductor along with a cast of young British singers and an augmented Scottish Chamber Orchestra – even doubling the main roles, making doubling even more of a secondary Festival theme!

There was some criticism of the 'student' quality of the singing but in truth, although it lacked the sheer scale of Birgit Nilsson with the Vienna Philharmonic at Salzburg, it seemed to me often musically better presented than some of the earlier Folkopera productions.

The Scotsman music critic disagreed with Verdi:

> *By placing the orchestra behind the singers this problem is exacerbated*, he wrote. *The point about opera is that the orchestra is meant to be in front, and it doesn't help to clarify the words (on this occasion optimistically sung in English translation) one little bit by putting the players in a wire cage at the back of the stage. All that happens is that the sheen of Strauss's music is lost and all that is gained is closer contact between the audience and the action.*

> *In Claes Fellbom's production, action is all. Like the blood in the closing scene, it spills all over the place: and it incorporates, between Salomé and John the Baptist, an orgasmically sado-masochistic interlude halfway through the opera, which is not only gratuitous and misconceived but makes nonsense of Strauss's scrupulously prepared ending.*

On the night I saw it the Salomé was Fiona O'Neill, the Jokhanaan Dmitri Kharitonov, the Herod Donald Stephenson and the Herodias Jady Pearl; the reduced score was one which Strauss himself had made shortly after the première for use in smaller German opera houses, and the result was a completely different *Salomé* from any I had seen before. Although the voices did not have the power of a full-scale production, they were certainly adequate for the size of the theatre.

The youthfulness of the singers restored the balance. Most Salomés need to impress with size and quality of voice to convey the sensuality and twisted desire of a spoiled and perverted teen-age girl and there have been plenty of interpretations where only the sheer brilliance of the singing has held the line against a ludicrous and incredible stage image. Fiona O'Neill was no Birgit Nilsson or Ljuba Welitsch but she began with the advantage of being young and comely and, in the nude dance sequence, imbued with a teasing, provocative and riveting sexiness far outstripping the tamely posed gesturing of Berkoff's vapid temptress. She sang the music rawly but with dramatic effect and captured tellingly the imperious shallowness and the lusty allure of this terrible child. It gave the opera a new dimension. Dimitri Kharitonov's brutal and inflamed Jokhanaan shed a new harsh light on the prophet, imposingly presented, Jady Pearl's Herodias simmered with base revenge and Donald Stephenson's carnal, neurotic and epicene Herod was very fine. The enlarged Scottish Chamber Orchestra under Kerstin Nerbe played with fiery intensity and maintained a dramatic balance which fed the sensuous score into the action without swamping the singers. A very unusual *Salomé* but a piquant interpretation.

The National Opera of Spain from Madrid brought a lively example of Spain's own music theatre, the *zarzuela*, to The Playhouse. The form takes its name from the Palace outside Madrid where the first performances were given before Philip IV and his court in the 17th century. The first *zarzuelas* were short and heroic in mould and mirrored Italian operas of the period but gradually they moved away towards a more *verismo* style and became popular rather than regal entertainment. *La Chulapona* (Back Street Woman) was written in 1934 and unlike most *zarzuelas* it ran for three hours. This proved rather too long for the colourful but light-weight tale of the rivalry of two laundresses for the hand of a butcher, even when spaced out with flamenco, the flutter of fans, the click of castanets and the bustle of Madrid street life.

At the King's Opera North offered three nights of Prokoviev's fairy-tale opera based on a play by Carlo Gozzi, *The Love For Three Oranges*, a sad skeleton of the programme at the 1962 Festival when the Belgrade Opera gave the work its British première along with five other operas filling 15 of the 21 nights. It was a good ensemble piece, imaginatively staged by the young producer Richard Jones as a dazzlingly costumed, slickly managed cartoon of grotesques recounting the tale of the Prince who could not laugh until he saw the witch humiliated and was then cursed to fall in love with three perennially thirsty oranges conjured up by Fata Morgana. A sprightly performance, it introduced a new theatrical device in a six-boxed card where you could scratch to produce a smell appropriate to the scene you were watching!

Anything which has a programme note by the composer which says ...

What has always struck me and now strikes me even clearer, about Wölfli's conception of himself is that, despite his obvious and indisputable madness, it more closely approximates reality, even 'non-mad' reality than that semi-conscious conception of the self as a single whole person 'myself', most of us confidently carry around with us. For that very reason The Divine Circus *is concerned only 'secondarily' with Wölfli's 'biographical fate' in super-realistic operatic form, but 'primarily' with the possibilities that such an opera has of throwing light on the multidimensional reality we all trundle around with in our daily life.*

... is something you approach with care, not to say apprehension.

Heightened by further reading which tells you that the central character Adolf Wölfli is a schizophrenic Swiss child-molester who wrote most of the text and some of the music, that the images of his insanity are the central preoccupation of the opera, it might well have persuaded you to go to *La Chulapona* instead or try some other festival where derangement did not seem to be the major theme.

However if you had done so you would have missed a strangely gripping piece, staged with acute invention and set to bizarre but haunting music which examines the fertile processes of a mind severed from reality which creates not one but several worlds of its own. It should have been presented within the circus ring promised in the brochure but Leith Theatre proved inadequate for that (as much else) but nevertheless Jutland Opera's showing of Per Norgaard's intelligent and probing work made a strong impression.

Another piece of music theatre was Duncan Youngerman's *soi-disant* opera-ballet *L'An Un* (Year One) which took its title from the French Revolution's attempt to re-write time by removing all Christian references, abolishing Sundays and religious festivals and re-starting the calendar. Like the new order time structure, it seemed pretentious and unproductive. Musically uninteresting and short on plot, the stringing together of a series of symbolic tableaux achieved nothing but a hotch-potch of boring images with only the Red Notes Dance Company providing any moments of liveliness or unaffected dramatic fire. By contrast the National Youth Theatre's mixture of masks, puppets, music and spirited acting in de Falla's *Master Peter's Puppet Show*, based on an episode in Cervantes's *Don Quixote* was done with great *élan* and not a little style, vivacity and pace.

Events in the concert hall were generally adjudged to be below Festival standard and deficient in programme interest. Although Mariss Jansons and the Oslo Philharmonic did their now-celebrated Tchaikovsky act and the 19-year old Norwegian pianist Leif Ove Andsnes gave a highly musical and unsplashy account of the Grieg piano concerto and Simon Rattle with his Birmingham Orchestra won acclaim for the maturing boy wonder and even grudging recognition from the more austere critics for playing Boulez, Webern and Takemitsu, it was felt that Dunlop's choice of the Gothenburg Symphony and the Nouvel Orchestre Philharmonique under Marek Janowski added little to the lustre of the Usher Hall programmes and there was sharp criticism of them at the final press conference.

Spain's National Orchestra, with the genial Rafael Frübeck de Burgos conducting, opened the Festival and was better received but no-one was convinced that it was an orchestra of world class. The programme too was loyal but patchy. *Atlántida*, the work to which Manuel de Falla devoted the last two decades of his life, had always been a mystery rather like the sub-ocean land after which it was named. Falla himself never seems to have decided whether it was an opera or an oratorio and called it 'a scenic cantata'. The London Symphony Orchestra under Igor Markevitch had given the first British performance at the 1962 Festival; in 1989 it was entitled Fragments from *Atlántida* which suggested uncertainty as to the quality of the whole which had been completed by his pupil Ernesto Halffter after Falla's death.

Dance seemed to have made a come-back into the programme with six companies, not counting the two Salomés. The biggest group, the Houston Ballet at The Playhouse, was disappointing in its European première *Gautama Buddha* (to music by an Indian composer, Naresh Sohal who lived in Edinburgh!) but the scurrying pseudo-Oriental dance patterns by Christoper Bruce provided a series of pretty images rather than a narrative structure to the film-score music. In a later programme their *Swan Lake* was adjudged pretty ordinary apart from Li Cunzin (who had also danced Buddha) as Siegfried. The Spanish National Ballet was all stomp and flounce and their *Bolero* was rated by ballet critic Christopher Bowen as 'With no exceptions, the campest thing I've ever seen at a Festival'. The stone-faced Cristina Hoyos brought her group and a rattling clicking, stamping condensation of *Carmen* to the Usher Hall together with *Suenos Flamencos* (Flamenco Dreams), all of which added up to a rather obvious *Viva Espana!* TV commercial. Kresnik's bloody *Macbeth* was impressive if you had not already supped full of horrors, but the big dance hit was Martha Graham's wonderful realisation of Hieronymus Bosch's famous triptych *A Garden of Earthly Delights*, a stunning fusion of dance, mime, music, aerial acrobatics and brilliantly imagined direction, at once horrifying and beautiful, making a haunting and mesmerising theatrical experience.

But the programme's saving grace was, as always in the Dunlop era, the theatre. There was no blockbuster from Japan that year but the Japanese were there in the stark confines of St Bride's Centre for matinees and evenings with the Yokohama Boat Theatre, and late night with Japanese pop star Epo, a giggly girl who sounded just like any other pop star but quieter and was about as Japanese as Phil Collins. The Boat Theatre was very different.

Their contribution to Festival Macabre was one of their own legends *Oguri Hangan, Terute Hime*. A love story set in mythic times, it portrayed the complex moral tale of Oguri, a nobleman already married 72 times, falling in love with Terute, a virtuous princess who redeems him by digging up his rotting corpse and taking it on a pilgrimage to the top of a holy mountain where he takes vengeance on his enemies. Man-eating horses, poisoned sake, slavery, a journey into hell to retrieve the loved one, lots of ominous percussion and nastily realistic death masks all came into it somewhere but it was rather difficult to follow the subtitles above the stage because so much was happening below. I could well have missed something significant. Although there was cherry blossom and sunlight on the mountain top in the final scene when Oguri's decomposed corpse triumphed, it was difficult to feel anything but a mixture of nausea and nervousness about the happy ending.

Unfortunately *Clyde Nouveau*, a new play by Iain Heggie, did not live up to the scabrous but hilarious promise of *A Wholly Healthy Glasgow* except in its casual use of obscenities. The Tron Theatre actors gave it plenty of vitality but they could not rescue it from a poor and sloppy script. Heliotrope Productions *Torchlight and Laser Beams*, a play fashioned by the brain-damaged Christy Nolan and Michael Scott from Nolan's life and epic struggle to express himself, suffered from inaudibility in Leith Theatre and occasional over-elaboration in direction. The character of his free spirit which shadowed the disabled Christy did not really work as a concept but the courage and emotion of the story of his life and struggle came through vividly.

Selling package tours to the Road to Damascus and like highways to faith and salvation was rubbished with enthusiastic savagery in Tim Robbins's *Carnage*, a thinly structured but sharply written narrative set around a couple out to save their marriage by a pilgrimage to God's Happy Acres theme park. The brash violence, noisy tacky rhetoric and ghastly geniality of the over-the-top evangelist was brilliantly captured by Lee Arenberg as the Reverend Dr Slocum Cotton, all of it was tightly directed by Robbins and much of it was very funny. The only problem was that American TV evangelism has by-passed parody, however ruthlessly incisive, because it is virtually impossible to satirise something which is already farce. Full marks however for a brave and accomplished try.

There were fine solo performances in the smaller prose recitals. Miriam Margolyes in *Wooman, Lovely Wooman, What a Sex You Are!* examined the women of Dickens, fictional and actual with a warm but beady eye; John Fraser made a sympathetic tribute to J. M. Barrie, a once-celebrated playwright completely neglected by the Festival and Dame Wendy Hiller provided some crisp reminiscences of George Bernard Shaw. Jerome Deschamps failed to repeat his comedy triumph of the previous year with *C'est Dimanche*.

Many operas begin as plays but if the opera is successful it often obliterates its ancestor. Who nowadays watches *Le Roi S'Amuse*, Hugo's play which gave Verdi the plot for *Rigoletto* or *La Tosca*, Victorien Sardou's drama which Puccini made into one of his greatest successes? Pushkin's play *Boris Godunov* was hardly known at all except as the source of Mussorgsky's opera and it was fascinating to see what the great Russian director Yuri Lyubimov, returning to the Taganka Company from which he had been expelled six years before, would do with it. In fact music played an important part in his production at Leith Theatre in bursts of *a cappella* song from the crowds on the stark stage. It had none of the gorgeous trappings of the Russian Orthodox Church, it was moved from the 16th century to 1917 with the message that even without a Tsar the spirit of the people of Russia would survive and conquer.

Despite the contortions inflicted on the plot to preach a present-century message, it was done with great power and authority, with dark volumes of sound booming from the stage, a dominating rendering of the title role by Nikolai Gubenko and the lighting casting long ominous shadows.

The most significant theatre came from Spain.

There was Els Comediants, a Catalan company from Barcelona, bounding, enthusiastic, athletic in D*imonis*, disrupting total theatre which opened with fireworks in a downpour in the grounds of George Heriot's School above the Grassmarket, in an explosion of demons

> *It is intriguing to learn*, wrote one reviewer, *that when first performed in southern Spain, it aroused fury and earnest prayers against the evil evoked. Such a reaction seems strangely inappropriate, even for a deeply religious or superstitious society, as evil is the last of the things on colourful display in the show.*
>
> *Abandon, yes, a certain lewdness, yes, but evil never: this is a glorious joyous party full of jolly dragons and fire-juggling goblins, in which any sudden scariness belongs to the long and dignified tradition of enacting and exorcising spirits in great communal festivals.*

Very occasionally, a little overt symbolism creeps in: a washing line hung with clothes joins the general fire, shreds of lettuce leaves are hurled into the crowd – a destruction, surely, of banal domesticity. Mostly, though, it is sheer effect. In a touch of final bravado, one of the demons scales the full height of the walls and from the dizzy top grandly declares the republic of demons and a fulsome toast to the Edinburgh Festival, to which there could hardly have been a more exuberant start.

Later that week they were in the Royal Lyceum to give one of their few indoor performances,*La Nit*, a representation of things that go bump, whoosh, bleep or whoof in the night.

There were more goblins, a moon blowing balloons, vampires aspiring to be rock-stars, miming and clowning and not enough language to erect any kind of barrier. Not a very quiet night but a sexy, enlivening and surreal one. Not a show where you were at all likely to nod off.

The Compania Nacional Teatro Classico from Madrid were very different. Created in 1986 specifically for that purpose, they were the proof that the validity of classical theatre, done in the context of its time, still existed and flourished. This they did in Edinburgh with two superb productions of masterpieces from the great depths of the Spanish dramatic repertory. *La Celestina* by the 15th-century Fernando de Rojas was written less as a play than a dramatic reading, but as it contains no description and no comments by the author but is entirely in dialogue, it is easily adapted to the theatre. Adolfo Marsillach directed this classic tale of young nobleman Calisto's lusty love for the young Jewess Melibea and his attempt to have the old bawd Celestina act as a go-between, with a rigorous clarity through which the undertones of lust and social and racial prejudice run all the way to greed, confusion and tragedy. The mixture of high sentiment and false *noblesse* of the upper classes and the low-life scheming mixed with superstition and dubious magic of the servants and Celestina were brilliantly contrasted. There was an enchanting Melibea, way beyond the usual dewy-eyed heroine class, from Adriana Ozores and a subtle and plausible Celestina of wonderful earthiness and cunning from one of Spain's most celebrated actresses, Amparo Rivelles but this was a strong ensemble performance without a weak link.

The Mayor of Zalamea is one of 17th-century Pedro Calderón de la Barca's most famous plays. It is a story of military occupation, seduction, lust, brutality and honour, written with an uncharacteristic economy and forthrightness but veined through with complex emotions, attitudes, vanities and obstinately held standards of belief.

It was directed by José Luis Alonso with great bravado and pace, with a fine eye for sweeping movement and the stillness of reflection and pain. Adriana Ozores was again the much-abused heroine and a superb Jesus Puente was her father, the Mayor, stubborn, loving, honourable, wily and compassionate.

This was a great performance set beautifully within the context of a great play full of humanity, mostly at its worst, but briefly and brightly sometimes at its best. If this is real Spanish theatre, give us more.

El Alade de Zalamea *(1989)*

There were two other Calderón plays, *Life is a Dream* from the Stary Theatre of Krakow in Polish and *Schism in England* in an English version by John Clifford. The Polish version reminded me strongly of the story about students of different nationalities asked to write an essay on 'The Elephant'. The Polish submission was entitled 'The Elephant and the

Polish Question'. Andrzej Wajda's version of Calderón's great play about the king who locks up his heir as a child for fear of assassination and the son's deprivation, loneliness and isolation was staged in a bizarre and confusing set and the attempt to relate it to Poland's problems was hardly more convincing. The National Theatre Studio's production of *Schism in England* was an historically interesting view of the Spanish attitude to Henry VIII's divorce of Catherine of Aragon. This adaptation, which probably following the original too closely, was verbose and flat, although it had a fine central performance from Geoffrey Bateman as Henry – it too made Calderón in Spanish seem the better option.

The exhibition in the National Gallery *El Greco: Mystery and Illumination*, although not a very wide-ranging show, reinforced the feeling that one of the glories of Spain is a special vision and conception of people, places and objects and their mysterious relationships with one another not altogether shared with other cultures.

XXIX

In his final two years as Festival Director, Frank Dunlop appeared to become a convert to the idea that music was an integral and vitally important part of the Edinburgh Festival programme and he devoted a great deal more attention and space to it. In 1990 there were no less than 15 orchestras, six companies from different countries doing eleven operas or music theatre works, eight dance companies and ten drama companies offering twelve productions. In 1991 there were only three opera companies but they managed to present eight works while eight dance or mime companies offered nine works and there were eleven orchestras and ten theatre companies as well as a number of plays in solo show form.

The Bolshoi Opera from Moscow was hi-jacked on its first-ever visit to Britain, on its way to Glasgow's City of Culture 1990 celebrations (a matter of considerable West Coast gloating over Edinburgh which had made little attempt to promote its title to this accolade, assuming it would fall to Scotland's capital and its Festival by right) with one opera comedy *The Betrothal in a Monastery*, a reworking by Prokoviev of Sheridan's play *The Duenna*. This was billed as a new *post-glasnost* production but it seemed rather old-fashioned and although agreeable enough, not of great significance. However, the support for the three performances ensured that the Bolshoi was invited back for 1991. *The Betrothal* was certainly better than the pretentious novelty of Gounod's *Faust*, the trite production and dreadful choreography of *Prince Igor* (attributed to Fokine who must have been sizzling in his grave), which despite some robust singing, marred the Slovak Opera and Ballet performances in the second week. Martinu's *Julietta* which ended their visit, was a different matter. It was strange, ingeniously presented and well sung by Eva Jenisova and Juraj Durdiak in the main roles, a weird surrealist tale of a Parisian bookseller returning after three years to a seaside town in search of a girl he remembers, whose beauty and whose singing have haunted him.

He runs into a wall of collective amnesia, a fantastical, contorted world where nothing is remembered but some things – such as the girl – are still there. An imaginative piece with some evocative music, it was accomplished but baffling without subtitles, unless you had done your homework thoroughly in advance. Martinu's *The Greek Passion*, based on Nikos Kazantzakis's powerful novel *Christ Re-Crucified*, the story of a village passion play, was given a rather staid concert reading by the Prague Symphony and a group of soloists from Welsh Opera who had been scheduled to bring it to the 1984 Festival but cancelled. *Juan Darién* from the Music-Theatre Group of New York was a complex Uruguayan mix of music, mime dance and puppetry, all, except the music, created by Julia Taymor. The story of a jaguar cub transformed into a child by the love of one human and changed back to a jungle beast by later cruelty, *Juan* was inventive, played and presented with imaginative flair, poignancy, charm and skill.

Having 15 orchestras was no guarantee of quality and the Festival was again diminished by performances which failed to reach the highest standards. The Bolshoi was billed as 'the finest opera orchestra in the world' (I wonder if the writer had ever heard of the Vienna Philharmonic ?) and under Alexander Lazarev it turned in acceptable performances of Rachmaninov, Tchaikovsky and a spirited Prokoviev's *Alexander Nevsky* with the Festival Chorus. But apart from Martinu, the anniversary of whose birth was being celebrated, there was very little that was unfamiliar in the concert programmes. A fine Isolde came from Lisbeth Balsev in Jutland Opera's concert performance of the complete *Tristan und Isolde* in the Usher Hall. Unfortunately the other soloists could not match her confident and wonderfully phrased singing and but the Aarhus Symphony under Francesco Cristofoli gave good support, lacking a little in the fine tracery of detail perhaps, but vigorous and musically effective in general. The outstanding events of the music programme were the recitals given by Monserrat Caballé and Teresa Berganza, rare chances in the current Festival fiscal climate to hear great artists still in their prime.

Up till now the drama had always been advanced as the justification of Dunlop's programming but in 1990 that excuse began to wear a bit thin.

What was announced as 'a two-year focus on the arts and culture of the countries of the Pacific rim' was made the excuse for his own production of Robert Louis Stevenson's *Treasure Island* in the Assembly Hall (about 100 years since Stevenson settled in Samoa). No-one much liked Hywel Bennett's Long John Silver but the most general feeling was that the pantomimic presentation was not worthy of the Festival. Unfortunately the rest of the Pacific did not really raise the standard.

Naturally Dunlop summoned help from the country which had given him his greatest Festival successes and with which he had established a particular and grateful relationship. In fact, the Japanese connection at the Festival went back 35 years to 1955 when the second Festival Director Ian Hunter brought the Azuma Kabuki company to Edinburgh. Peter Diamand also had the Hosho Noh Company from Tokyo in 1972 and there had been various other Japanese manifestations in other years.

But before Dunlop's time the Festival had seen principally drama from Japan in traditional forms such as Noh and Kabuki. Frank Dunlop introduced Western classics performed *à la Japonaise* in the Ninagawa Company's stunning productions of *Macbeth* in 1985, *Medea* in 1986 and *The Tempest* in 1988. Ninagawa returned in 1990 but now, wishing to reflect modern Japanese theatre in content as well as performance, he brought a modern Noh play *Sotoba Komachi* written by Yukio Mishima. Just what 'a modern Noh play' might be no-one was sure, but a little research suggested that Mishima might not be that 'modern' as he had committed ritual suicide 20 years before and written his Noh format play using an old tale of a famous beauty, Ono no Komachi, who boasts of her *affaires* to an impoverished poet in a park.

It was preceded by a traditional Noh play derived from the same story, played and danced by Yukio Yoshimura, Japan's most celebrated Noh performer, who had never before appeared outside his native land. Presumably 'played and danced' were courtesy terms, because in *Sekidera Komachi* the traditional Noh, Yoshimura squatted on the stage against a no-doubt-symbolical fence for around 25 minutes, virtually without moving. It was about as dramatically exciting as watching paint dry.

The modern Noh done to Western music was better. There were couples in smart Japanese suits necking on park benches while Ono ran through her tale of the conquest of the gallant Captain Fukakusa. A certain amount of ritual admiration was accorded to this, – 'beautiful lighting', 'sensitive combination of west and east rhythms' etc – out of a justifiable reverence for Ninagawa's great gifts as a director and the splendour of the previous Japanese theatre he had brought. But I thought it was only marginally less boring than the traditional Noh and I have never understood why each petal from the traditional cherry blossom of the trees in the park had to fall on the stage with a metallic clunk.

There were two other Japanese companies. The Chijikai came with a murderous comedy the *Great Doctor Kengyo*. Although it was billed as a modern play and had been written by the still-extant Hisashi

Inoue, it was set in the Edo period of the 17th century and was the story of a blind serial killer who slaughtered his way to the top. The Japanese theatre team which had played at the 1987 Festival with a space-travel fantasy, the young Yume no Yuminsha Company this time brought a truly modern drama about splitting-up Siamese twins *Hanshin* (Half-Gods), posing many questions within the choice of which twin do you save, Shura – wizened but brilliant – or Maria – beautiful but dumb? There was also a Japanese orchestra to open the Festival and a virtuoso Japanese percussionist, Stomu Yamash'ta who had a sound and vision show at St Bride's Centre, which was often dazzling but found its east to west culture bridge made of over-boiled rice.

The rest of the Pacific contributions more or less fell off the rim. New Zealand's *Hedda Gabler* lost its way in 1950s New Zealand: the beautifully costumed court and folk dances and ceremonial marches from Korea drew only polite applause. The best Stevenson commemoration was Tom Allen's superb account of the Vaughan Williams setting of *Songs of Travel* in his Queen's Hall concert.

The rest seemed curiously un-related to anything – the end of the Kenneth Branagh/Emma Thomson Renaissance Company world tour began a week before the Festival, among a flutter of previews, and puttered out in the King's Theatre with an indifferent *King Lear* and a jolly but tired *Midsummer Night's Dream*. The Dunlop programme offered two other *Lears*, one in stately Indian Kathakali format and the other the father of nonsense verse and limericks skilfully delineated by Nicholas Parsons. The Shakespearean version (well roughly) also appeared on the Fringe four times. There was a rather off-target *Danton's Death* from the Edinburgh company, Communicado. In modern dress and Scots, it was bitty and unfocused, more interested in Danton's sex life than his politics.

With their energy, the orange red and yellow blaze of the costumes and their facile evocation of animals and birds, the American Indian Dancers restored some life to the Pacific rim concept as, in a more static way, did the Inca and Chimu treasures ranging from sheet-gold gloves and sacrificial knives to stylised images of condors and llamas in the *Gold of Peru* at the City Arts Centre.

The finest show in the Festival was the magnificent exhibition, worthy of comparison with anything Edinburgh had put on in the past, of *Cezanne and Poussin, The Classical Vision of Landscape* at the National Gallery. Edward Gage provided this admirable introduction in *The Scotsman*:

Formal order is fundamental in all art. It is the whole subject in Abstract art (which Cezanne prefaced).

But one has only to peel a Della Francesca to find beneath its patent subject a secret of the creative process – a structural equation, a microcosm of universal order. Appreciation of this exhibition depends on comprehending this phenomenon. One must recognise the formal harmony and unity resident in Poussin's sparsely-peopled landscapes inspired by the Roman campagna and its classical ruins. Two centuries later and working on his own ground around Aix en Provence, Cezanne is quoted as saying he wanted 'to re-do Poussin according to nature'.

The ability and compulsion of the artist to make his own designs from what his eye sees and yet relate to others who look at his work was never more clearly on view. This was an exhibition which stays in the mind. Unfortunately, the *Cezanne and Poussin* show together with the fine *Scotland's Pictures* at the Royal Scottish Academy, *Dynasty*, a splendid assembly of portraits and artefacts from the years of the Stewart monarchy at the Scottish National Portrait Gallery and the sensational *Gold of Peru*, reflected little credit on the Festival organisation which had neither arranged nor funded them.

Two months after the end of the 44th Festival it was announced that Frank Dunlop's contract would not be renewed after the 1991 Festival. After years of bickering, perhaps the decision should not have come as a surprise but conflict with the City Fathers was endemic in the Festival Director's job and, as Dunlop had been making a three-year business plan with the Scottish Arts Council which would have taken him up to 1993, and had been heavily involved in the on-off-perhaps-on plans to convert the Empire into Edinburgh's long-desired opera house, the timing of the November announcement seemed odd. Perhaps the Festival Director's proposal that he should combine the post of running the new theatre with retaining some kind of control over the Festival through an executive deputy, proved the breaking point.

When it was revealed that the decision to end Frank Dunlop's contract had been taken at a Council meeting which had not been fully attended and which was not minuted, suspicions arose of an anti-Dunlop plot. However there were not too many heartrending elegies of regret at his departure.

The Scotsman's Arts Editor, Allen Wright gave a balanced assessment:

In the past year or two there has been a distinct decline in his authority as a drama producer. This had been the area in which he had been much stronger than previous Festival directors and yet he seemed unable to regain the high ground which he had himself staked out four years ago.

His buccaneering spectacle in the Assembly Hall and Kenneth Branagh's two Shakespeare productions at the King's Theatre may have been exceedingly popular last August but there were many who felt that the Festival deserved more than an adaptation of Treasure Island *on its main stage, and that the Festival should not be the last stop on a world tour by the Renaissance Theatre Company. Frank's latest world theatre season was but a pale shadow of the one he first mounted in Edinburgh four years ago.*

After praising the achievements of 1986 and other important drama years he continued:

A man of his experience, talent and temperament might never recognise, far less admit, that he had been too long in charge of the Festival to surprise us any more. Over the last year his conduct of Press conferences has been curiously defensive and sometimes embarrassing, but the popularity of this year's Festival was largely of his doing.

The next director must be as committed to the visual arts as he is to other art forms but it will be hard to find anyone like Frank who is both artistically accomplished and shrewd in the ways of showbusiness.

Music critic, Conrad Wilson's assessment was less merciful. Under the heading *Road to mediocrity* he wrote:

With Dunlop initially came the hope of a Festival less dependent on the expensive London orchestras, with their routine Festival Hall programmes, which had been a weakness of his predecessors. But after the excitement generated by his own production of Oberon, *a real vindication of Weber's much-maligned opera, the musical side of the Festival dwindled into mediocrity. Before Dunlop's time, the London orchestras may have brought routine programmes but they also brought outstanding conductors who in recent years have been sorely missed. The generally second-run foreign orchestras and conductors who have replaced them (also, quite often, with routine programmes) have been too often a depressing feature.*

Though shortage of cash has been blamed for some of the Festival's problems, most of the trouble it seems to me, has lain in Dunlop's over-emphasis on variety, his desire to put on quantities of low-budget events, even extending the duration of the Festival several days in the process. Quality control has become less rigorous and this is what the next director must rectify.

Much speculation ensued about Dunlop's successor. Among names bandied about were Bill Burdett Coutts, who in addition to making a great success of the Assembly Rooms venue in George Street had been director of Glasgow's Mayfest, Richard Demarco, Bill Bryden and Sheila Colvin, associate director to both John Drummond and Frank Dunlop, who had left Edinburgh in 1989 to be Director of the Aldeburgh Festival. Few people in Scotland had heard of Brian McMaster, since 1976 director of Welsh National Opera, when his appointment was announced. At his first press conference in May, this small quiet 48-year-old bachelor with an almost diffident manner, said that he had no idea why he had been appointed, no budget and no plans or policies. Later he said: 'It wouldn't be proper to say anything much until Frank Dunlop has retired'.

There was a final flurry of controversy before the last Dunlop Festival when a report that he had called the Fringe 'a third-rate circus' at a luncheon with London journalists, caused a spat with Lord Provost Eleanor McLaughlin; Bill Bryden's Ship's Company pulled out of their *Peter Pan* production at the Assembly Hall because no-one could find the £400,000 to put it on, and Dunlop hastily substituted Tom Fleming and the *Thrie Estaites*.

For his Edinburgh exit Frank Dunlop appeared to have given up anniversaries and decided to concentrate on global effect. In spite of the fact that Britain was hosting a Japan Festival, the Pacific Rim seemed to have sunk virtually without trace, its only manifestations in Edinburgh being the now inevitable Ninagawa production (this time in English) and a folk group from Korea.

The focus shifted to Eastern Europe again. The Bolshoi from Moscow and the Kirov from Leningrad brought operas. With the Lenkom from Moscow at the newly re-opened but not yet refurbished Empire Theatre in Ostrovsky and the Leningrad Philharmonic, they made up the Russian contribution to the rather loosely delineated theme, *East of Berlin*. The Czech Philharmonic and the Panocha Quartet, the National Theatre of Martin from Slovakia, Teatr Ekspresji and Kantor's Cricot Company from Poland, The Open Theatre of Belgrade and the Romanian National Theatre of Craiova filled out the pattern. Berlin itself appeared with the Ballet of the Deutsche Oper. There were additions with Mummenschanz from Switzerland, Compagnie Phillipe Genty from France, a pop star drama from Stratford East and a proper performance (as opposed to the previous year's reading) of R. S. Silver's *The Bruce* from the Brunton Theatre just down the road at Musselburgh.

Other dance companies came from Canada and Cuba. There were five British orchestras and Felicity Lott, Jessye Norman, Sheila Armstrong, Peter Donohoe, Nigel Kennedy, Igor Oistrakh and Tom Allen were among the soloists.

The only anniversary (not actually due until 1992) was celebrated by *Rossini at Home*, a travesty of a programme in the rather gloomy Royal College of Physicians, which failed utterly to mirror any semblance of what could have been the ambience of the famous *soirées musicales* with which Rossini entertained his friends after he stopped writing operas. The suggestion in the brochure that what Rossini called *les péchés de vieillesse* (the sins of old age) was a group of lewd songs was disgraceful but hardly more so than the matter of the performance which was feeble and inadequately presented. Bernard Bresslaw (about twice the size of the composer) did his best to convey some idea of the wit and spirit of the man who said of himself 'I no longer compose. At my age, you decompose'. Rossini's reputation as a writer of songs and occasional pieces was not enhanced by the other performers and his fame as a gourmet was as scurvily assaulted by the stodgy all-too-British pasta and indifferent wine served in the coarse of the entertainment.

East of Berlin was thrown into turmoil by the coup which deposed Gorbachev in the middle of the Festival on 19 August. This resulted in the Leningrad Symphony becoming once again the St Petersburg Symphony before they completed their three concerts under the mercurial and occasionally clownish Yuri Temirkanov. But his posturing was given poignancy and point when, in the last concert on the day after the coup, Dmitri Alexeev managed to infuse the Beethoven C major concerto with a kind of impassioned anger which pleaded for life and freedom to continue vividly. Before the concert Temirkanov said sombrely to the Festival Chorus 'It is well we sing a Requiem tonight'. With the Chorus in tremendous form, Termirkanov made the Mozart Requiem not a dirge but a reaffirmation of hope. It was an extraordinary evening. Michael Tumelty described it in *The Herald*.

If you cannot accept the principle of synchronicity – the coincidence of time, place and event – then don't bother reading on.

Last night the Leningrad Philharmonic Orchestra, as part of their final appearance at this year's Edinburgh Festival, and under the direction of their music director, Yuri Temirkanov, performed Mozart's Requiem to a packed and intense Usher Hall. As they finished, a Reuter's report came into The Herald *announcing that 'tracer bullets were going into the night sky' in Moscow as around 20,000 of Boris Yeltsin's supporters manned barricades outside the Russian parliament building.*

Last night Yuri Temirkanov, famed as a self-caricaturist and showman, dropped his act. Last night the Leningrad Phil players gave the performance of their lives. Last night the Edinburgh Festival Chorus – whether they were aware of it or not – transcended mere musical performance and laid out an experience which locked into the emotional and psychological mood of the times.

The great raw rush of sound which heralded the opening movement was beyond their normal levels of singing; the scalding intensity of the chorus's singing of the Kyrie, *the power and pleading in the* Confutatis *movement, the thunderously authoritative* Quam Olim Abrahae, *and the solid phalanx of sound in the* Sanctus, *all these amounted to more than the sum of their parts – it was like the gigantic reiteration of something immutable, something beyond the immediacy and urgency of current events. I wonder if the chorus has any idea of the quality and effect of what it achieved last night.*

This was a profoundly contemporary requiem we heard last night. I can't write any more.

For once, the opera programme was lavish and ambitious. The Kirov brought virtually the entire repertoire of their Mussorgsky Festival, mounted in Leningrad on the 150th anniversary in 1989. It included the Shostakovich orchestration of *Khovanschina* at the Playhouse, two concert performances of scenes from the recently discovered original score of *Salammbô* and *Sorochinsky Fair* at the Usher Hall and the one-act *The Marriage*, which had been seen as a play about the opera by Peter Ustinov at the 1982 Festival.

The politics of the plot of *Khovanshchina*, which are embroiled in the historic events following Peter the Great's accession in the 17th century, are very complex and although the action was rather static the opera was magnificently presented and costumed and finely sung with lots of impressive choruses and some striking solo performances, notably that of Olga Borodina as Marfa and Bulat Minzhilkiev as Prince Ivan Khovansky. *Boris Godunov*, the one Mussorgsky opera with which most music-lovers are reasonably familiar, was given in its full four-hour version in the concert hall. It was plagued by misfortune. A virus struck down the lead singer and the substitute had never sung Boris on stage before. He did his best but not all such crises end in raptures and instant stardom and this was one of them. Things were not helped

Yuri Temirkanov

219

by the fact that the printers did not deliver the programmes on time and for most people that meant they had little idea of what was going on. *Sorochinksky Fair* was a simpler plot of lovers attending a fair and circumventing parental suspicion, with a happy ending and lots of Ukranian folksiness in the score. *Salammbô*, based on Flaubert's powerful and passionate Carthaginian novel, promised to be more interesting but the scenes presented were lyrical but scrappy

Nevertheless it was an impressive programme musically. It seemed ironic that when Frank Dunlop had put together a bill of real musical interest, even if it was occasionally let down by indifferent performance, that it should be time for him to go.

The Bolshoi *Eugene Onegin* was rather slow-moving although the quality of the music and the dedicated way it was sung and directed by Alexander Lazarev pulled it together after the longueurs of the first act. Rimsky Korsakov's *Christmas Eve* was even slower and did not have the glue of a quality score to keep it together. With a rather heavy-handed production which ran well beyond its time it seemed hardly worth the elaborate staging

Scottish Opera, making its first appearance at the Festival for six years apart from a couple of one night stands in the Usher Hall doing concert versions of American musicals, produced a very pure and clean-limbed version of Mozart's *La Clemenza di Tito*, an opera for which I have never been able to summon up much enthusiasm. Stephen Wadsworth's production and the Scottish Opera Orchestra under Nicholas McGegan brought out the more rewarding parts of the score but did nothing to make any of the characters from this improbable chronicle of the history of Nero's friend any more credible or human. Scottish Opera, returning to the Festival fold after years of disagreement with Dunlop, deserved better than this.

There were good concerts from the Czech Philharmonic under Jiri Bĕlohlávek and Sir Charles Mackerras, particularly one conducted by Mackerras which combined a stirring account of Dvorak's dramatic *Seventh Symphony* and a splendidly sung *Glagolitic Mass* with four impassioned Czech soloists and the fervour and weight of the Festival Chorus. Maurice Bejart, too long an absentee from the Festival, lit up The Playhouse with a mammoth four-and-a-half dance reading of Wagner's *Ring* cycle called *Ring Round the Ring* from Berlin Oper Ballet.

Using libretto readings to a piano arrangement of the score as well as recordings of the operas, the emotions and the mythic aspects of Wagner's epic were touched in, slashed on, sometimes almost over-dramatised, sometimes derided or more gently mocked in a plethora of styles and dance techniques of quite dazzling imagination and invention. Brilliantly danced by a strong company which seemed not to have a weak link, it cast shame on the lack of first-rate dance programming at the Festival.

Once again Dunlop's strength, the theatre programme failed to sustain his reputation. It seemed strong on paper, the Moscow Lenkom Theatre in Ostrovosky's *Too Clever By Half*, a new Japanese play directed by Ninagawa in English, the Teatr Ekspresji from Poland in something described as 'A dance of life', Phillipe Genty whose *Derives* had been a hit at the last Festival, Kantor's last play, Marivaux and Brecht in Slovak, and an Anouilh play from Belgrade in Serbo-Croat.

Unfortunately the Ostrovosky was not clever enough by several fractions. Kantor's last play *Today is my Birthday,* played as the last rehearsal which the author directed, was a ghoulish disappointment and the Romanian, Serbo-Croat and Slovak interpretations of Jarry, Brecht, Marivaux and Anouilh emphasised a dramatic truth which world theatre seasons do their best to obscure. Scenery, costumes, lighting, gestures, grimaces, props and masks are not enough; theatre needs words.

They were there in *Tango at the End of Winter* written by Kunio Simizu in 1984 and adapted into English by Peter Barnes, writhing around the structure of an ageing actor losing his public because of the dreaded cult of youth, plagued by dreams and delusions of yester-year, and being set-up by his despairing wife in an affair with a young actress. It was always going to end in tears and the manner of its portrayal with flickering, fluttering narrative, haunting baroque violins by Pachelbel, in the verismo setting of a drab disused cinema in a remote northern Japanese town, only added to its problems. Alan Rickman, who is one of the finest actors in the world, as the ageing Sei somehow invented and sustained a character who almost carried this convoluted essay in sensual self-pity but the play drowned in a kind of hyper-analysis which made everything less real than the central problem. *Tango* received some of the most amazing mega-pseud reviews I have ever read, even allowing for the ingrained genuflection which the Ninagawa name had acquired in Festival Edinburgh. The Victoria Cross for Alan Rickman would not, on the other hand, have been too much.

BRIAN McMASTER 1992-
Ex Edinburgh semper aliquid novi

XXX

A new director with a background in opera following a controversial figure criticised heavily for his interest in music being at best vestigial, raised expectations that Brian McMaster would move swiftly to redress the perceived musical imbalance and win the plaudits of the opera buffs. But from the programme of his first festival in 1992 audiences somewhat bemusedly learned to expect from the quiet unflamboyant McMaster only the unexpected. True, there was a packing of the Festival team with select imports from the Welsh National Opera mafia. Richard Armstrong came to Scottish Opera as music director, Joanna Baker took up the new post of Director of Marketing and Public Affairs and there were other shufflings at Festival HQ in Market Street.

Rumour suggested that the new Director did not have a lot to work on, as what he inherited from the last incumbent left a good deal to do. He must also, of course, have been hindered by the long forward planning schedules of most major companies, to say nothing of the £179,000 deficit which was part of his inheritance. What he offered was certainly interesting, innovative and enterprising, showing little trace of the row of snorting old war-horses which might have been projected from his former career as Managing Director of Welsh National Opera.

Indeed the 1992 programme seemed to be designed to prove that McMaster was not the answer to the opera buffs' prayer. It seemed more structured to satisfy the supplications of the accountants, with curious genuflections of a mostly not too expensive nature

Brian McMaster

towards the unusual, the forgotten and the new. There were just seven sort-of-operatic performances of four-and-a-half operas, two of them in concert form in the Usher Hall and two double bills with one half devoted to ballet or something in that barely-defined field which lies somewhere between cabaret and *opera buffa*. And there was an awful lot of Tchaikovsky: the most 'accessible' (i.e. top of the pops) of classical composers.

The Tchaikovsky-fest included all six symphonies plus the *Manfred*, and the two completed piano concertos. Just eight of the Usher Hall concerts were without a work by Tchaikovsky and there were five concerts and recitals entirely devoted to the Russian composer, in all more than 50 works by Tchaikovsky, a Festival surfeit it ever there was one.

For two nights at the King's Theatre there was the sweet-sour combination of Cimarosa's *Il Maestro di Capella* and Poulenc's heart-rending *La Voix Humaine*, an evening of knowing hilarity as Claudio Desderi struggled to apply his old-fashioned conducting techniques to a recalcitrant and bolshy (definitely not Bolshoi) orchestra and brilliantly evoked despair as Elisabeth Söderström sought to recapture her abandoning lover by telephone.

The excuse for *Yolanta* and *The Nutcracker* coupling at the King's was that the one-act opera and ballet were the original commission which Tchaikovsky got from the Imperial Theatre in St Petersburg in 1892. *The Oprichnik*, Tchaikovsky's first real operatic success, was given a concert performance in the Usher Hall with the Scottish Opera Orchestra and Chorus conducted by Mark Ermler and a strong, largely Russian cast headed by the radiant Siberian soprano Galina Gorchakova who had recently made a sensational Western debut in Prokoviev's *The Fiery Angel* in London and New York. There was even a prize draw for a holiday in St Petersburg for those who booked for at least 12 events in the Tchaikovsky series!

The forgotten were commemorated on the drama side by 14 plays from two neglected playwrights, the English actor, director and writer Harley Granville Barker and the Glasgow-born dramatist C. P. Taylor. Barker was one of the outstanding figures in the British theatre in the early years of the century, an actor of distinction, a director of great insight and courage and an outstanding playwright who fought tirelessly against the restrictive practices of censorship but did not live long enough to see them abolished in 1968.

He was one of the first directors to train actors in the need to have a total conception of the characters they played, with an off-stage life colouring their interpretations. His plays were for the most part serious examinations of contemporary social morality and family crises. George Bernard Shaw, who worked with Barker in the Fabian-influenced Court Theatre in Sloane Square called him with Shavian irony: 'A cold-hearted Italian devil but a noble soul all the same. Altogether the most distinguished and incomparably the most cultivated person whom circumstances had driven into the theatre at that time.'

The Barker plays were given by various companies, three in full performance and four in rehearsed readings, well-cast and directed, with actors from the Lyric, Hammersmith, the Orange Tree, Richmond, the Royal Lyceum and the Royal National and although *The Voysey Inheritance* and *The Madras House* confirmed themselves as being the most distinguished of Granville Barker's plays, others like the ironic one-act comedy *Rococo*, about the vicarage funeral squabble over an old vase, underlined Barker's beady eye and acute ear for the nuances of English life shrewdly observed.

Cecil Philip Taylor grew up in Glasgow as part of a Jewish family which had fled from pogroms in Czarist Russia and was probably better known in Scotland than Granville Barker, for many of his plays had been performed at the Traverse in Edinburgh and in Glasgow. When he died in 1981 Benedict Nightingale wrote in the *New Statesman*:

> *Cecil Taylor wasn't the sort of dramatist who wrote with an eye to 'posterity', whatever 'posterity' is. Seventy plays in 30 years, constant creative work with children, the mentally and physically handicapped, young offenders, drama students, culturally isolated adults, everyone. He would have been too busy to worry very much about his future reputation, even if he had been temperamentally inclined to do so, which he wasn't.*

Nevertheless it seems a pity that he did not live to see the handsome retrospective with which the Edinburgh Festival provided him. He would have been just 62.

The Taylor-fest, like the other chunky programme sections of McMaster's first Festival, was uneven. *Good*, his last play, an intense and moving examination of a decent young German professor engulfed by the mood of the 1930s into the Nazi SS, was given a splendid production by Michael Boyd for Glasgow Tron Theatre with a fine, intellectually despairing, highly sensitive performance as Halder from Conrad Asquith. *Schippel*, adapted from the 1913 satirical comedy of 'bourgeois heroism' by the German playwright Carl Sternheim, was made by Taylor into an extraordinary 'serious farce' about a quartet of singers headed by a wealthy goldsmith in a small German principality, who are forced to recruit the local plumber, gifted with a glorious *heldentenor* voice, into their high bourgeois group when their tenor dies. The snobbish social dilemmas induced by this move to win the local *lieder* festival, gloriously complicated by Schippel's shrewd exploitation of the situation, love and the goldsmith's pretty sister, were brilliantly played and excellently sung by the talented singer-actors of the Greenwich Theatre directed by Jeremy Sams, with a lovely central performance from James Saxon as Schippel. Hamish Glen's production of *Walter*, reflections on his colourful life by an old Jewish Glasgow comedian, was unfortunately flawed by a highly eccentric on-off lighting plot, spoiling a fine performance by Tom Watson.

Scotland had a musical slot in five excellent concerts, *Scottish Music Through the Centuries*, inspired and organised by composer John Purser. They traced development and musical styles through songs and instrumental pieces from early Celtic chants honouring St Columba and St Kentigern; 17th- and 18th-century vocal music in the classical mode; mid 18th-century German-inspired songs, sonatas and piano music to concertos; and occasional pieces by modern composers ranging from Alexander Campbell Mackenzie to Thea Musgrave and James MacMillan.

Venues varied from Greyfriars Kirk to the Queen's and Usher Halls and forces employed to delineate our musical history included Capella Nova, Concerto Caledonia, the Scottish Chamber Orchestra and the Hebrides Ensemble

The new was effusively represented by the Mark Morris Dance Group in a balletic account of Purcell's opera *Dido and Aeneas* with the singers in the pit with the orchestra, while the dancers, in changing roles, pranced and pirouetted, stamped and glided the tale of Carthage's doomed queen. Very accomplished and sometimes both poignant and funny but a cultural cocktail not quite integrated enough to become an easily acquired taste.

The almost new (it had been an opera production from Deutsche Oper am Rhein in 1976), Schoenberg's *Moses and Aaron* in oratorio form in the Usher Hall as the Opening Concert was a singularly daring programme choice, viewed with some trepidation on many sides, but it proved to be one of the great occasions of this or any Festival.

Somehow the power of the great musical and liturgical struggle between the blind faith of Moses and the imagery and showmanship of Aaron for the soul of the Jewish people in their flight from Egypt and journey into the desert towards the promised land, became more vivid without the visual trappings of mountains, orgies, deserts, naked virgins and a calf of gold. Willard White's Moses, spoken and barely sung, was a towering figure of agonised truth, embracing the unknowable, despising the visual and tactile hype Aaron wished to put in its place, but despairing of communicating the great verities within him, felling the golden calf and smashing the tablets of the laws in the search for purity but unable to find means of conveying his trust and belief in an un-imaged God. There was a vain, puzzled but striving Aaron, brilliantly sung by William Cochran, and the Edinburgh Festival Chorus

Arthur Oldham, first and longest serving Edinburgh Festival Chorus Master, and Frank Dunlop on either side of the Chorus Sponsorship Cheque awarded by the Hamada Foundation

and other soloists sang the fiendishly difficult music with fervour.

The whole performance with the BBC Scottish Symphony and the RSO's Children's Chorus was melded together by Richard Armstrong into a performance of surpassing splendour. Brian McMaster presented all the chorus members with T-shirts inscribed 'I survived Moses and Aaron'. It was a momentous opening to his reign as Festival Director.

The 1993 Festival was fanfared into its first day in *Scotland on Sunday* by Robert Dawson Scott asking a question under the heading *McMaster Pieces*, which I cannot recall ever having been posed about any other of the Festival's seven Directors.

Can the new Festival Director do no wrong? Even the more outré accoutrements of Brian McMaster look set to vindicate his sense of adventure.

There are, let's face it, some pretty odd bits and pieces in the 1993 International Festival programme: a 1950s Variety show; a troupe of traditional Scottish story-tellers; a complete retrospective of a Scottish composer who is barely out of short trousers; an orchestra from Spain. the Orquestra de Cambra Teatre Lliure. that no-one can even pronounce never mind has ever heard of; and finally Lluis Llach – madre de Dios – a singer of Catalonian protest songs. Is Brian McMaster an aria short of an opera?

Leaving aside the inaccurate bravura which must never be allowed to besmirch a good journalistic intro, (youthful composer James MacMillan was in fact 34 at the time and Festival audiences over 47 years had managed to get their tongues round a few other challenging bits of articulation such as Chkhikvadze and Szymanowski without serious injury), it was undeniably a strange programme.

Unlike 1992 it opened with a curiously low-key event. The featured composers (in addition to MacMillan) were Janacek and Schubert, a very curious pairing particularly in view of the fact that they were at opposite ends of the 19th century and that Leos Janacek did not write any significant music until long after the age at which Schubert died.

The Royal Scottish National Orchestra under its resident conductor, Walter Weller, opened the Festival with the Festival Chorus and five soloists in a worthy but unexhilarating programme consisting of two pieces by Janacek and Schubert's Mass No Five in A flat.

Later there were more Janacek-Schubert programmes with the Scottish Chamber Orchestra, the Philharmonia, Scottish Opera Orchestra and the Royal Liverpool Philharmonic and a fine recital by Anne Murray and Philip Langridge of Janacek's dramatic song-cycle *The Diary of One Who Disappeared* and Schubert's flower ballad *Viola* with Peter Donohoe. The most bizarre coupling was the concert performances of two operas by the themed composers. Neville Garden wrote in *Scotland on Sunday*:

The Festival went out, courtesy of the Royal Liverpool Philharmonic Orchestra, as it came in – with performance of music by Schubert and Janacek. These two composers were yoked together for the entire Festival. It was a marriage not made in Heaven. The Festival Director, Brian McMaster was plainly anxious to make some kind of point with S and J, as they came to be known to concert-goers. But the pairing told us only how different they are – and we know that anyway. The evening in which Schubert's Friends from Salamanca and Janacek's Sarka were performed back to back was the best (or worst) example. Festival-goers emerged from the Usher Hall thinking only what a master of opera was Janacek, and how inept was Schubert.

Overall, some of the Festival's most memorable moments came during concert performances of opera, such as the marvellous accounts of Oberto Verdi's first opera and of Mozart's Così Fan Tutte in the Usher Hall. Of the staged operas the Canadian Opera Company's Bartok and Schoenberg bill were much admired as was the Welsh National Opera's Falstaff. Scottish Opera's account of Verdi's I Due Foscari was flawed by some silly visual effects.

225

In the Usher Hall, the Oslo Philharmonic Orchestra and its charismatic conductor Mariss Jansons delighted consistently. So did the Philharmonia of London, especially with music by the Scot James MacMillan.

But there was only one real no-no, the operatic double bill at the Traverse Theatre. James MacMillan's Tourist Variations *and Craig Armstrong's* Anna *were frankly, dire.*

Not a bad track record, then, for Brian McMaster. There's only one thing I must remember to ask him. This year's Festival was to see the debut of the new National Orchestra for Scotland, a body scheduled to rise from the ashes of the BBC Scottish Symphony Orchestra and the Orchestra of Scottish Opera. It didn't happen because these two sterling orchestras resisted the proposed merger.

So what happens at the Festival? The BBCSSO gives a performance of two operas (the Schubert and Janacek works) and the Scottish Opera Orchestra plays a selection of concert works. Could Mr McMaster – or somebody – be trying to tell the players something?

The 18 works by MacMillan given at the Festival got a mixed reception. The first concert in the Queen's Hall with The Chamber Group of Scotland conducted by the composer, was of early works, interesting in terms of an evolving musical voice and emotional and spiritual concerns. This impression was immediately trivialised by the one-act opera *Tourist Variations* to a text by Iain Heggie on a double bill with Craig Armstrong's *Anna*, a piece of unfunny and snobbish social comment portraying the boredom and pointlessness of tourism and its disciples in a formless score and a banal libretto. *Anna* was even worse because it lacked even the flickers of musical ingenuity which MacMillan occasionally produced. *Busqueda*, half of yet another double bill, based on poems by Mothers of the Disappeared in Argentina, was a non-opera stiffly presented but with haunted and moving music shot through with brutal terror. *Visitatio Sepulchri* the New Testament account of women finding Christ's empty tomb in the first Easter, was finely staged and developed with evocative and imaginative musical ideas.

In the Queen's Hall concert given by London Winds there was *Untold* a charming quintet using a cor anglais instead of an oboe, woven around the melody of an old Irish love song and *Tuireadh* a magnificent lament for the dead of the Piper Alpha disaster, full of grief and the terrible surging of the implacable sea. The same evening in the Usher Hall there was his thrilling witch-trial work, *The Confession of Isobel Gowdie*, the most widely known MacMillan piece, in a searing performance by the Philharmonia under American conductor Leonard Slatkin. This was followed by the most triumphant of MacMillan's new works in the world première of his trumpet concerto, *Epiclesis*, written for and played with incandescent brilliance by John Wallace and the Philharmonia. *Epiclesis* is the invocation of the Holy Spirit in the Catholic Mass, with the trumpet in the role of the priest and the orchestra the congregation.

On first hearing, the congregation seemed to have more to say and crave than the priest but the total effect was stupendous in a work that seems more relevant to the struggle of faith and earthly distraction than ritual. To follow this and *Gowdie* with Stravinsky's *Rite of Spring* was intellectually and emotionally brutal – to be battered by bigotry and cruelty, struggle in the fire of belief and then attacked by frenzied pagan carnality, all in one evening, was almost too much to bear. But wonderful.

Nor was it all. Making the role of the producer paramount in two pieces as cerebral as Bartok's *Bluebeard's Castle* and Schoenberg's *Erwartung* seemed unnecessarily luxurious and a kind of perversity to do in the theatre two operas often played in the concert hall. But Robert Lepage's stage invocations of these two psychodramas was disturbingly neurotic yet teetering on the edges of restraint and his handling of them did add something to their sinister and terrible unwinding. Verdi's *Falstaff* was given a fine lusty colourful production by Peter Stein for Welsh National Opera and offered a Festival first in Donald Maxwell's superb performance as the only Scots singer, I think, to have sung the rumbustious Sir John.

It also introduced us to a splendid new voice in Bryn Terfel whose Ford gave rich promise of great things to come.

The rest of the Verdi retrospective was 'a thing of shreds and patches'. Scottish Opera's *I Due Foscari* was so poorly received that the Royal Opera House, Covent Garden cancelled the co-production arrangement they had made to take it into their repertoire. The production was gimmicky with pop-up chairs for the council chamber and flying coat-hangers for the chorus to change costumes on stage. The music is fine if not inspired Verdi but it was poorly sung. Neither the Chinese tenor, Deng nor the heroine Katerina Kudriavchenko, who was inaccurate and squally, were in good voice. Only Philip Joll made the most of his role in a noble and poignant interpretation of the Doge but unfortunately he was singing half off-stage, score in hand and out of costume while the bronchitis-stricken Frederick Burchinal voicelessly (and badly) mimed the part in the middle. Richard Armstrong did his best to bring the opera to life by pointed direction of the orchestra, who played the vivid score with intensity and spirit but the whole thing had a doomed air. The Requiem, one of the Festival's staples down the years, was given the poorest performance I have heard. Despite some fine singing from Olga Borodina, Dennis O'Neill, Alastair Miles and the Festival Chorus, the fierce and vulgar tempo set by conductor Carlo Rizzi threw the whole marvellous piece out of kilter.

Oberto, Conte di Bonifacio, Verdi's first opera, on the other hand, was a rousing and splendid experience. Sung with lusty fervour by Dennis O'Neill, Alistair Miles, Maria Guleghina and Jane Henschel and played with tremendous *élan* by the RSNO under David Robertson, it could only have been Verdi with its splendid broad melodies, lyrical attack and vivid choruses. Verdi was only 23 when he wrote it but it is full of tuneful forecasts of the great composer he was to become.

Mark Morris, who has been a fixture at the Festival since McMaster became director, had to move his two dance programmes from the Playhouse to the much less comfortable venue of Meadowbank Sports Stadium. However the difficulties were surmounted with energy and style and his signature mixture of musicians and dancers was enthusiastically received. The first programme to Brahms's *Liebesleider Walzer* and *Neue Liebesleider Walzer* was beautifully sung by the quartet of Felicity Palmer, Amanda Roocroft, John Mark Ainsley and Thomas Allen and danced with romantic zest by Morris and his group.

In the second a clutch of new works were to music by Bach, American frontier songs and Lou Harrison, variously provided by country/folk-singer Michelle Shocked, bassist/composer Rob Wasserman, the Emperor Quartet and the Schola Cantorum of Edinburgh. Morris proved he is genuinely a new kind of dance experience, a fount of creative energy, a sometimes reverent, sometimes raucous partner to the music he sets.

Where Morris as a dancer is ironic, sometimes camp and as a choreographer sweeps from the jokey and athletic to devotional sensuality, the central component of Bill T. Jones's dance is anger. It infuses his pieces with silken energy when not with rage and even in the more lyrical pieces there was always a hard under-edge of something – vengeance, contempt, loss? It was hard to tell. At the King's Theatre his dances protested at mortality, homophobia, injustice, racism. It was uncomfortable but compelling because he left the audience nowhere to hide.

There was more protest in the theatre. Peter Sellars turned Aeschylus's *The Persians*, the oldest play in the dramatic canon, into a condemnation of America in the Gulf War. Aeschylus's play examines Persian defeat by the Greeks in terms of Athenian corruption, from the point of view of Xeres's court.

Sellars in Robert Auletta's mangling of the original almost obliterated the audience with a sound system with speakers under seats and almost everywhere else, blasting the deafening impact of Tomahawk missiles and other modern attack hardware. Outside the theatre the night I was there, groups of eminent and obscure drama freaks including one headed by Jeremy Isaacs and Murray Grigor, poked painfully at their eardrums and shouted at each other in condemnation, defence and vituperation. The last scene, powerfully played by John Ortiz as the Persian king and Cordelia Gonzalez as his mother, almost rescued the stark and noisy evening but by that time we were too painfully deafened to care.

The Persians *(1993)*

Peter Stein is less a political proselytiser than a theatre director. His productions are renowned more for getting the most out of the text of the plays he directs than for putting something in. He likes space and lots of it and he would have been wildly unhappy in the Lyceum. For the transfer of his celebrated 250-cast production of Shakespeare's *Julius Caesar* from the Salzburg Festival, he used the main exhibition hall at the Royal Highland Showground on the fringes of Edinburgh at Ingliston. There was still the question of language. Shakespeare in German is not to everyone's taste, let alone comprehension, and people did walk out. But those who stayed were treated to a tremendous spectacle and some superb individual and collective performances.

Michael Billington in *The Guardian* called it 'a downright, unforgettable masterpiece'.

> *Stein's determinist vision in no way precludes the detailed investigation of individual character. Thomas Holtzmann's magnificent Brutus, concave-featured like a younger version of Bill Deedes and round-shouldered as if weighed down by the burden of civic expectation, is a bookish idealist hopelessly ill-at-ease in the world of realpolitik: even his tenderness towards the boy Lucius speaks volumes about his character.*
>
> *Hans Michael Rehberg (a show-stealing Menenius in this year's Salzburg Coriolanus) makes Cassius a political obsessive wreathed in inviolable solitude. And Gert Voss is the best Mark Antony I have ever seen: as he lovingly explores the rents in Caesar's gown to excite the crowd, you realise he is the kind of man in whom friendship is inextricably mixed up with an awareness of his own dangerous charisma.*
>
> *Stein does not lock the play into a rigid concept. His greatness lies in his minute exploration of the text (his own adaptation of the Schlegel translation), his ability to make every moment live theatrically and his uncanny gift of suggesting that a play is an act of collective memory.*
>
> *For me the great moment is still that in which the senators, after the murder of Caesar, kick over their chairs while the conspirators look on his felled body in silent, dumbstruck awe. Time is suddenly suspended; and you feel this is how it must be after an assassination. Stein uses drama to reclaim history.*

The German theatre showed its international versatility with an extraordinary offering in American English at the Royal Lyceum, *Dr Faustus Lights the Lights*. In *The Observer* Michael Coveney wrote:

> *If you mixed and matched writers and directors until blue, green or red in the face, the primal posthumous alliance of Gertrude Stein and Robert Wilson would still sound*

like a dream ticket. Trance and repetition, an iterating pulse of spare and beauteous incantation, minimalism as an aesthetic fetish, a world of sighs and dreams: Dr Faustus Lights the Lights *was a real treat and artificial (high)light of the official programme.* With this extraordinary re-telling of the Faust legend, never performed in the author's lifetime, Wilson and the young company from the Hebbel-Theater, Berlin had an interpretative ball. Or perhaps interpretative is the wrong word.

The plot, if anything so bourgeois could be detected within these three acts, has Faust selling his soul not for riches, knowledge, intellectual dominance nor lustful dalliance with Helen of Troy but for the invention of the light-bulb, conferring on the old Wittenberg scholar god-like powers. Illumination in the form of brilliant lighting and silhouette staging there was in plenty, creating any number of bizarre and intriguing pictures and encounters with weird figures and dances with the Scarlet One and a scythe-bearing giantess on stilts, endlessly entertaining if somewhat lacking in narrative thrust. Deconstructionist shadow play to an accordion score by Hans Peter Kuhn, fascinating director-wallow, 'a stark visual thrill and the aural equivalent to pot smoking' as one critic described it. From an author who once suggested that Hitler should be nominated for the Nobel Peace Prize, it was certainly a tortured view of an old tale.

The Waking Dream, a magical exhibition which successfully projected a century of photography as a distinctive nostalgic and powerful art form, was blessed relief; as was the Tag Theatre's three-week long Assembly Hall all-singing, some-dancing showing of Alastair Cording's stage adaptation of Lewis Grassic Gibbon's trilogy of Aberdeenshire novels, *A Scots Quair*, in proving that a classic doesn't have to be put on the dissecting table to make an impact.

Other German contributions to Festival drama were less controversial than the Stein/Wilson *Faust* but directorial dominance was very clear in Philip Prowse's lavishly symbolic Citizens' Theatre *The Soldiers* written by Goethe's friend, the 18th-century *sturm und drang* man, Jacob Lenz. We had seen it all before in the Lenz derivatives, Buchner's *Woyzeck* (1973); Berg's operatic *Wozzeck* (1966 and 1980) and Zimmermann's directly adapted opera *Die Soldaten* (1972), and plenty of other tales of licentious soldiery at their worst across the centuries. There seemed no need for eviscerated war memorials and bellowing SS men. How many directors does it take to change a light bulb?

In fact either seduction or brutal soldiery (or both) seemed inescapable in Edinburgh theatres in 1993, even recurring in Heinrich von Kleist's ironic comedy *The Broken Jug* and the rehearsed readings of two other Lenz plays *The New Menoza* and *The Tutor*. Jimmy Logan's slick slice of nostalgia for Scottish music hall *The Fabulous Fifties*, with a host of still glittering vaudeville stars, blissfully managed to avoid them however, and was one of the few theatrical occasions when the unravaged audience left with a smile.

Someone else who was smiling was Brian McMaster. The 1992 Festival had wiped out the deficit he had inherited and carried forward a surplus of £10,000. In 1993 the sun had shone for 128 Festival hours and the takings were up by 20%. The new logo he had commissioned – a Picasso-esque bugling bug – seemed to be blowing a fanfare of triumph.

The star of the 48th Festival in 1994 was obvious before it began. It was – it had to be – the new glassy gleaming, plush and gilt Edinburgh Festival Theatre, the longest and most eagerly awaited cultural icon in the city's chequered artistic history, which had been a gleam in some ambitious planner's eye ever since the Edinburgh International Festival of Music and Drama first took off as a major world event in 1947.

In the end, all the grandiose plans for a completely new theatre, custom-built for large and spectacular productions suited to a festival of Edinburgh's eminence, staggered on to a few drawing boards, then withered and died. Projected and even chosen sites were cleared and built upon for some other purpose; the charges of cultural elitism levelled when the phantom was known as Edinburgh's 'Opera House' gradually fading in the miasma of shame as Scotland's capital and the world's most comprehensive Festival was not able to create a theatre fit and able to house the lavish productions which the world clamoured to bring to its miraculously surviving and internationally prestigious festival of all the talents.

But although the principal site for the Festival's original opera house is now the setting for a building perhaps closer to Edinburgh's steely commercial heart, what we could now rejoice in as the Edinburgh Festival Theatre was no mealy-mouthed compromise but an exciting and stimulating addition to the city's entertainment structure, created by an Edinburgh company of architects, The Law & Dunbar-Nasmith Partnership. The never-answered question however remained. Why did it take so long?

What we got was not a totally original building but the remaking of an old theatre with long and honourable associations with the arts. They may not have been the arts which the Festival is always accused of being elitist about, but Scotland had always felt more comfortable with comedy and the lighter theatrical textures than the air-rending clouds of tragedy be it Sophoclean, Shakesperean, Verdian or Wagnerian.

The Empire, as the theatre was known through three of its manifestations as music-hall declining into bingo, played an important part in the early Edinburgh Festivals when it annually shook off its red-nosed image to become a centre for ballet and occasionally drama and opera. Even before the Festival however Pavlova danced there (and is the subject of a delightful piece of Edinburgh balletomane anecdotage) and I remember Laurel and Hardy and Jack Buchanan as well as Constant Lambert, Margot Fonteyn and Moira Shearer treading its boards.

In its day the Empire was renowned for spectacle as well as a showcase and testing ground for comics, tap-dancers, Irish tenors and other ballad-singers and the new building with its lavish theatrical facilities and the largest stage in Britain offered the possibility of theatrical extravagance once again.

For although the decision to convert the Empire into the Festival Theatre may be disdained as a typical Edinburgh compromise, the actuality is a splendidly designed building which offered the best of most theatrical worlds.

The ambience of the old theatre was retained although it is now more comfortable than it was; the staging possibilities are completely new, spaciously of world standard: the front of house foyer reception and leisure areas with a luminous glass frontage and stairs visibly climbing to all levels of the house giving the building an exciting new dimension. There are spaces for smaller performances at cabaret and lecture/recital level and architect Colin Ross most admirably achieved his declared intention of creating an audience buzz on entering..

The programme outside the Festival three weeks for the first six months included eight operas, seven dance companies, several musicals and orchestras and bands galore, as well as plays and cabarets, chamber music groups, pop singers and choirs. In other words the Edinburgh Festival all the year round, in a bold attempt to refute comprehensively the much reiterated whinge that Scotland can only take one or two concentrated cultural bashes a year; to show that live theatre in the widest sense is part of our lives and that we have not all degenerated into couch potatoes or quasi-deaf zombies meandering the streets with our ears clamped. It just remained to be seen what Scotland – and the Festival – would make of it.

After a run-in season starting in June which included a fine Scottish Opera *Tristan und Isolde*, two other operas, three ballet companies, a number of recitals and Noddy, the theatre made its Festival debut on Monday 15 August 1994. The prospect of adding 24,000 seats to the Festival's capacity was celebrated with the only opera by the theme composer of the 1994 Festival, Ludwig van Beethoven. Scottish Opera's *Fidelio* was an admirable performance conducted incisively by Richard Armstrong and the acoustics proved excellent for the orchestra's sterling rendering of the score and the nobly sung Leonore of Elizabeth Whitehouse but Tim Albery's production with its drab quasi-Eastern Europe costumes, some cramped design and travel-snaps back projection, hardly showed off the large and capacious stage to advantage.

It took Australian Opera's colourful production of Britten's opera *A Midsummer Night's Dream* to do that. Mary Miller, *The Scotsman's* music critic, not famous for sparing an adjective when seven will do, called it 'brilliant, blazing, wildly funny, of a dreamy glistening beauty, hot and hazy, pink and twinkly, purple and erotic, spectacular and wonderful'. But she did add 'that is, if you aren't too keen on opera'.

Everybody enjoyed the production and most people agreed that Roderick Brydon, a very experienced Britten conductor, despite being set with his orchestra in an ornamental pagoda bandstand stage centre, all uniformed like a regimental band, conducted the music with great wit and flair, despite the competition from the sets, costumes and Baz Luhrmann's exotic production and some not very impressive contributions from a few of the singers. For this was no Athenian wood but the British Raj in India at the height of its splendour. Oberon and Tytania were Indian gods and the roguish fairies dark-skinned Krishna companions or *gopies* (it was explained very firmly to a colleague that they don't have fairies in Oz!). The artisans were Dad's Army soldiers in pendulous shorts tropical kit, Lysander was in the Indian Civil Service, Demetrius was an officer, Puck was winsomely and wickedly camp. Only Michael Chance's bell-like counter tenor, disdainfully outfaced the rompish comedy and provided a wonderfully sinister and other-wordly dimension. The comedy was often vulgar but entertaining and the ensemble of the setting and production was enchanting but Chance gave it a kind of verity as an opera it would otherwise have lacked.

The other productions at the Festival Theatre were court favourite Mark Morris's *L'Allegro, il Penseroso ed il Moderato* and Peter Handke's wordless play *The Hour We Knew Nothing of Each Other* – a title which seemed to run a bold risk of being prophetic.

Reviewing the dance programmes, Geoffrey West wrote:

The hype machine seems to be a finely tuned vehicle these days and the Mark Morris Dance Group has developed cult status in Edinburgh over the past two years, with tickets for his four performances of Handel's L'Allegro, il Penseroso ed il Moderato *among the fastest selling for this year's Festival. Constantly told that* L'Allegro *was his masterwork, many went along convinced they must concur, and dutifully offered a rapturous reception. But have we witnessed a masterpiece, or just a very successful publicity campaign to blanket our power for rational thinking?*

It would seem that despite the obvious attractions – a pleasing combination of music and movement, colourful Grecian-style chiffon costumes, and bright, ever -changing backcloths, Morris's treatment of an abridged reading of Handel's music does not so much enhance the score as sit alongside it. Watching the skipping dancers interweave across the stage, it is actually hard to engage with the music – finely played as it was by the Scottish Chamber Orchestra under Gareth Jones, with an excellent line-up of soloists and chorus. The undynamic nature of much of the choreography wasn't too far removed from the movement-to-music many of us suffered at school – everyone pretending to be a tree, or a rushing river. Although the music itself lacks

Mark Morris with Brian McMaster

231

drama, there seems to be no reason for the choreography to be so bland, apart from the joyfully constructed opening, and the hypnotically effective circling section within the finale. Pleasant in an unexciting way it may be, but masterpiece seems far too extravagant.

The Festival was developing a peculiar ambience. The Fringe had always been into the hype market, often from necessity because few people would come to many of the 500 or so shows scattered around town in everything from cellars to churches and 18th-century reception rooms, unless a loud and intriguing – and often blithely exaggerated – noise was made about its claims to superlative daring, obscenity, hilarity or other criteria of contemporary allure.

The city's recent image had been reformed by Irvine Welsh's acclaimed drug culture novel *Trainspotting*, (his *Guardian* column rated the Festival as 'a total pain in the arse'); the Film Festival's hit about murder among the Edinburgh chattering classes *Shallow Grave*, the summer invasion of In Yer Face (and any other part of your anatomy) comedians and their acolytes and lobbyists, and there were seriously weird people around in the Scottish capital in August. This meant that even the official Festival had now largely abandoned its discreet 'quality will tell' attitude and taken to bawling its wares from the rooftops, sometimes with as little justification as the more extravagant Fringe claims. One year it even brochure-boasted – in the Presbyterian form of a warning – of 30 seconds of nudity in a paralysing dull Polish show. O tempora! O mores! It was getting to us all. In a festival review for my column in *Scottish Medicine*, I wrote about it.

Now that lots of our gambled money is to be invested in such things as theatre and opera, perhaps it is time to take a widespread look at what goes on in such open spaces of artistic endeavour and whether we should be totally pleased about what is being done on those far from level playing fields.

During this year's Edinburgh Festival, newspaper columnistation reached new levels of frenzied irrelevance. For example, the much- admired or much-vilified Guardian (take your party pick) employed a series of self-publicising or self-abnegating (anyway self was a major ingredient) diary columnists, for the most part anon to me, who were so determined to be 'spaced out' (or whatever the current Ed-Fest argot is) and outrageous that they triumphantly listed their drunken etc cavortings in all the most outré Ed-fest places, reaching new heights of avant-garde obfuscation in being comprehensively incomprehensible. This may have performed a kind of social service as a guide to where to avoid if you were interested in civilised post-performance analysis but it seemed to me to reflect an unfortunate trend in the dramatic arts which we are now being encouraged so profligately to back.

The Festival from the beginning encouraged directors with new ideas but people like Carl Ebert, Tyrone Guthrie, Giorgio Strehler and Jean-Louis Barrault saw their role as interpreters and illuminators of the text to the performers and the audience, seeking to make it more accessible and more enjoyable and dramatic, not as a 'message for our times' but as wonderful and meaningful entertainment. Now, everything must have a 'message', social political or theatrically divisive. The text has gone out the window; the circumstances in which the play or opera was written, its origins are ignored. All must be hacked about to reflect the director's theories. Is this what the theatre should be saying? That writing, context, entertainment does not matter, only director's manipulation?

There was even a critic writing in the Festival Souvenir Programme who argued that Shakespeare in German was better than Shakespeare in English because the text was thus made clearer and more easily understood than Shakespeare's English to an

English-speaking audience! So we had the extraordinary spectacle of Antony and Cleopatra *set in the Western Desert circa 1942 with Enobarbus's lyrical description of Cleopatra ...*

The barge she sat in, like a burnished throne
Burned on the water: the poop was beaten gold,
Purple the sails, and so perfumed that
The winds were love-sick with them.

... delivered in platt-Deutsch by a squaddy in a khaki forage cap and baggy shorts. I felt it lost quite something in visual and literal translation.

Of course it is not only the Festival which is heavily into time, place and text distortion. Recently we had an otherwise admirable La Forza del Destino *set in the American Civil War and a* Fledermaus *in Bearsden from Scottish Opera:* Rigoletto *relocated to Brooklyn, Chekhov moved to Wales, 42nd Street and an Australian sheep station,* Romeo and Juliet *on German trapezes and* The Merchant of Venice *in Los Angeles with TV cameras showing newsreel footage of the LA riots during the trial scene.*

Festival theatre was not all Director's Cut and Stars in Battledress, although it was there too in the Australian Opera and it has to be admitted that sometimes it worked. Britten's A Midsummer Night's Dream *changed continents and centuries to the last days of the British Raj in India fairly successfully. The projected biggest numb-bum of the three weeks, the seven hour 50 minutes performance at Murrayfield Ice Rink of Aeschylus's* Orestaia, *a co-production between the Festival, Melopomene in Munich and the Academic Theatre of the Russian Army, was a ringing unforgettable afternoon/ evening, riveting and. against all seeming odds, not for a minute boring. Scenically it was of the Stars in Battledress school and also subscribed to the dogma that only directors matter, but the highly readable sur-titles were in noble English prose and the Russian was most sonorously spoken with a fine cadence of dramatic sense all the way from mumble to roar/scream.*

The magnificent male chorus wore long caddy coats and Borsalino hats and represented in turn an audience for the passionate harangues of anguish, justification, vengeance and triumph, a council of elders and the conscience and muddled morality of vox pop. The female chorus were no less – ululating wailers of doom and suffering, terrifying savage harpies of vengeance. A triumph which almost justified the Director's Cut school. It also evoked a comical knee-jerk reaction from a feminist critic who attacked Peter Stein's superb production because Aeschylus didn't leave the harpies victorious at the end. A rare example of obstinate fidelity to the text and a rather winsome instance of the harpy theorist's belief that it's a terrible game because our side didn't win.

Of course there are occasions when directors should be given their head. For example, if they have written the play. One of the greatest pieces of theatre I have seen in Scotland is a prime instance. The Big Picnic, *written and directed by Bill Bryden, was given in the vast engineering space of Harland & Wolff's engine shed in Glasgow's Govan. It is the story of the Highland Light Infantry, recruited largely from Govan in the First World War.*

It is real theatre because you can't do it just in words, not even write about it. It was full of courage and pity and danger, presented with music, some of Scotland's best actors and genius. It was brilliantly staged and directed and moving almost beyond tolerance. If anybody attempts to transliterate this to the Gulf or Vietnam so that those with short historical memories can keep up with the fact that non-Hollywood past people felt the same emotions and suffering as we do, despite not being hopped-up on drugs and what's-it-all-about-Alfie propaganda, I will personally call up the HLI commandos from present and past and join in their annihilation – despite the fact that I was in the Navy.

Perhaps back to basics ought to begin being applied to the theatre in more realistic terms than it has been focused on anything else. After all we are now all part of Luvvie-Support if we buy a lottery ticket, and maybe we would like to know what the original words sound like in the original context.

XXXI

Not everyone agreed with my antediluvian viewpoint. Michael Billington, one of the most distinguished and perceptive of festival reviewers, mellowed into the Forest of Arden's Duke (not yet presented to us in Serbo-Croat or Samurai form) finding ...

Sweet are the uses of adversity;
Which, like the toad, ugly and venomous,
Wears yet a precious jewel in his head:
And this our life, exempt from public haunt,
Finds tongues in trees, books in the running brooks,
Sermons in stones, and good in everything.

... praising Handke's wordless play as 'a masterpiece of skilled orchestration and one of the highlights of a lifetime of Edinburgh Festivals', being gently snide about Stéphane Braunschweig's Centre Dramatique National's French *Winter's Tale* from Orleans, but enthusiastic over Dublin's Abbey Theatre revival of Synge's 1905 ironic morality tale *Well of the Saints*, about a blind couple who have their sight miraculously restored but, having looked at the world and each other, opt for darkness again. He even unearthed a worthy contemporary motive in what many people found a stodgy and pretentious version of Goethe's *Torquato Tasso*, featuring the 16th-century Italian poet in Edwardian dress at the court of Ferrara, directed by Robert David MacDonald with the Glasgow Citizens' Theatre.

At a time when governments urge a return to private patronage, it is salutary to be reminded of its historical reality: the Prince not only views Tasso as a status symbol and source of personal prestige but proprietorially seizes on his newly completed epic calling it 'My work, as in a sense it is'.

I don't know how this went down with the Festival's sponsorship department but I did notice that Tasso was prudently sponsored by the Festival's own solicitors.

No-one was quite as certain about Robert Lepage's *The Seven Streams of the River Ota*, the world première of which was offered at Meadowbank Sports Centre, in just three of its projected seven one-hour parts. The River Ota runs under the city of Hiroshima and the play links the nuclear-bombed city with the mutual impacts of Eastern and Western half-worlds through a death-camp survivor, Jana Capek, a Jewish-Czech photographer, in music, prose and a series of striking stage images.

The work is in progress, wrote The Observer's Michael Coveney, and I hope it progresses a bit more and comes back next year. It says much for the adventurousness of Brian McMaster's third festival that it dares to open with such an obviously haywire but potentially organic piece of work.

234

William Gaskill, whose productions at the Royal Court in the 1960s helped establish many of the most important British post-war playwrights, directed the revival of John Arden's *Armstrong's Last Goodnight*, a re-telling of an old Scots Border ballad with the Royal Lyceum Company. He spoke out strongly against the concept of a director's theatre where the impact of the text is sacrificed to imposed interpretation and stage effects.

> *I am just not interested in productions that use a lot of scenery and effects. The design should be minimal. I am a great text man and my whole background and training has led me to a real sense of belief in the work of the writer. I'm too old to change now. It was ingrained in my work at the Court.*

Unfortunately his direction of *Armstrong* did little to support these sentiments. Despite fine robust performances from Stuart Hepburn as Armstrong and Alison Peebles as the strong-minded mistress of Sir David Lyndsay of the Mount, the young King James V's emissary to the Border reiver (and incidentally author of *Ane Satyre of the Thrie Estaitis*), the play and its narrative purpose got lost in a welter of period hose and doubletry.

Failing to proclaim the virtue of text-conscious theatre, it was, reluctant though I am to admit it, a lot less exciting than the weird stravaigings we had seen on other festival stages.

There was an element of serious over-kill on the music side. Beethoven was the featured composer but, given that he is not exactly neglected in the generally available concert repertoire, it seemed unnecessary to have all the symphonies and all the piano concertos, well played as some of them were, setting a new course record of 55 works throughout the Festival. Richard Goode played twelve of the piano sonatas including the *Moonlight, Les Adieux* and the *Appassionata* and the Borodin gave ten of the string quartets. There was a magisterial evening when Alfred Brendel, probably the greatest living Beethoven pianist, played five of the lesser-known piano sonatas with that particular emotional intelligence which approaches genius. The most remarkable piece of programme-making was Fidelio Day.

The tracing of the evolution of Beethoven's struggles to compose his only opera *Fidelio* occupied the whole of Wednesday 17 August 1994, 11 years compacted into 12 hours. It began in the Usher Hall at 10 am with a marvellous mixture of the jolly and the learned from one of the great musical communicators of our day, Professor H. C. Robbins Landon, an expert on Haydn, Mozart and Monteverdi among others; on this day he was a genial and eruditely populist guide to Beethoven and his titanic battle with the unfamiliar medium of opera. Landon was a joy but I wondered what he thought of the sloppy and shaky versions of two of the four overtures to the opera, *Leonores* Nos One and Three and the sombre *Cantata on the death of Emperor Joseph II* from which Beethoven mined a few ideas for the final *Fidelio*, as the opera was eventually called. The Scottish Chamber Orchestra under Martin André did not seem to be in its usual sparkling form although Alwyn Mellor and Phillip Joll did their best with the gloomy *Cantata*. Perhaps the anticipation of a whole day of unrelenting Beethoven was just too much. Perhaps they were just under-rehearsed

In the afternoon they were in much better form with Sir Charles Mackerras and the 1805 version of *Leonore*. Right from the start of the *Leonore 2* overture, they sounded more cohesive and throughout the length of the first *Leonore* (there was another version in 1806, a revision for a projected Prague revival in 1807 before it became the final *Fidelio* in Vienna in 1814), they played the often attractive score with verve and finesse. Almost an hour longer than *Fidelio*, there were nevertheless many fine moments in this *Leonore* – an impassioned prison duet for Florestan and Leonore was well sung by William Kendall and Janice Watson, an excellent Rocco from Franz Hawlata: Donald Maxwell was a fiercely embittered Pizarro and the Festival Chorus were in impressive collective voice. It was an illuminating experience and to conclude with the 1814 *Fidelio* in the evening at the new Festival Theatre was the culmination of a fascinating and rewarding day, although you might have wished to transpose some of the cast from afternoon to evening to make it triumphal.

It seemed a pity that the kind of imaginative planning which had gone into Fidelio Day could not have been extended into the rest of the Beethoven repertoire on view, to give us the Battle Symphony, the Choral Fantasia, some of the Scottish songs, the Triple Concerto and *Christus am Olberge*.

However there was also Chabrier. Opera North brought two Chabrier productions, *L'Etoile* and *Le Roi Malgré Lui*, the first conspicuously lacking the elegance, style and comic musical grace we had seen from Opera de Lyons in the 1985 Festival; and the second getting itself enmired in a new plot about socialist revolution, distinctly lacking in charm or accomplishment. Chabrier's unfinished *Briseis*, a much more serious piece based on Goethe's *The Bride of Corinth*, singularly tortuous in plot and quite different in musical dimension, reflected the composer's fascination with Wagner in large-scale orchestration and highly dramatic vocal lines of considerable power and beauty, magnificently sung by Joan Rodgers and Kathyrn Harries.

French music up-to-date was provided by Boulez at 5 pm in the Playhouse and three late-night recitals of Messaien's *L'Apparition de l'Eglise Eternelle* and *Les Corps Glorieux*. The Messaien recital, a wondrous if sometimes taxing ending to a Festival day, played on the church's great new red Rieger organ in the High Kirk of St Giles by Thomas Trotter, was profound new music in its ultimate setting. Boulez in the incongruity of the afternoon Playhouse with the Ensemble InterContemporain, pursued his ever-exploratory path through the two *Improvisations sur Mallarmé* and a quizzical ingenious piece for a clarinet and its electronic shadow to a development of *explosante/fixe*, once part of an epitaph for Stravinsky, now evolving into a more complex and decorative structure for flute and 24 players plus electronics of mesmerising strangeness.

In addition to the inevitable Mark Morris, there was a strong dance programme. Miami City Ballet glorious in spectacular routines in Balanchine's *Jewels* dazzled everybody with their scintillating costumes, youthful energy, technical mastery and superb female soloists and produced a whirl and stomp of purely American virtuosity in the hoe-down spins, kicks and joyous jumps of *Western Symphony*.

Leaving the glories of Miami City Ballet for the banality of Fondation Jean-Pierre Perreault, wrote Geoffrey West, *was rather like awakening from a sun-drenched dream to the dull reality of a dismal winter morning.*

Certainly the message of Quebecois choreographer Perreault in *La Vita* was one of gloom, fading hope and growing despair, contrasting starkly with the fizz and sparkle of the Miami dancers and his vision of life as portrayed by his drab-clad cast had some doomed power but no joy. Lucinda Child's minimalism did not offer much more cheer – somehow minimalism is the antithesis of cheerfulness – and the repetitive choreography to pieces by Ligeti, Gorecki, Xenakis and Philip Glass was often a contest in sometimes elegant but never very expressive confusion.

Merce Cunningham at 75 had become a legend but by 1994, creating dance/movement to computer programmed music which sounded like distorted mechanistic tapes played backwards, his dance designs, like the few movements he contributed personally, seemed pretty creaky and the ideas behind them impenetrable to an uncomfortable ear-splitting degree. It was a bold dance programme but rather short on delight except for the wonderful Miami dancers and their superb Balanchine season.

For the three years since Brian McMaster's appointment as Festival Director the contribution of painting, sculpture and exhibitions in general to the Festival had been a matter of some contention. They had not been part of the original Festival programme but that omission had been repaired by Ian Hunter in 1952 and in every year since, until 1992, there had been at least one official Festival exhibition. Exhibitions continued after 1992 on a self-support basis although some of them attracted sponsors, but not as an official part of the Festival and not conspicuously supported in the Festival programme brochures.

This was partly due to the insistence of Timothy Clifford, director of the Scottish National Galleries, that only his exhibitions should be included in Festival publicity, but also to the number of exhibitions clamouring for attention during the Festival period and the financial problems involved in mounting and insuring major shows. Although this caused some bitterness in the arts world, there were still important exhibitions to be seen in Edinburgh at Festival-time, notably in 1994 the magnificent *Monet to Matisse* in the National Gallery, covering the four decades of landscape painting between the first impressionist exhibition in Paris in 1874 and the start of the World War I. Backed by Fondation Elf, it ranged through impressionism, fauvism and cubism, Cézanne, Van Gogh, Matisse, Gauguin and Seurat, Picasso and Derain to less well-known masters.

There was also an important spread-over-two-galleries show *The Romantic Spirit in German Art 1790-1990* at the Royal Scottish Academy and the Fruitmarket Gallery, tracing a very long and tenuous route from the Gothic grandeur of Caspar David Friedrich through Kandinsky and Klee to Joseph Beuys. Richard Demarco, who introduced Beuys to Edinburgh in 1970, had more Beuys among his cluster of exhibitions at the Demarco European Art Foundation. And the erotic, exotic and fascinating *Visions of the Ottoman Empire*, added vast layers of oriental lure to dreams of Eastern promise at the National Portrait Gallery with a show which included Thomas Phillips's portrait of Byron dressed as an Albanian bandit as well as Delacroix's sketch for *The Death of Sardanapalus*, lots of harems and reverent vistas of the Holy Land as well as David Robert's magnificent paintings of monuments in Lebanon and Egypt.

By 1995 it was becoming clear that Brian McMaster's planning philosophy of something new and unique in Edinburgh every year was running into the sands. There were certainly works new to Edinburgh being performed, some of them new to Britain, but they were being done by the same people. Mark Morris had been in every McMaster Festival; Pina Bausch was back; Miami Ballet was back; Gert Voss reappeared with two Berlin companies. Boulez, Abbado and Gunter Wand returned as did Bill T. Jones, Sir Charles Mackerras, Termirkanov, Mariss Jansons, Donald Runnicles and Andras Schiff. The directors' gang were there in force, Peter Sellars, Peter Zadek and Luc Bondy, with a new recruit in the Frenchman, Patrice Chéreau. Apart from a series of awkwardly timed Scottish folk-song concerts in the Festival Theatre and the three Scottish concerts organised by BBC Radio Scotland in their Queen Street studio on Sunday afternoons, just two British composers featured in Festival programmes. The rarest performance language was English and one of the English-spoken plays was a translation from the German. In fact the Germans seemed to be taking over the Festival. There were four orchestras from Germany and Austria. Dvorak was the featured composer with 30 works but of the remaining 80 or so in the concert and recital list, 66 were by composers of the Teutonic school, either Austrian or German.

No-one with slightest claim to musical knowledge would deny that some of the greatest composers who ever lived spoke German as their native tongue and wrote wonderful music which can be listened to painlessly over and over again. But added to Shakespeare and Sacha Guitry in German and Johann Christoph Friedrich Schiller in English in the theatre and Pina Bausch from Wuppertal in the dance programme, plus the endless stream of German plays or theatre companies over the previous three years, it sometimes seemed a trend too far.

The 49th Festival, however, offered something different on the opera front with the Kirov from St Petersburg. They had been at Frank Dunlop's final festival in 1991, when in tandem with the Bolshoi they gave us two weeks of seven Russian operas by Mussorgsky, Tchaikovsky and Rimsky-Korsakov in ten performances. This time they brought two fully-staged works by Rimsky-Korsakov to the Festival Theatre, *The Legend of the Invisible City of Kitezh* and *Sadko* plus a concert performance in the Usher Hall of Glinka's *Ruslan and Ludmila*. There were two performances of Dvorak's *The Jacobin* by Scottish Opera also in the Festival Theatre and there was some comment that, after all the 40-year fuss about an 'opera house' for the Edinburgh Festival, six performances in three weeks seemed hardly to be making adequate use of the new facility. The new theatre's programme was filled up with six performances of Mark Morris's ballet *The Hard Nut*, 21 mostly late-night concerts of folk songs from north-east Scotland, Spanish and Portuguese folk songs and discussions. How was it that in past Festivals there had been 18 opera performances by Glyndebourne and a similar number by La Scala and Hamburg Opera in the 'inadequate' King's Theatre?

At the Royal Lyceum there was novelty, one of those is-it-an-opera, a-musical, a-play works with a fashionably long and beckoning title *I Was Looking At The Ceiling And Then I Saw The Sky*. The music was by John Adams, composer of the sensation of the 1988 Festival *Nixon in China*: the words were by June Jordan and the direction by Peter Sellars, so it could have been anything. But as Ms Jordan was described as 'librettist' it was presumed to be an opera with seven singers and eight instrumentalists.

The Kirov Opera was certainly big enough with 305 people in the company and with Valery Gergiev as artistic director and conductor, it was led by a musician of international stature and considerable interpretative power. But the trouble with Rimsky-Korsakov's operas is that although the melodies are often lovely the characterisation and the narrative impetus is paste-board thin. It was not helped by the stiff

I Was Looking at the Ceiling and Then I saw the Sky *(1995)*

and static nature of the productions and it was done to death in both the staged operas by the overwhelming chocolate-box scenery. *Kitezh*, first of the fully-staged Kirov works certainly filled the Festival Theatre stage but inevitably became known as 'The Visible City of Kitsch'. *Sadko*, a strange fairy-tale of market forces and insider dealing involving adultery, economy with the truth, Novgorod and the underwater Kingdom of the Sea King, (gorgeously gauzed for Sadko's submarine wedding to the Princess Volkhova, who obligingly solves the adultery and bigamy problem by eventually becoming a river), was a wonderfully sung, sumptuously presented pantomime. The singing had to be good because the acting was terrible, backed up by a great deal of what Michael Radcliffe in *The Observer* called 'choric mugging'. The scores often had resonances of Wagner but it was difficult to decide whether it was the attempted flattery of imitation or some kind of heavy-handed musical joke. In a way the simple earnestness was endearing and the singing, the generally superb orchestral playing and the riotous colour were enjoyable but neither of the theatre performances by the Kirov could be counted as an emotional experience.

By contrast there was plenty of drama in the Kirov's concert version of Glinka's *Ruslan and Ludmilla*, another opera plot haunted by the supernatural with good and bad fairies, wicked dwarfs etc., with an overture known to every concert-goer and not much else anyone in the West had ever heard before.

> *Gergiev conducted a fizzy and disciplined concert performance*, wrote Michael Radcliffe, *of Glinka's eccentric masterpiece of 1842 which speaks a vigorous and unpredictable operatic language stretching back to Mozart and Rossini and extending its own influence over the musical future as far as Stravinsky's Symphony of Psalms. There were no distractions for the chorus, which sounded firm, resonant and full or the orchestra whose virtuoso playing acquired a better balanced texture than in the*

theatre pit; all the singers sang with dramatic commitment to the text, whether they had much voice or not (which was not the case in the theatre); among those with both voice and commitment were the soprano Marina Shaguch as Ludmilla and the alto Larissa Diadkova as Ratmir, a travesti knight, Even the compulsory divertissements – 'magic' dances and 'oriental' dances – sustained a forward drive. More concerts please.

A great deal was written in advance about John Adams's new opera at the Royal Lyceum which appeared in the first week and boldly had three times the number of performances (six) of any other opera in the Festival. This at least meant that you had a chance to see it if Edinburgh's notorious galley wireless was complimentary, but there was a serious danger of it being explained away before it began. Director Peter Sellars told us all his ideas about it in a long article of high-minded and baffling analysis; Andrew Porter said he thought the libretto was 'banal' when he saw it in New York. Watching it, said *The Scotsman's* musical guru Brian Morton, 'will surely again confirm the enormous pleasure of finding that something old and improbable like opera still works and still has something to say about how we live now and what we feel about the world we uneasily inhabit.'

Oddly enough, *I Was Looking At The Ceiling And Then I Saw the Sky* survived all the advance hype and intellectual dissection and the composer's claim that 'it was aimed at college-age audiences', to be an impressive piece of music theatre using all kinds of musical idioms (gospel, jazz, rock, soul and minimalism) within a situation rather than a plot of danger and love.

Michael Coveney, a theatre critic at the opera, was enthusiastic:

The title derives from something someone said during the Los Angeles earthquake of January 1994. John Adams wrote the music, June Jordan wrote the libretto about seven young people at that appalling, life-changing moment. Peter Sellars directed the show.

Adams and Sellars have collaborated before on Nixon in China *(1987) and* The Death of Klinghoffer (1991). *This time it's the end of the world, and the millennium, and the start of new musics. Each song has a challenging flavour. You think of Sondheim a lot – good Sondheim Company – and of the gnawing, sometimes annoying, serial sounds of Philip Glass, and of Menotti, and of bebop jazz; and every item takes its model and pushes it aside. The characters – girl, boy, lawyer, priest and so on – live only in the music, which really grabs, or in my case, grabbed.*

The characters are looking for the sunlight, and the staging is impeccable. Californian primary colours are evoked in the terrific lighting of James F. Ingalls and an entire exhibition of paintings, cartoons and other art work. I absolutely loved the idea that a piece of what is off-puttingly referred to as music theatre should be so hip, so intelligent, so funny and so droll.

Scottish Opera's *The Jacobin* by the featured composer Antonin Dvorak, had an entirely German stage team, director Christine Mielitz with designers Reinhard Zimmermann and Eleonore Kleiber from the Berlin Komische Oper and was conducted by Richard Armstrong.

This impressive ensemble together with a fine cast of singers made heavy weather of this melodious and beautifully scored domestic comedy-drama about a sternly traditional father and his revolutionary son. Ponderous humour and a refusal to enjoy the sentiments of love and reconciliation combined with the singers' sombre costumes and the setting of a very un-Bohemian grey cave, did not stop you wanting to hear the music again, though more cheerfully presented.

Musically the Festival opened with a glowing, rapturous performance of Bruckner's unfinished Ninth Symphony played by the Gustav Mahler Jugendorchester founded by Claudio Abbado as a non-EC counterpart to the European Community Youth Orchestra which was also his creation. Bruckner and youth do not naturally seem to go together but Abbado drew from his dazzlingly accomplished young players a performance of striking musical intensity and splendour, followed by a tremendous account of the *Te Deum* with Jane Eaglen, Liliana Nichiteanu, Endrik Wottrich and Robert Lloyd and the Edinburgh Festival Chorus in thrilling voice, brilliantly trained by their new chorus-master, David Jones.

Dvorak did not fare quite as well in the concert hall. There was rather a chilly version of the Stabat Mater from John Eliot Gardiner and the Philharmonia although the Festival Chorus and Anne Sofie von Otter managed to infuse some humanity and pain into the work, written after the deaths of three of his children. The Requiem with the Royal Scottish National Orchestra under Sir Charles Mackerras was also rather pedestrian and careful rather than inspiring. It was the Liverpool Philharmonic, not heard too often at the Festival in recent years, under their Czech conductor Libor Pesek, which provided the most satisfying and inspired Dvorak evening, ranging through his versatility and strengths with three overtures, a splendid recital of the dark-coloured *Biblical Songs* by Peter Mikulas and a hugely impressive account of the Brahmsian Symphony no six played with a dedication and expressiveness which allied Germanic precision and Bohemian brio with fine passion.

Sir Charles Mackerras

The most complex and astonishing work in the programme was the end-product of a collaboration between the Festivals of Edinburgh, Salzburg, Paris and Berlin, the Kölner Rundfunk and the SWF Symphony Orchestra, Baden-Baden. Bernd Alois Zimmermann's *Requiem for a Young Poet* was written in Cologne in the two years from 1967-9, eight months before Zimmermann, like the three young poets who were his iconology for writing the Requiem, killed himself. He called it 'Lingual for Speakers, Soprano and Baritone Solos, Three Choirs, Electronic Sounds, Orchestra, Jazz Band and Organ, based on Texts by Diverse Poets, on Reports and Accounts (1967-9).'

Andrew Porter's review in *The Observer* described it in more detail:

> *A cry of 'Requiem' opens three of its movements, and the close is a desperate 'Dona nobis pacem', but it begins with Wittgenstein's reflections on Augustine (and the meaning of words); the recorded voices of Neville Chamberlain (on his way to Munich). Hitler, Churchill, Stalin, Pope John XXIII, a snatch of the Beatles Hey Jude, lines of Aeschylus, Joyce and Pound are among the multifarious elements in its making.*

> *Twice Zimmermann sets an imperative from* Revelations, *'I heard a voice from heaven saying unto me, Write.' The long-anguished Requiem seems to have been wrung from him by that imperative: a public proclamation of personal despair. It is at once a 'documentary', a chronicle of all the oppressions done under the sun (Nagy's and Dubcek's speeches as Russian tanks rolled into Budapest, then Prague, are both heard) and the cry of a Catholic artist whose faith has been tried beyond breaking point. Lines that Beethoven set affirmatively – 'Brothers, beyond yon starry vault there surely dwells a loving Father' – here ring out bitter and ironic. The final cry for peace rises from a din of super-imposed recordings of demonstrations in Paris, Prague and Vietnam.*

It is a good description but regrettably it is much more lucid than was the performance.

For the first 35 minutes the sparse orchestra and soloists sat unemployed on stage, the choirs around the hall virtually mute, only the mixing desk in the stalls was fully active as speakers played the electronic

240

text of voices, recorded music, multi-lingual gabble and synthetic sound. Most of the score was speech or noise, passages recognisable as music apart from fragments quoted from Milhaud, Wagner, Messaien and the Beatles were rare; the languages were Latin, English (Chamberlain and the Beatles – 60 seconds?), Czech, Greek, French and German. The live Speakers were both German. In the second part where the orchestra got to play and the soloists to sing (the Croatian soprano, Vlatka Orsanica to stunning effect), we even had Ezra Pound and Mao Tse-tung in German as well as an occasional flurry in Russian and Hungarian. I had not gone into this unprepared. Twice I listened to the recording made by the same forces when they performed it in Salzburg in March 1995. I understand the resonance of unknown languages being used as music up to a point. My wife, who sings in the Festival Chorus, told me how many of the audience in Berlin were in tears when it was performed there before the Edinburgh Festival. But if I had shed tears they would have been of frustration and bafflement. There were certainly moments of sonar power and drama but, for the most part it was like searching for minnows with defective radar in the Sargasso Sea. If the two live Speakers parts had been given in English, it might well have been moving and comprehensible but it seemed no service to Zimmermann that his doomed message, questions about us all rather than answers to anyone, should have been lost in Babel's discord.

There was some disillusionment with the Festival staples. Pina Bausch's 10,000 plastic carnation-strewn *Nelken* was rated disappointing; the exuberant fizz and sparkle so enjoyed in 1994 from the Miami City Ballet failed to return when they opened the dance programme at the Playhouse with George Balanchine's choreography for *The Nutcracker*, never before seen in Britain. 'It is a better version of the ballet than most, but not that much better,' Jann Parry said chillingly in *The Observer*. 'Ballet is poorly served by this year's programming.'

Bill T. Jones's controversial *Still/Here* with its video testimonies showing dying people, brought accusations of projecting himself as an HIV-positive martyr immune to criticism, in some quarters but did not arouse anything like the furore it did in the United States. 'It is surely arrogant to dismiss Jones's work as a con-trick or a cheap stunt,' Jann Parry said firmly.

Everyone however continued to love Mark Morris.

Terrific musical taste has always been Morris's trump card, wrote *Times* dance critic Debra Craine, *a fact which makes his company the ideal choice for a festival which takes its music seriously.*

Stephen Foster's popular love song 'Beautiful Dreamer' could be the title for Mark Morris's opening programme in Edinburgh. Morris's dancers dream of a world in which harmonious movement is as natural as breathing – and, just occasionally, the happy reverie becomes a nightmare, raved Ms Parry.

Although no less opposed than before to bringing the same people back to the Festival year after year, I thought *The Hard Nut* was suave, accomplished beautifully danced and costumed, and hilarious. Most parody and satire falls down on style and almost never quite 'rhymes' with whatever it is sending up. But Morris's glorious version of a ballet I have often found boring and seldom transfixing, was a joy.

The drama programme however was something else. Nor is that a reflection on its quality, it was just that it suggested that joy was a commodity in pretty short supply. There was only one inedible turkey, entirely home-reared, and that was Alasdair Gray's much-acclaimed novel *Lanark*, adapted for the stage by Alastair Cording with music by Alasdair Nicolson. I do not know whether it was an over-seasoning of Alasdairs but the spoiled broth was neither of an even consistency nor tasty.

One thing the stage can do is to interweave the two worlds and parallel characters that dominate the story, wrote Michael Billington. *We are introduced instantly to Duncan Thaw, the visionary artist who like Gray himself, grows up in Glasgow from the 30s to the 50s. At the same time we meet his alter ego, Lanark, who lives in the dark,*

241

grim, coldly cruel city of Unthank which is 'Glasgow as Hell'. By condensing time,
Cording's adaptation is able to put on stage simultaneously things that in the novel
happen sequentially. But the loss is greater than the gain. As in all adaptations, you
get the narrative events without the imaginative context.

Tony Graham's production also has little of the physical expertise that characterised
'A Scots Quair'. Laurence Rudic as Lanark, Tom Smith as Duncan Thaw, Carol
Brannan as the loves of their twin lives and, especially, Kern Falconer as both the
sharp-suited Sludden and a dilapidated minister do all they can. But Lanark is, in the
end, a joyless experience.

The Abbey Theatre's *Observe the Sons of Ulster Marching Towards the Somme* (it was the Year of the
Interminable Title) at the King's proved it still had an impact as powerful as when it had been launched
a decade before as the first play in which a Catholic southern nationalist had explored with empathy and
an extraordinary compassion, the loyalties of Ulster. It was compared with Bill Bryden's *The Big Picnic* to
the latter's detriment, but it seemed to me that there was something complementary about the two plays
about the sentiment and terror of war and the horror, chicanery and sectarian divide of organised carnage.
The Sons of Ulster was more political, poetical and close-focused than Bryden's play, beautifully acted
and directed with power and infinite discretion by Patrick Mason. It was more artistic and held you in its
grip, more like a play and less like a war but it is the unconfident banalities, the stark metal terror of battle
in Govan that brought back the war that I was in to me.

The Berliner Ensemble *Merchant of Venice*, adroitly directed by Peter Zadek was a yuppified slick
stock-exchange comedy of ironies, with little threat but a series of skilled performances, mobile phones
and brandished *Financial Times* which revealed nothing about the play or the characters which had not
been tiresomely exhumed before in a dozen updated versions.

The Citizens' Theatre 50th anniversary production of Schiller's *Don Carlos* showed the company at its
superb, lavish and scintillating best. Directed and designed by Philip Prowse in a vivid and elegant translation
by Robert David MacDonald, it was presented in a magnificent black and gold set which, in spite of the
Prussian uniforms, managed by some imperial metamorphosis to capture the Inquisition-dominated,
dangerous intrigue-soaked ambience of the 16th-century Spanish court of Philip II. The scenes between
Philip, wracked by jealousy, heresy and the doomed weight of devious power and the noble forthright
Marquis of Posa were brilliantly played by Giles Havergal as the King and Andrew Woodfall. The skill and
pace of the production carried the long five-act play and the whole thing was an unadulterated triumph.
For almost as long as the Festival has run I have been trying to persuade its directors and counsellors to
put Verdi's compelling and dramatic opera based on this play in the Festival programme. Now we have a
theatre in which it can be handsomely staged, is it too much to hope the Citizens might have provided an
electric prod in that direction?

Patrice Chéreau's production of *Dans la Solitude des Champs de Coton* could not have been less like
his cinema epic *La Reine Margot* or his celebrated *Ring* productions at Bayreuth. Just two people, one
played by Chéreau himself and the other by Pascal Greggory, in an empty, spot-lit drill-hall made an arena
of commerce, a dialogue of dealer and client, a bullying evasive market exchange of positioning and
pressures without a defined product, composed as combat, words as weapons and espionage.

In 1996 it was the 50th Festival, a time, it might be thought, for celebration allied with a little nostalgia,
reflection on past glories, that sort of thing. But Festival Directors have never been very enthusiastic
about past glories, perhaps because such triumphs smack of vanity if they have fallen within their own
time of office, perhaps because 'comparisons are odorous' as Dogberry says, or again that all directors
are so forward-looking they have little time for bygone events. Only Peter Diamand who encompassed
both the 25th and 30th festivals within his long reign as director, made acknowledgement of the past in

1976, when the first two Festival operas, Verdi's *Macbeth* and Mozart's *Le Nozze di Figaro* were again in the programme; the Vienna Philharmonic, stars of the opening Festival, returned and a French orchestra, L'Orchestre de Paris ended the Festival in memory of the one which had begun it in 1947. In ending my introductory article to the 1976 Souvenir Programme, I wrote:

> *It is talking half the night away on a point of interpretation, a quirk of characterisation, the way Edwige Feuillere fell backwards downstage on to a circular white rug as she died at the end of* La Dame aux Camellias, *the inflection Burton used in 'Get thee to a nunnery'. The tenacious hanging on to moments of musical and dramatic splendour you know you may never experience again. Instant sweetly bitter nostalgia made tolerable only by the sure knowing that although these moments may not recur there will be others. That is the Festival.*

Unfortunately when Frank Dunlop celebrated the 40th anniversary of the Festival in 1986, there was no looking back to 1947, only, on the Sunday of the last week, a tawdry, ill-rehearsed and thrown-together Gala Concert for which I was ashamed to have written the introduction in the programme.

In December 1995 I talked to Brian McMaster about his Festival policy. The emphasis on directors for example:

> *On the musical side, in the Australian* Midsummer Night's Dream *with the orchestra on the stage, that was only done after acoustical tests and it concentrated as much on the musical side as the theatre side. In the theatre – yes. One of the feelings I've had was that the work of some of the major directors had been very under-represented in Britain and that that was something we should put right. Particularly I think, given the situation in Edinburgh, where if you are young with ambitions to work in the theatre, the chances are you'll put together a production on the Fringe. Now that being so, I think we have the opportunity to have an influence, hopefully a positive influence, on the future of the theatre – by providing work that might have some influence on young directors and actors and theatre practitioners.*

I pointed out that most of the productions mounted by his prestigious directors had been new versions or adaptations of classical plays and that there was a long and honourable history of the Festival commissioning new plays. Are new plays a problem?

> *Well, it's not slavish. It's rather like everything else. One of the things I said to myself about the festival is – it's obviously quite sexy to do a new piece. It's much more difficult to give the second performance of something. It hasn't got the sexiness but it's the second performance very often that's been crucial in establishing a work in the repertory. So I said we'll concentrate more on giving second performances. In certain areas we've given first performances in the last four years but not very many. In the appropriate situation we'll do that. But I think that part of our job is to fill gaps in provision. There is quite a lot of new work performed. Far too much of it finds its way into the bottom drawer after it's been performed once.*

I agreed that he had changed the ideas of many people about Moses and Aaron.

> *Well, as it so happens, there have just been two major productions of it in Europe. But at the time we did it – well, the publishers told us we could have the music for free.*
>
> *Nobody was performing it and they were thrilled to bits that we were. And I think it is a major piece. It certainly is a piece that, more than an awful lot of operas, lends itself to a concert performance.*

In view of the large number of concert performances of operas in his programmes, I asked if this was something about which he felt particularly strongly.

Well, no, but I think there are different approaches. I mean Oberto *was to show in one festival how far Verdi had travelled in his creative life, So we did his first and last operas.* Leonore *was part of a particular project to show the creation of* Fidelio. The Mozarts? *Well, a belief of mine is that Sir Charles Mackerras is the greatest Mozart conductor in the world, and he was recording these things and we worked out a way in which we could get the benefit of the recordings, and have therefore been able to give some significant performances. And therefore each one has been in a different context.*

I asked why, except for Mozart in the concert hall, he had avoided mainstream opera, the classical favourite repertoire.

I think there are a number of reasons for that. One: situations change and Scotland did have and, hopefully still does have, its own opera company – which should do the main operatic repertory. There's also the problem that in the old days – and this was true in many areas – the Hamburg Opera, for example, would descend on the Edinburgh Festival and do a whole repertory of operas. But that's changed. We're talking to one of those opera companies now about the future and they say they'd love to come but they could only do one opera. But the prime reason is that I think if we do put on an opera – on whatever scale – it's got to be something special. Anything in the Festival should be a Festival event. Things change: in 1947 there was very little cultural life – and it was filling a considerable gap. Now the situation has changed. And I think we should fill gaps in provision – that each event should somehow be a Festival event – in the sense that it should be something different.

Something you could not encounter in another context during a normal opera season, concert season or theatre season. And that's how we try and do it. But those gaps will change. They do change. One of the things we've done in the last two or three years is to programme a certain amount of large scale dance – international dance. Because there is actually nowhere in Britain at the moment where the large-scale companies can perform. That will change when Sadler's Wells is rebuilt as a larger theatre. And the importance, our priority for doing that, will no doubt change.

I asked if he thought he had made the best use of the long-awaited 'opera house', his own large scale theatre.

Well, it is, of course, very expensive. And when it opened we were determined to programme it as an additional venue. And that costs us another £800,000, so the whole scale of the Festival went up that year. And it was wonderful how the Council of the Festival and the local authorities backed us to the hilt – but it was a hell of a gamble. But for two years it's paid off. For two years we have been able to make maximum use of that theatre.

Rather a lot of small items in the Festival Theatre's programmes, I suggested.

Well, there were some very small items in the foyer. And the fado and other similar things were there covering the technical rehearsals for The Hard Nut. *What we actually do is to programme that theatre rather more. In a normal time you put on the events and you'll have the technical rehearsals but what we've done and what we're planning to do again is to put on some events over the technical rehearsals.*

I said I had noticed in his programming that he did not seem to be such a believer in commemoration as some of his predecessors.

Well, that's just one of the nonsensical principles that I have in the back of my mind – a bit like second performances or whatever – in that I feel that when there is an anniversary there tends to be a lot of activity.

Other people celebrate anniversaries: so there's a lot of the music or whatever it is of the composer whose anniversary it is. We tend not to do things on the date of the anniversary. We break this sometimes – we did it in the case of Chabrier, when there wasn't much happening.

I brought up the perennial subject of money, reminding him that most of the problems directors have had to face in the past have had to do with finance.

Well, there will never be enough of course. I mean, it's a different sort of festival, but let's face it, it is one with which we are compared and with which we compete in terms of international culture tourists, but Salzburg has a budget of £28 million and ours is now £4.9 million. So that puts the whole situation in context. Equally, next year is our 50th festival and, as chance would have it, unfortunately it's also the year of local government re-organisation and the local governments are faced with a major problem in coming up with the level of funding we had in the last couple of years. It does create major problems. Compare that with Avignon, which was only a theatre festival until recently, with a budget of £2 million, but it has been given an additional £850,000 to celebrate its 50th. We won't get that. But where I think I'm extraordinarily lucky is in the extent to which the local authorities back the Festival. And they did increase the funding of it by 40 per cent in my first two years.

You'll be aware that next year is the 50th Festival and 1997 is the 50th anniversary of the founding of the Edinburgh Festival. Well, taking the view that we do, we think that the 50th Festival is a year to celebrate but that 1997 is also something to celebrate. In 1996 we're reflecting or attempting to reflect the ideas that led to the creation of the Festival and really looking to the future; in 1997 we're planning to look back and celebrate a complete 50 years – looking at the whole 50 years rather than just the first festival.

It was difficult to see how the 1996 programme fulfilled this plan. There was an attempt to link two items to the first Festival. At the Opening Concert Donald Runnicles conducted the Royal Scottish National Orchestra and the Festival Chorus in Schoenberg's eight-minute *A Survivor from Warsaw* which had been written in America in the month of August 1947 when the first Festival took place. It is a marvellous piece but it was hard to see its relevance as not a note of Schoenberg was played in Edinburgh in 1947. It was followed by Beethoven's Choral Symphony, a work of which we had certainly had enough in the immediate past, in full just two years before, and with endless repetition of its choral theme all the way through the football World Cup. The second link was a silent film of Richard Strauss's *Der Rosenkavalier* made in 1926 and provided with an adapted score by the composer. This was given two performances at the Festival Theatre with Ensemble 13 conducted by Manfred Reichert, as a tribute to 50 years of the Film Festival – a bizarre gesture in view of the fact that the opera has only been given once at the International Festival, by Hamburg in 1952.

It was rather like 'Apart from that, Mrs Lincoln, how did you enjoy the play?' There were two productions by ballet dancers of operas by Gluck, Mark Morris directed *Orfeo ed Euridice*, the three soloists were Christine Brandes, Dana Hanchard and Michael Chance, the Mark Morris Dance Group provided most of the action with Christopher Hogwood conducting the Handel & Haydn Society Chorus and Orchestra from Boston. *Iphigenie auf Tauris* with the singers in auditorium boxes and dancers doubling their roles on stage was directed by Pina Bausch with the Scottish Chamber Orchestra and the Chorus of Scottish

Opera in the pit. There was some attempt at visual characterisation in the Morris production and at least the singers were in costume and on stage. But this was much the mixture as before. We had seen it already in *Dido and Aeneas* and *L'Allegro, il Penseroso ed il Moderato* and the singers were lost in the dancers' swirl and the somewhat unfocused energy of the choreography. The Bausch I*phigenie* was simply dance with a vocal as well as an instrumental orchestra.

If this was looking at the future of opera, it was in recession; going backwards to the days when the laddish element in the audience demanded more dance so that they could be titillated by the flashing legs of the corps de ballet. It had nothing to do with music drama.

We had more Gertrude Stein and Robert Wilson at the Playhouse in Virgil Thomson's *Four Saints in Three Acts*. Miss Stein wrote the libretto for this curious piece which fused gospel hymns, marching band tunes and black American themes. The composer said of it 'Please do not try to construe the words of this opera literally or seek in it any abstruse symbolism'. It was a hit which reached Broadway in 1934. The simplest way not to be baffled by it is not to see it.

Inès de Castro, James MacMillan's first full-length opera which had its world première at the Festival Theatre at the 50th Festival is quite a different matter. MacMillan has established himself as one of the most interesting young composers of the decade, with a flair for dramatic and colourful music and his first attempt at a major theatre work was awaited with something between hope and trepidation. Even the critics were nervous. Michael Tumelty, music critic of *The Herald* and a MacMillan devotee, was almost desperate:

> *Stay with it*, he pleaded. *That's my advice to anyone going to see James MacMillan's new opera – a major piece – either tomorrow night or when it goes into repertoire with Scottish Opera. Ultimately it will draw you in, horrify you and break your heart.*

It was savaged with spluttering fury in *The Times* but, for the most part, first reactions were confused. The setting and the subject were severely classical, woven through initially with the *religioso* music structures we had come to expect from MacMillan. There was clever and incisive writing for the orchestra but the vocal parts seemed stark and solitary. Most of all it was difficult to see why the story of Inès de Castro, 14th-century Spanish mistress of Portugal's crown prince, murdered by the King and carried as a corpse to the coronation of her lover to be enthroned as a dead queen, had fascinated MacMillan.

It could have been a grim exercise in the macabre but the composer took the story from the play written by John Clifford where the finale played down the grisly coronation scene for a redemptive ghostly encounter with a child. The only real horror was in a brilliant but gratuitous solo for the executioner and the duet for Inès and the barren, cruelly named Queen Blanca. It was not in the least Portuguese and seemed irrelevant to historic time and somewhat lacking in the central dramatic elements of the story. But it was certainly a Festival occasion.

The MacMillan opera was dedicated to Sir Alexander Gibson, a familiar figure at the Festival and the man who had been the source and stimulus of much music in Scotland, who had died, much too young, in 1995. Other than *Inès*, the significance of most items in the 'celebration' 50th programme was hard to discern. In addition to Mark Morris and Pina Bausch making a ballet of opera and occupying the Festival Theatre for 11 of the 14 nights it was open for performance, there were three other dance groups. Tomoe Shizune offered Butoh, the first Japanese event in McMaster's programming, a new kind of oriental theatre dance, graceful, colourful, minimalist and beautifully lit, scored to running water and pounding drums for three nights

James MacMillan

246

at the King's. At the Playhouse, everyone, except the most Morris-mazed, was enraptured by the choreography of Jiří Kylián and the superbly honed ensemble of the Nederlands Dans Theater – 'a genuinely world-class event to be treasured for posterity,' said Geoffrey West in *Scotland on Sunday*.

Radical Graham – which followed the Dutch company – devoted to perpetuating the work and ideas of the diva of American dance, Martha Graham who died in 1991 aged 96, was criticised in some quarters for 'presenting antiques in a modern display case' but most people still related to the passion, the anger at war, injustice and oppression which inspired her work.

In the concert hall there was yet another *Fidelio*, a superb *Gurrelieder* from Abbado and the Gustav Mahler Jugendorchester and the Festival Chorus with Hans Hotter, venerable and splendid as the Narrator.

Bryn Terfel was in magnificent voice in the Choral Symphony, a recital of Schubert, Ibert and Vaughan Williams songs and the welcome return of Mendelssohn's *Elijah*, too long neglected but given a glorious performance by the Orchestra of the Age of Enlightenment and the Festival Chorus under Paul Daniel as the finale to the Festival. The New York Philharmonic, one of the great orchestras in the world, proved to be in stunning form under Kurt Masur, wonderfully crafted performances, held firmly but delicately in Masur's bear-like paws, releasing emotion, passion and head and heart-turning rhythms in Strauss and Beethoven, Prokoviev and Tchaikovsky of impeccable and noble authority.

There was another connection with the first Festival I suppose, because the very first piece played in 1947 was Haydn's Symphony no 94 in G Surprise, and it was duly played by the Orchestra of the 18th Century under Frans Brüggen. But adding another 69 works by Haydn to the Festival programme seemed a bit excessive. There was morning Haydn in the Queen's Hall, tea-time Haydn in St Cuthbert's Church, evening Haydn in the Usher Hall, late-night Haydn at St Giles and the Usher Hall: there was vocal Haydn, orchestral Haydn, instrumental Haydn and choral Haydn. There was also a good deal of pianist Andras Schiff who was beginning to look nearly as permanent a festival fixture as Mark Morris. Innovations of a kind were provided by concerts devoted to the music of contemporary composers, Portuguese Emmanuel Nunes and Romanian György Kurtag. Both had been heard at the 1995 Festival but they certainly colourfully represented the European *avant-garde*.

Initial hype about the International Festival however spot-lit the drama. As planned, it was a heavily director-loaded first week with Robert Wilson presenting Miranda Richardson in a stage version of Virginia Woolf's gender-altering journey through the centuries, *Orlando*; Robert Lepage appearing himself in his own solo version of Shakespeare's Hamlet, *Elsinore* and Neil Bartlett invoking *The Seven Sacraments of Nicolas Poussin*, paintings which are part of the permanent collection of the National Gallery of Scotland.

It seemed an oddly risky plan to arrange for three solo performances as the theatre offerings with which to begin the Festival and in due course the sword of Damocles which hangs over hubris struck. First Neil Bartlett was taken ill and Poussin was out.

Robert Lepage gave a pre-Festival interview to *The Scotsman* about his one-man Hamlet. 'I don't want to sound as if I'm shmoozing,' he said, 'but the Edinburgh Festival is a great platform for us and Brian McMaster is a wonderful guy.'

If only he hadn't used that word 'platform' or called his company Ex Machina – but the sword of hubris swung once again. The machine which rotated Lepage through 360 degrees in the process of being everyone in *Hamlet* broke down or it wouldn't function on the King's raked stage in spite (or because?) of being computer-controlled. At all events the *deus ex machina* had turned into a *diavolo*. First one performance was cancelled. Then the press conference to explain why the first performance had been cancelled, was cancelled. Then all five performances were cancelled, costing the Festival £100,000, it was rumoured – plus the money to be repaid on the 3,000 tickets sold.

That left Miranda Richardson, an actress seen principally in films and on television, rather tremulously on her own as the Festival theatrical entertainment for the first week. She succeeded brilliantly in a performance of polished verve and physical grace, irony and hybrid passion as she made her androgynous way through the centuries from the swaggering boyo of the Elizabethan court to the post-suffragette lady of the manor of 1928 in Woolf's curious quirky richly-embroidered love poem to Vita Sackville-West. It was admirable, enormously accomplished and inventive but curiously cold and thin of emotion, human warmth; exquisitely choreographed but detached from reality and just too long for the graceful whimsy of the material, like reciting Herrick by moonlight in a lace-fringed two hour chunk.

No-one seemed quite sure whether John McGrath's updating of Sir David Lyndsay's *Ane Satyre of the Thrie Estaites* was encouraged, commissioned or just appeared out of the Saltire blue of Wildcat's play provision section.

A Satire of the Four Estates was played in the new International Conference Centre. Much more comfortable for the audience but as a venue for pageant drama on this scale, not a patch on the old Assembly Hall on the Mound where the many memorable performances of the old Lyndsay play had been given. Reaction to its delineation of auld Scotland's modern ills should have depended largely on which side you were on. In some reviews, even while struggling to be fair to Scots aspirations towards autonomy, it did. In *The Independent* Robert Hanks wrote:

> Ane Satyre of the Thrie Estaites, *Sir David Lyndsay's morality play first performed in 1552, is one of the great landmarks of Scottish culture and Tyrone Guthrie's 1948 revival is one of the landmarks of the Edinburgh Festival. Given this history, you can see exactly why updating the play must have seemed an attractive way of marking the 50th Festival: it's harder to see how John McGrath's ragbag of truism and whinges, wrapped up in plodding doggerel, works as a tribute to anybody.*
>
> *So long as the allegory remains reasonably abstract, it's easy to go along with: McGrath, you learn, is in favour of Love and Respect, Charity Democracy and Equality, who all appear as characters in the play. He likes Humanity, the dethroned king who must be married to pretty Jenny McReddie if the New Scotland, of which she is the personification, is to be worth anything. What he doesn't like is the Fourth Estate, represented here by Lord Merde, a repellent Australian media magnate and his hangers-on. All this is reasonable; but as soon as the play descends into particularities, it's as if a drunk has barged into an argument on your side, making your own position seem embarrassingly crude.*

This was as near geniality as most reviewers from south of the Solway got. The English establishment press did not bother about being unprejudiced.

> *A silly, coarse and imaginatively monotonous spin-off (from an original which never loses its intellectual elegance and moral grandeur),* shrieked *The Times.*
>
> *Crude, predictable and awesomely unfunny and there are moments when you feel like screaming at its infantile agit-prop agenda ... to find it as one of the show pieces of the official festival beggars belief,* wailed *The Daily Telegraph.*
>
> *Full of noise and shallow clichés, it panders to people who like their prejudices and opinions confirmed in public – the culture of Sky and the tabloids deserves more effort than this,* trumpeted *The Sunday Times.*

Michael Billington was a lonely Sassenach figure dispensing generosity and comprehension in his *Guardian* review: 'It's the kind of show that English audiences will hate and Scottish audiences love, but it adds greatly to the fun of the Festival and passionately articulates the Scottish dream of independence.'

> *What impresses most ,*said *The Scotsman's* Colin Donald, *is the enormous attention to detail in the lines and the direction and the savage force and quality of the performances.*

Much of it had genuine bite and humour, some striking points were made; there was a brilliantly acrid performance from John Bett in half-mask as Lord Merde but the staging was inept, the set tawdry and although there were some inventive comic rhymes there were also quite a few that might have made McGonagall blush. It was not the vulgarity but the triteness and sentimentality which stuck in some of even the most patriotic gullets. Surely our case for national identity is stronger that this.

There was more unanimity about Nottingham Playhouse's version of Botho Strauss' *Time and the Room* which closed the Festival at the Royal Lyceum – and sent quite a few people home early.

Sooner or later, Mr Donald wrote, *the vexed question of the German sense of humour is bound to arise in discussing Botho Strauss and it has to be said that the production – generously received at the Lyceum last night – served as a reminder of how easy it is to make people laugh in the theatre, especially given a bit of Festival good-will.*

Dearly enamoured of a laugh myself I found Strauss's chic gallery-style room – superbly designed and lit by Wolfgang Gobbel though it may be – a completely humour-free zone.

The other play which prompted one critic to say that it was the second time in this festival that Brian McMaster had lost the plot, was Carles Santos's Catalan *L'esplendida vergonya del fet mal fet* (The Splendid Shame of the Deed Badly Done if you have to know, but you don't). The title didn't mean anything but it had not lost the plot because it never had one. This extravagant surrealist romp ran for an hour less than scheduled but that was just as well because its totally lunatic, barely laminated series of actions filled that space fairly precisely – not a word I would care to use about any other aspect of the show. It was colourful, wild, very well sung, zanily choreographed and 60 minutes of hoot and inventive vulgarity, roughly spiralled around a mobile pianola pursuing a violinist on a trapeze and a woman who kept her husband in an aquarium. I have no idea what it was about but it made me laugh – and after Botho Strauss, that was a bonus.

The final festival play broke the mould of bafflement, cancellation and other forms of disappointment by being absolutely superb. The idea of Anton Chekhov's *Uncle Vanya* in Italian may seem at first to be almost as quirky as some of the other offerings at the 50th Festival but Peter Stein's production with the Teatro di Roma and the Teatro Stabile di Parma was a joy. This subtle and poignant unravelling of unperceived and unrequited love and pain, caged within a social structure which diminishes yet somehow enhances the wastefulness of human exchange, was beautifully achieved with a rare intensity of performance and no tricks. The focus was on the two women: Sonya, played by Elisabetta Pozzi with an

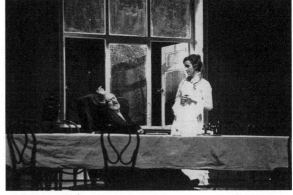

Uncle Vanya *(1996)*

enraptured devotion that added an extra dimension to Astrov's indifference, and Yelena, wife to the pompously smug Professor Serebryakov, who cannot resist the temptations of her own havoc-wreaking beauty, was realised with infinite nuances of vanity and desire by Maddalena Crippa.

The ending, with Sonya and Vanya's hopes breathlessly punctured into despair, was worth a thousand moments of stage trickery.

So the 50th Festival finished on an elegiac note in the theatre and a surge of spiritual triumph in Mendelssohn's *Elijah* in the concert hall. It had begun rather less auspiciously. At the end of the first week, former director Frank Dunlop proclaimed that the Festival had become too tame, too reliant on established names drawn almost exclusively from the Western European artistic canon. More fuss had been caused at the beginning of that week by the lecture on *Culture and Society*, given at the Festival's invitation, by the critic and writer, Professor George Steiner on the afternoon before the opening concert on the first Sunday. Sniping from the wings was not confined to Steiner and Dunlop.

The drama critic Michael Coveney, in a highly favourable review of *Orlando* said of the play:

> *With such work you regret nonetheless that it has not been originated in Edinburgh and that the director, Brian McMaster is directly responsible for no new work, no genuinely new commissioning, no real risk-taking. His festival has become a welcome haven for Mark Morris, Robert Wilson, Peter Stein and other avant-garde grandees. But he has merely brought us up to date. What is he proposing beyond them?*
>
> *It nearly pains me to mention George Steiner's bumbling, sycophantic and error-strewn lecture delivered last Sunday in the McEwan Hall of the university. In spite of himself and his blunders –* Beyond the Fringe *did not start the Fringe: Joan Littlewood did not have a triumph here with* Henry IV *– Steiner advocated self-questioning. And new work.* Virginia Woolf *and* Hamlet, *however you dress them up are not new. This postmodern affliction of nostalgia in the arts has taken over.*

There was considerable confusion about what Steiner had actually said. Certainly many of his references to Festival performances were wrong – many more than those quoted by Michael Coveney. No newspaper was going to print all of a lecture lasting 90 minutes, so the text was quarried for snappy paragraphs. This resulted in some reports that Steiner had suggested the Festival should cease because it had not succeeded in its immediate post-war desire to bring peace to the world and its components were not as interesting as science – the new arts field of the 21st century.

> *The* odium theologicum *which now emanates from the bitter quarrels between critical schools and movements in the humanities, the voluminous triviality of such, much that is produced in humane letters, art-history, musicology point to a Byzantine afternoon. As do the jugglers' ingenuities of deconstruction and post-modernism. Doing first-class science or technology is, visibly, enormous fun. It engages criteria of elegance, of beauty, of harmony in mathematics as old as Pythagoras or Plato but now hidden from all who cannot master the languages, dare one say, the poetry of algebra. That may indeed be 'no country for old men' as Yeats would put it, but it is brimful of laughter and sun-rise.*

He pursued the theme of the beauty of mathematics and science and summed up by saying:

> *To know when to stop is rare but vivid mark of honesty within excellence. Too many worn out ghosts of past or altered cultural ambitions and ideals litter the scene . It is precisely when it is still doing well, when its box-office is healthy, that an institution should draw a dangerous breath and ask of itself ' is my continued existence truly representative of both my initial aims? Are current realisations matching the excellence of the outset? These are not questions to be afraid of. It is the failure of nerve implicit in not posing them which could signal stasis or even decline.*
>
> *Only such clarity of view, I venture to believe, can fully allow the ancient cry of* gaudeamus igitur. *Let us therefore, rejoice. We are only 50 years young!*

This curious advocacy of middle-aged euthanasia was taken, not as some kind of philosophical flourish, but as literal advice to end the Festival. It was excellent leader-writer material but a student of festivals might have remembered that this was the Prof up to his own deconstructionist tricks again. A couple of years before at the opening of the Salzburg Festival, Steiner had delivered a similar lecture suggesting that almost all European culture is that of the museum and the archive and that the new vision of culture had to embrace the reality of the sciences. So this was well-trodden festival territory but for some occult superstitious reason, like the onset of the millennium, it made people think.

The future of the Edinburgh Festival is not in doubt. It is established firmly as one of the major cultural events in the world, the most comprehensive arts Festival; and there is no reason why it should not go on as it has done in the past from strength to strength. It is absurd to suggest that because it has not brought permanent peace to the world like some divinely esoteric United Nations, it has failed in its purpose. The aim of peace through culture was a pious hope not a direct festival objective. Much else has been achieved in the Festival's half-century.

There are issues to address; there always have been: there always will be. I rather doubt that they will or need include 'the poetry of algebra' but they must take account of the advent of technology. Global communication, from being an asset, could very easily become a menace to the arts. Enjoyment, moments of glory and rapture are not words and perhaps feelings which link too readily with the shorthand of global exchange on the internet.

Although in the context of contemporary artistic thinking, it may be a piece of nostalgic bourgeois self-indulgence to hope to come out of a performance of music theatre humming the tunes (Noel Coward famously said of *Camelot* 'I came out whistling the scenery') there is a sense in which this is a critereon of common appreciation which should not be contemptuously brushed aside. We must ask if the McMaster canon of festival programming *ex Edinburgh semper aliquid novi* followed down Steinerstrasse, could mean that events could come to us only on monitors and there would be no tactile, comprehensible memories of culture to take away from performances.

The Edinburgh Festival in all its diverse aspects – and only one of them, the central one, has been dealt with here – must retain two core characteristics – accessibility and choice. The scientific road – the information highway – is already comprehensively littered with garbage. Edinburgh may well face a struggle in the future to keep the art and purpose of live performance from extinction. Soon, we are told constantly, you will be able to get everything on the internet.

But for me that could not compete nor compare with the thrills and the joys which 50 years of the Edinburgh Festival have brought – to me and thousands of others. The richness and splendour of the offerings of these years will always be important to me as will the many fascinating people and dear friends I have met and made within these experiences and that time. For that reason there will always be some element of nostalgia in my assessment of the arts. The present and the future cannot exist without the past and its contributions – even if most of the scientists who ever lived are still alive today.

In each generation there will always be the desire to shake the tree of life and leave half its edible fruit rotting on the ground. But occasionally an apple may bounce from the head of a budding Newton and construe a new law of mental gravity – or comedy. Or a new Eve may offer a perfect undamaged fruit, caught in the air as it falls, to a new Adam, creating a fresh temptation, another beginning. The Festival should try to ensure that every year, it happens here.

Banquo on Thursdays